Heaven Has Eyes

Heaven Has Eyes

A History of Chinese Law

XIAOQUN XU

Oxford University Press is a department of the University of Oxford. It furthers the University's objective of excellence in research, scholarship, and education by publishing worldwide. Oxford is a registered trade mark of Oxford University Press in the UK and certain other countries.

Published in the United States of America by Oxford University Press
198 Madison Avenue, New York, NY 10016, United States of America.

© Oxford University Press 2020

All rights reserved. No part of this publication may be reproduced, stored in a retrieval system, or transmitted, in any form or by any means, without the prior permission in writing of Oxford University Press, or as expressly permitted by law, by license, or under terms agreed with the appropriate reproduction rights organization. Inquiries concerning reproduction outside the scope of the above should be sent to the Rights Department, Oxford University Press, at the address above.

You must not circulate this work in any other form
and you must impose this same condition on any acquirer.

Library of Congress Cataloging-in-Publication Data
Names: Xu, Xiaoqun, 1954– author.
Title: Heaven has eyes : a history of Chinese law / Xiaoqun Xu.
Description: New York : Oxford University Press, 2020. |
Includes bibliographical references and index.
Identifiers: LCCN 2020003949 (print) | LCCN 2020003950 (ebook) |
ISBN 9780190060046 (hardback) | ISBN 9780190060053 (updf)|
ISBN 9780190060060 (epub) | ISBN 9780190060077 (online)
Subjects: LCSH: Justice, Administration of—China—History. |
Justice, Administration of—China—History—20th century. | China—Politics and government. | China—Politics and government—1949–
Classification: LCC KNN1572 .X8 2020 (print) | LCC KNN1572 (ebook) |
DDC 349.51—dc23
LC record available at https://lccn.loc.gov/2020003949
LC ebook record available at https://lccn.loc.gov/2020003950

For Matti Zelin

Contents

Acknowledgments ix
Chronology of Chinese History xi

Introduction: Law and Justice in Chinese History   1

I. LAW AND JUSTICE IN IMPERIAL CHINA, 221 BCE–1911 CE

1. Five Punishments and Beyond: The Evolution of Penal Codes in Imperial China   7

2. From the Imperial Capital to the Magistrate's Court: Judicial Practices in Imperial China   40

3. The Emperor, the Family, and the Land: Law and Order in Imperial China   66

II. LAW AND JUSTICE IN LATE QING AND REPUBLICAN CHINA, 1901–1949

4. The Best of the Chinese and of the Western: Legal-Judicial Reform in the Late Qing, 1901–1911   101

5. The Rule of Law, Judicial Independence, and Due Process: Ideals and Realities in the Republican Era, 1912–1949   118

6. Bandits, Collaborators, and Wives and Concubines: Criminal and Civil Justice in the Republican Era, 1912–1949   146

III. LAW AND JUSTICE IN MAOIST CHINA, 1949–1976

7. "Contradictions between the People and the Enemy": Criminal Justice as the Proletarian Dictatorship   175

8. "Contradictions among the People": Mediation and Adjudication of Civil Disputes   207

IV. LAW AND JUSTICE IN POST-MAO CHINA, 1977–2018

9. The Legal System and the Rule of Law: Changes in Criminal Justice, 1977–1996 — 223

10. "Naked Officials" and "Heavenly Net": Changes in Criminal Justice, 1997–2018 — 256

11. "Look toward Money": Civil Justice in Post-Mao China, 1977–2018 — 285

Conclusion: Heaven Has Eyes — 303

Notes — 309
Selected Bibliography — 337
List of Chinese Characters — 353
Index — 359

Acknowledgments

This book results from an intellectual journey that began in classrooms. I first taught the upper-level undergraduate class Law and Justice in Chinese History in 2008, after my book on Chinese judicial reform in the early twentieth century was published, and since then I have taught the course periodically. The necessity of teaching the course as a survey of Chinese law from the imperial era down to the post-Mao era to undergraduates, most of whom did not have a background in Chinese history, pushed me to delve into the primary and secondary sources on the subject and try to present a coherent historical narrative and analysis. The experience of teaching the course, and the fact that most students received it positively, motivated me to attempt a book on Chinese legal history that is accessible to undergraduates and useful to postgraduates and scholars in China studies, and especially in Chinese law and history. A sabbatical from Christopher Newport University in spring 2015 allowed me to start drafting a manuscript that has finally evolved into the present book.

The book is a synthesis of my own research and the existing scholarship on Chinese legal history. Obviously it would not have been possible for me to write such a book without the important and exciting work produced by many scholars in the field in the past three decades or more. The selected bibliography is a testimony to the collective achievements of these scholars. I owe a huge intellectual debt to all of them. In a small way, the book serves as a tribute to their scholarship and acts as a signpost for the field of Chinese legal history marking this moment. Of course, none of the scholars whose work I have quoted and cited is assumed to agree with all or any of my understandings of Chinese law and history. In fact, many issues are worthy of scholarly debates, and new insights are to be gained from further research.

The book manuscript was accepted by Oxford University Press for publication thanks to two anonymous referees who recommended it. I am profoundly grateful for their support and for their constructive comments and suggestions. Additional written comments from two anonymous members of the editorial committee at the Press were also helpful. Nancy E. Toff, the editor of the book, spotted the potential of this project from the beginning, and she took great care in helping me fit the book into the OUP style of presentation and in guiding the cover design. The book would not have appeared in the present form without her sound judgment and able hands. The copyeditor further improved the text. I alone am responsible for any errors that may remain.

With warm regards, I dedicate this book to Matti Zelin, my mentor when I was a doctoral student at Columbia University in 1989–93 and since those memorable years.

Chronology of Chinese History

The Formative Period of China

Legendary sage rulers	?
Xia state	?–16th century BCE
Shang state	16th–11th century BCE
Zhou feudal system	1045–221 BCE
Western Zhou	1045–771 BCE
Eastern Zhou	771–221 BCE
Spring and Autumn period	770–475 BCE
Warring States period	475–221 BCE

The Imperial Era, 221 BCE–1911 CE

Qin dynasty	221–206 BCE
Han dynasty	206 BCE–220 CE
Three Kingdoms	220–280
Wei	220–280
Shu	221–263
Wu	221–277
Jin dynasty	281–316
Northern states and southern dynasties	316–589
Sui dynasty	581–618
Tang dynasty	618–906
Five dynasties	907–960
Song dynasty	960–1279
Yuan dynasty	1279–1368
Ming dynasty	1368–1644
Qing dynasty	1644–1911

The Republican Era, 1912–1949

The Beijing government	1912–1927
The National government	1927–1949
Second Sino-Japanese War	1937–1945

The People's Republic of China—The Mao Era, 1949–1976

The New Democracy	1949–1956
Transition to socialism	1956–1958
The Cultural Revolution	1966–1976

The People's Republic of China—The Post-Mao Era, 1977–Present

Deng Xiaoping as leader	1978–1997
Jiang Zemin as leader	1997–2002
Hu Jintao as leader	2003–2012
Xi Jinping as leader	2013–present

Introduction

Law and Justice in Chinese History

Law and justice are among the basic functions of the state in any country.¹ The state performs these functions in the context of multidimensional interactions within the state system and between the state and society, affecting people's lives in myriad ways. A grasp of the ways in which law and justice function in China enables us to better understand Chinese politics, economy, society, and culture. To that purpose, this book offers a history of Chinese law and justice from the imperial era to the post-Mao era. It addresses the evolution and function of law codes as well as judicial institutions and practices; examines the transition from traditional laws and practices to their modern counterparts in the twentieth century and beyond; and traces the interactions among official ideologies, political institutions, social-familial structures, laws and the judicial system, legal culture, and social-economic life.

From ancient times to the twenty-first century, there has been an enduring expectation or hope among the Chinese people that justice should or will be done in society, an expectation that is neatly expressed in a popular Chinese saying, "Heaven has eyes" (*laotian youyan*). What is justice, then? To the Chinese mind in the imperial era, justice was, and was to be achieved as, an alignment of Heavenly reason (*tianli*), state law (*guofa*), and human relations-feelings (*renqing*).² The notion suggests that enacting and applying state law that manifests Heavenly reason (ultimate morality) and takes into consideration human relations and feelings should be the way to achieve justice. Such a notion of justice ran through more than two millennia as the guide to law and justice, until the turn of the twentieth century, when Western-derived notions—natural rights, legal equality, the rule of law, judicial independence, and due process—came to replace the Confucian moral code of right and wrong. This was a fundamental shift in the philosophical and moral principles that informed law and justice. The legal-judicial reform agendas since the beginning of the twentieth century (and still ongoing today) stemmed from this radical change in Chinese moral and legal thinking, but to materialize these principles in everyday practice is much more difficult to accomplish, for a variety of reasons. Moreover, China in the turbulent twentieth century experienced the politically divided Republic (1912–1949) that endured civil wars and the Second Sino-Japanese War, the one-party People's Republic (since 1949) that saw Maoist Socialism and the Cultural Revolution, and finally the post-Mao economic reforms and opening to the world—all these events and developments influenced or conditioned how law and justice would function.

In the meantime, the traditional notion of justice as an alignment of Heavenly reason, state law, and human relations did not vanish but has remained an expectation, even if not always articulated as such. "Heavenly reason" has been conveyed by different vocabularies in prevailing ideologies of particular times since the early twentieth century. As an expression of ultimate morality to justify laws and juridical decisions, the term "Heavenly reason" was replaced by "modernity" and "judicial sovereignty" in the late Qing and the early Republic, "nationalist revolution" and "rule by the party" in the Nanjing era, "proletarian revolution" and "class struggle" in the Mao era, and "Socialism with Chinese characteristics" and "social stability" in the post-Mao era. Compared to these primary agendas for the state, such goals as the rule of law, judicial independence, and due process are secondary, even if they may be primary in the judicial field. From this perspective, no matter how "justice (what is just)" was and is defined, the saying "Heaven has eyes" always has resonance with varied meanings for different people in Chinese society; justice that manifests Heavenly reason is always expected or desired; and, last but not the least, the traditional Chinese legal thinking that prized substantive justice (however defined at a particular time) over procedural justice still casts a spell on Chinese minds in the twentieth century and beyond. Thus the history of Chinese law and justice highlights, in a crucial dimension, the theme of change and continuity in understanding Chinese history and culture.

More specifically, the present book aims to situate laws, judicial practices, and legal culture in the political-social-moral universe that has been particular to China's past and present. It explains the modern transformations of law and justice, with their achievements and defects, in the contexts of China's interactions with Western nations and of the legacies from the imperial era. One is not surprised to find that after the intellectual rupture of the Maoist era, laws and the judicial system and practices in post-Mao China have continued to function under influences from both the traditional and the Western models that serve in effect as moral-intellectual resources and inspirations, either explicitly or implicitly and consciously or unconsciously. As a corollary, tensions and debates (domestic and international) arising from the differences and interactions between the two sources have accompanied what has transpired as justice (in both meanings: what is just, and the judicial system and practices) in China.

The history of Chinese law may be broadly outlined as follows. First, the imperial era prior to the twentieth century (221 BCE–1900 CE) saw the evolution of imperial penal codes, the judicial procedures and practices, and the ways in which law and justice upheld the political, familial, and economic (especially landowning) systems. The legal development was driven by the intellectual debates since the pre-imperial era over morality and governance and by the political experiences of the imperial era. As a result, the imperial laws became more and more comprehensive and elaborate, but all were conceived within the framework of a penal code that covered criminal, civil, administrative, and procedural matters.

In the early twentieth century, the final decade of the Qing dynasty (1901–1911) and the era of the Republic of China (1912–1949) together constituted a transitional period, during which traditional Chinese law and justice were changed into modern forms and norms. While the reform in law and judicial practices during 1901–1927 were guided by the legal principles and models learned from Western nations (primarily continental law), their counterparts in the Nationalist (Guomindang [GMD]) period (1927–1949) functioned as a hybrid between Western-derived principles and Leninist theory and practices, the latter being a legacy shared by the Chinese Communist Party (CCP).

The Maoist era (1949–1976) of the People's Republic made a break in the trajectory of legal-judicial reform since the late Qing. Mao's theory and the CCP's practice of governing Chinese society through the Party and through a continuous revolution fundamentally shaped the way in which law and justice would function during the period. Mao's ideological position regarding the nature of the state (and law and justice as its functions) interrupted and blocked the hitherto ongoing legal-judicial reforms since 1901, while some sort of legal-judicial functions of the state had to be fashioned in order to govern the country.

In the post-Mao era (since 1977), the People's Republic of China (PRC) has remained a one-party state, but many changes have occurred in criminal and civil justice. Motivated by integration into the world economy and influenced by international human rights movements, legal-judicial reform has been advancing toward more safeguards for procedural justice, more legal responses to newly emerging crimes, and less severe punishments of criminal offenses than before. However, these changes did not reject the principles and practices of the CCP dominating policymaking regarding the development of Chinese society. In the meantime, there has been a dramatic increase in civil litigations, as China has morphed into a much more complex society than ever before, in an environment fostered by the ongoing reforms and opening since the late 1970s.

In the end, there would emerge four overlapping historical contexts within which one is to understand Chinese law and justice. First, the long imperial era witnessed the dynamic and evolving nature of Chinese law. Second, the political and cultural interactions between China and the West drove the twentieth-century legal-judicial reforms. Third, the interplays and negotiations between principal and agents within the state system and between the state and societal players actualized laws and justice as daily practices and lived experiences. Fourth, due to human fallibility, an inevitable reality is that justice can only be relative and imperfect, even under the best circumstances; at the same time, the inextinguishable human spirit to pursue justice—"Heaven has eyes"—suggests a prospect for progress in achieving more justice and more human rights protection in China as an ongoing and never-ending endeavor.

This book addresses primarily criminal and civil justice, leaving out other areas of jurisprudence in the Western tradition, such as constitutional, administrative, and commercial laws (including taxation, capital-labor relations, security and investment, etc.), for two reasons. First, the criminal and civil matters dealt with here were at the core of Chinese law and justice in the imperial era (when the notion of a constitution was absent, for example) and have remained so since the early twentieth century, even though there have been uneven and intermittent developments in constitutional, administrative, and commercial laws as necessary components of modernization. Second, criminal and civil laws and related court cases are more useful and interesting than other areas of jurisprudence in shedding light on Chinese history and culture because they tend to capture from critical and revealing angles the political, social, economic, and cultural lives of all social strata (elite and nonelite) in different time periods.

PART I
LAW AND JUSTICE IN IMPERIAL CHINA, 221 BCE–1911 CE

1
Five Punishments and Beyond
The Evolution of Penal Codes in Imperial China

Chinese law and justice are as old as Chinese history. One of the features defining an ancient civilization, including Chinese civilization, is the rise of the state (or the ruler), and law and justice are among the basic functions of the state. The history of Chinese law begins with the intellectual sources of law and justice in ancient China. Ruling elites conceived law as an instrument for maintaining a balance between two primal forces of the cosmos—yin (negative, feminine, the moon, waters, etc.) and yang (positive, masculine, the sun, mountains, etc.)—that manifested in human society as the existing political-social-moral order. Chinese penal codes appeared as prototypes in the pre-imperial era and then grew to be more and more elaborate and comprehensive throughout the imperial era. Indeed, the evolution of law and justice was part and parcel of a continuous development of the Chinese imperial system, despite periodic changes in ruling dynasties, and the dynamics of China's long imperial past before its modern transformations in the twentieth century.

Intellectual Sources of Law and Punishment

Heaven and Human Affairs

An influential Confucian creed, dating from the Zhou period (eleventh through third centuries BCE) stated that "only when minds are rectified [*zhengxin*] are persons cultivated [*xiushen*]; only when persons are cultivated are families regulated [*qijia*]; only when families are regulated is good governance [*zhiguo*] obtained; only when good governance is obtained is there peace all under heaven [*ping tianxia*]."[1] Connecting ideas of self, family, government, and the known world (all under Heaven), this statement succinctly conveys the moral foundations of Chinese society that law was to support: its family system, its social fabric, its morality, and its governance. In a nutshell, the political-social-moral order in imperial China was built on the notion of interactions and harmony between Heaven and human society, each underpinned by a balance of yin and yang, two primal forces of the cosmos, a conception the historian Benjamin Schwartz called "correlative cosmology."[2] Self, family, government, and all under Heaven thus constituted a coherent moral universe.[3] All these concepts originated in ancient China and are found in archaeological and written sources from the Shang (seventeenth through eleventh centuries BCE) and the Zhou (1045–221 BCE) periods.

The Shang and the Zhou kingdoms were founded, respectively, by Shang Tang and King Wu, after each led a rebellion against the sitting ruler of a previous ruling house. Shang Tang overthrew the last ruler of the Xia kingdom (circa twenty-first through seventeenth century BCE), and King Wu took over from the last ruler of the Shang. In order to justify his rebellion, King Wu made a claim to the Mandate of Heaven [*tianming*] and denounced the previous ruler for failing the will of Heaven and the wishes of the people, thus losing the mandate. (According to the Zhou sources, Shang Tang had made the same claim for overthrowing the Xia, which might have been a myth to reinforce King Wu's claim.)[4] Moreover, the belief in and the discourse on the omnipotence of Heaven was displayed in religious rituals, such as divinations, prayers, and offerings (including human sacrifices during the Shang), asking for blessings from Heaven for various important political, economic, and military activities, from warfare, hunting, planting and harvesting crops, to construction of palaces and tombs.

From those early ideas came the most influential beliefs and practices in imperial China: Heaven was the ultimate cosmic force or being, and the ruler was the Son of Heaven (*tianzi*); the patriarchal family system, Heavenly ordained and yin-yang–sustained, was the foundation of the entire political, social, and moral order all under Heaven. These two foundational notions were conveniently combined and personified in the ruler as the Son of Heaven and the parent of the people.

In the philosophical and political writings of the Zhou period (known as the classical sources), the Mandate of Heaven or the Way of the King (as the Son of Heaven) was closely connected with the well-being of the people. In the chapter "Grand Models" ("Hongfan") of the *Classic of Books*, it is stated that "the Son of Heaven serves as the parents of the people and therefore is the king of all under heaven."[5] Mencius, the primary propagator of Confucius's teaching, most forcefully articulated the idea that the role of the ruler as the Son of Heaven was to carry out Heaven's will and care for the people as parents, with benevolent governance.

Another rationale for the benevolent governance required by the Mandate of Heaven was developed by Xun Zi with a metaphor that would become a classic in Chinese language. In Xun Zi's account, the king of Lu state asked Confucius what dangers the king might be facing, and Confucius answered, "The ruler is a boat, and the common people are water; water can carry the boat and water can capsize the boat" (*shuize zaizhou, shuize fuzhou*).[6] Whether the metaphor originally belonged to Confucius or Xun Zi himself, it became a well-known and enduring political concept that "the people was the foundation of the state" (*minben*). Confucian scholars and officials in subsequent centuries would frequently cite it as a moral-political admonition to the ruler. The Confucian rhetoric would praise, as models of high morality, the legendary sage-kings and wise rulers prior to the Shang period—Yao, Shun, and Yu—as well as Shang Tang and King Wu. Thereafter the notion of benevolent governance became a centerpiece of Chinese political philosophy due to the lasting influence of Confucianism from the Han dynasty (205 BCE–220 CE) down. Throughout the imperial era the notion that the Mandate of Heaven could be lost due to failure to deliver benevolent governance and passed on to another Son of Heaven was repeatedly and routinely invoked by founders of new ruling houses to justify the overthrow of previous dynasties.

The Political Meanings of the Mandate of Heaven

Was the notion of Heaven-human interactions, as the logical premise of the Mandate of Heaven, a real belief or merely political rhetoric used by officials to compel the emperor to be benevolent and by the emperor to compel officials to perform their duties correctly? It was probably both, for the emperor and his officials, as the following examples suggest.

During the reign of Emperor Taizong (627–649) of the Tang dynasty, he issued at least six edicts of general amnesties; the first was to mark his ascendance to the throne and all the rest were in response to natural disasters in the country (storm and flooding, drought, locusts, etc.).[7] In 737 the Court of Judicial Review reported to Emperor Xuanzong that in the whole country only fifty-eight capital offenders were executed that year, and magpies built nests on the trees in the Court's garden where previously no birds had come due to too much "killing atmosphere" (*shaqi*) or yin. In response, the emperor ordered an elaborate celebration banquet and offered rewards to top officials in the capital.[8]

The notion of Heaven-human interactions was also used by high officials to nudge the emperor to be a benevolent ruler. Bao Zheng of the Song dynasty served in various positions in the capital and provinces. Known to be an incorruptible official [*qingguan*], Bao became a legend. Embellished stories in which he tried and punished wrongdoers entered the repertoire of Chinese popular culture down to the twentieth century, in theater and storytelling performances.[9] As a real person, on occasions of thunder in winter, solar eclipses, comets, and earthquakes, Bao did advise Emperor Renzong to reduce tax burdens on the people, listen to officials' honest opinions, pay attention to defense on the frontiers, and reward virtues and punish crimes, "in response to warnings from Heaven" (*yida tianjie*).[10]

Fast-forward to the Qing dynasty (1644–1911), and emperors exhibited the same belief. In 1697, on the occasion of receiving a report about a pending solar eclipse, Emperor Kangxi made the following comment:

> Solar eclipses can be calculated by humans, but since ancient times kings and emperors have always been awed and cautioned, and striv[en] to improve human affairs, in reverence for such Heavenly changes, whereas mediocre rulers would attribute human affairs to fate. This year there have been floods and earthquakes, and now a solar eclipse is predicted. I believe these happenstances result from the overabundance of yin. How can anyone say that they have nothing to do with human affairs?[11]

When Emperor Kangxi spoke of an "overabundance of yin," he meant that too many people might have been executed or wrongfully punished. In 1675 a drought occurred, and he ordered high officials to review all criminal cases to correct any wrongful convictions and punishments.[12] In 1695 an earthquake shook Shanxi province, and he ordered a general amnesty for "all under Heaven."[13] In these instances, the Qing emperors continued a time-honored tradition. As a conquest dynasty, the Manchu rulers claimed to have inherited the Mandate of Heaven and embraced the right and duty to uphold the Confucian political-social-moral order. They claimed to have subscribed to the Chinese notion of a cosmic order and the way it was reflected in the delivery of justice. The Qing emperors made it known that they were doing just that, either as manifestation of their true belief or as correct behavior to meet the expectations of Chinese officials and commoners.

Qing officials too acted accordingly. During the reign of Emperor Tongzhi, the imperial censor Hu Qingyuan submitted a memorial on issues of law and justice: that bandits be allowed to surrender themselves without time limit; that all shops, not just the thirty-six designated firms, be allowed to deal opium; that amnesty for female convicts should not cover murderers; and that jail guards who abused inmates be punished severely and their superiors lightly. To preface his memorial he cited the recent drought in the capital region as a sign of injustice being present in the country, and he argued that amnesty for murderers would cause the souls of their victims to form a malignant atmosphere (*liqi*), leading to floods, droughts, locusts, and diseases.[14]

In 1863 Shi Dakai, one of the Taiping Rebellion leaders, was captured near the Dadu River in Sichuan province because the river suddenly and unseasonably rose more than twenty feet, preventing Shi and his men from crossing the river. Luo Bingzhang, the provincial governor of Sichuan who captured Shi, submitted a memorial to the emperor, attributing the river phenomenon to Heavenly majesty (*tianwei*) being in agreement with the emperor's virtues, and requesting that a temple be built and dedicated to the Dadu River spirit.[15]

Books of model cases produced in the imperial era would also make connections between wrongful cases and abnormal weather patterns, such as droughts, storms, and floods. *Tangyin bishi*, a book compiled initially by Gui Wanrong of the Song dynasty, was re-edited and expanded by Wu Na, a Ming dynasty official, and then included in the *Complete Repository of Four Treasures* under Emperor Qianlong of the Qing.[16] However, in his commentary on two wise officials who righted wrongfully decided cases, Wu Na indicated that he did not think droughts and storms had direct connections with the delivery of justice, even though he would still commend those officials.[17] In the same vein, in books of model cases and other sources, wise officials would solve murder cases by resorting to methods other than judicial torture, including their manipulation of common folks' belief in the all-knowing power of local earth-gods, which suggests that those officials themselves did not believe in the earth-gods.[18] Nevertheless they shared the fundamental notion of justice as an alignment of Heavenly reason, state law, and human relations and as a balance of yin and yang.

In short, as either a belief or a political rhetoric or both, the entrenched notion of Heaven-human interactions played an important role in compelling both the emperor—the Son of Heaven–to act as a benevolent ruler *and* his officials to perform their duties to manifest and materialize the ruler's benevolence in everyday life.

Confucianism and Legalism

One key question about governance or benevolent rule was how to deal with delinquent behavior that violated a communal code of conduct defined by the elites. Varied answers to this question marked several schools of thought in the Eastern Zhou (770–221 BCE), the formative period of Chinese cultural traditions, and Confucianism and Legalism were the most influential. Both addressed how to maintain political-social-moral order and how to achieve good governance. In a broader sense, Confucians and Legalists, and all the elites in ancient China, agreed that the ruler or the elites needed to take care of (*yang*) common people in the same way as parents should take care of their children, which included protection, nourishment, education, discipline, and punishment. They differed, however, on how to do it.[19]

Confucians believed that humans were born to be good, even if "petty persons" were prone to going morally astray. A proper political-social order, therefore, was to be upheld by moral forces such as rituals and propriety taught through education. Logically, Confucianism placed emphasis on the ruler's moral example and the role of moral force to influence the people and prevent delinquent behavior. Confucius said that regulating people with orders and penalties would deter them from committing bad acts, but it would not teach them what was shameful to avoid; guiding people with virtue and propriety would teach people not to do what was shameful.[20] His ideal society was a hierarchy whereby morally superior men, whom he called *junzi* (gentlemen, as opposed to petty persons), would occupy higher positions.

Philosophically, Han Fei, a Legalist, shared with Confucians the notion of a hierarchical political-social order sanctioned by Heaven. Han Fei stated, for example, "Minister serves ruler, son serves father, wife serves husband—when these three matters are in order, there is peace all under heaven, and when these are not in order, there is chaos all under heaven. This is the eternal way of all under heaven."[21] This was a formulation very agreeable to Confucians. Yet Han Fei and other Legalists believed that human nature is inherently bad because humans have bodily desires. Legalists emphasized the role of law and punishment in bringing about peace and order. In their view, the deterrent effect of law and punishment would be such that in the end punishment need not be used when all people would learn to abide by the law, having seen examples of punishment. In other words, they were concerned about the end result: people abiding by law, from whatever motivation, which contrasted with Confucius's concerns.

Legalism would be adopted by the Qin state as the guide for policy, which helped the Qin strengthen its power and conquer six other states, resulting in the founding of the Qin dynasty (221–206 BCE), the first imperial state in China. The dynasty was short-lived, however. The Han dynasty, which replaced the Qin, was keen to draw lessons from its predecessor's quick collapse. The first three Han emperors favored Daoism, a school of thought attributed to Lao Zi that valued passivity and tranquility. But the fourth Han emperor, Emperor Wu, was persuaded by Dong Zhongshu, a Confucian scholar, to adopt Confucianism as the official ideology. This move once and for all established the dominance of Confucianism (despite its wax and wane in different periods) in Chinese tradition and of the notion of Heaven-human interactions and the importance of filial piety that both reflected and reinforced the patriarchal family system.

Legalism was by no means abandoned, however. From the Han dynasty down, each of the succeeding dynasties would use Confucian ideology for moral principles and Legalist practices as governing instruments, since both were indispensable to the ruler. Over the course of two millennia law and punishment evolved through all the dynasties to be more elaborate and more rational—within the framework of absolute monarchy. "Since the ancient times," reads the *History of Yuan*, written by Ming dynasty scholars, "whoever rules all under heaven, even if sage emperors and wise kings, cannot achieve good governance without law and punishment; that is why when the people do not follow the guidance of virtue and righteousness, they need be regulated by law, and when the law is violated, punishment need be applied, which is indeed something unavoidable. So the earlier rulers made law and punishment, not to establish authority, but to assist in good governance."[22] In short, Confucianism as a dominant ideology would justify the existing political-social-moral order, while law and punishment as governing instruments informed by Legalism would enforce the order.[23] Consequently, judicial functions of the state constituted part of the political order.

Centrality of the Patriarchal Family

In the year 210 BCE the first emperor of the Qin dynasty died of illness during a tour of the country. Having covered up the emperor's death, Zhao Gao, the chief eunuch, persuaded Li Si, the chief advisor, to let Hu Hai, the emperor's younger son, inherit the throne, whom they could more easily control than an older man. To tie up loose ends, Zhao and Hu forged an order in the name of the first emperor and sent it to Hu's elder brother, Fu Su, and a general, Meng Tian, who were both commanding troops at the Great Wall. The order told the two men to commit suicide. Suspicious about the order, Meng urged Fu that they should request a clarification. Fu replied, "When a father asks his son to die, there is no need to make another request." He killed himself.[24]

To understand Fu Su's conduct and, more broadly, to grasp the essence of law and justice in imperial China, it is necessary to highlight the centrality in Chinese life of the patriarchal family and the related discourse on filial piety, because they constituted the foundation of the entire political-social-moral order of the imperial era. Prior to the patriarchal society, matriarchal groups had probably existed in primordial China. Their traces were retained suggestively in fragmentary Chinese mythology, such as the story about Nü Wa, a female who patched up the leaking sky with stones and created human beings from mud. Yet the legendary sage-rulers and wise kings preceding the Xia, the Shang, and the Zhou were already father figures of ancient tribal societies. In Han dynasty funerary art, Nü Wa is depicted as the wife of Fu Xi, one of the early sage-rulers, a depiction that embodies "the linkage of the cosmic triad—Earth, Man, and Heaven—as well as the balance of *yin* and *yang*."[25] This historical transition decisively shaped the patriarch-centered system and ideology.

During eight centuries of the Zhou period, the patriarchal family system and the discourse on filial piety, along with the notions of the Mandate of Heaven and the Way of the King, were fully established and continuously reinforced. The moral implications of the patriarchal family and its ideology, filial piety, may be summarized as follows: An individual is inconsequential or unimportant unless as a member of a family; an individual is no more and no less than a link in the chain of a patriarchal family line to connect its ancestors and posterities, and continuing the family line is a man's primary moral obligation; women are indispensable in the reproduction of the family line but are subordinate and subservient to men, just as yin to yang; and last but not the least, it is imperative for children to *totally* obey and respect their parents, grandparents, and other family seniors—as Fu Su did.

The patriarchal family system, and the moral code that supported it, came to be deeply entrenched in the Zhou and after, partly due to the pivotal role of Confucianism. The state was simply conceived as the patriarchal family writ large; that is, the ruler was the Son of Heaven and the parent of the people at the same time. Fu Su's fate illustrates the power of this notion of ruler as parent and the compelling force of the ideology of filial piety. The discourse was especially effective with people who wanted to do right or to conform to the prevailing moral code. All the subsequent legal principles and penal codes would uphold both the imperial system and the family system as the core of a coherent political-social-moral universe.

Law and Punishment in the Pre-Imperial Era

Legendary Five Punishments

The earliest recorded law and punishment occurred with the emergence of rulers and social classes in the Xia kingdom when a hereditary ruling family was established for the first time. No conclusive archaeological evidence of the legendary sage-rulers prior to and including Yu, the founder of the Xia, has been found.[26] There is geological evidence of a cataclysmic flood around 2000 BCE, which, in the Chinese legends, was heroically tackled by Yu, who was said to have lived around that time.[27] References to the sage-rulers in the classical sources also suggest the existence of such tribal leaders in a time when a writing system had not been fully developed. In that context, the classical sources make reference to punishments even prior to the Xia. The "Book of Yu: Rules of Shun" in the *Classic of Books* vaguely mentions "five punishments," referring to beheading and mutilations.[28] It was debated in later times whether these penalties had been used under Shun; they were more likely used in the Xia in some form, even though archaeological evidence is lacking. They were certainly used in the Shang and the Zhou, as evidenced by both archaeological remains and written sources.[29]

Prototypes of Penal Codes

During the Spring and Autumn era (770–476 BCE), when earlier fiefdoms under the Zhou king evolved into separate feudal states, "written" laws began to appear. Several states made public their rudimentary penal codes, inscribed on bronze or iron structures. The *Law Books* (*Fajing*) compiled by Li Kui of the Wei state had far-reaching influences on subsequent penal codes. The *Law Books* did not survive, but they were quoted and cited by the authors of *History of Jin* (*Jin shu*) and of the *Tang Code and Annotations* in the seventh century CE. Those references indicate that the *Law Books* contained six books, covering robbery and theft, rebellion, detention, apprehension, various offenses (such as gambling, fraud, bribery, scaling city walls, and illicit sex), and the general principles. These categories were to remain central in the penal codes of the imperial era.

In terms of legal principles, lawmakers in the Zhou period already differentiated intentional from unintentional offenses, and recidivists from first-time offenders, the latter being punished more leniently. As for punishments, the early penal codes included the death penalty, bodily mutilations, tattooing, and enslavement. Less regular penalties included exile, whipping, flogging, and fines (to redeem mutilations and tattooing when an offender's guilt was less conclusive).[30] These precedents would be passed down to the imperial era.

Evolving Penal Codes in the Early Imperial Era

The Qin Dynasty (221–206 BCE)

Among the competing states of the Warring States era (475–221 BCE), the Qin proved to be the most successful in building up its economic and military power to eventually conquer the other states, due to its Legalist approach to agriculture, warfare, and statecraft, for which Shang Yang was responsible. Arriving from Wei, a neighboring state, Shang became the chief advisor to the Qin ruler and recommended new ways to expand state power. Among other things, his initiatives included the use of harsh laws and severe punishment to achieve the goals of the state. He advised equal application of law and punishment to all members of society and devised the system of collective responsibility among every ten families in a neighborhood for crimes occurring there. Shang's insistence on equality before the law led to a case in which, when the crown prince committed an offense, his two tutors were punished in substitution. After the prince ascended the throne, he retaliated against Shang and ordered his arrest for sedition. According to the historian Sima Qian of the Han dynasty, Shang was fleeing for his life when he stopped at a hostel for food and water; the owner, not knowing to whom he was speaking, said that under a law issued by Lord Shang, he (the owner) would be punished for catering to anyone without identification. Shang sighed at his own harsh law. In the end, Shang was forced to launch a real rebellion, which resulted in his execution in a gruesome manner.[31]

The use of harsh laws and severe punishments did not end with the passing of Shang Yang. Although the Qin state and the Qin dynasty (221–206 BCE) did not leave behind a complete penal code, many specific laws and ordinances were enacted. The Qin bamboo strips unearthed in 1975 from the Sleeping Tiger Tombs in Yunmeng county, Hunan province, contain laws and ordinances on agriculture, taxation, labor services, currency and markets, warehouses and storage, rewards and appointments, as well as on formats of legal documents and procedures of criminal investigation, interrogation, and trial. (Bamboo was the primary medium on which Chinese characters were written for records and communication before the invention of paper in the later Han dynasty.) The archaeological findings in Yunmeng and in Zhangjiashan offer solid evidence of an expanding administrative and legal system under the Qin dynasty.[32]

In the Qin law, categories of punishments expanded, and a lasting addition was penal labor, often meted out along with tattooing or mutilation. The most common type of penal labor for men was to work at construction sites of palaces, tombs, city walls, roads, and the Great Wall; the next common was to transport goods over various distances. Penal labor also included serving as soldiers on the frontiers. Penal labor for women meant working as slaves or servants for the state. Other penalties, such as exile, whipping, flogging, and fines, continued as well.

The Han Dynasty (206 BCE–220 CE)

While the early emperors of the Han followed Daoism in an effort to recover the economy and restore social stability after the violent transition from the Qin to the Han, they recognized the need for a new penal code, not only to deliver effective governance but also to symbolize the beginning of a new era with the Mandate of Heaven. Soon after the Han dynasty was founded, the *Law of Nine Chapters* was compiled. Its first six chapters were based on the ancient *Law Books*, and three new chapters were based on the Qin precedents. Thereafter the Han law would continue to grow, in the form of articles added to the code (*lü*), imperial edicts (*ling*), regulations on particular matters (*ke*), and trial precedents or analogies (*bi*). In addition, there were administrative laws on matters such as rituals, imperial palace security, and rules for officials to see the emperor. In all these the influence from of the Qin law was evident.[33]

As for penalties, the Han continued to apply the centuries-old five punishments until 167 BCE, when Emperor Wen reformed them to a degree. Tattooing was replaced with penal labor; losing one's nose and a left toe, with flogging; losing a right toe, with decapitation. Even though the spirit of the reform was to remove mutilations as penalties, two high officials at the time commented that the change would lighten penalties in name but increase executions in reality. In 156 BCE, in response to reports that many offenders were spared the death penalty but still died from flogging, Emperor Jing ordered that penalties of five hundred blows of flogging be reduced to three hundred; twelve years later Emperor Jing further reduced flogging of three hundred blows to two hundred, and two hundred to one hundred; the size of instruments used in flogging also became standardized.[34] These changes marked a pivotal turning point in Chinese conception and practice of punishment and set in motion a trend away from bodily mutilations toward other forms of penalties.

One of the ancient five punishments was castration. It was not in the early Han penal code but was added by Emperor Jing (r. 156–140 BCE). The court historian Sima Qian suffered the penalty ordered by Emperor Wu (r. 140–87 BCE) for defending a general who, having exhausted his supplies, surrendered to the Xiongnu, a nomadic group the Han was fighting on the northwestern frontier. In the later Han, however, castration as a punishment was again abolished.[35]

Another important change was that in the Qin dynasty penal labor was a penalty for life, and the Han began to set time periods for it. The heaviest sentence of penal labor for men was to do construction work with shaved heads while wearing chains, and for women was to grind rice for five years; the next was for men to do construction work, without shaving heads and wearing chains, for four years; then for men to gather fuel wood for temples, and for women to hand-screen rice, for three years; then for men and women to serve as city wall guards or sentries, for two years. The lightest was for men to do general labor or guard the frontier, and for women to do menial work within the palace, for one year.

One of the early legal principles was that officials were treated more stringently than common people. As early as the Warring States era, Legalist Han Fei commented that the king's interests and his ministers' were at odds: the king wanted to appoint capable people as ministers, and ministers wanted to earn an income even if they were incompetent; the king wanted to reward hard work, and ministers wanted to gain fortune without work; the king wanted the talented to be able to use their capabilities, and ministers wanted to form factions for private gain.[36] This insight points to what modern social scientists call the "principal-agent relationship"; that is, a principal (here, the ruler or the state) must try to monitor, at certain costs, his agents (officials) who tend to behave in ways that harm the principal's interests. That is why the emperor would always be suspicious of his officials' conduct and punish those who harmed his interests and undermined his Mandate of Heaven by misdeeds. From Emperor Wu onward, several categories of offenses committed by officials entailed severe punishments. These included situations where officials serving princes in fiefdoms did not report offenses committed by the princes, officials serving the emperor conspired with princes in fiefdoms to form factions, and princes unlawfully appointed officials. Separately, officials who shielded criminals, and officials who failed to capture rebels, would be executed. If officials, and anyone else, failed to report crimes they were aware of, they would be punished for the crimes under the law.[37] In short, there began to emerge types of offenses applicable only to officials or imperial clan members. They would grow into more systematic categories in later dynasties.

Between the Han and the Sui Dynasties (220–581 CE)

The end of the Han dynasty in 220 CE ushered in a period of political division, during which a host of rival states and brief dynasties came along simultaneously or in quick succession. The Han was succeeded by the Three Kingdoms: the Wei, the Shu, and the Wu. They were all taken over in 280 by the Jin dynasty, which had replaced the Wei in 266. The Jin ruled the unified country for only thirty-seven years, however. From 317 onward, North China was under a series of sixteen competing or succeeding states, most of which were founded by nomadic peoples who had invaded and settled in agrarian land in North China. In the meantime, what was left of the Jin in South China (known as Eastern Jin) ended in 420 and was followed by four brief dynasties: the Song, the Qi, the Liang, and the Chen. Not until 589 did the Sui dynasty in North China, having swept away rival states in the North in 581, conquer the Chen in the South to reunify China under one imperial state.

It was during the nearly four centuries of political division and ethnic assimilation that various states in the North and the South expanded their penal codes and developed their judicial practices. This happened because each rival state or brief dynasty regarded a new penal code as a way to symbolize a new and better government with the Mandate of Heaven. The end result was that Chinese law and judicial practices entered a maturing phase, and some important legal developments of this period would be inherited by the major dynasties to come.

One aspect of the legal evolution was that the penal codes conveyed, more than ever before, Confucian concerns about the patriarchal family system and the absolute power of the emperor as the Son of Heaven and the parent of the people, despite (or because of) the growing influence of Buddhism and religious Daoism (an outgrowth of philosophical Daoism) during the period. Significantly, lawmakers in those states, even ones founded by nomads, were Confucian scholars who facilitated the Sinicization of nomadic peoples.

The most important legal work of this period was the penal code of the Wei (220–265) of the Three Kingdoms. Reorganizing and adding to the Han code, the Wei code featured eighteen chapters. The first chapter was on legal principles, a change from the *Law of Nine Chapters* of the Han that discussed principles in the final chapter. The new code added nine chapters to categorize in greater precision various offenses and judicial procedures. Besides the penal code, the Wei compiled forty-five chapters of ordinances on local administration, and more ordinances on the central government administration and military affairs. The Wei code and ordinances amounted to more than 180 chapters.[38]

The Jin dynasty (266–316) that succeeded the Wei further revised the previous laws to produce the Jin code, with twenty chapters and 1,530 articles. In addition, the Jin compiled forty chapters of ordinances, covering such matters as state administration, official ranks and appointments, rituals, official conduct, educational affairs, household registration, taxation, transportation, medicine, palace security, military command and warfare, and imperial household and aristocracy. The subsequent dynasties would incorporate all these matters into penal codes.[39]

Zhang Fei, a judicial official of the Jin, wrote a preface to the Jin code to define and clarify important legal concepts and principles. He explained, for example, how to judge a criminal offense to be intentional or unintentional or negligent; what would constitute swindling, fraud, assault, unfilial evil acts, grave depravity, and so on; how to differentiate initiating a crime, conspiring to commit a crime, and leading the commission of a crime by a group; what would constitute robbery and ill-gained goods; how to punish a perpetrator of multiple crimes, and so on.[40] These legal expositions were to help officials grasp and apply the penal code properly. They formed a useful framework of legal theory for subsequent lawmakers to follow.

In aggregate, the changes and transformations in law and punishment during the period led to less severe and relatively more humane penalties for criminal offenders. From the Han dynasty through the period several heated debates occurred among high officials over whether bodily mutilations should be restored as punishments, and each time the opinions against restoration prevailed.[41] Notably, the Northern Qi (551–589) once again abolished castration as a penalty. Thereafter castration was never prescribed as a regular penalty in the penal codes of subsequent dynasties, even though it would be used as a rare and special penalty for certain offenses in the Qing dynasty.

In the meantime, punishments had transformed from centering around the ancient five penalties of bodily mutilations to the new five penalties: death; exile, with flogging; penal labor, with whipping or flogging; whipping; and flogging. In cases where mitigating circumstances existed, offenders (or their families) could redeem these penalties with fines. The penal code of the Northern Zhou (557–589) even set time periods for families of convicts eligible for redemptions to prepare the required money, from fifty days for the death penalty to ten days for flogging, and "the very poor may request exemption from payment."[42]

Confucian concerns for the family system may be seen in the following examples. In 488 Emperor Xiaowen of the Northern Wei (386–534) issued a decree that if a capital offender to be executed had old grandparents who had no other children and close kin, such a case be reported to the throne.[43] Presumably such an offender would be spared from death by an imperial pardon, even though the sources are vague on the point. The idea of allowing a capital offender to live in order to support his grandparents (or parents) was based on Confucian morals about filial piety and the patrilineal family line. This suggests the degree to which the Tuoba clan of the Xianbei, a non-Chinese nomadic tribe that founded the Northern Qi, became Sinicized, and the degree to which Confucianism (via Chinese elites) influenced the elites of nomadic peoples who established states in North China and tried to govern the people on the land. The practice, however, did not become standard in subsequent dynasties until the Tang.

Another provision in the penal codes of various states of the time was about the elderly and the very young. The classical sources had already noted that the elderly and the weak should not be punished. The "Zhou Rituals: Judicial Office" ("Zhouli sici") said that amnesty is first for the young and the weak, second for the elderly, and third for the mentally disabled. The principle was firmly established during the Han dynasty. By this time it had become common in all the penal codes that seniors of seventy and over and minors under ten were not liable for any offenses except treasonous crimes and murder. These provisions would feature in the subsequent penal codes.[44]

The period also saw the introduction into the penal code of "eight deliberations" (*bayi*) and "ten abominations" (*shi'e*). The eight deliberations first entered the code of the Wei (220–265), even though the concept originated in the pre-imperial era, or no later than the Han dynasty.[45] They referred to eight categories of people who, upon being convicted of offenses, should be considered for leniency in punishment. These included the emperor's relatives, the emperor's friends, highly regarded people, highly capable people, highly merited people, high officials, highly diligent people, and imperial descendants of previous dynasties. The concept and practice favored the imperial clan and other aristocrats but also treated talented people more leniently to serve the interest of the state. (How the "capable," the "merited," and the "diligent" were defined was at the discretion of judicial officials.)

The "ten abominations" first appeared in the Northern Qi code. The term referred to ten types of the most heinous crimes that deserved the most severe penalties, not to be redeemed by fines or given leniency due to the eight deliberations or an imperial amnesty. The ten categories were:

1. Attempts at rebellion: plan to harm or overthrow the emperor.
2. Attempts at seditious acts: destruction of imperial temples, tombs, and palace.
3. Attempts at treason: betraying the state and following a usurper.

4. Unfilial evil acts: beating or murdering parents or grandparents or their brothers and sisters, one's own brothers and sisters, one's husband or his parents or grandparents.
5. Depravity: murdering three people of a family or murder by dismembering or poisoning or using black magic.
6. Grave irreverence: stealing or forging imperial clothing or items, or failure to serve emperor properly in medicine, food, transportation, etc., or cursing emperor, or being impolite to an emperor's envoy.
7. Unfilial conduct: suing or cursing parents or grandparents, or taking family property from parents and not providing for parents, or getting married while in mourning period for parents, or not mourning for parents who died, or falsely reporting parents' death.
8. Unharmonious conduct: murdering or selling senior relatives, or beating or suing senior relatives.
9. Unrighteous conduct: killing local officials, teachers, or officials of the fifth rank and higher, or not mourning a husband who died.
10. Incest: having sex with family members and close relatives, including concubines of father or grandfather, or cousins, uncles, in-laws, etc.

Obviously the ten abominations were mainly designed to uphold the patriarchal family system and the emperor's status as the Son of Heaven and the parent of the people. Thereafter the eight deliberations and the ten abominations would become standard features in the penal codes of the major dynasties that followed.

Mature Penal Codes in the Mid-Imperial Era

The Sui Dynasty (589–617)

In 581 Yang Jian, a general of the Northern Zhou state, took over the throne and founded the Sui dynasty as Emperor Wen. By 589 Emperor Wen was able to conquer the Chen, the last southern dynasty, and reunify the country after nearly four centuries of division. The refounding of a single imperial state ruling over a reunified country was a momentous development that would leave lasting legacies. For one thing, a unified country under a single Son of Heaven came to be an accepted notion of normalcy and legitimacy or conventional wisdom in Chinese political imagination; a dynastic cycle or a Mandate of Heaven would mean a reestablishment of that political order. Second, the Sui dynasty is best known for building the Grand Canal (still in use today) that connected North China and South China, both politically and economically, more closely than ever before. This would facilitate to a degree the continuous integration of the country as a whole in the wake of a third development of historical significance: large-scale migrations of nomadic peoples into North China and of northern Chinese into South China as far as modern-day Guangdong, Guangxi, and Yunnan in the previous four centuries and thereafter. Many Chinese, including officials and commoners, intermarried with non-Chinese people. In fact, Yang Jian, the founder of the Sui, married a woman of mixed ancestry (Chinese and Xiongnu), and Li Yuan, the founder of the Tang, was himself of mixed ancestry (Chinese and Turkic), both attesting to the ethnic assimilations resulting from large-scale migrations of nomadic peoples during those centuries.[46] Many soldiers from the North who marched into the South and stayed there after their missions were over intermarried with native southerners.[47] Thus the Sui dynasty, and the Tang that soon followed, would see China grow as both a territorially more expansive empire and an economically and culturally more complex society with a more diverse population—up to 60 million people during the Tang. The economic prosperity (lasting at least until 755), cultural flourishing, and cosmopolitan outlook, for which the Tang dynasty was known, transpired in that historical context. All this would have implications for the functions of law and justice.

Although the Sui existed for only twenty-eight years, it did not fail to produce a penal code, under the order of Emperor Wen and his son Emperor Yang; as noted earlier, a new penal code had become a necessary symbol in establishing the legitimacy of a new dynasty. The Sui code was largely based on the Northern Qi code, but with some important changes. It streamlined the code, down to twelve books and five hundred articles. It reduced the number of offenses punishable by death, exile, and penal labor. Some cruel and unusual punishments, such as dismemberment, displaying a decapitated head, and enslavement of the family members of offenders, were abolished. Five punishments were simplified and better defined: death (strangulation or decapitation); exile (1,000 or 1,500 or 2,000 *li*);[48] penal labor (one to three years in five grades); flogging (sixty to one hundred blows in five grades), which replaced whipping; and light flogging (ten to fifty blows in five grades). Redemptions by fines were stipulated in grades for different penalties.[49]

Besides the eight deliberations and ten abominations, the code adopted a new rule: the redemption of penalties with offices, which had initially appeared in the code of the Chen (the last southern dynasty). Under the provision, officials of the seventh rank and higher who were convicted of offenses could receive a reduction by one grade in their penalties; the fifth rank and higher could offset two years of penal labor, and the ninth through sixth ranks, one year.

This rule shows clearly that the Confucian political-social order was based on a principle not of equality but of hierarchy, and the penal codes were not based on the notion of equality before the law either. The Legalist approach put forward by Shang Yang in the pre-imperial Qin state had been lost to the Confucian conception of a political-social hierarchy. On the one hand, political-social elites had legal privileges expressed in the penal code by the eight deliberations and the redemption with offices. On the other hand, the hierarchy also meant that higher standards of conduct were applied to officials, since certain articles in the Sui code, and additional ordinances separate from the code, were applicable only to officials and their job performances, not to common people.

The Tang Dynasty (618–907)

With the collapse of the Sui in the midst of widespread rebellions, the Tang dynasty came into being in a familiar pattern: a former general of the Sui, Li Yuan, declared the founding of the new dynasty in 618 and then successfully eliminated and co-opted rival contenders to the Mandate of Heaven. After the change in dynasty, the Tang continued the trajectory started under the Sui of political, economic, demographic, and cultural growth and transformation.

Several developments in the Tang were of historical significance. First, the Tang state made efforts to extend more effective control over land and population—as a tax revenue basis—through household registration and periodic land redistribution. It also regulated markets and set prices for basic commodities every ten days in the capital city Chang'an to ensure social stability. These measures were successfully implemented in the first half of the Tang and would deteriorate after the An Lushan Rebellion of 755.

Second, a civil service examination was finally institutionalized. It initially favored literary skills, especially poetry writing and calligraphy, of those already recruited from families of officials and aristocrats. It would then gradually open the path of social mobility to classes other than aristocrats and officials and thus change the social composition of officialdom and the political-social dynamics of imperial China in the long run.

Third, most of the Tang emperors promoted Buddhism, which had been the case under the Sui as well, until the backlash against Buddhism under Emperor Wuzong (r. 841–846). The result was a proliferation of Buddhist temples, monasteries, and cave shrines, with a growing following of the faithful. A parallel growth was religious Daoism, favored by Li Yuan, the founding emperor, and his successors. Emperor Taizong (r. 627–649) elevated the status of Daoist priests and nuns above their Buddhist counterparts'. Daoism became popular and fashionable among the upper classes; many high officials, and Li Bai, a famous poet, were followers of the faith. In the capital city Chang'an alone there were thirty Daoist temples.[50]

All these developments did not change the dominance of Confucian moral code as the intellectual source of law and justice, however. While Buddhism and religious Daoism were growing during the Tang and in the subsequent dynasties, Confucianism continued to inform the penal codes and legal practices. This was the case because of the compelling power of the ideology undergirding law and justice as part of governance and state legitimacy. The notions of the Mandate of Heaven, Heaven-human interactions, justice as an alignment of Heavenly reason, state law, and human relations, and the centrality of the patriarchal family in the political-social moral order continued to inform the rulers on governance. These ideological constructs were built around the "self→family→society→all under heaven" continuum, far beyond the concerns of Buddhism and Daoism as individualistic or self-salvationist religions, and the latter were not equipped to substitute the Confucian moral code as a guide for law and justice. Like the dynasties before and after, the Tang rulers adopted a pragmatic approach to governance by appropriating the accumulated wisdom in previous penal codes and judicial practices, which led to the further growth of the Chinese imperial law along the traditional trajectory. Buddhism and Daoism might have influenced to a degree the secular trend toward moderating harsh penalties from the Han dynasty down, but that influence is difficult for historians to pinpoint.

Under Emperor Taizong and Emperor Gaozong, two earlier versions of the Tang code, largely based on the Sui code, were enacted in 636 and 651, respectively. Finally, the *Tang Code and Annotations* (*Tanglü shuyi*) was enacted in 654. This work was a milestone in Chinese legal history. First, it was a culmination of all previous lawmaking efforts dating from the pre-imperial era, with maturity and clarity in legal conception and application, built on the moral and practical deliberations of more than a millennia. Second, the Tang code was the first Chinese penal code that would survive in its entirety through several dynasties into the modern era, serving as the model for the subsequent imperial penal codes. Third, the Tang code would project wide influence on the legal developments in neighboring countries, such as Japan, Korea, and Vietnam.

Inheriting all the legal work from the previous dynasties, the Tang code added to and systematized several important legal categories. In thirty chapters with 502 articles, the code covered twelve broad subjects: legal principles, defining the five punishments (death, exile, penal labor, flogging, and light flogging), the ten abominations, the eight deliberations, the redemption with offices, voluntary confession, exemptions of penalties (for seniors, minors, and the sick or disabled), and so on; imperial guard and prohibitions (i.e., palace security); administration regulations; household and marriage; public stables and warehouses; unauthorized levies; violence and robbery; assaults and accusations; fraud and counterfeiting; miscellaneous articles; arrest and flight; and judgment and prison.[51] Under Emperor Taizong's urging, the death penalty for brothers of an offender convicted of treason against the emperor (as a collective punishment) was changed to exile. This led to a wider revision of the law to be more lenient in punishment; the death penalty for ninety-two offenses under the Sui code was changed to exile, and the penalty of exile for seventy-one offenses was changed to penal labor.[52]

Significantly, the Tang code was the first to spell out an article that signaled what may be called "legal pluralism" in Chinese history, even though in practice it might have had earlier origins. Article 48 provided that if various uncivilized peoples (*huawai ren*, lit. people outside Chinese civilization) committed offenses within their groups, their customary rules (*sufa*) should be applied; if they committed offenses between groups, the Tang dynasty law (*falü*) should apply. The annotation under the article further explained that "uncivilized peoples" referred to those in non-Chinese states (*fanyi zhi guo*) that set up their own rulers, each having separate mores and customs and different systems and practices. If offenses occurred within such a state, the matter should be resolved under that state's system and in accordance with its customary practices. If offenses occurred between two peoples, such as Koguryŏ and Paekche (two states in the Korean peninsula fighting one another around that time), the offenses should be determined by using the Tang state law (*guojia falü*).[53] The reference to the two Korean states as an illustration of the legal provision reflected a notion of Chinese overlordship in relation to the Korean rulers that had caused the Sui emperor Yang's military misadventure there contributing to the fall of the Sui; the Tang ruling elites would continue to harbor that notion, albeit with a laissez-faire attitude. More widely, the development of legal pluralism was indicative of the more diverse population living under the Tang state due to the continuous migrations of non-Chinese into North China and Chinese migrations into South China since the end of the Han dynasty and an increasing number of foreigners sojourning in China, and the adaptation of the Tang state in law and justice (i.e., in governance) to that demographic reality.

The Song Dynasty (960–1279)

After the last emperor of the Tang was deposed in 907, a few short-lived regimes followed until 960, when Zhao Kuangying, a general of the Northern Zhou, took over and founded the Song dynasty. As a long dynasty comparable to the Tang, the Song experienced several historical developments. First, the migrations to South China further increased, and more important, the country's center of economic growth moved to the South to stay. In 980 the population under the Song reached around 100 million, and 62 percent of the population were living in the South.[54]

Second, the economy became much more commercialized than ever before, ushering in a "market revolution," complete with the use of paper money issued by the government (starting in 1023).[55] Along with commercialization came urbanization; not only officials but also merchants and absentee landlords clustered in growing cities where luxury and entertainment were thriving industries and where working-class people, including handicraftsmen, dockworkers, physicians, fortune-tellers, entertainers, prostitutes, and others, provided labor and services.

Third, in response to the spread of Buddhism and religious Daoism came a resurgence of Confucianism in the form of Neo-Confucianism, which became the subject of the civil service examinations; the exams were now the primary means of recruitment of officials in the Song. Officialdom was characterized, and valued as such, by cultural refinement and civility, while military services and careers were devalued and downgraded.

Fourth, ironically in view of the devaluation of military services, throughout the span of the Song invasions of nomadic peoples from the northern frontiers were a constant threat and therefore a continuous drain on state resources. In the end, the northern half of the country was lost to the Liao state of the Khitans in 1127, and what was left of the Song, known as the Southern Song, was conquered by the Mongols (who had swept away the Liao and the Jin of the Juchen) in 1279. These developments meant that Chinese society became more complex and fluid, which had implications for criminal and civil justice. But the rise of Neo-Confucianism would ensure the continuous dominance of Confucian moral and legal principles.

Within three years of the Song's founding, the Song code was enacted under the order of Emperor Taizu. The new code followed the Tang code in content but adopted a new format. The structure of thirty books was kept, but various articles in each book were appended with annotations (*shu*), edicts (*ge*), ordinances (*ling*), regulations (*shi*), and directives (*chi*) on the same subject. Thereafter the Song continued to compile legal and administrative directives (*chi*) and precedents (*li*) that emerged in daily governance, so that officials tended to use the directives and precedents instead of the code to adjudicate cases.[56]

Law and punishment in the Song regressed in several aspects from the earlier trend toward moderating harsh penalties. Tattooing was restored as a supplementary penalty (applied to those sentenced to exile and penal labor), as was slicing to death as one form of the death penalty for serious crimes. During the reign of Emperor Shenzong, the idea of restoring bodily mutilations as punishments was again proposed and debated but did not prevail. Under Emperor Shenzong, however, the Law on Severe Punishment of Robbery and Rebellion (*daozei zhongfa*) was enacted. In any region where, as designated by the central government, robbers and rebels were active, this special law, instead of the relevant articles in the Song code, would apply, and the penalties under the law were more severe than the Song code prescribed. When a robber was sentenced to death, for example, his family property was confiscated to reward informants, his wife was exiled for 1,000 *li*, and so on. In the end, much of the country became designated regions where the special law applied.[57] The adoption of the special law points to the emergence of peasant rebellions and riots due to poverty and desperation in many locales, despite the more general trajectory of economic growth, commercialization, and urbanization.

The Yuan Dynasty (1279–1368)

After the Mongols toppled the Song and established the Yuan dynasty, they ruled China as a conquered land and did not intend to integrate with Chinese society or assimilate into Chinese culture. Thus, unlike previous Chinese dynasties, the Yuan governance was based on ethnic hierarchy rather than on social hierarchy. The population was divided into four ranks: the Mongols, allied nomadic peoples, the northern Chinese (who had been ruled by two nomadic states—the Liao and the Jin—that were conquered by the Mongols), and the southern Chinese (who were conquered last). Under the Yuan law, the Chinese were punished more severely than the Mongols for the same offenses.[58]

The Mongols were less familiar with Chinese culture and language because the Liao and Jin states had acted as barriers before their conquest by the Mongols, and the Yuan chose to deny southern Chinese (who also chose to avoid) civil service positions after the conquest, both factors explaining a wide culture gap between the Mongols and the Chinese. The almost colonial situation and the limited capacity of the Yuan state led to a pattern of loose or light government and less heavy tax burdens on the people. The Mongol practice to govern China "cheaply" had at least one unintended consequence: in 1315 the Yuan state reinstituted the civil service exam and then issued an abbreviated curriculum based on the *Four Books* compiled by Zhu Xi, the prominent Neo-Confucian scholar of the Song, for candidates to prepare for the exam. The curriculum would become the core content of the civil service exams in the Ming and Qing dynasties.[59] Thus the Mongols unwittingly left a significant and lasting imprint on the Chinese imperial system.

The Mongol characteristics were also seen in the legal realm. The Yuan penal code was compiled in 1323, based on an earlier version enacted in 1291.[60] The code was a hybrid between the Chinese legal tradition and the indigenous Mongol practices. It had twenty books and 2,539 articles in three categories: edicts (*zhaozhi*), statutes (*tiaoge*), and precedents (*duanli*). The complete Yuan code did not survive; the available version is missing eight volumes. The code carried over many legal practices from the earlier dynasties but also departed from them in several ways. Punishments under the

Yuan code were somewhat lighter than under the previous penal codes; the death penalty was carried out by beheading or, in cases of treason and depravity, slicing to death, and strangulation was abolished.[61] The Ming scholars who authored the *History of Yuan* observed that imperial amnesties were issued in all dynasties, but only in the Yuan dynasty were there amnesties due to Buddhist festivals. (The Mongols had converted to Tibetan Buddhism.)[62]

One more precedent was set by the Yuan: In 1314 five brothers were sentenced to death for capital crimes. Upon reviewing the case, Emperor Renzong sighed, "It is a misfortune for this to happen to the family; pick one [of the five brothers] who was the least guilty to be punished by flogging and let him support his parents, so that the family will not end its line."[63] The intervention by Emperor Renzong revived in effect a long-lost concept that had first appeared in the Northern Wei, "One is spared from death to support parents" (*liucun yangqin*), thus leaving a critical legal principle to be incorporated into the Ming and Qing penal codes. It is instructive to see that the legal principle was first proposed by a Xianbei ruler and then revived by a Mongol ruler before it was established in the Ming and Qing penal codes; the fact that the Xianbei and the Mongols were non-Chinese speaks volume about the acculturating effect of Confucianism and about the multiethnic innovations that contributed to the Chinese legal tradition.

Culminating Penal Codes in the Late Imperial Era

The Ming Dynasty (1368–1644)

The Ming dynasty was founded when the Mongols were driven out of China by peasant rebellions in the fourteenth century. Zhu Yuanzhang, a former rebel leader from the bottom of Chinese society and the founding emperor of the Ming, turned out to be a vigorous and autocratic ruler. He hated his officials' corruption and disloyalty (the latter for any criticism of his policies or conduct) in equal measure and punished real and suspected offenders harshly and cruelly. His obsessive suspicions against corruption and disloyalty would also explain the centralization of power in the hands of the emperor vis-à-vis officials in the capital and provinces. His fourth son, Zhu Di, became the third emperor, known as Emperor Yongle, after taking the throne by force from his nephew, son of Zhu Yuanzhang's eldest son.

Emperor Yongle's reign saw the legendary "Seven Voyages to the Western Sea" (Southeast Asia, the Indian Ocean, and East Africa) in 1405–1433. The Ming state was able to register land and population more systematically than the previous dynasties and began in the 1530s to implement a new method of assessing and collecting taxes known as the Single Whip, which merged labor service into land tax as one single payment for each household, remitted in silver. (Actual methods of tax collection varied to some degree in local societies.) China's population would grow from 60 to 85 million to over 160 million during the Ming. In the meantime a "second commercial revolution" was underway, which was to be further facilitated by an increasing flow of silver into China from the New World after the mid-sixteenth century.[64] In short, under the Ming dynasty Chinese society was becoming more commercialized and therefore more complex and diverse, beyond easy control by the state.

Built after driving out the Mongols whom the Ming continued to fight along the northern frontiers, the new dynasty engaged in a conscious endeavor to restore Chinese tradition, even though certain Yuan legacies actually remained (such as the civil service exam based on the *Four Books*). The effort was manifested in law and punishment as well as in other fields. One year before proclaiming himself the founding emperor, Zhu Yuanzhang had a provisional penal code drafted (with 285 articles), the familiar pattern of issuing a new penal code to symbolize the Mandate of Heaven of a new dynasty. In 1374 the Great Ming Code was written, and its final version was unveiled in 1397.

The Great Ming Code was largely modeled on the Tang code, with some innovations. It had thirty books and 460 articles, organized in seven categories: principles; officialdom; household, with books on household registration and labor services, land and house, marriage, harvest and grain tax, commercial tax, money and debt, and market; rituals; military system, with books on palace security, military administration, crossings and docks, stables and grazing, and message transmission; punishment, with books on robbery and theft, homicide, assault, cursing, litigation, bribery, fraud, illicit sex, miscellaneous offenses, capturing fugitives, and adjudication; and public works, with books on construction and waterworks. Thus the Ming code took another step forward in rationalizing and systematizing the conception and organization of legal categories in the penal code.

Under Emperor Xiaozong, the Adjudication Substatutes (*wenxing tiaoli*) were compiled in 1500. This collection of substatutes (*li*) either added to or expanded the relevant articles in the Ming code, and it provided guidance for punishing offenses under circumstances that were not spelled out in the code. The collection was issued as a separate volume from the Ming code, and later the substatutes were appended to the relevant articles in the code. Officials tended to use these substatutes, rather than the articles in the code, to adjudicate cases.[65]

The Ming dynasty too dealt with the issue of how to treat ethnic minorities in law and punishment. The Ming code stated that the law was uniformly applied to non-Chinese (*huawai ren*).[66] But one substatute issued in 1426 was a guide for trying criminal offenses committed by the aborigines in Guizhou province (*Guizhou turen*, lit. Guizhou aborigines; the term referred to more than a dozen different ethnic minorities there; in contrast, *huawai ren* referred to nomads in the north-northwestern frontiers). Under this substatute, a death sentence would be commuted to penal labor for life; exile with flogging or penal labor with flogging, to penal labor only; flogging, to penal labor for ten months; and light flogging, to penal labor for five months.[67] This was done apparently to treat the ethnic minorities with more leniency than the Chinese population because the former were unassimilated into Chinese culture and unfamiliar with Chinese law.

The Qing Dynasty (1644–1911)

In 1644 the Ming dynasty was toppled by the combination of a peasant rebellion and an invasion by the Manchu, a non-Chinese ethnic group based in Manchuria. After chasing away the peasant rebels, the Manchu established the Qing dynasty in Beijing to govern an expanded China. The pacification of the whole country would take four decades, and the territorial expansion under the Qing would take another few decades. The Qing dynasty was unique in Chinese history, leaving lasting legacies to China as a civilization and a nation-state well into the twentieth century. Unlike the Mongols, who conquered China in the thirteenth century, the Manchu intended to fully integrate with Chinese society and culture in order to govern China effectively, while keeping their own Manchu identity by such practices as not marrying Han Chinese and prohibiting foot-binding for Manchu women, an effort that was successful at least for the Manchu imperial clan and nobles.

Not surprisingly, the Manchu who had been familiar with Chinese culture under the Ming claimed the Mandate of Heaven and embraced Chinese tradition, including Confucianism. This was consciously manifested in how law and punishment were designed and practiced in the Qing. Emperor Qianlong wrote a preface for the Qing code in 1740. Tracing the origins of lawmaking to the sage-kings described in the *Classic of Books* of the pre-imperial era, the emperor declared, "My imperial ancestors received a clear Mandate of Heaven to pacify and govern all lands, and enacted the Great Qing Code and Substatutes, so that benevolence, education, righteousness, and rectification are all in their proper places."[68] Ideological exercises for political legitimacy aside, the Qing dynasty did follow the Confucian tradition in governance and in legal-judicial practices, along with instituting its own innovations.

The first version of the Qing code, based on the Ming code, was completed in 1646. In 1679 Emperor Kangxi ordered the Board of Punishment to compile the Current Substatutes (*xianxing zeli*), which were worked into the Qing code ten years later. Under Emperor Yongzheng, the Qing code was revised again, in 1727. The final version was completed under Emperor Qianlong in 1740, known as the Great Qing Code and Substatutes. Like its Ming model, the Qing code had the same seven categories organized in thirty books, with 436 articles (24 fewer than the Ming code). The number of substatutes would steadily grow in number, and were added to the code periodically. By 1727 these had grown to 824 entries; by 1740, to over 1,400 entries; and by 1870, to 1,892 entries. The Qing being the last imperial dynasty in China, the Qing code was fittingly the final incarnation and culmination of Chinese lawmaking over the course of more than two millennia.

Besides the Qing code, at different times the Board of Punishment compiled several case collections as legal sources. The most influential was the *Conspectus of Penal Cases* (*Xing'an huilan*), a collection of over 5,600 criminal cases that the Board had reviewed and corrected between 1736 and 1834; more than 300 cases occurring between 1842 and 1885 were added later. Separately, the *Collection of Corrected Cases* (*Bo'an huibian*), a collection of 379 criminal cases, was compiled in the 1790s and reedited in 1883; it contained cases that Qing emperors personally reviewed and gave opinions on. Yet another important collection of criminal cases as a legal reference book was the *Board of Punishment Cases of Adding and Reducing Penalties by Analogy* (*Xingbu bizhao jiajian cheng'an*). It contained a total of 2,992 cases and was completed in 1843 by two officials with experience in trying criminal cases.

The case collections served as legal interpretations and precedents for officials to use. In one case in 1779, for instance, due to Emperor Qianlong's intervention, the previous practice that a person of ten or younger committing homicide would not be punished by death was changed by the Board of Punishment: henceforth such a person could face the penalty of strangulation awaiting autumn assizes (henceforth "awaiting autumn assizes" was expressed as "delayed"), depending on circumstances under which the homicide occurred; the new rule was to be followed across the country.[69] All these case collections were an integral part of the Qing law and were actually consulted in criminal adjudications, whether or not they may be considered "case law."[70]

In addition, there were regulations issued by provincial authorities and approved by the central government as supplements to or local variations of the Qing code for the purpose of dealing with situations particular to regional and local conditions. During the Qing dynasty no fewer than a dozen or so provinces issued such regulations. They were essentially the results of negotiations between the central government (the Board of Punishment and the emperor) and provincial governors and their legal staff over how to better apply the Qing law to many different circumstances under which criminal offenses occurred and that the code did not cover at all or failed to address adequately.[71] As such, the provincial regulations also served as a legal source in the Qing criminal and civil adjudications.

Of historical significance in Chinese history, the Manchu reconceptualized China as a multiethnic entity instead of solely Chinese. The Qing incorporated into its territory what the previous dynasties regarded as the frontier regions contested by nomadic peoples—Manchuria, Mongolia, Xinjiang, and Tibet—plus the island of Taiwan on the coast, thus defining what has since been considered China in the modern era. To govern these newly incorporated regions where non-Chinese ethnic groups lived, the Manchu rulers established the Court of Colonial Affairs (*Lifan yuan*) and adopted flexible approaches and practiced legal pluralism. Under the Qing code, the law was still applied to non-Chinese (*huawai ren*), but those administered by the Court of Colonial Affairs were governed by the *Mongol Statutes* (*Menggu li*).[72] In fact, there were other localized laws to govern non-Chinese ethnic groups. In Xinjiang, for instance, the *Chinese-Muslim Regional Statutes* (*Huijiang zeli*), as well as the *Statutes of the Court of Colonial Affairs* (*Lifan yuan zeli*), were applied. Criminal cases among the Mongols, Tibetans, Uyghurs, Kazakhs, and other ethnic groups were adjudicated and penalties meted out under their respective indigenous laws, and civil disputes were settled according to local customs. Sources of those different legal practices even included the Islamic law and ethnic traditions.[73] At the same time, the Manchu soldiers known as bannermen, separate from Chinese troops, were under a special penal code. In addition, there were legal exceptions made to the Qing code in the form of special substatutes applicable in the northern or southern frontier regions or in the metropolitan regions of Beijing and Shengyang (the Manchu native capital), either to make penalties to criminal offenses more severe (in Beijing and Shengyang) or to make criminal procedures and penalties more flexible, deviating somewhat from the Qing code (in the frontiers).[74] All these practices, called "legal pluralism" in Chinese legal history scholarship, echoed the Ming substatute issued for the Guizhou aborigines, but the Qing policy was implemented on a much larger scale and from a rather different perspective than the Ming's: that of a multi-ethnic empire.[75]

Cruel and Unusual Punishments

Here a summary of several cruel and unusual punishments throughout the imperial era is in order. First of all, a quick note on the methods of capital punishment: From the Sui to the Qing, except for the Yuan, all the imperial penal codes specified two regular forms of capital punishment, strangulation and decapitation. While both methods would result in death, strangulation was deemed a lighter penalty than decapitation because the former left the body of the condemned whole, while the latter severed the head from the body, hence their difference in symbolic implications for afterlife. The same logic explains the unusual punishment of desecrating a guilty person's corpse (*lushi*) and dismembering a convict (*lingchi*).[76] For a didactic effect on the public and a shaming effect on the guilty, most executions of the death penalty in both forms were carried out in public places, usually markets or intersections of major streets. In that context, when the emperor ordered a person (an imperial relative or high official) to commit suicide at home (e.g., Fu Su's death), it was considered a merciful favor, as opposed to being executed in public.

Besides the regular execution methods, from the pre-imperial through the imperial era some rulers would use certain cruel and unusual punishments, whether or not prescribed by the penal code of the time, to punish and deter certain offenses. Such punishments were often applied to people convicted of attempting to usurp the throne or murder a sitting ruler, or betraying a ruler to a rival regime or an invading force, or committing depraved crimes. A despotic ruler would cruelly punish officials who offended him by disagreeing with his conduct or policy.[77]

One cruel and unusual punishment was *lingchi*, known in the West as "death by a thousand cuts" or "slicing to death"; it was essentially dismemberment of a person's body after he or she was killed at the third cut by a knife. "At least as it was performed in the late Qing, *lingchi* was not a slow death, nor did it leave the victim 'lingering' at the death's door, nor did it involve a thousand cuts. It was a methodical and relatively swift technique for putting someone to death."[78] Although different ways of dismembering bodies as severe penalties had occurred earlier, its final form as *lingchi* originated in the Liao state (907–1128) and the Song dynasty as an ad hoc, exceptional punishment; while the practice became formalized in subsequent dynasties, its legitimacy was questioned by some officials along the way.[79] In the Yuan it was one of the two forms of capital punishment (the other being decapitation), and in the Ming and the Qing it was reserved as a more severe punishment than strangulation and decapitation for certain heinous crimes.

The Qing code listed seventeen offenses to be punished by *lingchi*. For instance, if a man killed three members of a household (including servants or hired laborers), he would be executed by *lingchi* and his severed head displayed in public; if he had wife and children, they would be exiled to the frontier as slaves to soldiers.[80] In 1788 a tenant farmer named Zhang in Henan province, angered by a bitter dispute with a neighbor, hacked to death three sons of the neighbor and left the seriously wounded fourth son for dead. The provincial governor applied the law and sentenced Zhang to death by *lingchi*, and his wife and two young sons to exile to the frontier as slaves. Upon reviewing the case, Emperor Qianlong opined that Zhang's two sons should be castrated. His reasoning was that Zhang killed his neighbor's three sons, and the fourth, still fighting for his life, might also die; such heinous acts of cutting off someone's family line could not be adequately punished without having the killer's family line also cut off. The emperor ordered that such a penalty for children of such killers be a substatute to be followed in similar cases in the future.[81] Qianlong's reasoning shows a sense of justice that valued the family line and was based on the notion of countering a vicious crime with a fitting penalty to restore the balance between yin and yang. But that was not a universal view. Some officials' criticism of *lingchi* was exactly that the state should not punish an offender by committing the same act; in other words, they opposed "an eye for an eye" or "mirror penalties."[82]

Another cruel and unusual punishment was desecrating the corpse of a convict, either as an additional punishment or because the guilty person was already dead. In the Yuan dynasty, for example, Qian Zhen, an official in Chaozhou, Guangdong province, tried and failed to seduce the wife of another official, Liang Ji. Qian then framed Liang and had him killed in prison. When his misdeeds were exposed, Qian committed suicide by drinking poison. Emperor Taiding issued an edict that Qian's body be desecrated. The case then became a legal precedent in the Yuan.[83]

Starting with the pre-imperial Qin state when Shang Yang was in power, one cruel and unusual punishment was to execute the adult male family members and enslave (to the state) the adult female and minor family members of an offender. This kind of collective punishment as retribution and deterrence was conceived in accordance with the discourse on the primal importance of the family line and on collective responsibility for an individual's conduct. In the earlier dynasties family members and relatives thus punished would include three branches (and up to five, seven, and nine branches). How those branches were counted was a matter debated by scholars in the later dynasties. It was generally agreed that the "three branches" likely referred to relatives of father, mother, and wife of the offender. Throughout the imperial era, collective punishment occurred sporadically, typically when an emperor was offended either by a conspiracy or his paranoia thereof, or by an official who criticized the emperor's policy or conduct. The Ming dynasty saw the last events of this nature.[84]

Down to the Qing dynasty, punishing convicts of heinous crimes would still involve exiling their family members to the frontiers as slaves of the state. More severe punishments of family members (including minors) and close relatives of those who committed treason, rebellion, sedition, corruption, and mass killing (three or more members of a family) included the death penalty and castration, even though castration was not in the five punishments of the Qing code.[85]

Two additional penal practices were used in various dynasties, whether or not they were within the "five punishments" in the code, and were applied as supplementary penalties under the Qing code: wearing a *cangue* (a wooden board into which a convict's neck and hands were locked) in public, at the gate of the county government, for varying periods of time, and being tattooed with the Chinese characters for "exile" on the face, or "robbery" or "theft" on the right forearm, for related offenses and penalties. These add-on penalties offered more grades of punishment to better fit offenses committed under varied circumstances. In addition, wearing a *cangue* in public and bearing the tattoos were forms of public shaming as penalty for wrongdoing, with a didactic effect on the public, which the state took seriously. Under the Qing code, for an ex-convict to remove the tattoos without authorization was an offense by itself that was punished by sixty blows and reapplication of the tattoo.[86]

Three key points in the development of Chinese law and justice stand out. First, the notions of the Mandate of Heaven and Heaven-human interactions informed the conception of the political-social-moral order in a way that centered on the imperial system and the patriarchal family system. Justice was conceived to have three functions: to punish deviations from that order, to properly fulfill Heavenly reason and adjust human relations, and to rebalance yin and yang. Second, over the course of two millennia, Chinese penal codes grew more and more elaborate and comprehensive. By the Tang dynasty in the seventh century, if not earlier, a penal code would cover all aspects of the political-social-moral order, including administrative, civil, and criminal matters. Third, regular punishments for criminal offenses shifted from bodily mutilations to more rational and humane forms of penalty for most offenses, even though certain cruel and unusual punishments remained and flogging to inflict bodily pain was still used as a penalty for lesser offenses. Penalties could be redeemed with fines for elderly or disabled offenders or for amnesty or other circumstances. Imprisonment was not conceived as a penalty.

The penal codes provided legal penalties for acts or conduct that violated norms in all matters of the political-social-moral order in imperial China, from marriage, property, succession, inheritance, debt, taxation, bribery, official misconduct, and treason against the emperor, to violent crimes such as rape, murder, robbery, and assault. Before looking into how such offenses were punished under the law, we need to understand how such cases were adjudicated, that is, how the judicial system was set up and how judicial functions were performed in imperial China.

2
From the Imperial Capital to the Magistrate's Court

Judicial Practices in Imperial China

An understanding of law and justice in imperial China must address how the law was enforced and by whom, that is, what institutions performed judicial functions and how they operated. Institutionally, the system comprised judicial bodies of the central government in the capital and the administrative hierarchies across the country where law and justice were carried out and procedures and practices developed. Along with the penal codes, judicial practices in imperial China evolved through the ages and became more elaborate and more regulated; from our perspective, some aspects of the system and practices were deeply flawed. The judicial practices, as well as the penal codes, help explain how the Chinese imperial system operated and why it lasted so long.

The Judicial System in Imperial China

Judicial Bodies of the Central Government

Judicial independence was a modern concept of Western origin. In imperial China, judicial affairs were part of the responsibilities of administrative officials at all levels of the state and were dealt with as such. Certain institutions at the imperial capital would supervise judicial matters in the country, but across the country judicial functions were performed by provincial, prefectural, and county officials, who were assisted by judicial officers and/or private staff.

In the Qin and Han dynasties (221 BCE–220 CE), the top judicial officer in the government was the chamberlain of law enforcement (*Tingwei*), who was among the Nine chamberlains (*jiuqing*) at the imperial court.[1] Assisted by subordinate officials, the court lieutenant would adjudicate cases arising in the capital as well as serious or difficult cases sent to the capital from the provinces. The emperor would personally examine important cases and make decisions on them.

During the period between the Han and the Sui dynasties (220–581), the judicial bodies in the capital were largely a continuation of the Han model, with two new developments. In the Wei state (of the Three Kingdoms), an official called the erudite of law (*Lüboshi*) was added to the Office of the Chamberlain of Law Enforcement, which suggests an increased attention to the study of legal theory. In the Northern Qi (of the northern states and southern dynasties period), the Office of the Chamberlain of Law Enforcement was changed to the Court of Judicial Review (*Dalisi*) and became a larger central government institution. This set a model for the subsequent dynasties.

During the Sui and the Tang dynasties (581–907), the central government had three judicial bodies, with overlapping and counterbalancing responsibilities: the Court of Judicial Review, the Board of Punishment (*Xingbu*), and the Department of Censors (*Yushitai*). The Court of Judicial Review was a trial organ, responsible for trying cases involving central government officials and cases of common crimes occurring in the capital that entailed penal labor, exile, and the death penalty. Decisions on such cases would be reviewed and concurred by the Board of Punishment before they could take effect; capital punishment had to be approved by the emperor. Besides serving in the capital, the Court of Judicial Review had six "officers in charge of righting wrongs" (*sizhi*) and eight arbiters (*pingshi*) who would tour provinces to function as circuit courts.

The Board of Punishment was one of the six major administrative ministries of the central government. Its main function was to administer judicial affairs in the country. Besides promulgating substatutes and judicial ordinances, it would review cases tried by the Court of Judicial Review and cases entailing penal labor, exile, and the death penalty tried in the provinces. When the Board found doubtful or wrongful cases, it would either send them back for retrial or try them by itself. When the Board approved death sentences in capital cases from the provinces, such cases were then reviewed by the Court of Judicial Review before being sent to the emperor for approval.

The Department of Censors would supervise all government officials, including those serving in the Court of Judicial Review and the Board of Punishment, and impeach any officials who committed misdeeds and abuses. It would participate in the trial of serious cases and handle administrative lawsuits against officials.

The evolution of central government judicial organs into three bodies in the Sui-Tang period was an important development. It created a sort of "checks and balances" in administering justice: the Court of Judicial Review and the Board of Punishment checked on one another's delivery of justice according to the law, which would help reduce, not eliminate, wrongful convictions and punishments and improve state judicial functions. Both bodies were under the supervision of the Department of Censors that communicated directly with the emperor, which ultimately strengthened the emperor's control of all state institutions.

The Song dynasty (960–1279) saw some shifts and adjustments of judicial functions of different institutions. In 991 the Judicial Control Office (*Shenxing yuan*) was created inside the imperial palace, which would review cases that the Court of Judicial Review and the Board of Punishment were reviewing, thus adding another layer of judicial review, until it was abolished in 1080. In addition, the Department of Censors would try officials who were accused of crimes and review wrongful cases at all levels that were appealed to the Department.[2]

The Yuan dynasty existed for eighty-nine years. During the period multiple institutions in the capital had overlapping judicial functions, signaling an underdeveloped state system that was trying to rule a vast empire. The Yuan kept the Board of Punishment and the Department of Censors, but the Court of Judicial Review was gone; other agencies, such as the High Court of Justice (*Dazongzhengfu*) had judicial power over the entire country, but from 1272 onward it would try only cases involving Mongols, and from 1328 onward, only Mongol officials. The Executive Council (*Xuanzheng yuan*), as the central government agency for religious affairs, would try cases involving Buddhist monks, as would the Bureau of Military Affairs (*Shumi yuan*) try cases of military personnel.[3]

The Ming (1368–1644) and the Qing (1644–1911) dynasties made another change to the judicial functions of the central government. The Court of Judicial Review would only review capital cases, not try any cases. The Board of Punishment now became the trial organ. Besides adjudicating cases occurring in the capital, including those involving officials, it had thirteen (in the Ming) and seventeen (in the Qing) departments. Each department would review and retry cases sent from a province it supervised. Several additional offices were in charge of matters such as preparing the Autumn

Assizes, reducing and redeeming penalties, administering prisons, capturing fugitives, and keeping confiscated goods and money. The Department of Censors (now called *Ducha yuan*) remained the emperor's "eyes and ears" overseeing all officials, including those of the Board of Punishment and the Court of Judicial Review.

The Ming-Qing period also saw special courts in the capital outside the three bodies noted. The Ming emperors allowed palace eunuchs to establish special services whose mission was to spy on and hunt down any real and imagined enemies of the emperor. Known as "the Guards of Embroidered Uniform," "the Eastern Plant," and "the Western Plant," these agencies could arrest, torture, and execute anyone with impunity, and the three judicial bodies had no control over them when they committed such abuse of power and corruption.[4]

Seeing the corruption by eunuchs in the Ming as a lesson, the Qing dynasty made it a rule from the beginning not to give eunuchs special powers. Emperor Shunzhi had his edict to that effect engraved on an iron tablet installed within the imperial palace compound, to be followed by generations to come.[5] The legal pluralism in the Qing, however, entailed certain agencies that performed judicial functions. Along with the Board of Punishment and the Board of Revenue, the Imperial Clan Court (*Zongrenfu*) would try and punish the imperial clan members who committed offenses. When Manchu bondservants of Manchu nobles committed offenses, they would be tried and punished by the Imperial Household Department (*Neiwufu*).[6]

Judicial Functions beyond the Capital

Below the central government, the administrative hierarchy had two or three levels in different dynasties. From the Qin through the Sui dynasty, prefectures and counties functioned below the central government. In the Tang and Song dynasties, the administrative level above the prefecture was called a circuit (*dao* or *lu*). The head of a circuit was the military commissioner. He did not have the powers of the provincial governor of later dynasties and did not perform judicial functions. Instead the circuit department of trial and punishment would supervise the judicial activities of prefects and county magistrates in the circuit. In mid-Song the circuit began to have a judicial commissioner to supervise judicial affairs of prefectures and counties and review cases tried there.[7] The Yuan dynasty created four levels below the central government: provinces, circuits, prefectures, and counties. In the Ming and the Qing the imperial capital commanded provinces, prefectures, and counties, without circuits. (The Qing had circuits between provinces and prefectures for revenue collection purposes, not as an administrative level.)

From the Qin dynasty down, chief administrative officials were empowered to perform judicial functions, but they usually let their judicial officers or legal assistants play that role, a practice that continued until the Song dynasty. In 995 Emperor Taizong issued an edict that chief administrative officials must personally try cases. In 1120 Emperor Huizong further ordered that any prefects and county magistrates who did not personally try cases and let assistants do so instead be punished by two years of penal servitude.[8] Thereafter it became the norm that chief officials would personally try cases. In the Ming and Qing dynasties the provincial governor and the prefect reviewed serious cases from the counties. The county magistrate, who was assisted by his private staff as well as county runners, handled arrest, investigation, interrogation, prosecution, adjudication, and civil mediation, having the most direct impact on how justice was delivered. The Qing penal code specifically provided that county magistrates must personally try civil (as well as criminal) cases.

Below the county government, township leaders and constables would handle civil disputes, help capture fugitives, confiscate criminals' properties, detain criminals' family members, and so on. These mechanisms of dispute resolution and law enforcement in local society were crucial because of the population increase. due to territorial expansion, land reclamation, and introduction of higher-yields grain strains from the Song down. The sheer size of the population (around 400 million by the mid 19th century) was translated into state undercapacity by the Qing era and manifested in the larger numbers of households under the county magistrate's jurisdiction.[9] Under such circumstances, those township leaders and constables either belonged to or were beholden to local elites who were often from entrenched lineages. As "natural leaders," local elites were most concerned about maintaining the legal and moral order in local society as a "public" matter, and they would either volunteer or be asked to mediate and settle civil disputes without involving the magistrate. These local elites were not above bending the law in their own interest when they or their relatives or clients were involved in lawsuits. This social dynamic would condition to a large degree what transpired as justice in local society.

In this connection, the rule that chief officials must personally try cases did not work as well as designed. From the Tang through the Qing, chief officials were mostly appointed after they passed civil service exams. Such exams tested candidates' mastery of Confucian classics and skills of writing and calligraphy, not their legal skills and knowledge. As Confucian generalists, county magistrates were usually unfamiliar with the penal codes and legal ordinances. A county magistrate would typically rely on his private assistants and county runners to perform his judicial functions. Furthermore, due to the rule of avoidance—requiring that governors, prefects, and magistrates could not serve in their native places—the county magistrate was an outsider to local society, while his county runners were local men rooted in local power networks and controlled by local elites. Thus the county magistrate would often face challenges from local elites if he wanted to handle judicial matters impartially and according to the law.

Officials' Judicial Functions and Liabilities

Officials had many responsibilities and were liable for failings in performing their duties, including their judicial functions. As early as in the pre-imperial era, officials would be punished for mishandling cases due to five misdeeds: abusing power, using public office to settle private scores, allowing wife or concubines or their relatives to interfere with cases, taking bribes, and accepting illegal requests. The penalties of an official for such misdeeds would be the same as for the crime in question.[10]

In the Qin dynasty miscarriage of justice by officials was classified in three categories: punishing serious crimes lightly or punishing minor crimes severely; minimizing crimes to let offenders get away; and unintentionally misjudging offenses and penalties. The first emperor of the Qin punished officials for such failings by exiling them for labor services at the construction site of the Great Wall or for military services in the southern frontiers.[11]

The Han dynasty lawmakers reconceived judicial misconduct. They used the concepts of "let off" (*chu*; to let offenders get off with lighter or no punishment) and "frame in" (*ru*; to convict and punish the innocent or punish an offender more severely than the law prescribed). Intentional deviation in either direction would be punished, while unintentional mistakes were not.[12]

Of course, to prove whether or not mistakes were intentional was complicated rather than straightforward, and was up to the judgment of superior officials.

The Tang code was the most clear and logical in defining judicial misdeeds and penalties for them. First, an official could only try an offense of which a suspect was accused, not other offenses; otherwise it would be considered a "frame-in" misdeed, entailing penalties. Second, an official who intentionally let off or framed in someone would be punished for the same offense; for example, if an official had an innocent person executed (framed in), the official would be punished by death; if he gave one year of penal labor to an offender who should have gotten three years (let off), he would be punished by two years of penal labor. Third, for committing frame-in due to unintentional error, the penalty would be reduced by three grades; for committing let-off due to unintentional error, by five grades. Fourth, if an offender to be executed by strangulation was beheaded, or vice versa, or an offender to be executed in either way committed suicide, the official responsible would get one year of penal labor.[13] These rules would be retained in some form in all subsequent penal codes.

Despite these norms or their representations in the penal codes, the reality of imperial justice was not exactly their mirror image. Studies on the Qing law and judicial practices show that in certain criminal matters aside from serious offenses such as murder, rape, robbery, and rebellion, county magistrates tended to go easy on (i.e., let off) accused offenders. The cases in point were the offenses of getting married during the mourning period for diseased parents or husband (*sangqu*) and of marrying the wife of a diseased brother (*shouji*). Under the Qing code, the *sangqu* offense called for a penalty of one hundred blows on both parties before the marriage was dissolved; the *shouji* offense called for strangulation; in either case, if the offense occurred under the care of a senior family member, the penalty fell on the latter.[14] In reality, Qing magistrates often declined to take up such cases when reported or imposed no penalties on the offenders. They did so because they faced more important matters to deal with while having limited resources at their disposal, *and* because such "offenses" were often long-standing local customs among nonelite families, primarily due to economic necessity, even though magistrates and local elites were intellectually and morally opposed to such marriage practices.[15] This illustrates how Qing magistrates, in their daily work, perceived and acted on the perception of an alignment of Heavenly reason, state law, and human relations. It may be reasonably assumed that similar scenarios occurred in previous dynasties as well, which is yet to be confirmed by research.

Another area of the emperor's concern about how officials performed their functions was the efficiency by which court cases were processed, because a delayed case, especially a criminal one, would mean a wrong was not righted; as a result, the emperor's power and wisdom, indeed his Mandate of Heaven, would be questioned. So the central government pushed hard to minimize and clear up case backlogs and trial delays at various jurisdictions. In the Qin law, if the accused was detained for a long time without trial, officials in charge were held accountable. In the Han dynasty, the first emperor issued an edict declaring that when "cases were difficult to decide [due to lack of evidence], officials may not dare to decide, so that the guilty were not convicted, and the innocent were not cleared, for a long time"; such cases were sent to superior officials to be resolved.[16] Again it was the Tang dynasty that laid down for the first time the limits to how long various cases should take to be closed: the Court of Judicial Review should try a case within twenty days, and the Board of Punishment should review a case within ten days; if the Board's review disagreed with the trial results, the Court was to retry the case within fifteen days, and provinces were to retry the case within seven days.[17] The Song dynasty under Emperor Taizong revived the Tang rule on time limits for various criminal cases to be closed.[18]

The Ming code for the first time provided penalties of officials for case delays. If officials committed case delays, they would get twenty heavy blows; every three additional days would add ten heavy blows, up to sixty in total. If a suspect died under detention because of case delays, the official responsible would be punished by flogging and up to one year of penal labor, depending on what offense the suspect was charged with.[19] This article was retained in the Qing code.

The law on the book was one thing; whether the law was followed or enforced was another. The Song dynasty, for instance, saw repeated memorials from high officials addressing the fact that criminal cases were often delayed at every stage of the trial and review process, stretching out as long as one or two years. It often occurred that a convict who was finally spared the death penalty or given a reduced sentence by the Court of Judicial Review for reasons of mercy had already died in prison. Such memorials did not change the situation, however.[20]

Judicial Effect of the Censor System

From the Qin through the Qing, the central government always had a department of censors (its name varied in different dynasties) because of the "principal-agent relationship." A ruler (or a state) as the principal must rely on agents (officials) in order to govern, but agents do not always act in the best interests of the ruler. Inherently, the ruler does not have as much information on what is going on locally as agents do (what is called "information asymmetry"); therefore it is necessary for the ruler to monitor and discipline agents, which is an indispensable task with unavoidable costs for any ruler or state. The existence of censors in the imperial dynasties illustrates how Chinese emperors tried to deal with this universal issue in governing a country.

The censor served as the "Son of Heaven's eyes and ears" by monitoring all officials' conduct and impeaching their misdeeds, such as bribery, embezzlement, violation of rules and regulations, and dereliction of duties. Since judicial functions constituted an important part of the duties of governors, prefects, and magistrates, these officials' judicial performance did not escape the censor's watchful eye. The Department of Censors participated in reviews of capital cases and other joint reviews by high officials of serious cases. Circuit censors from the Department would tour provinces within each circuit, inspect prisons and interview inmates, and hear wrongful cases when they received complaints. All this weighed heavily on the shoulders of administrative officials handling judicial affairs.

In the Ming and the Qing dynasties, in addition to the Department of Censors, six boards had their own censors. Their job was to monitor any and all things they saw fit within their board and make comments, suggestions, or impeachments directly to the emperor. Revising a practice from the Tang and Song dynasties, Emperor Kangxi of the Qing in 1700 ordered that circuit censors and ministry censors should report officials' misdeeds, even if based only on hearsay (*fengwen*, lit. "heard in the wind"), but any false reporting motivated by private agenda would be punished under the law.[21] How this order was followed may be glimpsed in one case. In 1726 Xie Jishi, a circuit censor, impeached Tian Wenjing, a provincial governor, for corruption, without any evidence beyond hearsay. The ensuing investigation found Xie's accusation to be false, and the Board of Punishment decided that Xie should receive the death penalty with immediate execution because he had conspired and formed a faction with other high officials against Tian. Emperor

Yongzheng commuted Xie's death sentence to exile to the frontiers for military service, and other officials involved were given various penalties.[22] The case shows that censors would also have to walk a fine line in performing their duties for the emperor.

One of the mechanisms used by Qing emperors to control officialdom and gain sensitive information was the secret memorials system that Emperor Yongzheng developed. Certain high officials, such as provincial governors, governors-general, senior censors, and provincial education commissioners, could send memorials directly to the emperor on any issue they wanted to report. Later Emperor Qianlong would chastise a provincial governor for using secret memorials to accuse a county magistrate of abusing his office. The emperor issued an edict to explain his view: when officials used secret memorials to make accusations without stating their sources of information, it was impossible to verify the information; the practice encouraged disciplinary proceedings based on hearsay. In this instance, Emperor Qianlong contradicted his grandfather on hearsay, even though the latter was referring to the censor's job. Qianlong's concern was not about the rights of the accused but about the correct rules and therefore the legitimacy of the central government or the imperial power.[23] Nevertheless all these were concerns about and approaches to the issue of principal-agent relationship.

Judicial Procedures in Imperial China

Jurisdictional Hierarchy

Since chief administrative officials performed judicial functions, jurisdictions for handling criminal and civil cases were determined by administrative hierarchy. From the Han to the Tang there was a three-level and three-trial process: the first trial by the county magistrate, the second trial after review or appeal by the provincial governor, and the third trial after review or appeal by the judicial bodies in the imperial capital. From the Song to the Qing the system was a four-level and four-trial process, at the county, the prefecture, the province (or the circuit in the Song), and the capital. Multiple trials and reviews applied to criminal cases entailing penal labor, exile, and the death penalty. Lesser penalties and decisions on civil disputes were decided by one trial at the jurisdiction where such cases were filed, even though dissatisfied civil litigants could appeal to higher officials, although usually no higher than the provincial governor.

These rules were not clearly defined and strictly adhered to until the Tang dynasty. Under the Tang code, if a person filed a lawsuit above the proper level, both the person and the official who accepted the case would be punished, each by forty blows. On the other hand, if a lawsuit was filed at a proper jurisdiction and an official in charge made excuses to reject it, the official would be punished by fifty blows.[24] In the Ming and the Qing, the penalty for skipping lower-level jurisdictions became more severe: fifty heavy blows.[25]

Direct Appeal to the Emperor

Seemingly contradictory to the prohibition of skipping lower jurisdictions, in most dynasties ordinary people were permitted to make a direct appeal to the emperor. The premise was that a person or his relative had followed proper procedures to file a lawsuit, or had been prosecuted, at a proper jurisdiction, but the person or his relative was wrongfully treated, and his appeals to higher-level jurisdictions were wrongfully rejected, so that appealing directly to the emperor for intervention was his last recourse. When such an appeal was accepted and processed, and the case was corrected, the official of the original jurisdiction would be penalized. Thus the practice was a mechanism for the emperor or the central government to bypass the bureaucracy to get to the bottom of a wrongful case, and was another mechanism to monitor the conduct of officials at all levels.[26]

According to the classical sources, the practice of ordinary people appealing to the Son of Heaven originated in the Zhou period. It continued into the Han dynasty, as the *History of Han* (written by Ban Gu in the first century) recorded the following instance. In 167 BCE Chun Yuyi, a well-known physician and one-time local official, was accused of misconduct and sent to the imperial capital for trial and corporal punishment. His youngest daughter, Tiying, fifteen, went with him to the capital. She submitted a petition to the emperor, arguing that executed people could not be revived and mutilated bodies could not be restored, so the punished had no way to reform their behavior. She requested that she be allowed to substitute for her father and be penalized by serving as a slave of the state so that her father could reform himself. Emperor Wen was moved by her petition and ordered the changes that led to the abolition of bodily mutilations.[27]

Appealing to the emperor as a practice was developed after the Han and institutionalized in the Tang. People had three ways to appeal to the emperor. First, there were two big drums at the front entrance of the imperial palace, which people could beat to call the emperor's attention to their cases. Second, people could submit written appeals to other designated recipients. Third, people could kneel on the side of the road and shout when the emperor's convoy was passing. Under the Tang code, if an official of the original jurisdiction for a case did not act immediately after a direct appeal to the emperor was accepted, the official's penalty would be raised by one grade from the penalty for dereliction of duty. If the appeal proved to be untruthful, the petitioner would get eighty blows. By the Qing dynasty, the penalty for a false appeal to the emperor had been raised to one hundred blows and exile to the frontier.[28]

One case in the Song dynasty shows how the procedure would work for people who were wronged. In 984 Woman Liu of Kaifeng, the imperial capital, accused Wang, her late husband's son from a previous marriage, of poisoning her so that she was dying. Arrested and interrogated, Wang denied the charge. But having been severely tortured by another official, Wang admitted to the charge. In the meantime Woman Liu died. When Wang's case was reviewed by the Court of Judicial Review, his conviction was found to be doubtful for lack of evidence of poisoning. Wang was not acquitted, however, but his sentence was reduced to penal labor. That was when Wang's wife, Woman Zhang, beat the drums at the entrance to the imperial palace. Emperor Taizong personally questioned Woman Zhang to learn about the case. The ensuing investigation discovered that Woman Liu had engaged in a sexual affair and feared that Wang knew about it, which was why she tried to frame Wang; she died of illness resulting from her extreme stress over the affair. Pursuant to the investigation, all the officials and staff who had wrongfully handled the case—some had taken bribes in the process—were punished, up to exile to the frontier.[29]

Appealing to the emperor without first going through proper judicial procedures at proper jurisdictions, however, was a punishable offense. In 1751, for example, when Qing emperor Qianlong was touring southern China, two elderly peasants intercepted his convoy to submit a petition on behalf of local people about tax disputes with local governments. The merit of their petition aside (the matter was investigated separately), for the act of directly petitioning the emperor without prior legal steps, the men were punished. Mr. Kong was to receive one hundred blows and exile to the frontiers, but the penalties were to be redeemed with money because he was over seventy; Mr. Liu was exempted from the same penalties for being over eighty. The emperor approved the sentences.[30]

Restrictions on Filing Lawsuits

The Tang code stated that family members and direct relatives living together should not report to the state on one another for committing offenses other than the first three of the ten abominations (rebellion, sedition, and treason).[31] The principle originated in these words of Confucius: "Father shields son and son shields father, wherein uprightness exists."[32] Emperor Xuan of the Han dynasty issued an edict in 66 BCE to the effect that if children shield parents, wives shield husbands, or grandchildren shield grandparents, they would not be punished; if a father shields a son, a husband shields a wife, or grandparents shield grandchildren in capital cases, such cases should be handled by the chamberlain of law enforcement as special cases.[33] Thereafter the principle would be a standard feature in the penal codes of subsequent dynasties. Suing parents was an offense among the ten abominations. The principle conveyed the idea that in matters of law and justice, filial piety and loyalty to family would trump the interest of the public or society at large, but would not trump the interest of the emperor as parent of the people. This reveals in a particular dimension what the alignment of Heavenly reason, state law, and human relations meant in traditional China.

A parallel restriction was that servants could not report on or file a lawsuit against their masters. Under the Tang code, a servant was permitted to shield his master's commission of offenses; if a servant reported on or filed a lawsuit against his master on offenses other than rebellion, sedition, or treason, he would be punished by death; if he went against his master's direct relatives, by exile; if he went against his master's indirect relatives, by one year of penal labor.

Another restriction was based on the lack of physical or mental fitness. The Tang code prohibited three categories of people from reporting offenses committed by others, unless they were victims or the offenses were rebellion, sedition, or treason. These included seniors of eighty and above, minors of ten and under, and those who were blind or mentally unstable or whose two limbs were disabled.[34] This was consistent with articles in the code that people in these categories were not to testify in civil and criminal trials and were not to be punished for offenses other than rebellion, sedition, or treason. Qing legal scholars explained that the restriction was to prevent or curtail false accusations, since these people would not be punished even if they committed that offense. The restriction would feature in the subsequent penal codes, and the Ming and the Qing codes added women to the three categories because women were allowed to redeem penalties for certain offenses (including making false accusations).[35] As case records from the Qing indicate, however, the restriction on women launching lawsuits was not always followed by the county magistrate, especially when widows were suing on behalf of their young sons or for their own property rights.

One case in the Song dynasty is illustrative of how the restrictions were applied. Mr. An sued his stepmother for taking all the property of his father for her own son. The Court of Judicial Review agreed with the rulings at lower levels that An was to be punished by death for suing his stepmother. Emperor Taizong had doubts about the case and ordered further discussion among high officials. There emerged an opinion from forty-three officials: An's birth mother was a concubine; he sued his stepmother because what she did would deprive his birth mother of livelihood; that is, he did so out of filial piety to his birth mother, for which he should not be punished. The solution to the case was to let his father's property stay with him, and his stepmother to live with him, so that he would inherit the property and his stepmother would be taken care of for life. The emperor agreed with the opinion and had two officials of the Court of Judicial Review who had earlier ruled against An disciplined: they lost one month's salary.[36]

Finally, under the law in all dynasties, making a false accusation was a punishable offense. In general, a person who falsely accused another of an offense would be given the penalty prescribed for that very offense. That is, if a person falsely accused a neighbor of a murder that entailed the death penalty, the person would receive the death sentence when his charge against the neighbor proved to be false. False accusation of any kind against parents or grandparents would entail death by strangulation. A case in Henan province in the Qing dynasty is illustrative here. In 1775 Mr. Guan, who had sold himself to Mr. Dou as servant two years earlier, was caught trying to steal money from the house. Dou beat Guan and expelled him from the house. Guan then falsely accused Dou of forcefully taking Guan's wife. Under Qing law, a servant was considered a family member, and his or her relationship to the family head was the same as children to parents. Yet both the county magistrate and the provincial governor failed to consider this point in the law, so Guan was sentenced to exile as if in a regular case of making a false accusation. In reviewing the case, the Board of Punishment spotted the error. In response, the governor requested that he himself be disciplined for the error and Guan's sentence be changed to death by strangulation. Emperor Qianlong approved the sentence.[37]

Criminal Procedure at Magistrate's Court

Since the county magistrate's court was the place where most criminal cases would originate, what was the standard procedure there? The extant imperial penal codes provided specific articles and substatutes regulating how criminal cases should be handled to catch and punish the guilty and prevent or minimize wrongful convictions and punishments. A summary of the procedure follows.

When a criminal case was brought to the magistrate's attention by any source, he was required to take action or he would be punished with one year of penal labor.[38] The first thing was for the magistrate to determine whether the case was a prosecutable or punishable one by learning the identities of and the relationships between the accused and the alleged victim. As noted earlier, in a case where Person A beat Person B, for example, it would be no crime under the law if A was the father and B was the son and the latter was beaten for unfilial acts such as disobeying his parents.

The Tang code also provided that officials should try a criminal case only for an offense of which a defendant was accused; if officials were to seek convictions beyond the offense, they would be held accountable for the "frame-in" offense.[39] If a case involved offenses that occurred in two jurisdictions, it should be tried at one jurisdiction after another, and serious offenses would take precedence over lighter offenses, more offenses over fewer offenses, and earlier offenses over later offenses. If a case involved two jurisdictions more than one hundred *li* apart, it would be tried separately. Violation of the rule by officials would entail one hundred heavy blows.[40]

When a case of homicide was reported, the magistrate was required to personally arrive at the scene, with a county coroner, to examine the dead body and determine the cause of death. A coroner's report in the late Qing would include the names of the coroner, the next of kin of the dead, and any available neighbors (as witnesses), and detailed descriptions, on a preprinted form, of the body in eighty-three lines (ten fingers and ten fingernails were two separate lines, for instance), each marked as lethal or nonlethal (if wounded). Finally, there was the coroner's handwritten conclusion.[41]

When it was determined that a crime had occurred, the magistrate would hold preliminary hearings to question the accuser, who was required to state clearly the facts and circumstances of the crime, including the date, without expressing doubts, or risk the penalty of fifty light blows. Thereafter the magistrate would arrest the accused and hold trial. When the magistrate reached a verdict and decided on the sentence, under the law (from the Tang through the Qing) he would cite specific articles or substatutes or regulations in his sentencing, or risk the penalty of thirty light blows. *The Tang Code and Annotations* explained the rule by noting that conviction and sentence should be based on articles of the code, and if the law was not explicitly cited, errors and wrongs could result.[42] In other words, punishment must fit the crime, according to the law.

If there was no relevant article or substatute in the code that properly fit an offense, the magistrate was to rule by analogy to find an applicable article or substatute to cite. Another avenue of legality for punishment was to cite a catch-all article in the code, that is, "doing what ought not be done." Depending on the severity of the offense, its punishment could range from forty light blows to eighty heavy blows, under the penal codes of the Tang, the Ming, and the Qing (not in the Song code).[43] In 1819, for instance, Zhao Chunling, a banner officer, died of illness. Qi Cheng'e, his subordinate, intended to kill himself to serve Zhao in the afterlife because Zhao had treated Qi well. Qi informed the unit commander of his intention so that his death would not be investigated as a homicide. Qi was arrested as a result. Because what he tried to do was not an offense covered by the code, he was punished by analogy to the offense of "doing what ought not to be done" and given eighty heavy blows.[44]

When verdict and sentence were decided, the magistrate would announce them to the convicted offender and his or her family members to seek his or her agreement to submit to the punishment; if the offender did not agree, the magistrate would hear the offender's reasons and further examine the case accordingly. The Tang code and the Song code provided that officials violating this rule would be punished by fifty light blows for cases entailing penalties of exile and penal labor, and one hundred heavy blows for cases entailing the death penalty; in the Ming and the Qing, the penalties were reduced to forty light blows and sixty heavy blows, respectively.[45]

Legal Scribes' Role

Prior to the twentieth century there were no lawyers in China, since such concepts as legal counsel and defense were absent; instead legal scribes were necessary and available in the judicial process. For a person to launch a criminal or civil lawsuit was essentially to submit a written text presenting one's complaint to the county magistrate. Being illiterate and having no legal knowledge, a vast majority of Chinese litigants would need legal scribes to write complaints for them in order to pursue legal recourse. Legal scribes were called by their clients "litigation masters" because their legal knowledge and rhetorical skills would determine to a large degree whether a case would succeed in court. Those who lost cases due to their opponents' legal scribes would call the latter "litigation sticks." County magistrates would routinely denounce "litigation sticks" as a low-life type who made money by inciting lawsuits at the expense of government resources as well as of people who were dragged into lawsuits. For all the pejorative labels in official rhetoric, legal scribes were never specifically banned by any law in any dynasty, but making false accusations or inciting people to do so was a punishable offense. Under the Tang code, for example, for falsely adding offenses when writing a complaint on behalf of an accuser, a scribe would be punished by fifty heavy blows, and for falsely adding names of accusers, fifty light blows.[46] In short, legal scribes remained a feature in the social landscape and legal arena of the imperial era (and beyond).[47]

Forensic Evidence

In homicide cases, the judicial authorities required the use of forensic evidence to determine causes of death and detect perpetrators. The Qin bamboo strips from the Sleeping Tiger Tombs yielded records of homicide investigations describing in great detail crime scenes and conditions of dead bodies. The records may be considered the earliest efforts at forensic evidence in homicide cases. By the Song dynasty the practice and experience in forensic investigation had attained a quite sophisticated degree, as seen in such books on forensic investigation as *Parallel Cases Ruled in the Shade of the Pear Tree* (*Tangyin bishi*), compiled by Gui Wanrong in 1213, and *The Washing Away of Wrongs* (*Xiyuan luji*) by Song Ci in 1247, the latter being the best known reference book for officials handling judicial affairs.[48] The Song law prescribed detailed rules and procedures for officials to follow in conducting investigations of homicide cases and the examination of corpses.[49] The Ming and the Qing penal codes contained an article stating that officials in charge of judicial affairs personally go to the scene of a homicide and direct coroners to conduct a forensic examination and collect evidence. The Qing article prescribed a penalty of sixty to eighty heavy blows for officials failing to abide by this rule, and further required coroners to study *Xiyuan luji* as the textbook in their training.[50]

Of course, forensic investigation at that time did not have the benefit of modern sciences and technology; nothing like what the TV series *CSI* or *Forensic Files* portrays existed, but many practical techniques were developed and successfully used in homicide cases. In one case, a woman reported that her husband died in a house fire, but the man's family accused the woman of murder. When the victim's body was examined, no soot was found in his mouth. (His lungs were not examined since dissecting a dead body was not acceptable.) To prove what that fact would mean, the county magistrate had two pigs—one was alive and the other dead—burned and then compared their mouths. The one that was burned alive had soot in its mouth, and the one that had been killed before being burned did not. Facing this evidence, the woman confessed that she had murdered her husband before setting the house on fire.[51]

Judicial Torture

Under the judicial rules in imperial China, in capital cases and other serious cases, even with forensic evidence or eyewitnesses, confessions from perpetrators were required in order for conviction and sentence to be considered valid by superior officials, including those of the three judicial bodies in the imperial capital. For this reason, torture in trial was permitted for obtaining confessions from the accused. For imperial Chinese jurists, substantive justice (finding out who committed a crime and punishing the guilty) was more important than procedural justice (fair and humane treatment of the accused).[52]

Imperial lawmakers and high officials were aware of the obvious irony—that the accused might make false confessions to end suffering from torture, resulting in wrongful convictions and thus defeating the purpose of achieving substantive justice. That is why the imperial government highly commended obtaining confessions without resorting to torture. One document on judicial rules in the Qin bamboo strips from the Sleeping Tiger Tombs stated, "It is the best practice to pursue the words [of the accused] to obtain the truth, without using torture; it is a mediocre practice to use torture [to do so]; it is a failure to bluff [the accused]." Another Qin document on the bamboo strips prescribed techniques of interrogation: let the accused speak as much as he will and write down all that he says; question him on inconsistent statements and write down all his answers; further pursue inconsistencies in all his subsequent statements; when all inconsistencies are exposed and the accused continues to be untruthful, then torture may be used; the interrogation record should note that torture was used because the accused gave conflicting statements.[53]

Since solving criminal cases without resorting to torture was highly commended, cases in which officials accomplished such feats were compiled into reference books. One case took place in Taiyuan, Shanxi province, during the Qing dynasty. Woman X and her sister-in-law, Woman Y, were both widows and lived in the same house. Y had an affair with a man in the village. X scolded Y for it. In retaliation, Y falsely accused X of having an affair. When asked who the man was, Y said she did not know his name, but X should know. When X was brought in, she indeed named the man but said it was Y who was having an affair with him. When the man was arrested, he admitted to an affair with X, to shield Y. The magistrate chose not to use torture (for the offense both the man and the woman would be punished by eighty blows). Having placed knives and pieces of rocks of varying sizes in the courtroom and brought in all three suspects, the magistrate asked the two women to attack the man in any way they wanted—even killing him would be acceptable, since the man had brought shame to their family. Woman X was so angry at the man she tried to kill him with a sharp knife. Woman Y hesitated and threw only a small piece of rock at the man's buttocks. Seeing who was guilty, the magistrate stopped the action. Thus cornered, Woman Y confessed.[54]

From the Qin to the Tang dynasty, to prevent the abuse of torture, the state developed increasingly more defined rules on using judicial torture. Under the Tang code, the rules on using judicial torture included the following: First, torture could be used only after all other forms of evidence were exhausted. Second, the use of torture must be preceded by a written statement of the cause (which the Qin document had already prescribed) and a superior official's approval, or it could be applied with the presence of several officials. Third, torture could not be used in excess: no more than three times, with twenty-day intervals, and total blows not exceeding two hundred; for cases entailing flogging as penalty, blows for torture could not exceed those for penalty; if the person still did not confess, he had to be released on bail. Fourth, seniors seventy and older and minors fifteen and younger were not subject to torture, and their conviction required three witnesses' testimonies; if witnesses were fewer than three, then the accused could not be convicted and the accuser could not be punished for making a false accusation. Fifth, pregnant women and women who had given birth within the previous one hundred days were not subject to torture. If an official violated these rules, he would be punished by thirty blows; if a defendant died of torture, the official would get one year of penal labor.[55]

Most of these rules were retained in the subsequent penal codes; the Song code retained the rule on pregnant women, and the Ming and the Qing codes retained the rule on seniors and minors, as well as other provisions. Under the Yuan law, even tying ropes on suspects, having suspects kneeling on sharp objects, and beating suspects on the back were prohibited as "cruel methods."[56] The Qing code provided that the torture instrument, a wooden rod for squeezing fingers, should be used only in robbery and homicide cases, and no more than twice.[57] Whether the regulations were always followed by county magistrates or enforced by their superiors is another matter. Sources suggest that most county magistrates in all the dynasties tended to rely on judicial torture to obtain confessions, and there did occur some cases where magistrates were punished for using torture improperly.

Case Review Procedures

The possibility of wrongful conviction and punishment due to judicial torture or due to officials' mistakes or corruption in judicial processes was partly countered by a critical mechanism: the case review process that became established in the Sui dynasty. All cases from the provinces entailing penal labor, exile, and the death penalty were reviewed by the judicial bodies in the capital and finally by the emperor. Officials not reporting criminal cases that should be reported would be punished one grade below the penalty entailed in the case; not reporting a capital case, for example, would result in the official being punished by exile for 2,000 *li* under the Tang code.[58]

Under Emperor Taizong of the Tang dynasty, a man named Li was prosecuted for speaking heresy about the pending arrival of a new era, which would mean the end of the current dynasty, and therefore was considered to be inciting sedition. Zhang Yungu, a deputy head of the Court of Judicial Review, sent the emperor a memorial saying that Li was diagnosed to be mentally ill and should not be punished under the law. Yet a censor alleged that Zhang shielded Li because Li's brother was the prefect of Zhang's hometown, meaning that Zhang was currying favor with the prefect. Incensed by Zhang's alleged corrupt conduct that involved manipulating the emperor, Emperor Taizong had Zhang executed immediately, only to regret his rash decision at a moment of anger. Thus he made it a rule that officials should resubmit to the emperor any death sentence already approved, three more times for cases from the provinces and five more times for cases in the capital, to get confirmation each time, before execution could be carried out. This was to allow the emperor to reflect on the case in calm and to change his mind as appropriate. Soon, however, Emperor Taizong found that officials would resubmit approved death sentences three times in quick succession, which defeated the purpose of the procedure. He ordered that henceforth such death sentences be resubmitted five times in two days and another three times on the day of execution. If there were capital cases with extenuating circumstances, they should be brought to the emperor's attention.[59]

Later, a rule was established so that even when an official in charge of execution received the final confirmation from the emperor, he was to wait three days before carrying out the execution. Under the Tang code, an official who had a convict executed before receiving the final confirmation from the emperor would be punished by exile for 2,000 *li*; an official who had an execution carried out without waiting for three days after receiving the final confirmation would receive one year of penal labor.[60] The Song code borrowed the Tang article as a substatute, but it was not consistently followed so that at different times high officials called for a full restoration of the Tang rule.[61] The Ming and the Qing codes revived the Tang article but reduced the penalties for failing to follow these rules from exile and penal labor to eighty heavy blows and sixty light blows, respectively.[62]

In the Ming dynasty, a practice called "imperial court trial" (*chaoshen*) was established by the founding emperor, Taizu. Once a year the heads of the three judicial bodies and other high officials would meet at the imperial court to collectively review and decide on capital cases of common crimes that occurred in the capital. Another practice was called the "nine high officials trial" (*jiuqing huishen*): when a capital case was difficult to convict for a lack of evidence and confession, the heads of the three judicial bodies and other five administrative boards (rites, revenue, war, civil service, and public works), plus chief minister, would meet to review and decide on the case.[63]

The Qing dynasty inherited the "imperial court trial" (for capital cases occurring in the metropolitan area of Beijing) and the "nine high officials trial" (for special cases involving high officials) and developed another practice called the Autumn Assizes (*qiushen*) for capital cases from the provinces. The Assizes took place in the ninth month of the lunar calendar. When such cases arrived at the Board of Punishment, they were placed in two categories: to be executed immediately with the emperor's approval, for offenses listed among the ten abominations, especially rebellion, sedition, or treason; or to be reviewed at the Autumn Assizes. The three judicial bodies and other high officials of the central government would gather to review these cases and place them in four categories for the emperor to approve: verified (*qingshi*); stayed (*huanjue*); pitied (*kejin*); and spared (*liuyang*). The convicts in the first category would be executed after the Assizes (the waiting procedures prior to execution would still apply); those in the second would be held in jail for the next year's Assizes; those in the third were commuted from death to lesser penalties for extenuating circumstances; and those in the last group were spared death for being single sons of elderly or sick parents or grandparents who had no other kin (although this consideration was denied to convicts of certain offenses listed in the ten abominations).[64] All these cases going to and returning from the emperor would be copied and filed by the Criminal Section (*Xingke*) of the Grand Secretariat. (Thus the archives of the Criminal Section became one of the major depositories of criminal case files known as *Xingke tiben*.)

The Autumn Assizes had unintended consequences. On average each year two thousand to three thousand capital cases went through the Autumn Assizes, and executions resulting from the procedure fluctuated between 12 and 40 percent of those cases.[65] The largest percentage was the second category, *huanjue*, to be reviewed the following year. Some death row inmates would survive the Autumn Assizes year after year and stay in jail as long as twenty years or until they died, thus in effect resulting in a penalty of long-term or life imprisonment that was not in the penal code.[66]

Another issue concerned those spared death. In 1724 Emperor Yongzheng issued an edict to the Board of Punishment, saying that thanks to the "spared" category, some single sons might commit intentional homicide, counting on escaping the death penalty; so in the future a convict who was spared the death sentence to care for elderly parents must pay sufficient monetary compensation to the victim's family, or the convict would still be executed.[67] To standardize the criteria by which officials on the Board of Punishment would review capital cases consistently, a set of Articles of Autumn Assizes (*qiushen tiaokuan*) was compiled in 1767 and revised in 1784; 1909 was the last revision, into 165 articles.[68]

The capital case review process reflected a cautious attitude on the part of Chinese rulers in meting out the death penalty, aiming to make punishments fit offenses properly so that yin and yang would be balanced: too many executions would mean too much yin in the form of death, but perpetrators of heinous crimes not being punished properly would mean too much yin in the form of evil.[69] The following episode shows how one emperor perceived that balance and how he reacted to a perceived criticism that he lacked compassion. In 1729 Yang Bao, a circuit censor, submitted a memorial to Emperor Yongzheng, proposing that those convicts whose executions were stayed by three consecutive Autumn Assizes be commuted to lesser penalties (and presumably be released thereafter) so that they would not die from illness in prison. In response, the emperor issued a sharp rebuke:

> The law has long since been clear that killers should be punished by death. Of all people under Heaven, who does not have a father, a brother, and a child. If killers could safely get away, without paying a price, who [of the victims' families] would be satisfied? The convicts, after having taken other people's lives, are lucky for not being made to pay the price at the Autumn Assizes, and why should they feel that getting ill and dying from illness are hardships? Furthermore, giving leniency by stretching the law would only spawn criminality. I am afraid that after leniency is given, there will be more offenders.

The emperor then accused Yang Bao of having the evil intent of buying fame for being benevolent and making the emperor look ruthless. He ordered that the Board of Punishment come up with a proper punishment for Yang. The Board decided that Yang be exiled to a postal station in Xinjiang (in the remote northwestern frontier).[70] Aside from Yang's alleged intent to buy fame at the emperor's expense, Yongzheng's point was that those who committed homicide but were spared death due to imperial mercy should be grateful, even if they would suffer or die in prison, and that leniency beyond the law would spawn criminality.

Finally, all executions were to be carried out in at a proper time. In the Qing that meant the winter, after the Autumn Assizes; immediate executions for treason, sedition, or rebellion could be carried out in any season, but not on certain "no-execution days" (*jinxing ri*) in each month. Officials who violated these rules would be punished under the law. This practice again reflected the Chinese cosmic view of interactions between Heaven or nature and human affairs, underpinned by the notion of yin and yang; the winter season was the yin time proper for executions of capital offenders, and certain days in each month (even in the winter) were the yang time, when no execution should occur. Despite the rule, specifics were not always the same in all dynasties. The Song dynasty was known to have executions on more days in the year than the Tang dynasty, for example, and the argument for the more frequent and therefore speedier executions was that delaying executions would cause undue suffering of death row inmates in jails—an admission that prison conditions were horrendous.[71]

Prison Conditions

The criminal penalties evolved from the old five punishments (death and bodily mutilations) to the new five punishments (death, exile, penal labor, flogging, and light flogging), and imprisonment in itself was not considered a penalty. Yet criminal suspects, and often witnesses in cases of homicide or other serious offenses, would be detained before the case was resolved, and convicts would be held awaiting punishment. Some inmates would stay in jail for years before they were tried and convicted; some even died there. The spirit of the law meant that detention itself should not be harsh on inmates, since it was not a penalty. Under the Tang code, prison officers would be punished by sixty blows for inmates' deprivations, by one year of penal labor for an inmate dying from deprivations, by fifty blows for stealing inmate rations, and by strangulation for stealing inmate rations and causing inmates to die of hunger.[72] Similar articles existed in the Song, Ming, and Qing penal codes. The Yuan dynasty rules provided that inmates who had no relatives or whose relatives had no means to support them should be provided with food, clothing, and medicine or medical care as needed.[73]

The spirit of the law was rarely followed, however. In all the dynasties, prison conditions in many locales were miserable, but cases of punishing officials for inmates' suffering or death were rare, even though some cases were recorded in the Qing dynasty.[74] One typical depiction of abuses inside prisons in the imperial era is found in the *Song History* penned by Ming scholars, even though the abuses were by no means limited to the Song:

> Although law did not provide imprisonment [as penalty], to deal with violent crimes such as rebellion and robbery, [officials of] prefectures and counties would imprison offenders whose crimes did not entail exile, for one to two months or for one quarter to a half year, for them to repent; even longer imprisonment would have a time limit; and all inmates were fed. However, these days [under Emperor Lizong, r. 1225–1264], [officials of] prefectures and counties were so cruel that offenders were imprisoned without time limits, and they were not provided with food, until they died in jail. Some runners would beat up and use restraining devices on inmates for private gain. Local powerful families would bribe officials to frame innocent people and make them die in jail. Even litigants of familial and marital disputes were imprisoned. Some inmates died of hunger for lack of food and water. Others died of physical abuse as they lacked resources to bribe runners. When some inmates died of suffering due to runners taking bribes, the runners would report that the inmates were ill and under medical care, to prevent the truth from coming to light, while the inmates were already dead. In reports such inmates were said to have died of illness, but in reality they were intentionally killed. By the time of Emperor Duzong [r. 1265–1274], repeated edicts were issued to stop such abuses in jails, but to no avail. And the dynasty fell [in 1279].[75]

While the Ming scholars made a connection between the prison abuses and the fall of the Song that lost the Mandate of Heaven, such conditions as described were actually common in all dynasties, including the Ming. That is why Ming and Qing officials would conduct "hot reviews" (*reshen*) in summer to speed up processing defendants waiting for trial and convicts who would receive penalties below penal labor to "clear jails," since inmates tended to die of diseases in the summer heat.[76] The dreadful prison conditions gave rise to many criticisms from some officials and social elites in the imperial era, which contextualizes the Qing censor Yang Bao's proposal that those who survived three Autumn Assizes be given lesser penalties so that they would not die in prison. Emperor Yongzheng did not dispute the premise about prison conditions, arguing only that those who survived the Autumn Assizes and died in prison had nothing to complain about. This mentality, probably shared by many officials and runners, was one of the reasons prison conditions remained horrible throughout the imperial era (and beyond).

How should the judicial systems and judicial practices in imperial China be assessed? As two scholars noted, speaking of the Tang code, "the criminal procedure shows a very rational system of justice.... Both the accuser and the officials involved had to be careful lest they themselves face punishment."[77] There was a manifest effort on the part of all dynastic rulers and their officials to deliver justice as they collectively understood it. Their understanding was underpinned by enduring notions of a cosmic order mirrored in the existing political-social-moral order and of Heaven-human interactions. Given these larger historical contexts, how did law and justice actually uphold the Heavenly ordained order in human society?

3
The Emperor, the Family, and the Land
Law and Order in Imperial China

To the elites in imperial China, the cosmic order engendered a corresponding political-social-moral order in human society. Concretely, that order comprised the imperial system and the family system, both of which were headed by a patriarch, the emperor and the father, representing the primal force of yang. Law and justice as governing instruments of the imperial state were to uphold and protect that order. The legal cases include those involving offenses against the imperial system, the family system, and the socioeconomic system (the landowning system in particular), all interwoven in an overarching moral order. In Western legal terms, these were criminal and civil cases, but for Chinese elites in the imperial era, there was no such divide between the two categories. The Chinese would regard all cases of criminality, illegality, and immorality as offenses to varying degrees in a continuum undermining the Heavenly ordained political-social-moral order, to be dealt with as such.

Law and the Political Order

The first and foremost function of law and justice in imperial China was to maintain the imperial system whereby the authority of the emperor as the Son of Heaven and the parent of the people would prevail over everyone and everything. The emperor was above the law, or rather his will made the law. Such offenses as rebellion, sedition, and treason were among the ten abominations and punished most severely. No later than the Sui dynasty, Chinese lawmakers consistently conceptualized offenses against the emperor (rebellion, sedition, and treason) and common crimes such as robbery and theft in the same criminal category in penal codes, while offenses against the familial order were placed in separate categories.

Equally significant is that the emperor had great concern about officials harming the imperial authority or interest by committing corruption and abuses or violating rules and norms, causing the people to be resentful against the state and thus threatening the emperor's Mandate of Heaven. In the penal codes, books on punishing offenses committed by officials preceded books on punishing rebellion and robbery, which suggests that officials' failings in either morality or judgment were perceived to be more harmful to the political-social order than commoners' failings.

Civil Service Exams and Corruption

From the Sui and Tang dynasties down, Chinese officials were selected through an elaborate system of civil service exams. To ensure that these exams were fair and impartial so that the best and brightest were selected to serve the emperor, cheating was strictly forbidden, and precautions against cheating were steadily institutionalized. By the Ming and Qing dynasties, candidates would take exams incommunicado for the duration (up to three days in certain exams), and examination officers would grade exams blindly, with candidates' names on exam papers being covered. Not surprisingly, however, cheating by candidates still happened, as did corruption on the part of officials administering exams. Both kinds of conduct were punishable offenses under the law because they were ultimately attempts at deceiving the emperor and undermining his authority and interest.

The Tang code had an article on punishing officials who would recommend unfit people and not recommend qualified people to be candidates for offices; the penalty was one to three years of penal labor. The article was not always strictly enforced, however. Under Emperor Xuanzong of the Tang dynasty, for instance, two officials in charge of civil service exams, in order to curry favor with Zhang Qi, a censor trusted by the emperor, ranked Zhang's son the first out of sixty-four candidates who passed the national-level exam, causing a public outcry. In response, the emperor personally gave a written exam to all sixty-four candidates. At the end of the exam, Zhang's son was still holding a blank paper! Yet, for such blatant corruption Zhang Yi and the two officials were only dismissed from their offices in the capital and sent to provincial posts, which was deemed a form of banishment but was much more lenient than the penalty of penal labor.[1]

The Song code did not contain this Tang code article, but the Ming and the Qing codes revived it. The Qing code further included seven substatutes under it, referring specifically to irregularities in civil service exams: cheaters would be punished by one hundred blows and wearing a *cangue* for one month, up to exile to the frontiers; any officials who allowed or participated in cheating would be dealt with by the central government. The articles on legal principles specified how to treat officials committing offenses. One article states, "Of all officials of high and low levels in the capital and provinces, if anyone commits public or private offenses, his superior official shall write a detailed report and submit it to the imperial court for instruction and shall not resolve the matter without authorization." A substatute explains, "Of all civilian and military officials, *juren, jiansheng, shengyuan* [three types of civil service degree holders], *guandai guan* [officials with scholarly honors], and county runners, prison officers, and soldiers–all personnel serving the government—if anyone commits illicit sex, robbery, fraud, deceit, and all other offenses of obtaining ill-gotten goods, he shall be stripped of office or title to become a commoner. If the person is granted amnesty, his office or title shall not be restored."[2] In addition, articles on bribery and ill-gotten goods covered corruption in civil service exams.

In the *Conspectus of Penal Cases* compiled by the Board of Punishment of the Qing, cases under the article on officials recommending unfit candidate for offices were all about the punishments of civil service exam candidates for cheating. Cheating acts included carrying cheat sheets into exams, hiring someone to impersonate oneself to sit for exams, stealing another candidate's exam paper to submit as one's own, and creating disorder during exams. The penalties ranged from one hundred blows and wearing a *cangue* for one month, up to one hundred blows and three years of penal labor.[3]

When bribery of officials was involved in cheating on civil service exams, both the cheaters and the officials would be punished severely. In 1712 a serious cheating and bribery case took place in Jiangnan province (future Anhui and Jiangsu provinces). The "nine high officials trial" held at the capital duly submitted the sentences of the convicts to Emperor Kangxi as follows: two officials—Zhao, an Imperial Academy scholar (*bianxiu*) serving as the deputy exam officer for Jiangnan, who took bribery, and Wang, the Gourong county magistrate, who alerted Zhao to the exam paper by a candidate who had paid money for the favor—received death by decapitation with immediate execution; Wu, the candidate, and a certain Yu, who arranged the payoff, received death by strangulation delayed; Fang, the Shanyang county magistrate, was also to die by immediate decapitation for alerting Zhao to the exam paper by Cheng, another candidate seeking favor; Cheng, the candidate who had buried cheat sheets in the courtyard where the exam was held, received death by strangulation delayed; two other candidates who cheated on their own without trying to bribe any officials were punished by flogging; and Zuo, a deputy capital censor serving as the chief exam officer for Jiangnan, was fired for failing to detect and prevent the corruption and cheating on his watch. In a separate case in Fujian province that year, Wu, an exam officer who took a bribe, was sentenced to immediate decapitation; Wang, a cheating candidate, and Lin, who arranged the payoff, were sentenced to death by strangulation delayed. Emperor Kangxi approved all the sentences in both cases.[4] It is worth noting here that from 1772 onward, under the Articles of the Autumn Assizes, capital offenders who were officials would be, without exception, placed in the *qingshi* (verified) category (i.e., they were to be executed), while offenders who were common people might be spared death at the assizes.[5]

Officials Abusing Power

Besides civil service exams, officials, especially county magistrates, had daily opportunities to commit corruption or abuse their power. Two cases will illustrate what constituted such offenses and how officials were punished for them. In 1818 Mr. Xiong accused a wealthier neighbor, Mr. Zhang of gambling, a punishable offense. County Magistrate Gu conducted a trial during which the charge was found to be false and Zhang was acquitted. To thank the magistrate, Zhang gave Gu 600 tael of silver through Gu's family servant Chen. When his acceptance of the silver became known, Gu was dismissed from office and investigated by the provincial governor. Gu promptly surrendered 600 tael of silver to the provincial treasury, and the investigation did not find that he bent the law in order to receive a bribe. Still, for obtaining ill-gotten goods without bending the law, Gu was sentenced to exile to Xinjiang for labor service. Gu's servant Chen was also exiled to Xinjiang as a slave of the state for inducing his master to commit wrongdoing.[6] Evidently the emperor wanted officials to manifest his benevolent rule and did not tolerate either corruption or the mere appearance of corruption.

Officials were prone to abuse their power, even if they intended only to do their jobs effectively. In 1812 County Magistrate Ma led his men to arrest a known gambling operator. In his escape, the gambling operator went through a kiln owned by Mr. You. When Ma and his men wanted to enter the kiln, You stopped them, saying the fugitive was already gone. Ma arrested You to bring him to the county office. On the way You and Liu, one of Ma's men, argued, and Liu hit You in his chest with a piece of wood, injuring him badly. At the county office, Ma still wanted to question You, while You was unable to answer due to the pain in his chest. Ma had You beaten for refusing to answer. Later You died of his injury to the chest. The governor sentenced Liu to death by strangulation delayed for detaining and causing death to an innocent person with intent, and Magistrate Ma was given one hundred blows and exile of 3,000 *li*. In reviewing the case, the Board of Punishment raised Ma's sentence to exile to Xinjiang for labor service.[7]

The Ming and the Qing codes provided that if an official governing the people (i.e., a governor, prefect, or county magistrate) failed to take care of them (*yang*) as a parent, or acted illegally, thus causing the good people to rebel and take over a city, the penalty for the official was death by decapitation.[8] While such cases were rare in the records, the spirit of the law permeated many other articles in the penal codes. One article in the Qing code, for instance, concerned unequal taxes and labor services imposed on the people, a common cause of peasant rebellions and riots. All taxes and labor services were to be assessed based on family members, land owned, and crop yield, according to which each household was assessed as upper, middle, or lower grade. If an official did not charge the rich and placed burdens on the poor, or committed fraud such as falsely switching grades of households, the poor people who were thus harmed could report on the official from the local level up. The guilty official would be punished by one hundred heavy blows. A superior official who refused to take up such a case would be punished by eighty heavy blows. If these officials received goods in return for their acts, they would be punished to the fullest extent under the articles on receiving ill-gotten goods—up to the death penalty.[9]

Although there are some case records from several dynasties that describe the punishing of officials, there is not sufficient data to ascertain what percentage of officials were corrupt and abusive and what percentage of corrupt or abusive officials were brought to justice in a given dynasty. How and why wayward officials were dealt with may be illustrated by one emperor's approach. Emperor Kangxi of the Qing dynasty was one of the more capable rulers who tried to live up to the Confucian model of benevolent governance. After assigning his bondservant Li Xu to the job of procuring textiles in Suzhou for the imperial palace and then of managing the state salt monopoly in Yangzhou, the emperor frequently asked Li for information (through confidential memorials) on particular officials and local opinions about them. On one occasion the emperor asked Li to verify one official's rumored corruption, but after Li's report simply stated that the official greatly enriched himself during his tenure, the emperor did not take action, as the official was already very ill and would die two months later.[10] On another occasion, Kangxi asked for information on Zhang Yingzhao, another official in charge of managing the salt monopoly, because the emperor heard about Zhang's bad reputation. Li reported that the official was not competent in doing his job, but said nothing about Zhang's ethics, and Kangxi took no action.[11] Referring to accounting discrepancies in county and provincial treasuries, the emperor once observed that in monitoring officials' conduct, many things could not be scrutinized too closely: "Under the law, for instance, a county government ought not to take for itself even one percent of a surcharge on taxes, and in daily socializing, officials ought not to accept even ten or twenty coins as a gift, but if such cases were all pursued according to the law, all people would be guilty and no one would know how to conduct themselves." On another occasion he said, "Incorruptible officials tend to be too strict, and being too strict makes subordinates' life very difficult. The best approach [to governance] is to be both incorruptible and tolerant [of subordinates]."[12]

These comments amounted to a recognition of the gap between ideal and reality and of the inevitable conflict of interest between the principal and his agents. The recognition would suggest how and why law as an instrument of governance was applied to officials selectively and deliberately rather than consistently and impersonally. Both human resources and organizational logic would dictate that punishment of agents by the principal was always and could only be selective. In the end, as the historian R. Kent Guy points out in a study of the punishment of certain provincial governors in the Qing, disciplinary actions and/or legal penalties against high officials were used by the emperor "at occasions of political stress to dismiss officials dramatically and peremptorily to highlight imperial political agendas."[13] The pattern was by no means limited to the Qing dynasty.

Rebellion and Treason

As the substatute under the article on "causing good people to rebel" made clear, in the imperial era rebellion and treason for any reason, including officials' misdeeds, would not be tolerated but suppressed, and rebels would be given the most severe punishments. Luo Shengfu of Nanchuan county, Sichuan province, started a cult in 1830. He claimed to have acquired magic power during a trip to Yunnan province and be able to let people acquire martial arts instantly by drinking a special liquid he concocted. When Luo gathered more than one hundred followers, he set up an armed camp, coerced local people to move into it, and killed two men who resisted. Having heard about these events, the county magistrate went to the camp to investigate. Using firearms, Luo and his men shot and killed more than ten soldiers. Later government forces stormed the camp. Luo and forty-one of his followers (men and women) were killed, another twenty-some men and women were burned to death when explosives stored in the camp caught fire, and Luo's son and another seventeen followers were captured.

Under the law, Luo was to be punished by slicing to death for rebellion; since he was already dead, his body was desecrated and his head was cut off and displayed in public. Luo's son and seventeen followers were beheaded on the spot. Another fifty-eight people who had been told by Luo to join the group and had not done so were judged to have committed the offense of knowing and not reporting a rebellion and were sentenced to one hundred blows and exile to Xinjiang as slaves of the state. Some laborers who had been hired by Luo to do menial jobs but were not at the scene during the fighting were sentenced to one hundred blows and three years of penal labor, also for not reporting a rebellion.[14] The case is just one example from the Qing dynasty, but it is typical of the way rebellion, sedition, and treason were dealt with throughout imperial China.[15]

Law and the Familial Order

Parental Power

The story of Fu Su, the elder son of the first emperor of the Qin, will make more sense when we get a full view of the parental power granted by the imperial penal codes. Under the Qing code, if children cursed grandparents or parents, or a wife and concubines cursed the husband's grandparents or parents, the penalty was death by strangulation, but only if the grandparents or parents personally filed the charge; grandparents or parents would not be punished for beating and causing death to children or their wife and concubines who cursed them. If children beat grandparents or parents, or wife and concubines beat the husband's grandparents or parents, the penalty was decapitation; if they killed the grandparents or parents, the penalty was death by slicing—both offenses were listed under the ten abominations. On the other hand, if grandparents or parents beat, and unreasonably killed, children who disobeyed their instructions, the penalty was only one hundred blows; if they intentionally killed children who did not disobey parental instructions, the penalty was sixty blows and one year of penal labor. Thus parents (and grandparents) and children (and grandchildren) were emphatically not equal before the law. How did the law play out in real life?

In 1789 Mr. Zhang's eleven-year-old son stole crops from a neighbor's field. The neighbor asked Zhang for compensation. Zhang was so angry at his son, who had often stolen goods in the community, bringing shame to the family, that he strangled his son to death. The Zhili (now Hebei) provincial governor ruled that Zhang should receive no penalty since he killed his son who was already "guilty" under the law. In reviewing the case, the Board of Punishment disagreed with the governor's ruling and made a correction. Zhang's son was guilty of stealing, the Board reasoned, but not guilty of cursing his parents, an offense that would have given his father immunity for killing him. It was incorrect for the governor to omit the words "cursing parents" and cite only the word "guilty" in the code. Furthermore, Zhang did not beat his son for disobeying parental instructions, causing the latter's death by accident, but strangled his son, intending to kill him. The Board decided that Zhang be punished by one hundred blows for unreasonably killing his son.[16]

In a case that occurred in 1826, Wang Chaodong asked his younger brother for money, and the brother refused. Wang Chaodong chased his brother with a knife in his hand, but was stopped and tied up by their father, Wang Qing. The father scolded his elder son, and the latter talked back. Unable to control his anger, Wang Qing buried Chaodong alive. The provincial governor ruled that Wang Qing should be punished by one hundred blows for unreasonably killing a son who disobeyed parental instructions. The Board of Punishment changed the ruling to nonpunishment, arguing that since the son cursed his father, a father killing such a son was not to be punished under the law.[17] These cases show the length to which the imperial penal code would go to uphold a father's authority over his children, and to which the state would go to enforce the law.[18]

Lineage and Its Patriarch

Patriarchal power was also legally granted for extended families and their larger descent groups, known as lineages (*zu* or *zongzu* or *shizu*). Lineages or patrilineal kinship networks became increasingly important in local society from the Song down. It was one of the ways for local elites to maintain and exercise their power in local society. The power was reproduced generation after generation through a variety of mechanisms and actions: maintaining a genealogy or patrilineal registry (*zupu*), an ancestral hall, a cemetery, and a lineage estate (its income would support the next two categories); sponsoring schools to support youngsters in the lineage to be successful in pursuing civil service exams; holding ancestral rituals, festivals, and celebrations; mediating disputes among lineage members; meting out penalties to wayward lineage members; engaging in or settling disputes and feuds with other lineages or social actors; intervening in lawsuits involving lineage members; and so on.

Based on the traditional customs regarding kinship, the Qing code officially prescribed five layers of kinship relationships marked by mourning clothing of five different materials (*wufu*), which was used to determine how to punish a perpetrator of a crime on the basis of his relationship with the victim. The systematic differentiations implied the assumption of the extended family and lineage in the minds of lawmakers; beyond that, however, articles in the penal code still focused on the household. The flourishing of lineage activities did not bring changes to the codes, but the power of the patriarch of a lineage came to be reckoned by the Qing state during the Qianlong reign, if not earlier. The state would officially establish the patriarch of a lineage as the authority figure over the lineage (*zuzheng*) who was to enforce the "community compact" (*xiangyue*) as well as state law, and as such he was a quasi-official accountable to the state for the actions of lineage members while having the power to discipline or punish wayward members. The Qing state took such actions for the purpose of social control, in response to the widespread phenomenon of lineage feuds in such provinces as Guangdong, Fujian, and Jiangxi.[19] The territorial expansion and the demographic growth under the Qing tended to outstrip the state's capacity to govern effectively, so that the Qing state was willing to mobilize local elites in maintaining the political-social order.

A natural lineage patriarch (*zuzhang*) was not empowered to kill wayward lineage members, however, and if he did, he was subject to criminal prosecution and punishment. In at least four cases, from Henan, Sichuan, Yunnan, and Anhui provinces during the Jiaqing reign (1796–1820), a lineage patriarch who caused the death of a lineage member was punished under the code. Although the lineage member had wrongfully taken the lineage property or funds and been confronted by the patriarch and other lineage members, killing such a lineage member was a homicide. In the four cases, the penalty was death by strangulation delayed, for fighting to cause the death of a lineage kin, for conspiring to beat a person to death, or for killing a guilty person without authorization (*shansha*); other participants in the fights or beatings received lesser penalties.[20]

Prohibition of Revenge Killing

As these cases show, while the authority of the patriarch in family and lineage and the moral code of filial piety were upheld by the law, they were trumped by the state's power or the authority of the emperor as the Son of Heaven and the parent of the people. This fundamental relationship in law and justice can be further seen in the prohibition of revenge killing that evolved in the imperial era.

Blood revenge is a tradition found in many ancient societies, including ancient China. Classical sources already dealt with the issue of revenge killing, with conflicting moral stances toward it: the morality of filial piety that called for avenging a father who was wrongfully killed versus the authority of state law that prohibited murder.[21] From the Qin and Han dynasties down, however, private vendetta or revenge killing was no longer legal and would be punished under the law, because revenge killings as private acts meant a negation of the emperor's authority in punishing all offenses and resolving all disputes. After all, it was the purview of the Son of Heaven to maintain the cosmic order by deciding life and death.[22]

With filial piety as a cardinal principle, however, the debate over the morality versus the legality of revenge killing continued as late as the Tang dynasty, while successive dynasties' penal codes evolved on the issue. Under the Tang code, if a grandparent or parent was assaulted, his grandchild or child would not be punished for fighting back attackers when no tooth or limb was lost; if someone lost a tooth or a limb, the penalty would be reduced by three grades from regular assault cases; only if someone lost his life would the penalty be the same as in regular cases. The Song code kept this article, and the Ming code deleted it. The Qing code revived the article but added that if grandparents or parents were killed by a perpetrator, and a grandchild or a child privately killed the perpetrator later, the penalty was sixty blows; if the killing of the perpetrator took place on the spot, there would be no penalty. The substatute under the article noted that if the perpetrator was already punished under the law but was not executed due to amnesty, and then was killed by his victim's child or grandchild, the latter would be punished by one hundred blows and exile of 3,000 li.[23] Thus, after the penal codes of different dynasties went back and forth over the issue for centuries, the Qing code made it unequivocal to punish revenge killing so as to assert the primacy of state authority over the punishment of homicide perpetrators.

Yet in judicial practice the way revenge killing was dealt with depended on individual cases, and often the avenger was spared the death penalty for being filial to parents who had been murdered. In a case during the Sui dynasty, Mr. Wang was murdered by his cousin and the latter's wife. Wang had three young daughters, ages seven, five, and three, who were brought up by relatives. When they were teens, Shen, the eldest of the three girls, refused to marry, despite urgings from her relatives. One day she told her two younger sisters that she wanted to avenge their father, and the younger girls agreed to go along. They killed their father's murderers and turned themselves in. The county and prefecture officials were unable to decide their punishment. In the end, Emperor Wen pardoned them. Similar revenge killings and pardons occurred in the Tang, the Song, and the Ming.[24]

During the reign of Qing emperor Qianlong, the punishment for revenge killing became harsher than the Qing code prescribed due to the emperor's intervention in one particular case. In 1777 Shen San broke into Wang Tingxiu's home at night to steal, and was chased and killed by Wang. For this unlawful killing, Wang received one hundred blows and three years of penal labor, per the Qing code. More than ten years later, Shen Wanliang, Shen San's son, killed Wang to avenge his father. The Zhili provincial governor cited the article in the code and sentenced Shen to one hundred blows and exile of 3,000 li. The Board of Punishment disagreed, believing the article did not apply to the case. Agreeing with the Board, Emperor Qianlong made a critical point on prohibiting revenge killing: Shen San was committing a crime when Wang killed him, and Wang was punished for the killing; the case was thus closed—the penalty fit the offense and no reason for revenge existed. (One might say that yin and yang were already balanced.) Qianlong continued:

> Our dynasty has strict laws and transparent punishments, both being well thought out and comprehensive, and all decisions on life and death are made by judicial officials, so how can we tolerate a person's unlawfully taking private revenge? Moreover, when the state's law is affirmed, private anger is vented, and the cycle of revenge killing should not be started, about which my instructions cannot be clearer. In the case of a son taking revenge, if his father died a wrongful death, and the perpetrator escaped the law so that the son had no other way to right the wrong, then there might be revenge to speak of. Now that Shen San was a criminal to begin with and Wang Tingxiu was punished under the law [for killing Shen without authorization (*shansha*)], the case was closed and Wang was no longer a convict [after serving out his sentence], but Shen Wanliang still killed him with intent. Shen should be punished for intentional homicide. If he was punished by flogging and exile as the governor decided, it would start a trend—since all people are children of parents, all could harbor personal anger to commit violence and intervene in the law in the name of revenge, where would all this end?[25]

He ordered that Shen be given death by decapitation delayed (the standing penalty for intentional homicide per the code) and that such a penalty be the precedent for similar cases in the future.[26]

Another intervention from Emperor Qianlong came in 1792, when a similar case took place in Shaanxi. For killing Dadian, Bimai had been sentenced to death by strangulation but the sentence was commuted to exile. His exile was further reduced to ten years due to an imperial amnesty. After Bimai returned to his hometown Zongkong, Dadian's son, killed Bimai for revenge. Per the 1777 imperial order, Zongkong was sentenced to death by decapitation delayed. In reviewing the case, Emperor Qianlong reaffirmed the message that private revenge killing would not be tolerated after "public righteousness" (*gongyi*) was asserted. At the same time, Qianlong said, considering Zongkong's motive, he could not bear approving the execution. He ordered that Zongkong be imprisoned for life and similar cases be dealt with in the same way.[27] Thereafter the ruling became a substatute added to the

Qing code, thus creating a legal base for life imprisonment in a particular category of offenses, even though the regular five punishments in the code did not include any imprisonment.[28]

Prohibition of Private Castration

Another intersection of the interest and authority of the emperor and those of the family patriarch was the imperial control over who would become eunuchs. In the larger context where the patrilineal family system was of the utmost importance, the status of the emperor as the Son of Heaven and the parent of the people entailed a sacrosanct requirement that the male imperial family line must be pure as well as continuous, or a usurpation of the throne would occur. The fact that the emperor always had many concubines made it especially imperative to ensure that no other men had sex with the emperor's women. Hence the use of eunuchs—castrated men—in serving the emperor and his family in the imperial palace.

The first emperor of the Ming dynasty issued an edict in 1372, saying that rich and powerful families in Fujian, Guangdong, and Guangxi often sought young men from poor families and had them castrated to be servants (men in such wealthy families usually had multiple concubines), and people who did so should be punished by castration and enslavement to the state. The Ming code provided the penalty for the offense: one hundred blows and exile of 3,000 *li*.[29] In 1492 a substatute was added to the article in the code to prohibit self-castration. The Qing code inherited the prohibition.

In the imperial era, selecting eunuchs was a process controlled by the state. Eunuchs were usually from poor families that had more than one son, and their fathers absolved them of their obligation to continue the family line so that they could earn a living by serving the emperor personally. Under the Ming (after 1588) and Qing codes, only when a family had four or five sons and was willing to offer one of the sons as a candidate for eunuch could it inform local officials of the intent. After official approval, the son's name would enter an official registry as a candidate to be selected as a eunuch. If any man had himself castrated without permission in order to be a eunuch, he would be given the death penalty by decapitation and his whole family would be exiled to the frontiers for military service; the penalties would apply to the man and anyone who performed the castration on him. At the same time, anyone outside the imperial family who used eunuchs as servants would be punished by one hundred blows and exile of 3,000 *li*.[30]

These prohibitions reflected two concerns: On the one hand, it was the emperor's exclusive prerogative to use eunuchs, and anyone else using eunuchs would be committing an act of usurpation and had to be punished.[31] On the other hand, the law was designed to deter any man from abandoning his filial obligation to continue the family line just for the sake of earning a living for himself as a eunuch. "One who would self-castrate to seek employment," said Emperor Renzong of the Ming in an edict, "merely aims for a life of fortune and power by rejecting his parents and ancestry. Ancient sages would seek loyal ministers among filial sons. Since such people did not even care about their parents, how would they be loyal servants to the emperor? From now on those who self-castrate shall not be forgiven."[32]

Marriage and Gender Inequality

For the continuation of the patrilineal family line, marriage was an obligation, not a personal choice. (That the extremely poor could not afford to marry was a separate issue.) Marriage was a family matter arranged by parents or grandparents, and the woman and the man to be married had no say in whom they would marry. The law codes from the Tang through the Ming assumed that arranged marriage was the norm and provided that if an improper marriage (such as one between close relatives or incompatible social classes) was arranged by parents or grandparents, the bride and the groom would not be punished.[33] In the Qing dynasty the code expressly stated in a substatute that all marriages were to be arranged by grandparents or parents, and if an unmarried person lost parents and grandparents, his or her marriage was to be arranged by other senior relatives.[34]

Men and women were not equal under the law. From the Tang through the Qing, a married woman could not ask for a divorce unless her husband had disappeared for three years and the case had been officially reported. On his part, no later than the Han dynasty, a husband could divorce his wife for any of the seven causes: barrenness, licentiousness, being impolite to in-laws, being gossipy, committing theft, being jealous, and being incurably ill.[35] A husband divorcing his wife without one of the causes would be punished by one and a half years of penal labor under the Tang and the Song codes, and by eighty blows under the Ming and Qing codes. However, from the Han down, any of the seven causes would be an insufficient ground for divorce if one of the following three conditions existed: the wife had mourned the deaths of parents-in-law; the husband had moved from rags to riches after marrying his wife; and the wife had no home to return to. If a husband divorced his wife despite one of these conditions, the penalty was one hundred blows in the Tang and the Song, and sixty blows in the Ming and the Qing, and the wife was returned to her husband.[36]

The seven causes for a husband to divorce his wife were not without controversy in the imperial era. At least one debate is known: Liu Ji, a late Yuan scholar-official who contributed to the founding of the Ming dynasty, opined in one of his books that of the seven causes for divorcing a wife, being incurably ill or barren was not an act of ill will, like the other five causes, but a misfortune of the wife. He asked, "Is it in accordance with Heavenly reason for a husband to abandon his wife for her misfortune?" To this argument, Wang Yi, another scholar-official of the same background as Liu, countered that the seven causes for divorce were qualified by the three conditions, which was very generous: "Which wife does not have one of the three?" More important, being incurably ill a wife could not take part in ancestral rituals with her husband, and being barren she would end her husband's family line, so she was rejected by nature or Heaven (*tian*) from fulfilling either moral duty; also, to reduce seven causes for divorce to five would depart wildly from Confucian propriety (*li*).[37] Thus the well-established moral imperatives of maintaining the patrilineal family line and ancestral rituals as filial piety would trump other arguments.

Under the Qing code, mutually agreed divorce was permitted; if a wife committed moral betrayal (*yijue*)—adultery or cursing parents-in-law—and ought to be divorced but the husband did not divorce her, he would be punished by one year of penal labor in the Tang and the Song, by eighty blows in the Ming and the Qing. A wife (or concubine) running away from her husband would be punished by two years of penal labor, and running away to remarry, three years, in the Tang and the Song; under the Ming and Qing codes, however, the penalty for a wife running away to remarry was death by strangulation.[38]

A husband was entitled to have concubines, a practice justified by the filial obligation to continue the family line; to have more sons would enhance the odds against disease and death. But a wife was required to be faithful to her husband. Under the Ming and the Qing codes, if a husband caught his wife in bed with another man and instantly killed both (supposedly at the moment of shock and anger), he would receive no penalty. The origin of this legal principle is obscure. The Tang and Song codes did not mention the matter. The Yuan dynasty established the practice and, in doing so, cited an "old statute," which might have been the law of the Jin state of Juchen, conquered by the Mongols.[39] The Qing code further provided that if the husband killed one of them or both later (i.e., premeditated murder), he would be punished for homicide (one hundred blows and exile of 3,000 *li* or death by strangulation delayed).[40]

Legally, a wife and a concubine were not equal, the latter having an inferior status. Under the Ming and Qing codes, a husband making his wife a concubine or making a concubine his wife would be punished by one hundred and ninety blows, respectively. True to the supposed purpose of having concubines, the children of concubines were legitimate under the law—all sons had equal right to inherit their father's property.

The Ming and Qing codes strictly prohibited marrying a former wife or concubine of a deceased or divorced kin, for such unions were considered crimes of incest (one of the ten abominations), and the penalties ranged from eighty blows to death, depending on the degree to which the offender was related to the woman's former husband or master. Marrying a former concubine of a father or grandfather, or a former wife of any paternal uncles, would entail death by decapitation without delay; marrying a former wife of a brother, death by strangulation without delay; and marrying a former concubine of an uncle or a brother, penalties reduced by two grades.[41] In practice, the county magistrate, if he did not ignore such cases altogether, tended to impose lighter penalties than what the law prescribed on those who married the wife of a deceased brother due to ignorance of the law or for economic reasons. On the other hand, the Board of Punishment and the emperor tended to adhere to the code in cases involving such offenses.[42] In fact, it is after Emperor Qianlong reviewed a case and made a ruling on it in 1784 that a substatute was added to the code: even if presided over by his parents or other relatives, a man who married the wife of a deceased brother would receive death by strangulation delayed, and his relatives and the local headman (*dibao*) who allowed the marriage to take place would each receive eighty blows for the offense of "doing what [one] ought not to do."[43]

A starker aspect of gender inequality before the law was that if a husband killed his wife or concubine who had cursed his parents or grandparents, his penalty would only be one hundred blows; if he scolded such a wife or concubine, who then committed suicide, there was no penalty. In contrast, otherwise causing someone to commit suicide would entail penalties from flogging to decapitation, depending on circumstances and victims' relations to offenders. On the other hand, if a husband killed or beat to death his wife or concubine without cause or without authorization even if his wife or concubine had faults other than cursing parents-in-law, he would receive death by strangulation delayed. To prevent a husband from killing his wife or concubine and then claiming she had cursed his parents or grandparents, the law required that only after his parents or grandparents personally reported to the magistrate the woman's misdeeds could the case of her verbal abuse be established to lessen the penalty of the husband who killed her. This would imply a legal nuance that cursing parents- or grandparents-in-law would actually mean cursing them directly. A couple of cases will illustrate how these scenarios would occur and how the law was applied.

One case transpired during the reign of Qing Emperor Jiaqing. Liang Zixin had a son, Liang Youfu, from his first marriage. His second wife, Bai, verbally abused Youfu frequently. Hoping to ameliorate the situation, Liang agreed that Youfu marry Zhang, Bai's daughter from her first marriage, and all four people lived in the same house. This did not help Zixin and Youfu (father and son), however, as Zhang also verbally and physically abused Youfu, while having a sexual affair with another man, an act that was caught by Zixin. Bai and Zhang (mother and daughter) then tried to kill Youfu by lacing his food with arsenic, but it was detected by Zixin, who did not do anything other than report it to a local constable next day. That night Zhang again physically attacked Youfu, with Bai cursing him on the side. At that point Zixin snapped. He strangled Zhang to death; then Bai madly rammed into him, and he strangled her to death as well. He then turned himself in. When the case was reviewed in the capital, Emperor Jiaqing opined that Zhang had tried to poison her husband to death, which was a capital crime in the first place (for attempted murder of a husband, the penalty was decapitation); Bai had intended to see her husband lose his only heir by participating in the murder plot, which was also a capital crime; and it was out of righteous anger that Zixin killed the two women. If Zixin was convicted of killing his wife unlawfully, his penalty (death by strangulation) would be commuted at the Autumn Assizes for extenuating circumstances, but the name of his offense would not properly fit what had happened. The emperor agreed with the Board of Punishment that Zixin be punished by one hundred blows and exile of 3,000 *li*, and the emperor further commuted the penalty to one hundred blows and three years of penal labor, "to convey my utmost desire to clarify penalties to assist in nurturing [the people] and uphold moral order" (*mingxing bijiao, weichi fenghua*).⁴⁴ The last sentence was a stock phrase of the official rhetoric on law and order in imperial China, and in this case the moral order referred to the wifely way Bai and Zhang were supposed to but failed to follow.

Another case took place also during the reign of Emperor Jiaqing. Fan Wenming compelled his reluctant wife, Gong, to go with him to clear weeds in the family's field. On the way Gong stopped and sat down to rest. Fan urged her to go on, but Gong did not respond. Agitated, Fan beat her with a wooden stick. Gong began to curse Fan and his parents. Fan then beat her to death. The provincial governor ruled that the case was a husband killing his wife who had cursed his parents, with no penalty. Reviewing the case, the Board of Punishment disagreed. Fan's parents did not report their daughter-in-law's alleged cursing, and there was no witness to what happened, so Fan should be punished for killing his wife without cause or authorization. Thus the implied legal nuance of the article in the code was applied here. In this case (and in another), the Board made a general argument, as follows: In handling cases of husbands killing wives for cursing parents-in-law, whether parents personally reported the cursing was the key evidence upon which to make a ruling. If parents did report, the penalty was one hundred blows for the killing; if not, the penalty was death by strangulation delayed; at the Autumn Assizes any evidence of the wife being otherwise unfilial could result in the death sentence being commuted to lesser penalties as a "pitied" case. Usually, the Board stressed, family quarrels varied in countless scenarios, and parents tended to be indulgent and not clear-minded, prone to making up excuses to save their sons. That is why the law required parents to personally report misconduct of a daughter-in-law prior to her being killed, which had profound implications.⁴⁵ Clearly, the Board of Punishment tried very hard to give guidance to governors, prefects, and magistrates on how to properly interpret and apply the penal code that could not possibly cover all scenarios of family disputes and domestic violence.

With the simultaneous existence of generational inequality and gender inequality before the law, when the principle of a senior family member taking legal precedence over a junior conflicted with that of a family male over a female, the former would prevail. In a case dated 1802, for example, Li Zhiguang argued and scuffled with his cousin because Li wanted to cut down a tree that was in the cousin's courtyard. The cousin's mother, Woman Qiu, tried to stop their fight. Li pushed her to the ground and beat her. Woman

Hu, wife of the cousin's brother, came to the rescue of Woman Qiu, her mother-in-law, and struck Li with a wooden object on the back of his head. Li died later. In short, Woman Hu killed a male cousin of her husband's. Upon reviewing the case, the Board of Punishment, the Court of Judicial Review, and the Department of Censors all agreed that Woman Hu killed a person while acting in an emergent situation to save her mother-in-law, equivalent to a son saving his mother, for which her penalty should be reduced (from death by strangulation) under a substatute on homicide. The emperor approved that Woman Hu be spared from death and the reduced penalty (which would be one hundred blows and exile of 3,000 *li*) be redeemed with payment according to the law.[46]

Punishing and Tolerating Illicit Sex

Given the paramount importance of the patriarchal family order, all the imperial penal codes would prohibit and punish various sexual relations detrimental to that order, which culminated in the most systematic fashion in the Qing code. In essence, nearly all sexual acts outside the legitimate union between a husband and a wife (or concubine) were considered illicit and punished accordingly.

First of all, penalties for sexual assaults were straightforward: a rapist would receive death by strangulation delayed; an attempted rape would result in one hundred blows and exile of 3,000 *li*; having sex with a girl of twelve and under was rape; and victims of rape were not punished. To establish a case of rape was far from straightforward, however. The law required that there must be signs of violence and that the victim was unable to get free of the alleged rapist; the incident must be known to someone; there must be physical evidence such as bruises or torn clothing before a man was convicted as a rapist and sentenced to death by strangulation.[47] In reality, women often fell victim to rape but had no easy way to provide the evidence required by the law, and they either would not report their case or would commit suicide to clear themselves because a nonconviction in a reported rape case would imply that the woman herself was immoral and impure, bringing shame to the family. A rape victim might commit suicide with the idea that she would take revenge against the rapist by haunting him and his family as a ghost.[48]

The law would also punish men and women for having consensual sex outside legitimate unions. Under the Qing code, both the man and the woman would receive eighty blows for having a sexual affair (in contrast, under the Tang code the same offense would be punished by eighteen months of penal labor); if the woman was married, her penalty would be ninety blows; a woman who was seduced to leave home and have sex with a man would receive one hundred blows. If a married woman had illicit sex, the husband had the choice to sell or keep her; if the husband sold or married her to the man with whom she had had illicit sex, both the husband and the man would receive eighty blows.[49]

The logic of the last provision becomes clear relative to another article in the law: A husband would be punished by eighty blows for allowing his wife or concubine to have illicit sex with another man. If a husband (or an adoptive father) forced his wife or concubine (or adoptive daughter) to have illicit sex, he would receive one hundred blows, and the man involved, eighty blows, and in such a case the woman was considered a victim and given no penalty. If a man had illicit sex with a woman inmate in prison, his penalty would be one hundred blows and three years of penal labor, and the woman would receive no penalty. An official who had illicit sex with a wife or concubine or daughter of his subordinate would be punished two grades more than the regular penalty for illicit sex (one hundred blows instead of eighty). These articles in the Qing code suggest that Qing lawmakers reckoned that under the patriarchal family system women were often not in a position to decide for themselves whether to have sexual relations and should be protected by the law in such situations, and that a husband or a father who sold his wife or concubine or daughter as a sexual commodity should be punished.[50]

Punishments for illicit sex also reflected legal inequality between social classes or social statuses. For a man having illicit sex with an official's wife, the penalty for both the man and the wife was death by strangulation delayed. In contrast, for having illicit sex with a commoner's wife, an official would be dismissed from office and given one hundred blows, and the wife would receive one hundred blows and made to wear a *cangue* for one month. A slave or servant having illicit sex with the woman of the house would be punished by one grade more than penalties for illicit sex between a man and a woman of the same social status, a man of good family having illicit sex with a slave or servant, one grade less.

The imperial penal codes did not prohibit prostitution, but the Ming and the Qing codes would punish by one hundred blows anyone who forced or sold women of good families into prostitution. Under the Qing code, those who bought women and forced them to have sex with others to make a profit would be punished by three penalties combined: one hundred blows, wearing a *cangue* for three months, and exile to the southern frontier. This prohibition initially did not apply to hereditary "debased households" who made a stigmatized living through prostitution, until the early eighteenth century, when all households were covered by it. Under the law, the Qing officials and their children would be punished by sixty blows for having sex with prostitutes, but the penalty did not apply to common people.

Among the rural poor during the Qing dynasty (if not earlier), a husband would invite another man into the household to share his wife in order to gain an additional laborer, or sell his wife to another man in order to pay off a debt; in other words, such things were done as survival strategies, mobilizing the wife's sexual and reproductive labor. Marriage and sex work were often indistinguishable in many variations of such practices. The social contexts of the practices were the uneven sex ratio (more males than females) and the extreme poverty. The elite moral orthodoxy condemned and criminalized such practices, but county magistrates in local societies often allowed such practices to exist when lawsuits were brought to their courts by disputes arising from various arrangements, such as the seller of a wife asking additional payment from the buyer, or the natal family of the wife challenging such a deal. The magistrate would adjudicate such cases without applying a blanket rule but on a case-by-case basis; the preference of the wife in such a case would often shape the magistrate's decision to let her return to the first husband or the second husband or the natal family. (The second outcome meant allowing the sale of the woman.) In most cases the magistrate did not confiscate the bride-price as stipulated by the law but ordered the seller to refund the buyer. The corporal punishment provided by the law was often applied to the seller, the buyer, and the matchmaker, in the form of slapping instead of flogging. In short, understanding the social reality of rural poverty, the magistrate took a pragmatic and lenient approach to the offenses of illicit sex committed by the poor as survival strategies, not as sexual extravagance.[51]

Homosexuality and the Qing Law

The imperial penal codes never prohibited homosexuality per se, because it was not perceived to be a threat to the patriarchal family order under normal conditions. As men and women would enter heterosexual marriages as obligations to their families, regardless of their sexual orientation, men having homosexual affairs was deemed inconsequential, and was even favorably written about in literary works. Only when men remained single due to poverty or other circumstances *and* engaged in homosexual acts did the matter become a perceived threat to the patriarchal family order and thus a concern to the state. The concern grew strong enough in the course of the early Qing that the matter finally entered the Qing code in 1740.[52]

The traditional tolerance of homosexuality per se can be seen in the roundabout way certain homosexual acts by certain men were punished under the Qing code. A substatute under the article on punishing extortion for money categorized a type of offender as "vicious bare sticks," and the punishment for such behavior was exile to the frontier for servitude to the state. "Bare stick" was a colloquial and figurative Chinese term referring to a single adult man who had no prospect of getting married due to poverty. From the Ming to the Qing, the term acquired a legal meaning and entered the penal code. The Qing code defined "bare sticks" as people who were prone to getting into brawls, making trouble, committing violence, and harassing or harming good people for no reason. "Depending on the crime, bare stick would be better translated as hoodlum, rapist, swindler, extortionist, or gangster."[53] Another substatute under the same article enumerated various acts that bare sticks might commit in gangs. For such offenses, a gang leader would receive death by immediate decapitation, and gang members, death by strangulation delayed. Fathers and elder brothers of such offenders would all receive fifty blows, unless they reported the offenses.

From these provisions stemmed a further legal step: a substatute under the article on punishing illicit sex provided that perpetrators of gang rape were punished according to the substatute on bare stick gangs. Another substatute related to sodomizing young males kidnapped from good families, for which offenders were punished as bare stick gangs: immediate decapitation for the gang leader and death by strangulation delayed for gang members. For raping a young boy (or girl) under ten, the penalty was immediate decapitation, and for raping those between ten and twelve, decapitation delayed. The substatute also provided that consensual sodomy between males would be punished by analogy to "illicit sex between military personnel and civilians," which called for one hundred blows and one month of wearing a *cangue* for both parties.[54] Obviously the tortuous legal steps starting under a substatute and then resorting to an analogy to another substatute in order to punish consensual sodomy simply meant that the act was not a crime in its own right. In practice, the analogy part of the substatute would be applied only when the matter came up in other related offenses. The following are a few cases to which the substatutes just cited were relevant.[55]

In 1819 Zeng, a young Buddhist monk, was sodomized by Jie, another monk, and Lü, a layman, and Zeng beat and injured Jie thereafter. On Lü's advice, Zeng disguised himself as a woman to flee (to escape the penalty for injuring Jie), and when caught, Zeng accused Jie of sodomizing him when he was twelve. Zeng was found guilty by analogy of "using heretical methods to fool people" (disguising himself as a woman) and was given a penalty reduced by one grade: exile for 3,000 *li* and wearing a *cangue* for two months. Lü was guilty of inciting someone to make a false accusation that would entail the death penalty for the falsely accused (for sodomizing a boy of twelve and under), and he was punished by exile of 3,000 *li*. The case file sent by the provincial governor to the Board of Punishment did not mention the issue of coerced sodomy, the root cause of the whole case, nor what should happen to Jie, one of the two rapists, and the Board too did not comment on either point.[56] Under the Qing code, a perpetrator of two offenses would be punished for the one that entailed the more severe penalty.[57] Here, of the two offenses—a monk disguising himself as a woman and making a false accusation, and a monk and a layman committing coerced sodomy or gang rape—the latter was more severe. The officials probably believed that the relationship was actually consensual if the alleged victim was older than twelve, so they dealt with the first offense only. Yet Jie could have been separately punished by one hundred blows and wearing a *cangue* for one month for consensual sodomy, and he was not. It would appear that when the officials determined that the alleged rape did not occur, they had no interest in pursuing the matter of consensual sodomy.

Although consensual sodomy was not always punished, it would downgrade the social status of a person in such a relationship, in terms of criminal justice. In a case dated 1815, a man who was a victim of rape by another man but had been in a homosexual relationship with a third man was punished for consensual sodomy (the third man was not dealt with since he had died), and the second man's penalty for coerced sodomy was reduced by one degree because the victim was no longer deemed a person of good standing (*liangren*).[58]

In 1818 a case arrived for review at the Board of Punishment. Lu Jiahui, a *juren* degree holder and Confucian teacher, seduced and sodomized his private pupil, Lu Lianfang, age fourteen. When Lianfang's father transferred his son to another teacher because the son was not making good progress in his study, Jiahui filed a false accusation against the father in order to have Lianfang stay with him. The provincial governor noted in his review that the Qing code had no article or substatute on punishing a teacher for sodomizing his student. He ruled that the case be analogized to illicit sex between relatives (someone having sex with his brother's wife). Jiahui was to be punished by one grade less, from strangulation delayed to exile of 3,000 *li*, and Lianfang, by the same penalty but to be redeemed with a fine by his family.

The Board disagreed and held that the governor used the wrong legal analogy. A Confucian teacher was supposed to be a moral example, the Board reasoned, similar to officials being the parents of the people, so the proper analogy for Jiahui's offense was an official having illicit sex with the wife of his subordinate. It was beyond despicable, the Board further noted, that Jiahui seduced and sodomized a student learning Confucianism from him, and that he then made a false accusation in order to keep Lianfang available to him for abuse, which made him "almost a vicious bare stick." As such Jiahui should be punished severely, by exile to the frontier for military service so that "the warnings to others would be made clear." Again, the teacher was punished for a more severe offense of sexually abusing a student and a minor, which eclipsed the offense of consensual sodomy. On the other hand, Lianfang was punished for consensual sodomy by analogy to "illicit sex between military personnel and civilians," per the substatute noted earlier. At fourteen, Lianfang was said to be young and innocent and was given one hundred blows and forced to wear a *cangue* for one month, both to be redeemed with fines by his family.[59]

More revealing is yet another case, dated 1819, involving five bannermen in Fengtian (Liaoning) province. Ji Lin'a falsely accused Zha Buzhan of stealing his money. An investigation found that Zha forcibly took Ji's homosexual partner Guang Ning and, along with two more men, forcibly sodomized Guang—a case of gang rape of an adult male. The three offenders were punished by analogy to "gang rape of a woman who had committed illicit sex": Zha was exiled to the frontier to be a slave to soldiers and the other two were punished by one hundred blows and exile for 3,000 *li*. Ji's offense of making a false accusation was excused because the alleged offense (robbery) would entail a lighter penalty (penal labor) than what the three offenders deserved and received (exile). Yet for his homosexual relationship with Guang, Ji was punished by one hundred blows and forced to wear a *cangue* for one month. Paradoxically, Guang Ning was not punished for consensual sodomy; he was only deprived of his bannerman status for his "lack of shame in the extreme" in repeatedly receiving penetration by Ji.[60] Neither the provincial governor who forwarded the case to the Board of Punishment nor the Board that reviewed and approved the sentences commented on why Guang was not punished for consensual sodomy. It could be that because Guang was a victim of gang rape in the case, he was treated leniently, and also that Qing officials tended to regard male homosexuality per se more as a matter of personal shame (for the penetrated in particular) than a crime, and therefore the enforcement of the law on consensual sodomy was inconsistent.[61]

Law and Landownership

The penal codes in imperial China covered a wide range of offenses, some of which arose from civil matters, such as marriage and inheritance, and had a bearing on the maintenance of the patriarchal family order. Local officials would also face cases that arose from civil disputes and escalated into physical assault and homicide, for which criminal penalties must be applied. More frequently, local officials handled civil disputes that entailed no or light penalties under the law but required a ruling by an official to be settled. Contrary to an earlier view in the West that traditional Chinese law did not address civil disputes, archival sources that became available in the past three decades or so show that disputes, litigations, and adjudications over what imperial lawmakers called "minor matters" routinely occurred in imperial China.[62] At the same time, litigants would often defy rulings by magistrates in civil cases, and such defiance often led to violence and homicide, as seen in the Qing dynasty records.[63]

One thing that assisted to a degree in adjudicating civil cases including land disputes was the widespread use of contracts. From no later than the Han dynasty down, almost all significant economic transactions, from selling and buying slaves, properties, and goods to hiring laborers, renting land and other property, borrowing money, and indeed arranging marriages (as socioeconomic transactions between families), required written contracts.[64] Written documents were the most important evidence in civil litigations. These included contracts, tax payment receipts, land registration records, wills, and lineage registry. Physical objects such as tombstones and land boundary demarcation stones were also relevant as evidence to civil adjudications.⁶⁵ Officials who tried civil cases would take contracts most seriously. If contracts were officially certified, with a contract tax paid to the state, called "red contracts" (*hongqi*), they would have stronger legal effect in lawsuits. Officials would dismiss cases for a lack of credible contracts or other written records. If a litigant was found to have presented forged or altered contracts or other written documents, officials would have such papers voided by marking a cross with ink over them so that they had no legal effect any more; these were then physically preserved in case files as evidence of fraudulent conduct. Those who submitted false documents would lose their cases but normally would not be punished as criminal offenders.⁶⁶

As might be expected, officials were not always fair and impartial in judging civil cases, for a variety of reasons. A county magistrate might be motivated by personal greed (taking bribes) or faced with pressure from powerful local elites who wanted him to bend the law in favor of their families or relatives. Since such misconduct was a criminal offense, officials who committed these acts ran the risk of being exposed by complaints from victims and ensuing investigations by superiors and punished under the law. Indeed some officials were thus exposed and punished. The county-level judicial process would be further perverted by county clerks and runners who earned low wages and derived their illicit but tacitly accepted supplementary income from controlling access to the magistrate's court.⁶⁷

Beyond the scenarios of corruption, what would normally guide a magistrate to make rulings on civil disputes? Typically the magistrate would consider both laws and local customs, in accordance with social norms, in an effort to align Heavenly reason, state law, and human relations. This alignment came to permeate society to influence both elites and nonelites. This may be glimpsed in a land sales contract dated 1744 between two peasants in Guangxi province, far away from political-economic centers. At the end of the contract and before the seller's signature was written the phrase "[I sign in the presence of] Heavenly reason–human conscience" (*tianli ren liangxin*).⁶⁸ A look at what kind of civil disputes would usually occur and how they were normally settled by the judicial process will shed more light on the role of law and justice in maintaining the system of private landownership and the prevailing moral universe in imperial China.

Real Estate Disputes

By the Qin and the Han dynasties, private ownership of land and free sale of private land had been established and protected by law, along with public or state-owned land. Thereafter disputes over land (and houses) were the most common civil disputes in imperial China, an agrarian society prior to the twentieth century.

Two historical conditions particular to Chinese tradition are noteworthy in considering land disputes in the imperial era. The first was that no later than the Tang dynasty, imperial law always mandated equal division of family land and properties among all sons, including those born of concubines. Even daughters without brothers—that is, when a father had no sons—could inherit one-quarter, a third, one-half, or the whole of family property under different conditions and in different dynasties. From the Song dynasty down, widows could keep their late husband's property if they did not remarry. Furthermore, a father without sons could adopt a son of his brother's as heir; the guiding principle or Heavenly reason was again the continuation of the patrilineal family.[69] The law on equal inheritance led to a phenomenon that a family's properties would disperse over a few generations and each household in each generation would have less land than the previous generation, unless a man was able to increase the size of his land at the expense of his brothers or someone else, if not from reclamations. This would explain to a degree the incentives on the part of landowners (including powerful lineages) to acquire as much land as possible by legal or illegal means, which contributed to land disputes.

The second condition was that no later than the Song dynasty a landowning practice had been established as a social custom accepted by the law—a conceptual and legal separation of the right to "subsoil" and the right to "topsoil."[70] Subsoil was the physical land owned by a person, and topsoil referred to the surface of the land tilled by someone, typically a tenant who bought the right to work on the land for a certain period of time (say, twenty years), during which he would pay annual rent. The owner could collect rent but could not evict the tenant during those twenty years. The tenant's right to topsoil could be inherited by his sons or other family members or sold to a third party. Subsoil and topsoil were often transacted separately. The owner would sell his land (subsoil) or pawn it (*dianmai*, also called conditional sale) for a period of time (say, fifteen years), while the tenant continued to till the land, unaffected by whoever owned the subsoil. The owner could redeem the land he had pawned at the end of the specified period, or could lose it forever if he did not redeem it at that time. He could pay more to redeem it ahead of schedule if the other party agreed. Sometimes a tenant would sell or mortgage or use as collateral for loans his right to topsoil without informing the subsoil owner. A holder of the pawned subsoil would transact his fixed-term ownership in similar ways, especially when he figured that the original owner would be unable to redeem the land. These complex and bewildering relationships among the owner, the user of the land, and other possible parties also contributed to land disputes.[71]

One land-dispute case in the Song dynasty reveals how landowners would try to use documents to hide their property in order to evade taxes. Zhuan sold three pieces of land to Mao, but Lü sued at the county magistrate's court, claiming that he was the owner of those properties and that Zhuan sold them illegally. At the trial, Zhuan presented deeds to the properties dated 1189 and 1194 and a property registration record dated 1240 to support his claim. On his part, Lü showed contracts dated 1219 and signed by Zhuan, which pawned the properties to Lü's father (and presumably Zhuan never redeemed them, which the source did not make clear). But neither man could come up with any records to show that he had paid taxes on the properties, which would have been effective evidence of ownership. The magistrate concluded that the case arose from tax evasion committed by Lü and Zhuan, who both had used their respective documents to disclaim the properties to evade taxes but now tried to claim their ownership. Under the law, the magistrate reasoned, hiding properties to evade taxes was a punishable offense, so neither Lü nor Zhuan should keep the properties, or it would amount to rewarding wrongdoers. He ruled that the new owner, Mao, who was innocent of all wrongdoing, should be given official deeds to the properties; the money that Mao paid Zhuan for the land be confiscated by the county government; and Lü's and Zhuan's fraudulent documents be voided and put in the case file. Zhuan and Lü would have been punished for fraud and tax evasion, but Zhuan had died before the case was closed, and Lü was not punished due to an imperial general amnesty. The case gives us a glimpse into tax evasions that the magistrate said were common; he marveled at the fact that the two men would turn against one another, bringing themselves to official attention and penalties.[72]

Another case shows how a magistrate made his ruling on a property dispute out of his sense of right and wrong as well as his understanding of the law. Zhang Guangrui and Hong Baisi were next-door neighbors. For some time Zhang had wanted to acquire Hong's house. When Hong was sick and dying, his sons, Qian'er and Qianwu, were worried that they didn't have enough cash to properly bury their father. Seizing the opportunity, Zhang had his son draft a contract, but in the name of his son-in-law (to hide his role), offering cash to Hong's sons in exchange for their house. He also persuaded Hong Baisi's elder brother to lean on his nephews to accept the deal. Unexpectedly, Hong Baisi's stepson, Zhou Qian'er, who had been married out of town, returned home and stopped the transaction from being completed. An angry Zhang physically drove away Zhou.

Soon afterward Zhou and Hong Qian'er sued Zhang for having shocked their father to death. At the same time, they put together the money they owed Zhang to settle the matter. The magistrate ruled that Zhou and Hong falsely accused Zhang of shocking their father to death, but their action was caused by Zhang's extortionist scheme, so both parties should be punished; now that Hong and Zhou died one after another during the lawsuit, they were already punished by Heaven, and their house was confiscated as a symbolic penalty; Zhang, his son, and his son-in-law conspired to extort, but Zhang was the mastermind to be held accountable and his penalty was one hundred blows of light bamboo.[73]

The magistrate's ruling may well be questionable in today's court, either in China or elsewhere, but it precisely shows the large latitude of discretion the county magistrate had in making rulings on civil disputes according to his sense of right and wrong (or Heavenly reason) more than his reading of the law. Significantly, this case was in a reference book of exemplary adjudications from the Song dynasty.

Disputes over properties could and often did escalate into violence and become criminal cases. A case dated 1787 involved a dispute over water usage for farm land and is noteworthy because the case resulted in a new substatute added to the Qing code. Yuxiu and Shide were neighbors. They both dug ponds to irrigate their adjacent farm fields. One day in April, Shide pumped water from Yuxiu's pond to irrigate his own field. Upon seeing what Shide was doing, Yuxiu first tried to stop him and then tried to break the earthen barrier between their fields to let water go out of Shide's field back to his field. Shide began to curse Yuxiu's parents and physically attack Yuxiu. In the ensuing scuffle, Yuxiu hit Shide in the head with a spade, killing him. The trial by the county magistrate and the review by the provincial governor agreed that Yuxiu committed homicide in a fight, and his penalty was death by decapitation delayed. The Board of Punishment disagreed: Shide stealing water from Yuxiu was a crime, so Yuxiu's killing him was not homicide in a fight, but killing a criminal without authorization (*shansha*) and his sentence should be death by strangulation delayed. The Board made a further point: stealing water from a neighbor's field was a worse crime than stealing money and things since the consequence was no harvest from the field for the victim. In this case, Yuxiu was to be punished, but his family would suffer a poor harvest from Shide's criminal act. The Board proposed that a substatute be added to the code: for stealing water from farm field, the penalty would be two years of penal labor plus fifty heavy blows for one affected *mu* (one-sixth acre) of field, and for every additional five *mu*, an additional ten blows, up to eighty blows. Emperor Qianlong approved the Board's decision on Yuxiu and the new substatute.[74]

Succession and Inheritance

Property disputes were often related to succession and inheritance. As one historian summarized, "The basic principles of Chinese household division practices were three: living parents received support, unmarried siblings received marriage expenses or dowries, and all sons inherited equally."[75] These principles constituted the moral universe that informed the county magistrate's rulings on succession and inheritance disputes in varied situations on which the law was silent. A case in the Song dynasty offers an example. Wang Wansun had a son, Wang Youcheng, who failed to support his parents. Wansun and his wife had to move in with Li, his son-in-law. Wansun willed to Li his topsoil right to a piece of government-issued land (*zhitian*), a subsidy for having been an official. (In theory the subsoil was still owned by the state.) After Wansun passed away, Youcheng sued Li for the land. The magistrate ruled against Youcheng, with a moral reprimand: Youcheng should ask himself why his father did not live with him and eat food provided by him but with and by a son-in-law. Youcheng should have regretted to death his behavior toward his parents instead of seeking the land right left by his father. The land in question was a piece of government property that Li had been tilling, the legitimacy of which was attested to by his father's will, his mother's testimony, the government records, and previous magistrates' rulings. In the face of all this, Youcheng still brazenly went against his parents' wishes and repeatedly burdened the state with his meritless lawsuit, for which he was given twenty light blows.[76]

Another case from the Song, with a contrasting outcome, would again contextualize the moral universe in which county magistrates would make their civil rulings to achieve justice and upheld morality as they understood it. Widower Tan married a second wife, Ah Wei, who had a son, Li, from her first marriage. Manipulated by Li and his mother, Tan drove away two sons of his first marriage and gave all family property to Li. After Tan died, one of his elder sons sued Li at the county office. Li presented eleven contracts and deeds, four of which had Tan's signature, purportedly ceding all Tan's property to Li. But the magistrate simply rejected these documents on the ground that Tan could not and should not have written or signed them because it was both unreasonable and unlawful for Tan to deprive his elder sons of all properties (against the principle of equal inheritance among sons). The magistrate attributed Tan's behavior to the tricks played by Li and his mother to alienate Tan from his elder sons. He praised the two sons, who had been ill-treated, for not challenging their father when he was alive, out of filial piety. (Actually, if they did, they would have been punished under the law.) He ordered that Li's documents be voided and placed into the case file and that the elders of Tan's lineage preside over dividing Tan's properties equally among his three sons, including Li. He also ordered Li to be given one hundred light blows for sowing discord in Tan's family.[77] This case shows that the county magistrate could throw out signed deeds or contracts that he believed had violated law and morality in the first place. It also suggests that in the Song dynasty the lineage elders were important, but they were not in a position to settle such disputes and therefore a ruling by the magistrate was required.

These two cases tell us that the county magistrate had much discretion to make rulings on civil disputes, as opposed to criminal trials. In both cases, the guiding principles for the magistrate were the paramount interest of the patrilineal family and the sanctity of filial piety. In the first case, the magistrate endorsed the father's will in favor of the son-in-law because he judged that the son had forfeited his right to inherit his father's topsoil by failing to support his elderly parents, while the son-in-law, by his filial acts, earned the right to inherit it. What had probably happened but was not mentioned in the case file was that the son had already inherited his parents' house, which made it easier for the magistrate to make his ruling. In the second case, elder sons were driven out by a father who, in the magistrate's opinion, was manipulated by a second wife and a stepson. A father depriving his elder sons' inheritance also violated the law on inheritance. It was therefore moral and just to restore these sons' legitimate rights to inheritance.

Disputes over land and inheritance often intertwined with a widow's rights to her late husband's property. The following case in the Qing dynasty was typical of such scenarios in imperial China. In 1759 Ge Jicheng died without an heir. His wife, Guan, committed to widowhood, and the lineage selected a branch nephew as Ge Jicheng's heir. The nephew and Ge Jicheng's mother, Lu, lived with Guan. Five years later, Ge Jirong, Ge Jicheng's younger brother, schemed to take over his brother's properties from Guan, after Jirong had squandered his inheritance. Ge Jirong invited his mother to move to his place, and then claimed that she agreed to marry Guan to a man named Qi. The truth was that Jirong sold Guan to Qi for 10,000 copper coins. On an agreed day, Ge Jirong, Qi, and several of their helpers took Guan by force from her home to Qi's home. Due to Guan's incessant cries and struggles, members of Ge Jirong's lineage were alerted, and they intervened to rescue Guan from Qi's home.

The county trial and the provincial review brought Ge Jirong a penalty of one hundred blows and exile to 3,000 *li*, a reduced penalty (by one grade) for the offense of "junior or distant kin forcibly selling [a woman of the family] in order to take over property." Ge Jirong's penalty was reduced one grade because he was the sole remaining son of his mother, but the Board of Punishment held that Ge Jirong did not deserve the penalty reduction since his brother's widow, Guan, was supporting his mother. Ordered to reexamine the case, the provincial governor changed Ge Jirong's sentence to death by strangulation delayed, the full penalty for the offense. Qi, who paid to buy Guan, was given thirty blows and three months wearing a *cangue*. Emperor Qianlong approved these penalties.[78] This case points to a pattern: the law, and the officials who enforced the law, in late imperial China would support widows' rights to property, consistent with the Neo-Confucian ideology exalting widow chastity as a virtue for correct familial-social order.[79]

The criminal and civil cases in the imperial era show moral imperatives as well as legal reasoning behind the penal codes and their implications in Chinese life. It should be clear by now that the central concern of the imperial dynasties was to use law and justice as governing instruments to maintain the existing political-social-moral order, namely, the imperial system, the family system, and the landowning system, all surrounded and undergirded by an encompassing moral universe in which the patriarchal authority occupied the center, personified by the emperor and justified by the cosmic order or Heavenly reason.

The legal and judicial system in imperial China operated as well as it might have done under any circumstances, as long as China's imperial system and its moral universe were not fundamentally challenged from outside. This was indeed the case for many centuries, until the arrival of Europeans in the sixteenth century. Western powers and the Qing dynasty would come into conflict over the design and effect of Chinese law and justice. That conflict contributed to the Opium Wars and the resultant unequal treaties in the nineteenth century and eventually to Chinese legal-judicial reforms in the twentieth century.

PART II
LAW AND JUSTICE IN LATE QING AND REPUBLICAN CHINA, 1901–1949

4
The Best of the Chinese and of the Western
Legal-Judicial Reform in the Late Qing, 1901–1911

When Europeans arrived in China in the early sixteenth century and after, they inevitably either observed or personally experienced Chinese law and justice. Although at that time many aspects of Chinese law and justice were similar to their European counterparts, such as numerous capital offenses, corporal punishment, and judicial torture (e.g., the Inquisitions and "divine ordeals"), Europe was going through a transformation into modernity during the seventeenth to the nineteenth century. Following religious wars, legal-judicial reforms, Scientific Revolution, Industrial Revolution, and political revolutions, European states and societies had experienced profound changes. In the meantime, exploring and expanding to the rest of the world, Europeans practiced imperialism and colonialism. These events and developments constituted the historical contexts in which the European encounters with Chinese law and justice took place, with far-reaching consequences.

Conflicts began to arise in the eighteenth and nineteenth centuries between the Qing dynasty and Western powers over Chinese law and justice. These conflicts contributed to the Opium Wars and the resultant unequal treaties signed in 1842 and 1860. At the turn of the twentieth century, driven by a desire to gain equality with Western powers, the Qing dynasty launched a legal-judicial reform (1901–1911), based on Western models, to modernize legal codes and judicial institutions and practices, as part of a comprehensive reform program called "New Policies." As the principles of the rule of law, judicial independence, and due process guided the legal-judicial reform, a new conception of justice (what is just) came into being. In a sense, the new legal principles now functioned as alternative "Heavenly reason" or ultimate morality, since they were promoted as the international standards for "all under heaven," which was now Planet Earth instead of a Sino-centric world. Both the reform agendas and the principles that guided them produced long-term legacies that would survive the Qing dynasty into the Republican era

(1912–1949) and beyond. The traditional notion of justice (what is just) as an alignment of Heavenly reason, state law, and human relations did not vanish, however; beneath the rhetorical surface it continued to resonate with Chinese legal minds.

Encounters between Chinese Law and Western Powers

Changing Western Narrative on Chinese Law

Prior to the European exploration of the entire planet in the Age of Discovery, direct contact between Europe and China via the Silk Road was sporadic at best. Information about China that Europeans were able to glean from reports by the Franciscan friar William of Rubruck and the Venice merchant Marco Polo in the thirteenth century and after was fascinating but remained sketchy. Only with the maritime explorations in the Age of Discovery did some European sailors, traders, and missionaries begin to arrive in China. They wrote to a limited European audience about what China was like. As far as Chinese law and justice were concerned, reports by Jesuits and others were mixed. One example of a positive assessment of Chinese law was from the German philosopher Gottfried W. Leibniz:

> What we call the light of reason in man, they call commandment and law of Heaven. What we call the inner satisfaction of obeying justice and our fear of acting contrary to it, all this is called by the Chinese (and by us as well) inspirations sent by the Xiangdi (that is, by the true God). To offend Heaven is to act against reason, to ask pardon of Heaven is to reform oneself and to make a sincere return in word and deed in the submission one owed to this very law of reason. For me I find all this quite excellent and quite in accord with *natural theology*.[1]

Such views reflected a more philosophical and theological perspective in the intellectual context, where criticism of the existing political and religious order in Europe required a foil or countermodel. On the other hand, both positive and negative views of Chinese law and justice penned by Europeans who actually traveled to China and experienced or witnessed its legal practices voiced varied individual perceptions. Galeote Pereira, a Portuguese soldier and trader, spent several years in the mid-sixteenth century (the

Ming dynasty) in a Chinese prison for smuggling but had positive things to say about Chinese justice. Pereira observed that Chinese officials held open court sessions where common people could watch the proceedings, so that what was said in the court would be recorded truthfully, which was not the case in his own country. He also related that two Chinese local officials were punished for falsely accusing him of certain crimes. At the same time, Pereira depicted Chinese corporal punishment (flogging) in gruesome detail.[2] The mixed views of Chinese law and justice expressed by European traders and missionaries in the sixteenth and seventeenth centuries reflected a time when Europeans were more impressed by the economic wealth and political order in imperial China compared to a Europe torn by religious wars and other strife.

That historical context had changed by the eighteenth century, as European nations were transitioning into modern forms with the Scientific Revolution, the Enlightenment, the Industrial Revolution, and penal-judicial reforms.[3] Thereafter the European attitude toward China in general and Chinese law and justice in particular became more and more negative, even though Chinese judicial practices and their Western counterparts, especially regarding the severity or cruelty of punishment, were not markedly different in the eighteenth century.[4] In the meantime, an increasing number of European travelers to China for trade opportunities and Christian missions invited more frequent encounters between the two sides in the realm of law and justice. As a study of European depictions of Chinese punishments during those centuries summarizes, this body of verbal and pictorial literature "displays a marked shift in emphasis, from highlighting the rationality and orderliness of Chinese punishments in the early modern period to stressing the cruelty involved, from the late eighteenth century onward."[5] In fact, the Western narrative and representation of the cruelty and barbarity of Chinese law and punishment in popularized formats such as paintings and photographs would continue unabated well into the twentieth century. In the representation of backward Chinese law and judicial practices, China and its people were featured as "bloodthirsty, barbarian, pitiful and lamentable, needing redemption by the West."[6]

One important factor in this negative turn in the Western narrative of Chinese law and justice was a strategy adopted by the British East India Company to defy Chinese legal sovereignty: a demand for extraterritoriality, justified by a European discourse on "Asiatic" or "Oriental despotism." George Thomas Staunton's English translation of the Qing penal code published in 1810, which was an achievement in itself, only reinforced the British view that China was inferior in legal as well as other aspects of human endeavor.[7] In 1834 Lord Napier, the first British trade representative in East Asia, communicated to Prime Minister Earl Grey that the Qing state, which was stupid, depraved, and ignorant of international law, should not be treated according to the rules accepted and practiced among civilized nations.[8] J. F. Davis, an official of the British East India Company, argued specifically for extraterritoriality in his book on China published in 1836.[9]

From one scholar's perspective regarding extraterritoriality as a manifestation of legal imperialism, the assertion of extraterritoriality in Asian countries by the British in the eighteenth century resulted from both the theoretical premise of legal positivism (sovereignty was based on law and law was made by a sovereign) and the practical convenience that would benefit European colonial expansion: "British legal positivists were heavily involved with imperialism. . . . The imperial vision held by these men shaped their encounters with Asian law; their studies of Western and Asian law then shaped colonial politics."[10]

Concurrently the Qing dynasty wanted to maintain its sovereign power and imperial authority vis-à-vis all foreigners by enforcing Chinese law when Europeans committed criminal offenses in China, through the established judicial procedures. These competing agendas and perspectives led to numerous cases of legal conflicts, of which the best known was the *Lady Hughes* Incident.[11]

Lady Hughes was a merchant ship that belonged to the British East India Company. Anchored in the water near the city of Canton (now Guangzhou) on November 24, 1784, the ship's guns fired in saluting, and one shell landed on a Chinese boat lying on the side of *Lady Hughes*, killing one Chinese and injuring two (one of whom died later). Chinese local officials requested that the responsible gunner be handed over for a judicial inquiry. The British captain and supercargo refused to cooperate. After a six-day stand-off, the British finally handed over the gunner to the Chinese authorities on November 30. The gunner was found guilty and, under order of the emperor, was executed by strangulation (one grade below decapitation) for unintentional homicide.

The British narrative regarding the case was that the incident was an unfortunate accident and the gunner was innocent of any criminal intention. Yet both English law and Chinese law reckoned criminal liability of varying degrees in cases of "accidental homicide." Under English law, a person who caused someone to die in the course of committing a felony was guilty of murder, even if the person did not intend to kill. In the case of *Lady Hughes*, prohibition of discharge of firearms in Chinese territories was well known to the British, and therefore firing guns in saluting was illegal to begin with. The commanding officer was informed of the presence of the Chinese boat nearby and ordered the firing nonetheless, which suggested a foreknowledge and a disregard of possible harm from gun shells to Chinese lives.

A more generalized British narrative was that the Chinese law was unduly severe in punishment and the gunner would not receive fair treatment in the Chinese court. In fact, however, Chinese local officials did not treat foreigners unfairly in criminal cases, and often considered mitigating circumstances and meted out more lenient penalties to foreigners in cases of physical fights between Chinese persons and foreigners resulting in homicide or injury. Their mentality was to minimize any conflicts between foreigners and the Chinese and prevent any larger fallout thereof, or they would be blamed for being ineffective, as shown by the fate of Lin Zexu, who was punished for bringing the first Opium War upon China. That is why they would act in a more conciliatory manner toward foreigners than they were supposed to under the Qing law.

Yet all this was irrelevant, since the British were not interested in assessing Chinese law or its enforcement. Motivated by a determined agenda to defy Chinese law and sovereignty, the British had constructed a lasting narrative of Chinese law and justice being arbitrary and barbaric, a narrative that would lay the ideological ground for the Opium Wars and the resultant unequal treaties in the nineteenth century.

The Opium Wars and Aftermath

The direct causes of the Opium War of 1840–1842 were the illicit opium trade conducted by British merchants in Canton and the Chinese enforcement of opium prohibition carried out by Lin Zexu, the imperial commissioner, in 1839. For the British, the conflict over opium trade and prohibition offered a convenient opportunity to tackle a larger issue: to open China for trade in general by dismantling what was called the "Canton system." Under the system set up by the Qing in the eighteenth century, only one Chinese port, Canton, was open to Western merchants, who were placed under various restrictions. This explains why the Treaty of Nanjing (1842) and its supplement treaty (1843) resulting from the Opium War did not mention the opium trade at all, but achieved the larger British objective of removing the Canton system through concessions exacted from Qing China in return for nothing—hence the term "unequal treaties."

One of the key concessions in the Treaty of Nanjing was extraterritoriality, a goal that the British had long pursued with the discourse on barbaric Chinese law and justice. Different from "diplomatic immunity," extraterritoriality was a legal right, by which British nationals were not subject to Chinese law and judiciary—as if they had been on British territory. If they committed a crime in China, they would be tried under British law by British consuls in treaty ports. (Five Chinese ports were opened to the British under the Treaty of Nanjing.) By signing similar treaties with Qing China in 1844, France and the United States obtained the same concessions, including extraterritoriality.[12] By these treaties they also acquired most-favored-nation status, a status that would then become a standard feature in all treaties subsequently signed between various Western nations and Qing China, so that any concessions or favors the Qing gave to one nation would be automatically shared by the other nations as well.

The Second Opium War (1856–1858) took place because Great Britain and France wanted to revise the earlier treaties to expand their privileges in China. The war led to the 1860 Convention of Beijing, under which ten more treaty ports were opened and opium trade was legalized. Foreign powers benefiting from these treaties included Britain, France, the United States, and Russia. More significant, by the time of the Treaty of Shimonoseki resulting from the Sino-Japanese War (1894–1895), in which Japan defeated the Qing, the number of treaty ports had grown to several dozen, along not only China's coast but also the Yangzi River. Foreign warships as well as merchant ships could freely sail to and anchor at those ports.[13]

One of the consequences of the unequal treaties was the gradual alienation of treaty ports from Chinese sovereignty. In Canton, Shanghai, Tianjin, Qingdao, Xiamen (Amoy), and other cities, parts or the whole of the city became foreign enclaves beyond the Chinese authorities due to either long-term leases or outright encroachment by foreign powers. The best known of such places were the International Settlement and the French Concession in Shanghai, which came into being through foreign encroachment. The two sections, with both Chinese and foreign residents, constituted a larger part of the city than the Chinese section. The International Settlement was administered by the Shanghai Municipal Council, made up of foreigners, and the French Concession under the Municipal Administrative Council, made up of the French. Each body had its own police force and court of law known as the Mixed Court. In the International Settlement both Chinese judges and foreign consular representatives used to sit and try criminal cases involving Chinese suspects and civil lawsuits between Chinese litigants or between Chinese and foreigners. After the 1911 Revolution, the Shanghai Municipal Council completely took over the Mixed Court, where Chinese law was selectively applied. "Frequently, the court applied simply its own sense of justice, without citing any authority whatsoever for its decisions. . . . In the International Settlement, the foreign residents were not only exempt from Chinese law but defined what *was* Chinese law, and then applied it to Chinese subjects living on sovereign Chinese territory."[14] It is in view of these (and other) conditions under the unequal treaties that China of the late nineteenth and early twentieth century is often called a "semicolony."

The Qing government accepted the extraterritoriality in the Treaty of Nanjing and subsequent treaties because it was forced to after suffering military defeats, but also because at that time Qing emperors and high officials did not find it particularly objectionable. The Qing dynasty practiced legal pluralism; that is, it allowed different ethnic groups other than Han Chinese to use their own laws and customs. Given that experience, in the eyes of Qing emperors and officials, allowing foreign consuls to try their nationals in China under their own laws did not seem very different from the Qing tradition.[15] Only after having learned about the law of nations and the concept of "national sovereignty" (the American lawyer and diplomat Henry Wheaton's *Elements of International Law* [1836] was translated into Chinese in 1864) did Qing emperors and officials realize that extraterritoriality was harmful to national sovereignty and degrading to the nation. But the clause and the practice had already been fully entrenched in the treaty system governing Sino-Western relations.

The Significance of Late Qing Reform

The Origins of Late Qing Reform

On January 29, 1901, the Empress Dowager Ci Xi issued an edict:

> We have now received Her Majesty's decree to devote ourselves fully to China's revitalization, to suppress vigorously the use of the terms "new"

and "old," and to blend together the best of what is Chinese and what is foreign. . . . We therefore call upon the members of the Grand Council, the Grand Secretaries, the Six Boards and Nine Ministries, our Ministers abroad, and the Governors General and Governors of provinces to reflect carefully on our present sad state of affairs, and to scrutinize Chinese and Western governmental systems with regard to all dynastic regulations, national administration, official affairs, matters related to people's livelihood, modern schools, systems of examination, military organization, and financial administration. Duly weigh what should be kept and what abolished, what new methods should be adopted and what old ones retained. By every available means of knowledge and observation, seek out how to renew our national strength, how to produce men of real talent, how to expand state revenues, and how to revitalize the military.[16]

Her action was an attempt to save the dynasty in the wake of the Boxer debacle in 1900 that caused tremendous harm to the dynasty's legitimacy as well as China's national interests. In response to Ci Xi's call, high officials submitted reform proposals, which led to the reform known as the New Policies. These policies would promote industry and commerce, Western-style education, and military modernization, and the centerpiece was to transform the Qing government into a constitutional monarchy. Zhang Zhidong and Liu Kunyi, two governors-general, submitted three memorials on reform measures, including a sharp critique of the existing judicial and penal practices, thus triggering the legal-judicial reform as part of the New Policies.

At a deeper level, the legal-judicial reform, as well as other programs, would not have happened if it had not been for the intellectual rumination and fermentation in the previous decades during which Chinese elites, including scholars, officials, and merchants in treaty ports, became increasingly informed of Western practices in law and governance as well as in industry and commerce. The efforts by foreigners (mostly missionaries) and Chinese to translate Western political and legal concepts into Chinese language had begun even prior to the Opium Wars but intensified after 1860. Among the most important fruits of these efforts were *Wanguo gongfa* (Public Law of All Nations), translated from Wheaton's *The Elements of International Law*, and *Faguo lüli* (Laws and Statutes of France), translated from six French law codes, both published by the Translation Bureau (*Tongwen guan*) of the Qing in 1864 and 1880, respectively.[17] *Wanguo gongfa* was quickly translated into Japanese and played a role in the legal reform in Japan.[18]

In 1887 Huang Zunxian, a *juren* degree holder (someone who passed a provincial-level civil service exam) and a diplomat stationed at the Chinese Embassy in Tokyo for five years (1877–1882), published his *Riben guozhi* (A History of Japan) after witnessing the Meiji Reform firsthand. In the format of traditional dynastic histories, Huang's book featured a "treatise on law and punishment" (*xingfazhi*), which contained, with annotations, the Criminal Code (*xingfa*) and the Criminal Procedural Law (*zhizuifa*) that were modeled on the Continental Law and newly adopted in Japan.[19] Transliterating from *kanji*, Huang popularized some of the Chinese terms of Western legal concepts that would later appear in the Chinese law codes.[20]

Zhang Zhidong was another prominent figure among those who were informed of Western practices in legal and other fields. Zhang actively led Self-Strengthening projects during his tenure as governor-general in Guangdong and Guangxi and then in Hunan and Hubei (1883–1894), during which times his staff included 398 Chinese and 239 foreigners, the latter presumably being his sources of information on the West and Japan.[21]

Before the turn of the twentieth century, those reform-minded Chinese elites were already discussing the need to reform in various fields in light of Western practices, not only for the reforms' practical applications but also for their intrinsic merit. Zheng Guanying, a scholar, entrepreneur, official, educator, and writer, was another practitioner of Self-Strengthening. His widely read book published in 1894, *Shengshi weiyan* (Speaking Dangers in the Prosperous Era), contained a chapter titled "Administration of Punishment" (*xingzheng*) wherein he compared Chinese and Western law and justice. Praising Western judicial practices, he criticized their Chinese versions, from judicial torture and harsh punishment to horrible prison conditions and opium policy, and argued for reform in all these practices.[22]

Reform was more decisively reinforced by a desire shared by all Chinese elites to end extraterritoriality, a symbol of China's inferiority to Western powers and Japan. After the reform was signaled by the Qing government, Great Britain, the United States, and Japan conveyed their support for it. In their commercial treaties signed with China in 1902 and 1903, the three powers promised that given the Chinese government's desire to reform the judicial system "to bring it in accord with that of Western nations," they would relinquish extraterritoriality "when the state of the Chinese laws, the arrangement for their administration, and other considerations" warranted such actions.[23] From that point onward, to abolish the foreign privilege of extraterritoriality was the most politically compelling argument cited by reformers in Chinese debates on reform: a modern judiciary modeled after Western counterparts would remove foreign powers' justification for keeping extraterritoriality. The point was directly articulated by Shen Jiaben to none other than the empress dowager when Shen submitted the draft criminal code to the throne in 1907.[24]

"Rights" Concept and Reform Goals

After fierce debates over how and to what degree Western models were to be adopted and Chinese practices to be preserved to achieve "what is the best of the Chinese and the Western," Qing high officials on both sides of the debate generally agreed that the reform of Chinese law and justice was to be guided by the principles of the rule of law, judicial independence, and due process. Besides that, the ideas of protecting "human rights," "the people's rights," and "the people's civil rights and private rights" were voiced for the first time in these debates. Acquired from the translated law books, including *Wanguo gongfa*, the rights concept seemed similar to, but was actually different from, the Confucian statecraft theory about "the people being the foundation of the state" (*minben*): the latter underscored the importance of the ruler being benevolent toward the people, whereas the former started from the notion that rights were endowed by nature and therefore inalienable from each human being. In June 1908, for instance, the Commission on Studying Constitutional Government (*Xianzheng biancha guan*) and the Government Advisory Council (*Zizheng yuan*) presented to the throne an "Outline for the Constitution" for the projected constitutional monarchy. It contained a chapter on "the rights and obligations of officials and the people" as well as a chapter on "the ultimate power of the sovereign." The memorial that preceded the Outline stated, "The constitution is to consolidate the power of the sovereign and to protect the subjects. . . . Listing the rights and obligations of the subjects is to make clear the principle of the people being the foundation of the country" (*yishi min wei bangben zhi yi*).[25] Thus the concept of rights was said to be based on traditional statecraft theory, even when the Western constitutional models were invoked at the same time. By blurring the subtle difference in Chinese philosophy behind the *minben* concept and Western philosophy behind the rights concept, the reformers were able to forestall possible opposition to the rights concept. In fact, whether or not all Qing officials grasped the difference between Chinese and Western philosophies, no one refuted or challenged the rights concept.

In this context, Ze Gong, a Qing high official in charge of screening reform proposals, was able to claim that "all constitutional countries took as their priority the revisions of law to protect human rights. In order to use laws to protect human rights, they all established separate judicial institutions to gain the trust of the people, because only judicial institutions could follow the law and only the law could protect human rights." Equally significant, Ze argued for the universality of judicial independence as a principle: "Judicial independence is not to respect judicial officers but to respect the law. No matter what the governmental system, [the goal of] respecting the law of the land was the same in all countries. Whether it can be achieved depends on whether judicial institutions are independent."[26] These statements reflected a new vision of the functions of law and justice as protection of human rights, which was a new kind of Heavenly reason, very different from the traditional conception of law as an instrument for upholding the political-social-moral order.

Certain concerns remained, however. Some Qing officials warned against the danger of blindly copying Western models and emphasized the importance of making law and justice suit the conditions of Chinese society, culture, and tradition in order for them to function properly and effectively. An example of the concern was the fierce opposition to the draft criminal code completed in 1907, causing the draft to be shelved; at the same time, deliberate caution was taken in the drafting of a civil code, which was preceded by a nationwide investigation of local customs in civil and commercial matters.

Despite debates and certain disagreements among Qing high officials on specific issues regarding the reform, a broad set of reform agendas was accepted and set in motion, as follows:

1. Separating criminal justice and civil justice and drafting respective law codes.
2. Establishing a court system with four levels, independent of the administrative offices.
3. Introducing due process, with criminal and civil procedural laws, which banned torture in trial, allowed legal representation and defense, and established judicial procedures, including an appeal process through the court system.
4. Abolishing cruel and unusual punishment (slicing to death, displaying a decapitated head, and desecrating a corpse) and corporal punishment

(flogging); making imprisonment the primary form of punishment for criminal offenses; and replacing public decapitation and strangulation with hanging on prison grounds as the only form of the death penalty.
5. Reforming the prison system and improving incarceration conditions.

Thus the late Qing reforms started an ambitious program to remake Chinese law and the judicial system and, impressively, achieved some of the most important goals within a decade.

Criminal and Civil Codes

In 1904 the imperial court appointed Shen Jiaben and Wu Tingfang as the heads of the Law Codification Commission responsible for drafting new laws. (The men were the same generation as the reform-minded Zheng Guanying; all three were born and grew up after the first Opium War.) Shen was a legal scholar versed in Chinese imperial laws and familiar with Western and Japanese legal practices. Having passed the national-level civil service exam with a *jinshi* degree, Shen had been a deputy chairman of the Board of Punishment in 1901. He would become the head of the Supreme Court in 1906 while concurrently serving on the Law Codification Commission until 1910, when he became the deputy chairman of the Government Advisory Council and then the deputy minister of law in 1911. Thus Shen was the main architect of the legal reforms. His colleague Wu Tingfang had received legal training in England and practiced law in Hong Kong. Wu served as minister of foreign affairs and in other capacities while working with Shen until 1907. Under Shen and Wu, the draft criminal code was completed in 1907.[27]

The draft code immediately confronted strong criticism. The imperial penal codes, including the Qing code, upheld the imperial system and the patriarchal family system with provisions on "unfilial" and "unwifely" offenses and with generational and gender inequality in punishments for offenses. Guided by the principle of the rule of law (where equality before the law inhered), the draft code abolished all the said provisions and penalties. Some high officials denounced the draft code for undermining the very fabric of Chinese society and sowing social disorder. The critics argued that the result would be to harm, not strengthen, the nation. The opposition was so fierce that the draft code was withheld from enactment. In December 1909 the reformers presented to the throne an alternative, the Current Penal Code of the Great Qing (Daqing xianxing xinglü), a revised Qing code containing less radical changes than the draft code, and it was approved in May 1910.[28]

A civil code came along much more slowly, for important reasons. Drafting a civil code separately from a criminal code was one of the major agendas of the late Qing reforms. On the one hand, "the Western language of constitutional government and rights pervaded the political and legal discourse of the day. They came close to standing for universal values that could no more be questioned than industrialization or economic development. That language was what set the context for the rights approach to civil law embodied in all three drafts of the civil code."[29]

On the other hand, given the debate on how much Chinese tradition should be preserved within the legal reforms, the reformers working on a draft civil code emphasized the importance of Chinese local customs to civil justice. The Law Codification Commission set up bureaus in all provinces to investigate customs in civil and commercial matters. This cautious and deliberate approach delayed the drafting of a civil code, while the collection of local customs was not completed until nearly two decades into the Republic. When three books of the draft civil code, *General Principles*, *Obligations*, and *Rights in Rem*, were presented to the throne on October 26, 1911 (the books *Kinship* and *Succession* were soon to follow), the anti-Qing Revolution had broken out in Wuhan sixteen days earlier. Therefore the 1911 draft civil code remained an unfinished product at the end of the Qing dynasty.[30]

Court System

In 1906 the Court of Judicial Review became the Supreme Court as the highest court in the land, paired with a General Procuracy, while the Board of Punishment became the Ministry of Law for judicial administration without trial functions anymore, except that it would continue to review capital cases for the Autumn Assizes. Such was the beginning of separating courts from administrative offices, the institutional prerequisite of judicial independence. One significant break from the past occurred in 1910: the Autumn Assizes, the nine high officials trial, and the imperial court trial were abolished, and the Ministry of Law would review all capital cases as the end point of the criminal procedure.[31]

In 1907 a four-level court system began to be built: the court of first instance, the district court, the provincial high court, and the Supreme Court.

Each court was paired with a procuracy. At the provincial level, a department of justice would run judicial administration, reporting to the Ministry of Law, and its counterpart in trial function was the provincial high court, under the Supreme Court. Below the provincial level, a district court at a county seat would serve as the appellate court for a number of neighboring counties where courts of first instance tried minor cases. The four-level judiciary was not easy to construct, as it required a huge amount of financial and human resources. By 1911 the established courts numbered 345, and the country had more than 1,700 counties. Where courts did not exist, county magistrates continued to perform judicial functions along with administrative duties, as before.

At the courts established during 1907–1911, criminal and civil cases were tried according to the law in transition. Civil cases were adjudicated with multiple legal sources, since a civil code was not yet available. A collection of 117 criminal and 78 civil cases tried at three levels of courts in various provinces during 1907–1911 shows that 42.3 percent of civil cases were decided by reference to social norms or common sense (*qingli*), 18 percent by applying the parts on civil matters of the Current Penal Code of the Great Qing, 14 percent according to customs (*xiguan*), and 10.3 percent by invoking legal principles.[32]

Due Process

A Chinese term for "due process" was not coined at that time, but certain issues arising from the reforms fit the category. The first was a need for procedural laws in criminal and civil justice. Under Shen Jiaben and Wu Tingfang, a draft criminal and civil procedural law was completed in 1906.[33] It contained jury trial and legal representation by lawyers of defendants and litigants. In response to a call by the imperial throne for comments on the draft law in 1907, however, all provincial governors urged a delay of its enactment on the ground that the law would cause many inconveniences, manifesting a widespread resistance among officials to procedural justice that would more or less obstruct substantive justice as they saw it. In 1909 a criminal procedural law and a civil procedural law were separately drafted and distributed to provinces, but they too were not officially enacted.

The second issue was judicial torture. It was part of the traditional criminal procedures, but its legitimacy or efficacy had been questioned by some high officials from the Song dynasty down to the Qing.[34] In 1901 Zhang Zhidong and Liu Kunyi submitted their memorial, which set the legal reform in motion, and one of their proposals was to abolish judicial torture. In 1904–1905, when asked to comment on the Zhang-Liu proposal, Shen Jiaben and Wu Tingfang forcefully supported banning judicial torture on several grounds: it was the most notorious of Chinese legal practices criticized by foreigners, so it must be abolished in order to end extraterritoriality; the existing law did not require torture in all cases but emphasized the importance of willing confession, which by definition was not obtained through torture; and in any case, torture would not assure justice but only err either by freeing the guilty (who survived torture) or by wrongfully convicting the innocent (who made a false confession to avoid or end torture). The imperial throne approved their position.[35] Thus judicial torture was rendered illegal normatively, even though some county magistrates would continue to use it, in violation of the prohibition, well into the Republican period.

The third issue was long-term detention of criminal suspects. The imperial penal codes did not provide imprisonment as a penalty, but criminal suspects could be detained indefinitely before trial due to unavailability of a key witness to or a key suspect in a case. In 1909 Chen Shantong, an imperial censor, submitted a memorial to the throne asking for a change to the practice. "Such detainees committed offenses that would not result in the death penalty," wrote Chen, "but were imprisoned for life, or as long as ten or even twenty years, often dying from illness; even if they were luckily released before dying, the long-term imprisonment already rendered their bodies useless, making them unable to sustain a livelihood. Essentially, they were punished no less cruelly than decapitation and strangulation, which is really pitiful." Asked by the throne to give an opinion on the issue, the Ministry of Law fully concurred with Chen's view and ordered provinces to process all detained suspects waiting for trial within three months and detain criminal suspects in accordance with the law, as the Current Penal Code of the Great Qing already provided that suspects of robbery waiting for witnesses for trials would be detained no more than three years; either they would be given reduced sentences or released on bail.[36] This issue would become part of the effort to deal with trial delays and case backlogs and lead to regulations on time limits of cases to be tried in the Republican era.[37]

The fourth issue was summary execution of robbers and bandits, which would not be resolved, due to a number of factors, for the duration of the Republic.

Prison Reform

Like Europe before the eighteenth century, in traditional China imprisonment was not a form of punishment for crimes but an incidental condition in the judicial process. People were confined to *wait* for trial (or retrial) as defendants or to be questioned as witnesses or to be punished as convicts. Jails and unofficial confinement facilities were known to be crowded, filthy, disease-prone, and full of abuses; inmates often died from starvation, abuse, or disease. "Good people could not bear seeing such places and would equate them with hell; especially foreigners criticized them relentlessly," said Zhang Zhidong and Liu Kunyi in their memorial of 1901.[38] They requested that provinces be ordered to raise funds to make jails roomy and clean, provide daily rations and special provisions for summer and winter, and prohibit abuse of inmates, with severe penalties for any violations. Unofficial detention facilities, if necessary to keep, should be formalized and regulated in the same way as regular jails, while their irregular varieties would be strictly banned. In 1904 Shen Jiaben and Wu Tingfang fully endorsed the Zhang-Liu proposal on prison reform. Since the criminal code was to make imprisonment the main form of punishment, Shen submitted a memorial on the issue in May 1907. He observed, "In Western constitutional countries prison stands in a triangular relationship with the judiciary and legislature. If there are comprehensive legal codes and wise and fair judges but no proper prisons to carry out punishment, then to reform [convicts] into better persons will be merely empty words."[39] Shen could invoke "Western constitutional countries" as models to reinforce his proposal since a constitutional monarchy was the key project of the New Policies. He proposed to establish new prisons, train prison officers, enact prison regulations, and compile prison statistics. In his view, every provincial capital and every treaty port should have a model prison, and prisons should be different from workhouses. His memorial was endorsed by the Ministry of Law.

In 1910 a draft Great Qing Prison Law was completed, with an invited Japanese advisor as its main author. The draft law laid out the fundamental principles for a modern prison system based on the Western model. The document embodied the notion that incarceration was to both punish and reform convicts, through work and moral education; the notion and related practices were to endure through the Republican era into the People's

Republic.⁴⁰ It conveyed compassion in providing sanitation standards and medical care for the sick in penal institutions. The draft prison law was not enacted before the Qing dynasty fell, but the document offered a blueprint for prison reform in the Republican era.

The late Qing reforms of Chinese law and justice left behind a lasting legacy. In retrospect, the project of the rSeforms enjoyed broad support among Qing high officials beyond the leading reformers Shen Jiaben and Wu Tingfang. Notably, Shen, and many other high officials, did not have training in or direct exposure to Western laws and legal institutions but were familiar with Western legal-judicial practices. This suggests a deep level and a wide scope of transnational circulation of legal ideas via translations by Chinese and foreigners alike. Along with Shen and Wu, some Qing high officials understood the importance of judicial independence and supported the legal equality embodied in the draft criminal code. In essence, the reformers, the imperial court, and many Qing high officials came to accept the principles of the rule of law, judicial independence, and due process. The theoretical premise of these principles—the concept of natural rights or human rights—was a reformulated Heavenly reason, as it were. The reform was to revise state law to match it, while considering how the law would harmonize with human relations or China's social-cultural conditions as well.

The willingness of many Qing high officials to follow Western models to reform Chinese law and judicial practices had limits, for both ideological and practical reasons, as shown in the opposition to the draft criminal code and the resistance to the procedural laws. In such cases, Shen Jiaben, Wu Tingfang, and other reformers were able to argue skillfully for their reform agendas and make concessions on certain aspects of them, to win approval from the imperial court. In the end, what was articulated as the principles of the reform and what was actually achieved laid the foundation for the continuation of the reform in the Republican era. As we shall see, however, an underlying tension would persist between the Western models that were consciously adopted and the Chinese practices that were rooted in China's political, economic, and social-cultural conditions.

5
The Rule of Law, Judicial Independence, and Due Process

Ideals and Realities in the Republican Era, 1912–1949

The anti-Qing Revolution broke out in October 1911, and the Republic of China was proclaimed in January 1912, with the revolutionary leader Sun Yat-sen as the provisional president. In February, Yuan Shikai, a Qing high official, persuaded the Qing imperial house to abdicate; in return Sun ceded the presidency to Yuan. After Yuan died in 1916, squabbles and civil wars among provincial military commanders known as warlords dominated the political scene, and the central government in Beijing (claimed by whichever warlord) was unable to govern the country as a whole until the Nationalist Party (Guomindang or GMD) under Chiang Kai-shek founded the National Government in Nanjing in 1927. The GMD initially cooperated with the Chinese Communist Party (CCP), founded in 1921, but turned against it in 1927. After a protracted civil war between the GMD and the CCP, which was suspended during the Second Sino-Japanese War (1937–1945), the Communist forces led by Mao Zedong would finally defeat Chiang's government in 1949.

Despite the political turbulences and divisions from 1912 to 1949, continuity prevailed by and large in modernizing Chinese law and justice. The transition from the Qing dynasty to the early Republic was almost seamless in the legal-judicial field, where the New Policies were more significant than the 1911 Revolution. What late Qing reformers had envisioned and partially achieved in fashioning modern forms of law and justice framed the legal principles, laws, and judicial system in the Republican era. The new Republic simply inherited the reform agendas and their rationales from the New Policy decade.

The Beijing government (1912–1927) developed more specific rules and regulations for judicial institutions and procedures in the spirit of the rule of law, judicial independence, and due process. In working out the details of the reform, the judiciary encountered many difficulties and invited new challenges, partly because conditions in local society did not favor reform initiatives and partly because the central government in Beijing was unable to tap into tax revenues across the country, which was in the grips of warlord politics. With limited resources, the plan for building and formalizing judicial institutions and normalizing judicial procedures was implemented unevenly in the country.

Yet an in-depth look into the operations of the judicial system during 1912–1927 corrects an impression left by earlier scholarship of an absence of central government authority amid political divisions (the "China in disintegration" thesis). In the legal-judicial field, the laws, rules, regulations, orders, and directives issued from the national capital reached and were followed within the judicial system at the provincial level and down to the county level, where district courts and their branches were established. In places where courts had not been built and county magistrates performed judicial functions, reform initiatives issued from the central government were carried out to a larger degree in procedural normalization and to a much lesser degree in institutional formalization; noncompliance usually resulted from a lack of resources. "In such cases, it would be inaccurate to conclude that the central government failed to 'reach' the county level."[1] From a larger historical perspective, one observes a paradox in which the modernizing Chinese state was setting up ambitious state-building goals that could not be adequately matched with available resources, and therefore the modern state-building project would inevitably look and feel more like a failure than a success.

From 1927 onward, the National government carried forward the same project and faced many of the same problems as did its predecessor, while inventing peculiar laws and judicial practices due to its ideology as a revolutionary party-state. Unlike the Beijing regimes that did not have a political ideology as such, the government in Nanjing under the Nationalist Party had a political ideology to guide its revolution and state-building. The ideology included the Three Principles of the People and the theory of a three-stage revolution. While one of the Three Principles was democracy (an electoral constitutional government), it was qualified by the theory that the Nationalist Revolution would move from a military campaign, through a tutelage period, to reach a constitutional government. The founding of the National government in Nanjing in 1927 was proclaimed as the transition from the military campaign to the tutelage period, during which the GMD would exercise state power on behalf of the people and rule the country through the party (*yidang zhiguo*).

Applied to law and justice, this theory contradicted the principles of the rule of law and judicial independence. The National government tried to strike a balance between its monopoly on political power and its continuation of legal-judicial reforms. Thus law and justice during 1927–1949 unfolded in two major dimensions. One was to politicize the judiciary to make it a tool to deal with political foes, and the other was to continue the reform initiatives started by the late Qing New Policies and carried on by the Beijing regimes, in order to elevate China's international standing and abolish extraterritoriality. A combination of the two agendas produced peculiar legal-judicial practices that pioneered what was to come under the CCP before and after 1949.

Law and Justice under the Beijing Government, 1912–1927

Provisional New Criminal Code

In March 1912 President Yuan Shikai ordered the enactment of the draft criminal code of 1907 as the Provisional New Criminal Code (PNCC), deleting references to the imperial system.[2] Importantly, Article 10 of the PNCC spelled out the principle of legality (no crime unless law [so says]; *nullum crimen sine lege*, in Latin).[3] The article meant that the traditional legal practice of adjudicating by analogy was abolished, to the credit of Shen Jiaben in the New Policy decade. (The principle would be inherited by and more precisely expressed in the 1928 and 1935 criminal codes.)

The effect of the article on real life may be seen in two cases. In 1916 A's nephew was beaten to death by B and C. Because A received money from B and C to settle the matter privately, he falsely accused D and E for the murder. Several years later D and E died while at large, and the case was closed. Then the victim's son came forward to name B and C as killers of his father. The Hubei Provincial High Procuracy asked the Supreme Court for instructions. The Court replied that the lawsuit filed by the victim's son should be accepted, but A's private settlement with B and C was not a crime in the PNCC.[4] It is worth noting that what A did—private settlement of homicide and false accusation—were both punishable offenses under the Qing code.[5] In another case, dated 1918, a poor peasant in Qian county, Zhejiang province, handed his wife to another man as a "conditional sale" (*dian*), and the magistrate inquired how to deal with the case. The Supreme Court replied that although selling a wife was an offense, if the transaction was indeed conditional (the wife to be returned within an agreed time period), then the husband was facilitating illicit sex for money (*deli zongqian*), which was not an offense in the code.[6] Again, the deal would have been an offense under the Qing code.

Modeled on Western and Japanese criminal codes, the PNCC revised detailed articles and substatutes of the Qing code into more generalized categories of offenses, separated penalties from various offenses, and made penalties for various offenses more flexible depending on circumstances, whereas matching a specific penalty with a specific crime had characterized the imperial codes. On homicide, for example, Shen Jiaben argued to the throne in his presentation in 1907 of the draft criminal code that it was unnecessary to differentiate premeditated murder from intentional homicide, killing by poison from killing by other means, killing an official from killing a civilian, or killing ordinary people from killing family members of lower status. As for "mistaken killing"(*wusha*), it was uncalled for, since there was no such a thing as "mistaken robbery" or "mistaken abduction."[7] Thus in the PNCC homicide fell into only two categories, intentional and negligent killings, instead of at least five in the Qing code. These changes in the names of crimes and in punishments gave judges far more discretion in assigning guilt and penalties, causing problems for undertrained judges and an underbuilt court system in the early Republic and inviting criticism. Some of the issues were partially addressed in the 1928 and 1935 criminal codes.[8]

Incomplete Civil Law

At the founding of the Republic, there was only a draft civil code of 1911. When the PNCC replaced the Qing code to guide criminal justice, no counterpart in civil justice was available to courts. In late March 1912 the Ministry of Justice (the former Ministry of Law) issued a directive to all provincial departments of justice that civil cases be adjudicated "according to good customs in respective provinces, and in reference to the Japanese civil and commercial laws," and that the judicial procedures follow the draft criminal and civil procedural laws.[9] In April 1912 the Government Advisory Council adopted a resolution to echo Yuan Shikai's March 21 order to enact the PNCC, and it added that the parts of the Current Penal Code (of Great Qing) on civil matters still in effect (Xianxing lü minshi youxiao bufen) should apply in civil cases.[10] The law's articles on civil matters were indeed applied in courts, and a practicing lawyer compiled them into a book, along with the Supreme Court interpretations and the Board of Revenue Regulations, and privately published it in 1918.[11] The status of the 1911 draft code was not clarified, however, until July 1914, when the Supreme Court stated, "Although the draft civil code has not been enacted, its articles fitting national conditions and legal principles may be considered and applied as legal grounds."[12] Thus from 1912 to 1929 local customs, the relevant parts of the Qing law, the draft civil code, and foreign laws were all used as legal sources in civil litigations, and the Supreme Court frequently offered interpretations on all of them, in response to inquiries from lower courts.

In the meantime, the Law Codification Commission under the Beijing government was working on a second draft civil code to replace the 1911 draft. The effort led to the 1925 draft civil code. The authors of the new draft made certain changes to the earlier draft to address what they regarded as flaws due to an indiscriminate application of Western legal principles to China's social conditions. First, they downplayed the individual rights to emphasize the primacy of family and added the concept and articles about "patrilineal succession" (*zongtiao jicheng*) that included *jiantiao*—a male succeeding both his father and his uncle who had no male heir, even with two wives for producing heirs for both branches of the patrilineal family—a custom that had been allowed by the Qing state. It also gave the family head more authority over children, including their marriages, than the 1911 draft code did. Second, they changed the book *Rights to Debt* to *Debt* and revised relevant articles therein to balance the rights of the creditor and of the debtor. Third, in the book *Rights in Rem*, they deleted the section on debt in land, a concept adopted from the German civil code, and added a chapter on "rights to conditional sales of land and house" (*dianquan*), a long-standing Chinese practice.[13] These changes may be seen as a move against the alleged "total Westernization" and a pragmatic approach to aligning state law with Heavenly reason and human relations in Chinese society as these lawmakers understood. The 1925 draft civil code was not enacted but circulated by the Ministry of Justice in 1926 to the courts as a legal reference. The second and third changes would be incorporated in the Civil Code of 1929–1930.

Building Courts and Prisons

Building more courts and prisons was a priority for the reform, as the New Policy decade saw only 345 courts in the country. In 1912 the Ministry of Justice unveiled a plan for building new courts and new prisons. It envisioned that courts, procuracies, and prisons be established in all provinces, except Mongolia, Tibet, and Qinghai, between 1914 and 1918. Each of more than 1,700 counties was to have a district court with one or more courts of first instance, totaling over 2,000 courts. In counties where courts did not exist yet, three special trial officers would try cases so as to separate judiciary from administration and prepare for courts to be established. As for prisons, Beijing was to have a model prison in 1912 (already built). Provincial capitals and commercial metropolis should improve existing new prisons and build another sixty in 1913–1914. New prisons should be built for counties in 1915–1916, with one prison for every six or seven counties, totaling over 240 prisons.[14]

Not surprisingly, this ambitious plan (aimed more at impressing foreign powers than being realistic) never materialized during the Republican era due to a lack of financial and human resources. Many courts were set up at the county level in 1912–1913, only to be dismantled in 1914 in a financial retrenchment. What came out of the retrenchment was a system whereby the county magistrate's trial would serve as the court of first instance for minor cases that would, on appeal, arrive at the district court for a second trial and end at the provincial high court for a final trial; both the county magistrate and the district court would conduct the first trial of major cases that would go through the high court (or their branches) and end at the Supreme Court. Some semblance of the four-level court and three-trial system was kept, but the institutional content changed from the original plan.

The efforts to build a modern prison system fared worse. The Ministry of Justice issued Regulations on Prisons (1913), based on the 1910 draft prison law, and many other rules and regulations to modernize provincial prisons and county jails (for convicts) and detention houses (for defendants). It mandated separation of convicts and defendants, of male and female inmates, and of juvenile and adult inmates, among others. It introduced moral education for and productive work by inmates within prisons. It prohibited abuse of inmates and mandated investigation of inmate deaths. It instituted periodic inspections by provincial judicial officials of all penal institutions and courts to enforce compliance with the regulations. Yet, as inspection reports revealed, noncompliance was common at the county level, mainly because the standards set by the central government were far from the reality of local social-economic conditions.[15] Nevertheless, even halfway (or less) compliance was an improvement over previous conditions.

Regulating Judicial Officers

The Ministry of Justice placed emphasis on qualifications of judicial officers. In 1912 it dismissed judicial officers at top posts in Beijing and installed their replacements. The new appointees were educated in law in Japan or Western countries and had work experience in Chinese law and judiciary. Justice Minister Xu Shiying urged heads of all high courts and procuracies to seek qualified and morally upright people to be judicial officers as "the foundation of the judicial reform."[16] In 1925 among 955 judges and procurators in the country, 211 were graduates of law schools in foreign countries and 770 received higher education in China (some did both).[17]

Equal to, if not more than, the imperatives in the imperial era, mechanisms were built to discipline judicial officers for misconduct, such as the Commissions on Disciplining Judicial Officers, Senior Civil Servants, and Ordinary Civil Servants. Starting in 1921, the regulations on judicial officers covered county magistrates and trial officers in counties where courts did not exist. County magistrates were also under other regulations against bribery, corruption, and dereliction of duties, such as the Law on Punishing Officials for Bribery; the Supreme Court ruled in 1915 and 1921 that the law would apply to county policemen, clerks, runners, detention house guards, and government workers appointed to handle ad hoc tasks.[18]

The Law on Organizing Courts of 1910 that the Republic inherited from the Qing dynasty prohibited judges from being a member of political parties or of the Parliament or provincial and local assemblies. The rule was enforced by the Ministry of Justice from December 1912. In March 1914, "in the spirit of judicial independence," President Yuan Shikai also issued an order to bar judges from joining political parties.[19] In January 1915 the ban was extended to cover adjudicating county magistrates.

Another measure to prevent corruption in the judiciary was the "rule of avoidance." In January 1914 the Ministry of Justice issued an order to lay down the rule as follows: judicial officers (judges and procurators) at the provincial level should not serve in their native provinces; those at district courts and procuracies should not be natives of the area their institutions served; and those at both the provincial and district levels who had close relatives serving in the same or immediate superior institutions should ask for transfer. In 1919 the Ministry extended the rule to cover court clerks. The concept of the rule of avoidance was not new; in the imperial era, provincial governors, prefects, and county magistrates were all forbidden from serving in their native places. In the Republican era, however, only judicial officers and adjudicating county magistrates (and lawyers) were subject to the rule of avoidance, while administrative officials in all posts were not. This was therefore a measure specifically designed to help ensure the judiciary's integrity and independence.

Lawyer System

Legal defense, including defense lawyers cross-examining witnesses, was first introduced by Shen Jiaben in a chapter on lawyers in the draft criminal and civil procedural law of 1906.[20] The Law on Organizing Courts of 1910 also assumed lawyers' presence in courts. In September 1912 the Ministry of Justice issued the Provisional Regulations on Lawyers, recognizing and regulating the legal profession for the first time in Chinese history. Thereafter several sets of regulations and rules were enacted on lawyers' qualifications, examinations, ethics, obligations, supervision, and discipline.[21]

A different rule of avoidance was applied to lawyers. In 1915 the Ministry of Justice ordered that lawyers who had served as judges, procurators, or court clerks could not, within three years of leaving office, practice in the same area over which their former employers had jurisdiction. In 1916 the Ministry revoked the rule without explanation. Then in September 1918 the Ministry reinstated the rule, noting that some lawyers would use their connections with former offices to get inside information about cases and advertised such connections to gain clients. One month later the rule was extended to cover lawyers who were former court bailiffs.[22]

One issue in regulating lawyers had an impact on due process. Under various rules, lawyers could represent clients in criminal and civil cases at formal courts but could not appear in trials conducted by county magistrates. The Ministry of Justice repeatedly refused to remove that restriction, believing that the lawyer would be able to manipulate the law and outwit the county magistrate who was not sufficiently trained in law, and only a legally trained judge in a formal court could balance the role of the lawyer. The situation made legal scribes (who wrote complaints for litigants) indispensable players in the county judicial process, as was the case in the imperial era, despite magistrates routinely disparaging legal scribes as inciters of lawsuits.

Judicial Procedures

To ensure due process, in 1912 the Ministry of Justice issued orders to remind all courts and county magistrates that under the PNCC and Article 50 of the Provisional Constitution, criminal and civil trials should be open to the public and no torture and physical abuses during trials would be tolerated; those who violated the rules would be prosecuted and punished. Courtrooms were required to have seating space for the public to observe trials. In 1915 the Ministry ordered that sentencing documents at trials should be written in concise and plain language so that ordinary people would understand. In 1917 it ordered that conviction and sentencing of criminal cases be orally announced and then posted in public. These orders aimed at making judicial procedures fair, transparent, and user-friendly.

Trial delays and case backlogs—a perennial issue in the imperial era—also plagued the Republican judicial system. It became an even greater concern to the state as an issue of state legitimacy as well as judicial efficiency. Under the 1915 Regulations on Trial Deadlines for Criminal Prosecution, all courts and procuracies should finish investigation of a criminal case, pretrial hearing, and trial in ten days each (twenty days for trials of homicide and robbery). The county magistrate should close a criminal case within sixty days of receiving it. Magistrates, judges, and procurators were subject to disciplinary action for violating the rules. In 1927 another order required courts to send files of appeal cases to the appellate courts within five days of appeals.[23]

To help reduce trial delays and case backlogs, summary procedures for minor cases were introduced in 1914. A summary chamber with one judge would try cases where evidence was clear, and penalties would not exceed fourth-degree prison terms (twelve to thirty-five months), and no pretrial hearing was required. A procurator would prosecute a case within two days of receiving it. Trial would be conducted orally, with written proceedings for the record. The judge would pronounce the sentence within two to five days of taking a case. When the judge pronounced the sentence, the defendant would be asked whether he or she wished to appeal, and if not, the case was closed. Similar procedures were set up for civil litigations. These summary procedures were further standardized under new regulations in 1922.

One way to reduce the caseload and backlog was mediation for settlement out of court. Traditionally, mediation was conducted by local elites in the community. In 1914 the Ministry of Justice and Ministry of Industry and Commerce jointly issued the Regulations on Commercial Dispute Arbitration Offices, officially empowering local chambers of commerce to mediate and arbitrate commercial disputes. The Ministry of Justice called for active mediation and settlement of civil disputes, but cautioned against coercing litigants to settle. In 1916 the Supreme Court instructed that if a civil ruling contradicted a settlement agreement between the litigants, the ruling should not be enforced.[24]

Enforcing Civil Decisions

One challenge to the court system was the enforcement of court rulings in civil cases. That litigants refused to accept court rulings was as common in the Republican era as in the imperial era. Litigants would treat litigation as a game, and an adverse court decision as another hurdle to jump over in the game, by defying the ruling, delaying its execution, dragging out the case, and wearing out the opponent. To uphold the authority and credibility of the law and courts, the Ministry of Justice tried to tackle the problem through legal means. In July 1913 the Capital District Court proposed ways to enforce civil decisions, as the existing law was vague on this. In the court's opinion, properties to be sealed to pay debts should correspond in value to the amount awarded by the court, and the debtor's minimum living should be maintained. Auction of properties should be handled by a local chamber of commerce and supervised by court-appointed personnel. Since "Chinese people have a very thin notion of obeying the law," said the court, to prevent someone from physically resisting enforcement police officers should be present to deal with such situations.[25] The Ministry ordered that the proposed measures be followed by all courts as standard operating procedure to enforce civil decisions. Thereafter the civil enforcement measures grew more systematic, culminating in detailed regulations (with 130 articles) issued in 1920 and amended in 1927.

Appeal Process

In the imperial era, criminal cases entailing penal labor, exile, and death were reviewed by superior officials, and capital cases were reviewed all the way up to the eyes of the emperor, but there was no appeal or review of civil cases. Now under the criminal and civil procedural laws, most criminal and civil cases could be appealed to superior courts. After a criminal trial, either the defendant or the procurator could appeal within ten days, but this was limited to sentences heavier than detention and fine. After the second trial, either party could appeal for conviction and sentence being at odds with the law. After the third trial, either party could file an appeal to the Supreme Court for the illegality of the trial. In civil cases, litigants could appeal within twenty days of the first trial and within twenty days of the second for cases with remedies of ¥100 and above.

The appeal of criminal cases tried by county magistrates was more complicated. A rule was set in 1912 that criminal cases tried by the magistrate for penalties from prison terms of five years and up should be reviewed by the provincial high courts, even if the convicted did not appeal. Starting in 1914, all criminal cases with convictions at county trials would be reviewed. The high court would either approve of the former ruling, order a retrial, or change the sentence. Where high courts were few and far between, neighboring county magistrates would serve as appeal courts for county trials; as more branch high courts and district courts were built, the practice ceased in 1921, with certain exceptions. In general, the appeal and review process helped correct wrongful cases. During the 1920s and 1930s, for instance, the Jiangsu Provincial High Court corrected around one-quarter of cases tried by magistrates.[26]

Foreign Responses to the Reform

As legal-judicial reforms were taking place in the early Republic, the government pressed foreign powers on the issue of ending extraterritoriality. At the Washington Conference of 1921–1922, the efforts led to an agreement, in reference to the commitments made by Britain, the United States, and Japan in their treaties with China signed in 1902–1903, that foreign powers would investigate the conditions of Chinese law and judiciary and of extraterritoriality to determine whether it was time to end the latter. The Commission on

Extraterritoriality in China (with members from twelve nations plus China) conducted on-site visits from May 15 to June 15, 1926, and issued its report on September 16. At the time, thirty-five Japanese, twenty-six British, nineteen American, eighteen French, seven Portuguese, and five Italian courts were operating in China to try criminal and civil cases involving their nationals. In addition, Belgium, Denmark, Netherlands, Norway, Spain, and Sweden had similar consular jurisdictions in the country.[27] The report identified a number of problems in the practice of extraterritoriality in China and found some progress in Chinese laws, courts, and prisons since the founding of the Republic. But it also pointed out continuing flaws in the Chinese system: absence of a working constitution and presence of political divisions, frequent interference by the military authorities in court cases, absence of a criminal code that should replace the PNCC, failure to follow enacted laws in practice, inadequacy of judicial personnel and funding, and more. Based on these observations the foreign powers decided not to relinquish extraterritoriality until these flaws were corrected, to the disappointment of the nine Chinese delegates (headed by Wang Chonghui and Zheng Tianxi) on the Commission. Wang, who signed the report, made a note that his signature did not imply his approval of the report's entire content.[28]

Law and Justice under the Nationalist Government, 1927–1949

Rule by the Party versus Judicial Independence

Compared with judicial officials of the Beijing government, GMD party-state officials were more ambivalent about, and even critical of, the Western models of law and justice. They did not consider Western legal principles universally valid or necessarily superior to the Chinese legal tradition. Some GMD officials were critical of what they saw as the procedural formalities copied from the Western models that, in their view, ill suited China's social conditions and only caused judicial inefficiency, case backlogs, and extra burdens on people involved in criminal and civil lawsuits.[29] In short, they might as well have argued that state law based totally on Western models would not align well with Heavenly reason and human relations in Chinese society—now that Heavenly reason or ultimate morality was the GMD party ruling the country on behalf of and for the benefit of the people.

Upon establishing itself in Nanjing, the National government abolished the ban on judicial officers being political party members, and officially called for "partyizing the judiciary" (*danghua sifa*). Ju Zheng, a GMD veteran who became the minister of justice in October 1934, defined the term as "not to make a judiciary of party members, but to make a judiciary of party doctrines."[30] Nonetheless the GMD required that not only judges should apply party doctrines to adjudication, but also as many judges as possible should be recruited from those who understood and would carry out party doctrines.

Despite efforts at training party members to become qualified judicial officers, it was practically impossible to staff all judicial institutions, or other branches of the state system, with party members only. In 1929 a Training Institute for Judges was set up, open solely to party members, but it had limited impact. From 1930 to 1935 the institute graduated 428 judges, 75 prison officers, and 61 court registrars, while the entire judicial system had 2,382 judges and 1,071 procurators in 1936. Similarly, in 1934, of all 248 employees in the Ministry of Justice, only 104 were party members. Obviously there was a pragmatic policy to recruit qualified nonparty members as judicial officers and personnel—a balance or compromise between political allegiance and professional competence.[31]

What partyizing the judiciary actually meant for the GMD may be illustrated by the story of the Provisional Court. The International Settlement and the French Concession in Shanghai were under foreign administration, and the foreigner-dominated Shanghai Municipal Council controlled the Mixed Court in the Settlement. In January 1927, after negotiations with consuls from various foreign powers in Shanghai, the Chinese provincial government in Jiangsu was able to reorganize the Mixed Court into the Provisional Court with a Chinese president and Chinese judges. After the GMD settled in Shanghai in April 1927, Lu Xingyuan, who had obtained a master's degree from Oxford and served in various judicial posts under the GMD authorities in Guangzhou, was appointed the court president in May. At Lu's inaugural ceremony, a GMD party head in Shanghai praised him as a faithful follower and devoted disciple of Sun Yat-sen (founder of the GMD) and went on to say, "Now that the Government has appointed him to this important post, we have no doubt whatever in our minds but that he will do his utmost to uphold the doctrine and the traditions of the [GMD] in the administration of justice according to the law."[32] Reporting the occasion, the foreign press in Shanghai questioned how Lu could advance the interest of a political party and administer impartial justice at the same time. Indeed just five months later Lu was fired from his post because he adhered to the rule of law and judicial independence and refused to hand over Communist suspects arrested in the Settlement by the Municipal Police to the Chinese military authorities.

Lu was succeeded by He Shizhen, an American-educated law expert and GMD party member, who pledged that he would abide by the party's decisions and do his best to carry out the party's principles. He might have thought he could uphold judicial independence and be a good party member at the same time. Yet after one year on the job, He resigned in August 1929 because his idea of judicial independence clashed with frequent interference from the GMD, and even from Chiang Kai-shek personally, in court cases and in his duty as the court president.[33] A few months after He's resignation, on April 1, 1930, the Provisional Court was incorporated completely into the Chinese judiciary, while the Settlement was still under the Shanghai Municipal Council. The story of the Provisional Court is complex since the issue of judicial independence intersected that of China's judicial sovereignty, but it was clear that with the principle of ruling the country through the party, the GMD state was to use the judiciary to crack down on its political foes as part of normal functions of state governance.

Political Crimes and Punishment

To fully grasp why Lu Xingyuan was fired in 1928, one needs to look at how the GMD state began to create categories of crimes that were politically defined in terms of people's ideologies and political affiliations. The essence of classifying certain groups of people as political offenders was to allow the state to go beyond the regular laws, court system, and due process to eliminate or "reform" people thus identified.

A category of "local bully and evil gentry" came into being in 1924, when the Nationalist Revolution led by the GMD was in full swing. At the time there was no legal basis to prosecute a "local bully and evil gentry," but demand from local activists for dealing harshly with known bad guys in local society was such that in May 1927 the provincial government in Anhui, a province that had come under the GMD control, adopted the Provincial Regulations on Punishing Local Bully and Evil Gentry. The document listed several categories of vaguely defined offenses, including taking advantage of intellectual, political, and economic privileges to oppose revolution or engage in counterrevolutionary propaganda; conspiring with bandits to terrorize local society; oppressing the common people (including physically hurting or killing people; infringing on others' rights, property, and reputation; forcing marriage on women); and inciting litigation to swindle and extort people. Yet the provincial document could not be considered a statute applicable in the court, and it only added to legal confusion, as inquiries addressed to the judicial authorities and the GMD party center attested.[34]

In August 1927 the National government issued the Regulations on Punishing Local Bully and Evil Gentry, and set up the Special Provisional Criminal Courts to try the related offenses; the earlier provincial regulations now became the law. "Local bully and evil gentry" were defined by what the offenders did: dominating the countryside and oppressing the common people; forcing women to marry against their will; depriving debtors of personal liberty; obtaining profits from usury; facilitating opium-smoking and gambling; inciting and scheming to incite lawsuits; controlling public offices and embezzling public funds; and so on. Many of the rich, the powerful, and the resourceful in local society would easily fall into the category, leading to local power struggles now waged in a new name. A party to an ordinary dispute over properties would often launch a lawsuit accusing the other party of being a local bully and evil gentry, only to have the case rejected by the court, as seen in Jiangsu province.[35] Such local struggles would push the GMD to scale back the rhetoric on the local bully and evil gentry so as not to undermine the local social order and power structure considered crucial for the consolidation of the GMD party-state.

In the meantime, a separate category of political offenders, the "counterrevolutionary," was introduced. In March 1928 Nanjing enacted the Provisional Law on Punishing Counterrevolutionary Crimes. The law targeted primarily Communists and secondarily other political dissidents, including those opposed to Chiang Kai-shek within the GMD. Offenses under the law were tried by the special criminal courts, with severe punishment. In November 1928 the special criminal courts were abolished, but not the special laws. Cases of counterrevolutionary acts would be tried at provincial high courts, and those of the local bully and evil gentry at district courts.

According to a government report, in 1929 the judiciary prosecuted seventy-two defendants (including two women) under the law against the local bully and evil gentry, and 897 suspects (thirty women) under the law against counterrevolutionaries. These numbers represented only cases tried by regular courts, not those handled by the military and security forces.

Under a special order from the National government dated December 1929, all cases of CCP suspects arrested in Shanghai were to be processed by the Shanghai-Wusong Garrison Command; less serious cases would go to regular courts for trial, and serious cases would be tried by military courts. In fact, prior to and after the order, the military authorities would arrest and execute Communist suspects with or without trial. In 1930, for instance, local gentry in Taixing, Jiangsu province, organized a Provisional Relief Association Office to work with the government troops and local security forces to fight Communist guerrillas. Certain villagers were executed without trial as Communist suspects, which caused local people to launch a lawsuit against a key gentry figure for indiscriminately killing innocent people.[36]

In 1931 Nanjing enacted the Emergency Law on Crimes against the Republic, which superseded the laws on punishing counterrevolutionaries and local bullies and evil gentry. It provided the death penalty and heavy prison terms (fifteen years to life) for offenses against the National government, the GMD party, and party doctrines. The offenses included organizing activities against the state and making and spreading print materials in violation of the Three Principles. Those offenses were broad and vague and could be stretched to cover anything and everything that the GMD party-state deemed objectionable. Between July 1933 and June 1934, the Jiangsu Provincial High Court tried ninety-one defendants charged under the emergency law and convicted fifty-nine of them.[37]

The GMD party-state set up special penal institutions to incarcerate and secretly execute Communists and political dissidents outside the regular judicial system. These included military prisons run by the military authorities, concentration camps and labor camps controlled by the secret services, institutes for repentance administered by the Ministry of Justice, and detention centers attached to the military police or security and garrison forces. The GMD state would use extralegal apparatuses and practices, as well as special laws, to secretly imprison, torture, and execute (or simply assassinate) Communist suspects and left-wing writers.[38]

A historical context was that both the GMD and the CCP were not the kind of debating parties in electoral politics typical of Western democracies at that time, but two armed groups baptized in Leninism and fighting warlords in the mid-1920s. From 1927 onward they engaged in military as well as political struggles against one another for state power, or the Mandate of Heaven. The way the GMD state treated the Communists as rebels or bandits was well within imperial tradition, even though China had become a Republic.

The Criminal Code

Aside from dealing with political opponents with special laws and courts, the National government continued the legal-judicial reforms it inherited from the late Qing and the Beijing government. Upon its founding in 1927, the government decreed that all laws and regulations that were previously in force should apply in courts for the time being, except those incompatible with the GMD party doctrine and any laws newly enacted by Nanjing.

One milestone in Chinese legal history is that the Criminal Code replaced the Provisional New Criminal Code in 1928, and it was accompanied by the Criminal Procedural Law.[39] The code continued to uphold the principle of legality, with Article 1 providing that an act that is not under penalty by express language in the law when it is committed is no crime. GMD officials emphasized that the new code moderated penalties and limited a judge's discretion in imposing harsher sentences. The code was also celebrated for other characteristics: it was informed by a recent trend of legal developments in foreign countries and new theories of criminology and penology; it responded to the legal culture among the Chinese people; it enforced the fundamental principles of the GMD party; and it reflected the changed and changing social conditions, including new forms of crimes.

In 1935 an amended version of the Criminal Code replaced the 1928 version. The 1935 code further expressed the principle of equality before the law, and gender equality in particular. Having concubines was now illegal, for instance. Married men taking concubines and being sued by their wives could be convicted of adultery and punished under the law, although this law could not be retroactively applied. These provisions had important implications for women's rights in the legal arena. If the new criminal code and the criminal procedural law were indeed progressive and more in tune with Western models, precisely for that reason the GMD state would deem the code inadequate for punishing all common crimes, let alone political offenses, and it resorted to special laws on certain violent crimes as well as on political offenses.

Although the Criminal Code of 1928 (and the 1935 amended version) was a clear break from the Qing law, Republican judges were able to achieve certain legal outcomes in criminal cases that the Qing law was designed to achieve; for instance, a parent killing a wayward son would be lightly punished or not punished at all.[40] Yet influences from the legal tradition in general, rather than particular articles in the Qing code, might have been at work, as shown in a case where a woman convicted of murder was lightly punished, but for reasons opposite to the Qing law. Lü Ming, thirty-four, a divorced man, signed and then dissolved a marriage agreement with Liu Jinggui, twenty-four, an art school teacher, in April–May 1933, before marrying Teng Shuang, a middle school teacher, in November 1933. After his marriage with Teng, Lü carried on a sexual affair with Liu, who hoped to win him back. On March 16, 1935, Liu impersonated a student to enter Teng's school and killed Teng with a handgun by firing seven bullets into her. In late April 1935 the Beijing District Court convicted Liu of intentional homicide but sentenced her to only twelve years in prison, citing "pitiable circumstances"; in the meantime, Lü was accused of using tricks to rape a woman, but was aquitted of the charge because evidence showed that Liu voluntarily had sex with him. The district procurator appealed Liu's light sentence and Lü's acquittal to the Hebei Provincial High Court, and the second trial sustained Lü's acquittal but changed Liu's sentence to life imprisonment. The sentence was upheld by the Supreme Court against Liu's appeal.[41] Given that Article 284 of the 1928 Criminal Code prescribed the death penalty specifically for premeditated murder or cruelty in committing a homicide, Liu's life sentence was still lenient, in stark contrast with the Qing law (under which she would have been sentenced to death by decapitation delayed). Besides the progress on gender equality being a factor (Lü was considered at least partly responsible for what happened), it would appear that Republican judges were swayed not so much by the Qing code as by the notion of the alignment of Heavenly reason, state law, and human relations. The notion was not articulated as such but was expressed in articles of the 1928 Criminal Code on reducing penalties, even in murder cases, for mitigating circumstances, ignorance of the law, and voluntary surrender after committing an offense, all of which were invoked by Liu's lawyers in defending her.

The Civil Code and Civil Justice

An equally important milestone, and the fruit of assiduous work by a generation of legal reformers, was the enactment of the Civil Code in 1929–1930. Based on and improved over the 1911 and 1925 draft civil codes, the Civil Code contained five books: *General Principles, Obligations, Rights in Rem, Kinship,* and *Succession.* The Civil Procedural Law followed in 1930–1931.[42]

The Civil Code set forth the principles in civil adjudications as follows: where the law was clear, it should be applied; where the law was silent, local customs should be taken into consideration; and where neither was available, legal principles should be the guide for judges to adjudicate. Equally significant was that several articles referred to "custom" (*xiguan*) either as an exception to or as the basis for their provisions. Under Article 428, for instance, repair of rental property should be done by the proprietor unless there was a special clause in the rental agreement or "a different custom." Under another article, if a holder of rental rights on land failed to pay rent for two years, the landlord could terminate the tenancy, "unless there [was] a different custom," and the holder of rental rights could transfer his right to another person, "unless there [was] a different stipulation in the tenancy agreement or unless there [was] a different custom." These and other, similar provisions echoed civil rulings by magistrates in the Qing and judges in the Republic that invoked custom as a legal ground, manifesting how customs actually "hardened" into law.[43]

Not all customs were embraced, however. The GMD lawmakers noted that custom could be a legal ground for civil rulings only if it did not undermine public order or good social mores. The principle was indeed carried through in the making of the Civil Code. The case in point is the age-old custom of *jiantiao*: a male could succeed both his father and an uncle who had no son and even have two wives for producing heirs for both branches of the patrilineal family. The custom had been accepted by the Qing state, and, based on the Qing precedents, some county magistrates continued to rule for it in the early Republic.[44] The 1925 draft civil code also allowed *jiantiao*. The Supreme Court endorsed *jiantiao* provided by the parts on civil matters of the Current Penal Code, but ruled that having two wives for *jiantiao* was bigamy; if such unions had occurred prior to the Republic, the second wife should be deemed a concubine, who could ask for divorce for being cheated into bigamy.[45] It was the authors of the Civil Code who finally rejected *jiantiao*, because it contradicted the principle of gender equality.[46]

In civil justice, the GMD continued another practice under the Beijing government: reducing the number of civil litigations through civil mediation and arbitration. The Law on Civil Mediation of 1930 mandated establishment of a civil mediation office in the court of first instance. A judge would serve as chief mediator, and each party to a civil dispute would recommend one mediator, who could not be a lawyer or a judicial officer. The mediation period would be seven days unless the two parties agreed to extend it further.

This law formalized mediation in civil disputes, which would weaken, but not eliminate, the role of local elites in unofficial mediation.

One development in civil justice was that a civil defendant who resisted civil enforcement or refused to honor a civil ruling would be detained. Yet the related regulations provided, and the Ministry of Justice emphasized, that a civil detainee could be held no more than three months, even if he or she did not find a guarantor or come up with payment to honor the court decision by then. (Recall that the 1927 law against local bullies and evil gentry made it an offense to deprive a debtor of his or her personal freedom.) This was supposed to address instances of a losing party to a civil lawsuit defying the court ruling, but it could hardly be effective since some defendants would rather sit out the three months than make payments. The result was that some courts would hold civil detainees beyond three months, a violation of the regulations, and other courts and county magistrates simply gave up on enforcing civil decisions altogether. Both scenarios contributed to case backlogs because these unenforceable civil cases could not be closed and filed away.

The Court System

Under the National government the judicial institutions continued to expand, even if short of the stated goals. After many years of debate among judicial officials and legal scholars, Nanjing opted to abolish procuracies in 1928 to reduce the cost and streamline the operation of the judiciary, by attaching procurators to the courts. In the meantime, the Supreme Court had expanded by 1934 from one criminal chamber and two civil chambers to four criminal and four civil chambers, with five judges each. One more civil chamber and three more criminal chambers were added in 1935. In that year the Supreme Court disposed of 8,823 civil cases and 5,852 criminal cases.[47]

The Ministry of Justice also announced a plan to expand the court system across the country, but it was utterly unrealistic and probably designed to impress Western powers for the purpose of ending extraterritoriality, as was the 1912 plan under the Beijing government. For instance, the goal of every county having a court was never reached. Of seventy-five counties in Zhejiang province (which was economically more developed), only eleven had courts or their branches in 1927, and seven years later some forty-three counties in the province still had no courts. As of 1934 the nation's court system had a total of 12,349 judicial officers and staff; 1,045 counties had no courts but employed a total of 5,719 judicial personnel. Measured by numbers, however, the state's judicial capacity was still growing: whereas all courts combined handled 52,322 criminal and 64,667 civil cases in 1930, the numbers almost doubled in 1935, to 111,843 criminal and 120,646 civil cases, excluding trials by county magistrates.[48]

The Prison System

In 1927–1937 thirty prisons, seventy-five detention houses, and ten institutes for repentance were built, bringing the total to 60 new prisons, 11 new branch prisons, and 101 new detention houses. In most of more than 1,700 counties, old county jails remained the norm. Conditions of provincial prisons and county jails did not improve significantly. Such problems as shortages of inmate rations, overcrowding, and unhealthy confinement conditions continued to plague the prison system.

In the mid-1930s the government came up with three new practices to alleviate crowding and reduce the cost of inmate rations. The first was to move inmates to remote areas to reclaim wasteland, which was not actually done until 1941. The second was to allow parole for common criminals who had served one-third or at least six months of their sentences, which was a reduction from "half of term or at least twelve months" provided by the Criminal Code. The third, after the Sino-Japanese War broke out in July 1937, was to recruit inmates, under certain criteria, into the army; such military service would be considered serving prison terms. These efforts did not make much difference, however.[49]

One particular dimension of these problems was that in the mid-1930s the National government launched an antinarcotics campaign. It was conducted by the military and security apparatus under Chiang Kai-shek's personal supervision. These institutions did not take care of drug offenders sentenced to imprisonment; such inmates were sent to the regular prison system administered by the Ministry of Justice and provincial high courts. At the Jiangsu First Prison in Nanjing, for instance, the number of inmates sharply increased between mid-1935 and early 1936, way over the prison's designed capacity. The female quarter was designed for 116 persons, but in April 1924 was holding 142 women, of whom 104 were drug offenders and

17 were military and political prisoners sent by the military and security apparatus to serve long terms. The south quarter was designed for 208 men but was holding 484; the east and west quarters each was designed for 240 men but were holding 290.[50] Prison crowding was a perennial problem that never went away. At the end of 1946, the prison system held no fewer than 161,675 inmates, compared to 49,303 in 1936.[51] Overcrowding made all other goals in prison administration difficult to achieve, from providing adequate inmate rations, moral education, and space for prison work, to controlling bullying and violence among inmates and preventing abuse by prison guards.

The Chinese Judiciary under the Japanese Occupation, 1937–1945

The achievements in modernizing Chinese law and justice from the late Qing to the National government may be further appreciated by looking at the way the judiciary operated in coastal provinces under the Japanese occupation during the Second Sino-Japanese War (1937–1945), when the National government was relocated to Chongqing, Sichuan province, in southwestern China.

The Japanese Occupation

The Second Sino-Japanese War broke out in the wake of the Marco Polo Bridge Incident near Beijing in early July 1937. From August through November, the Japanese forces and the Chinese forces engaged in a fierce battle in and around Shanghai. In mid-November the Japanese controlled the city and the surrounding areas, but did not take over the two foreign concessions until after the Pearl Harbor attack in December 1941. Advancing from Shanghai, the Japanese forces entered Nanjing on December 13, 1937. The infamous Nanjing massacre ensued for six weeks. By May 1938 the Japanese nominally occupied Jiangsu province and beyond but did not control many rural areas where Communist and non-Communist resistance persisted. To administer the occupied territories, the Japanese immediately built up Chinese collaboration regimes in various locations. By 1938 the Reformed Government of the Republic of China had been proclaimed in Nanjing. Two years later the regime was replaced by another, under Wang Jingwei, a GMD veteran and high official who had defected to the Japanese.

Under the Japanese occupation and Chinese collaboration regime, the judicial system largely maintained its prewar institutional structures, continued its regular functions, and operated under the established procedural norms. In terms of judicial administration, the two special district courts and their appellate courts (the former Mixed Courts) in the International Settlement and the French Concession were not taking orders from the Ministry of Justice of the Wang Jingwei regime in Nanjing, but from the Ministry of Justice of the GMD government, which had moved to Chongqing. Only after the Japanese completely took over the foreign concessions in Shanghai following the Pearl Harbor attack was the Wang Jingwei regime able to extend its judicial arm into both foreign concessions in 1942.

A symbolic move took place in August 1943. The Shanghai High Court was established as the appellate court for the Shanghai District Court and other district and county courts or county judicial sections in surrounding counties, and the special district courts and their appellate courts in the International Settlement and the French Concession (the former Mixed Courts) were abolished.[52] The change erased the special status of the former foreign concessions that were now integrated into the Shanghai Special Municipality, a goal that had long eluded the GMD government. The development fed into propaganda about Japan's mission to liberate Asian countries from Western imperialism, part of a larger competition with the Allies in winning over Chinese minds; for the same political-diplomatic calculus as the Japanese, the United States and Great Britain agreed in January 1943 to end the extraterritorial rights of their nationals in China, and Japan, Italy, and Vichy France soon followed suit.[53]

The Chinese Judiciary

To understand how the war and occupation affected the operation of the Chinese judiciary, one needs to separate the Chinese institutions from the Japanese actions during the occupation. The Japanese occupiers and the Chinese collaborators did arrest and execute anti-Japanese guerrillas, but did so by military and extralegal means rather than through the judicial system. The judiciary under the collaboration regime processed only common criminal and civil cases, as the war and occupation separated these cases more sharply from political offenses than before. During wartime, political offense primarily meant resistance against or collaboration with the Japanese occupiers, a conflict that was dealt with by both sides outside the judicial process, until the Chinese trial of collaborators after the war. By the same token, the Japanese military personnel who committed common crimes in the occupied territories were off-limits to the Chinese courts, despite the supposed renunciation of Japanese extraterritorial rights in 1943. That is why the Japanese did not intervene in the Chinese judiciary dealing with criminal and civil cases. Indeed allowing Chinese law and justice to operate as normally as possible would be consistent with the Japanese objective of "pacifying" the occupied territories.

For the judiciary under the collaboration regime, the chain of command ran from the Ministry of Justice in Nanjing to the heads of the provincial high courts that the Ministry appointed, and further down to district courts and counties, the same way the judiciary had operated in the prewar years. They functioned by the principles and tried to abide by the judicial rules and regulations established long before the war. In August 1939, for instance, the Ministry of Justice asked for information on the dates on which county jails were restored to their normal functions after the disruption by the war in 1937. In May 1940 the Ministry issued an order to the provincial high courts. It noted that under the Regulations on Prisons (dating back to the Beijing government), inmates in prisons and jails should be housed in separate quarters or cells in accordance with categories of offenses and age; since the war and occupation, however, the prisons that were restored in haste tended to make do and house all inmates in the same cells regardless of the differentiations specified in the prison regulations. The order asked for reports on the matter from all jails under the purview of the provincial high courts. In February 1943 the Ministry issued an order to reiterate the long-standing prohibitions against using hardened, long-serving inmates as "cage heads" to control other inmates in jails and prisons. Inspections of the county-level judiciary by officials from the high court, and moral education of inmates in prisons, both practices dating back to the early Republic, also continued. In short, the prewar rules and regulations, and institutions and procedures remained in force under the Japanese occupation. A few cases at the Songjiang District Court in Jiangsu province will illustrate how the court worked during 1938–1945.[54]

Criminal and Civil Cases

One case occurred in early 1940. Mr. Li worked in a rice shop in the county seat of Songjiang. He was asked to ship rice by boat from another rice shop on the western side of the town back to his shop. When the two other boats with the same task returned but Li's boat with 35 *dan* (about 4,700 pounds) of rice did not, the manager of his shop reported the case as possible theft to the county police bureau. Before the bureau took action, Li's boat was intercepted by a patrolling police squad because his travel pass indicated that he was supposed to travel from the western to the eastern side of the town but his boat was going north, away from his destination. Li readily confessed that he owed gambling debts of over eighty *yuan* and intended to sell the rice in another town at a slightly higher price and then come back to buy the same amount of rice again to ship back to his employer, hoping to make a small profit to pay off the debts. The police forwarded the case to the Songjiang District Court, and Li was charged with embezzlement. At the police bureau, Li's employer requested that Li be prosecuted, but at the trial, the employer asked for leniency since Li had an elderly mother to take care of. The court convicted Li but sentenced him to a prison term of six months suspended for two years, on the ground that Li was a first-time offender and his employer did not sustain actual loss and had asked for leniency. The entire criminal proceeding was in accordance with the procedures established before the war, and an unspoken effort at aligning Heavenly reason, state law, and human relations is discernible.

Continuity can also be seen in the local legal culture, in how ordinary people used and abused the judicial system as one more tool in their repertoire of social interactions and negotiations. One feature of the legal culture was making false accusations, including using a false identity to do so, to settle private accounts. People who engaged in such behaviors tended to be nonelite members of local society who lacked other resources to achieve their objectives. Such behaviors persisted under the occupation. In December 1939 the district court and the county government received a petition accusing a peasant and his two sons of beating to death another man who had stolen cotton from the peasant's family field. It also alleged a cover-up by the police precinct. When the summons were sent to the accused and the supposed accuser, the latter refused to accept the summons because he never wrote the petition and knew nothing about the alleged case; he then wrote a letter to the court stating the fact. Yet the court insisted that all four people named in the petition should appear in the court to answer questions. In the end, only the peasant appeared in the court. The courtroom session revealed that the allegation was fabricated. To make sure the alleged homicide did not happen, the court's procurator ordered the police precinct to report whether it knew of the case and what was the daily conduct of the peasant and his sons. Only after the police precinct reported that it knew nothing about the case and that the three men were good citizens did the procurator drop the case. What is striking is not that someone used a false identity to make a false accusation, but the way the court handled the case. As was the norm in the prewar period, the court treated all petitions seriously, especially those involving an alleged homicide. It would investigate alleged cases to err on the side of caution rather than let potentially guilty persons go unpunished. All the work in such cases was a waste of resources, but it was also the supposed function of the court.[55]

Perhaps more than criminal cases, civil lawsuits occurring under the occupation would suggest that most Chinese civilians tried to get on with their lives as normally as possible to survive the war. In 1940 Mr. Zhang petitioned the district court to issue a civil order to Mr. Lu for debt payment. Lu did not respond, and Zhang requested civil enforcement on July 5 and asked that Lu's wife be responsible for paying the debts. On July 23 Zhang sent another petition to the court for the same purpose. The court decided that since the previous decision on civil enforcement compelling Lu's wife to pay the debts was still in effect, there was no need to issue another civil order. As no further documents were filed for the case, Zhang probably did not get what he wanted. In other words, just as in prewar years, the unenforceability of civil rulings by the courts remained common, and parties to civil lawsuits continued to play the same old game of defying the court.

A case of civil mediation will illustrate the proceeding. On March 26, 1942, a woman named Liao, through her lawyer, petitioned the district court to mediate in a dispute between her as landowner and seven tenants. What Liao wanted was for the seven tenants to make additional payments as rent deposits because of the high inflation in recent years. The court session for mediation took place on April 8, 1942. Of the seven defendants, only two were represented in court by their sons, since their fathers had passed away years earlier (which meant that rental rights were inheritable). Liao's lawyer was also present. The civil court judge asked the two defendants whether they were willing to make additional payments as rental deposits, and the defendants said no. The judge ruled that the mediation was unsuccessful. It appears that Liao made a half-hearted attempt to pressure the tenants to pay additional rental deposits and the court judge made a half-hearted effort to mediate, and both were unsuccessful, as might be expected. Neither law nor local custom gave Liao any ground to compel her tenants to pay additional deposits because of inflation. The court judge probably anticipated the outcome and therefore the mediation session was largely a formality to end the process. Yet Liao's action and the court's practice show clearly how such civil cases were handled under the procedures established in prewar years.

What was accomplished in legal-judicial reform during 1912–1949 was broad in scope and significant in achievement, albeit with obvious limitations. The reforms were meant to achieve the following: ordinary people had access to an independent court system; judicial personnel were ethical and competent; judicial process was impartial, transparent, and efficient; criminals were punished according to the law, but not beyond the law (special laws were resorted to when the Criminal Code was deemed insufficient); the innocent were not wrongfully punished; and the judiciary was not overburdened by frivolous lawsuits and marred by case backlogs. To achieve all these goals, the central strategy of the Republican state was to establish, wherever possible, the forms and norms of judicial institutions and procedures that were informed by the Western models but inevitably modified by local conditions. The project required a huge amount of resources. The reality of insufficient resources forced the state to scale back the project while trying to hold up a partially established system and make it work.

Intellectually, the Republican-era legal reformers no longer used the vocabulary of an alignment of Heavenly reason, state law, and human relations; the term "Heavenly reason" disappeared altogether from legal parlance. In essence, "Heavenly reason" was substituted by the rule of law, judicial independence, and due process, but these principles did not negate the need to align them with both state laws to be enacted and human relations to be found in Chinese society. From this perspective, the repeated revisions of the Criminal Code (1907, 1912, 1928, and 1935) and the slow drafting of the Civil Code (1907–1930), along with the criminal and civil procedural laws, since the turn of the twentieth century were continuous efforts to arrive at such an alignment, one that could never be perfect in any case, especially in a rapidly changing society. Those judges and county magistrates who were conscientious may also be seen as striving on a daily basis to achieve the alignment when they made rulings in criminal and civil cases.

Ultimately the Republican state was engaged in a transformative project inherited from the late Qing: modern state-building. The difficulties it encountered were inherent in such a project and were aggravated by unfavorable circumstances, domestically and internationally. In summary, a general pattern of law and justice in the Republican era was a running paradox: the state set up institutional and procedural standards that state agents were unable to measure up to, and the reform created increasingly greater societal demands for judicial services that the state was hard-pressed to provide with adequate supplies.

6
Bandits, Collaborators, and Wives and Concubines

Criminal and Civil Justice in the Republican Era, 1912–1949

The legal-judicial reform from the late Qing through the end of the Republican era unfolded in a continuous trajectory. As might be expected, such a transformation of law and justice would face obstacles and pitfalls. The rule of law, judicial independence, and due process were intellectually accepted as the principles to guide law and justice, but they were not materially realized throughout the judicial system or in all legal practices. Besides the issue of financial and human resources, the forces of Chinese legal tradition and political, social, economic, and cultural conditions in local society would shape how law and justice, while being reformed, would work and how deviations from the newly established norms and forms would occur. The aggregate effects of such factors in bringing about actual outcomes of criminal and civil justice in the Republican era may be illustrated by three broad issues.

Defining and Punishing Robbers and Bandits, 1912–1949

The definition of robbers and bandits and the punishment thereof evolved over time from the late Qing into the Republic, owing to three historical factors.[1] First, robbery and banditry were endemic in the Republican era, primarily but not exclusively due to pervasive rural poverty; particular ecological and socioeconomic conditions in a given region could also spawn banditry, as was the case in Heilongjiang province.[2] Faced with the problem of banditry, administrative officials and military commanders at the provincial and county levels demanded that they be given power to carry out summary executions of robbers and bandits. Unlike legally minded judicial officials who were not responsible for maintaining public security, administrative officials such as provincial governors and county magistrates as well as local military commanders had to combat violent crimes and maintain peace and security as their daily job. The military wanted quick justice and harsh punishment as the most immediate and effective tools to suppress banditry.

Second, the criminal code and procedural law and the court system resulting from the reforms since the late Qing had paradoxical consequences: On the one hand, judicial officials, especially at the national and provincial levels, tended to insist on following judicial procedures, with only limited success. On the other hand, when and where those procedures were followed, the judiciary seemed ineffective and inefficient, especially in the eyes of local officials, for helping keep peace and security in local society.

Third, because formal courts were not established in all counties across the country and county magistrates as administrative officials performed judicial functions in most places, it was conceptually more acceptable for central government officials to grant county magistrates (and local military commanders) the power to execute violent offenders outside the judicial system and criminal procedures. It was also institutionally easier for local officials to do so.

The Late Qing Practices

Under the Qing law, capital cases would go through an elaborate review process from the prefecture to the central government. At the same time, military commanders had the power to carry out summary executions—"execution on the spot" (*jiudi zhengfa*)—of any rebels or robbers who would fight government forces or resist arrest. Such an execution still required approval by provincial authorities but was not subject to the regular review of capital cases. In the imperial penal codes the term "rebel" (*zei*) referred to someone who attempted to overthrow the state or harm the imperial family, while a "thief" or "robber" (*dao*) was someone who would steal or plunder. Yet all these types were subsumed under the same category in the law: "rebel-robber-thief" (*daozei*).

In 1853, amid a great peasant rebellion known as the Taiping Rebellion (1851–1864), the Qing government authorized provinces to apply summary execution to "local bandits" (*tufei*) who were taking advantage of the rebellion to disturb local society. The practice of summary execution became widely used and continued well after the rebellion was suppressed. Provincial and local officials would often stretch the rule and apply summary execution to many types of offenders other than rebels and bandits. Some high officials questioned the validity of the practice, but provincial governors resisted any suggestions to cease the executions. The debate on the issue led to no resolution before the Qing was replaced by the Republic in 1912.

Defining the Bandit in the Republic

Under the Provisional New Criminal Code (PNCC) enacted in March 1912, the death penalty was reviewed by the Ministry of Justice, execution was to be by hanging, and mentally ill people and pregnant women were not to be executed (as was the case under the Qing law). It was not clear, however, whether summary execution of rebels, bandits, and robbers was allowed by the PNCC since the code did not contain the word "bandit" (*fei*).

When the issue was referred to President Yuan Shikai in April 1912, he replied that if the guilt of a captured bandit was proven by solid evidence and confession, he should be punished by military procedures so as to deter hardened criminals; "military procedures" was a euphemism for summary execution. Thus "bandit" became a category of criminals to be harshly punished, even though it was still not in the criminal code.

The Ministry of Justice tried to limit the applicability of summary execution by defining "bandit" more narrowly as someone who committed serious crimes to harm public security directly or indirectly where martial law was in force; everywhere else regular courts should prosecute and try robbery cases under the law. The ministry's order was met with strong opposition from provincial governors. Seeing the inevitability of local and military officials executing robbers and bandits, the ministry hoped to separate robbery and banditry cases from other criminal cases and protect the latter from interference by nonjudicial officials. The compromise resulted in the Law on Punishing Robbers and Bandits (LPRB), known as the "Bandit Law" in the Western press, in 1914. The law harked back all the way to the Song dynasty's Law on Severe Punishment of Robbery and Rebellion that was applied, beyond the Song penal code, in regions where robbers and rebels were active.

The LPRB created a special category of offenders called "robber-bandit" (*daofei*), to be punished with draconian harshness. It took effect permanently throughout the country, not just in martial law areas and periods as the Ministry of Justice had initially hoped. It mandated the death penalty for armed robbery of a home or on the road by a group of three, and other offenses. It allowed county magistrates and military commanders to execute such offenders, after getting permission from provincial governors or superior military officers. There was no legal counsel and defense in such cases, nor appeals. The detailed implementing rules for the law further allowed a county magistrate, who believed a swift execution imperative for local security, to execute an offender charged under the law by sending the provincial governor a telegram, instead of the entire case file, requesting permission. The military always had leeway to execute people as rebels and bandits, but now the LPRB legally sanctioned the practice and allowed county magistrates and military commanders to use and abuse this power. The Ministry of Justice knew there were too many such executions, but the law gave it no room to intervene.

After the GMD government was established in 1927, it continued the Bandit Law in a new guise, called the Provisional Regulations on Punishing Robbers and Bandits (PRPRB). It was "provisional" in that it was supposed to expire after six months, but it was in fact renewed every six months for the remainder of the Republican era. The law expanded punishable offenses from nine to sixteen. One supposed safeguard against wrongful cases was that the death sentence given by a court or a county magistrate would be reviewed by the provincial high court and approved by the provincial government before the execution could be carried out. But if an offender was in the military, he would be tried and executed by the commanding officer after the sentence was approved by the unit's highest ranking commander.

The law was useful to administrative and military officials because its broad and vague coverage allowed them to execute anyone they claimed to be robbers-bandits. In the PRPRB of 1927, the term "robbers and bandits" continued to cover rebels and subversives. True rebels and subversives (such as Communists and dissidents) were treated as political criminals under special laws; in practice, however, political opponents or rebels or subversives could be conveniently called bandits and dealt with under the PRPRB, and vice versa—common criminals or marginal social elements could be summarily executed as supposed Communists. The two categories became interchangeable precisely because both were outside the criminal code.

Punishing Robbers-Bandits

After 1914 every county magistrate functioned within a legal and institutional context—the Bandit Law and the absence of a formal court in most counties—that enabled him to apply the law more frequently than was warranted, such as in cases where the guilt of the accused was still in question. Since the law did not allow appeals and did not go through regular reviews of capital cases, wrongful convictions and executions became more likely. The men, and sometimes women, arrested and executed under the Bandit Law were often either destitute people in rural society who carried out robberies, kidnappings, and other crimes, or just innocent peasants who were wrongfully accused. Two cases illustrate some common scenarios.[3]

On April 18, 1924, the Jiangsu Provincial High Court received a telegram from a peasant named Chen, saying that he had been falsely accused of being a bandit and tortured into confessing. The court ordered the county magistrate, Xu, to handle the case according to the law and report back as soon as possible, but Xu did not respond. On May 8 Chen sent a second telegram, desperately pleading to have his case moved to another jurisdiction to save him from a conspiracy. The court issued a second order to Xu and asked for a copy of the entire case file. Xu kept silent until June 18, when he simply notified the high court that Chen's case had been processed under the Bandit Law and approved by the provincial governor and that the case was now closed. That is, Chen had been executed. While the truth about Chen's guilt or innocence may never be known, Xu's behavior was suggestive, since he obviously prevented the high court from looking into the case and his action was authorized by the Bandit Law.

The PRPRB of 1927 allowed the high court to review death sentences in bandit cases and the provincial government to approve such sentences, but the procedure was no guarantee against arbitrary execution that was made possible by the law. In June 1929 the Jiangsu provincial water police force arrested Lin, a young man of twenty-one from Shandong province, inside a temple in Gaoyou county, and rescued a kidnapped nine-year-old boy held there. At a trial by the magistrate, Lin confessed that he was asked to join three other men to kidnap the boy and that he had also participated in an earlier kidnapping of a six-year-old boy and got his share of ¥12 from the ransom. The victim of the recent kidnapping and his father positively identified Lin at the trial, but none of the victims of the earlier kidnapping was present. Lin was sentenced to death for two counts of kidnapping for ransom under Article 2 of the Bandit Law and Articles 9 and 42 of the Criminal Code. In its review, the provincial high court found discrepancies between the victim's testimony and Lin's confession about the date of the recent kidnapping and noted that the identity of the earlier victims was uncertain. The court recommended a retrial to get all the facts, but the provincial government commission voted to approve the death sentence.

In fact, the provincial government commission's meeting records show that in the 1930s it routinely approved, with little discussion, death sentences imposed under the Bandit Law. Twenty-eight of the thirty meetings in a six-month period (October 24, 1933, to February 13, 1934), for instance, considered death sentences in robbery-banditry cases; only on two occasions was a case put aside for further investigation, while all the other death sentences under review were approved.

Of course, not all robbery and banditry suspects were executed; a majority of common criminals was sentenced to prison terms. At least to a degree, conceivably, the pressure to clear case backlogs and reduce the inmate population in county jails and detention houses, plus the fear of bandits escaping from county jails, might have pushed some county magistrates to convict and execute robbery-banditry suspects on less than sufficient evidence. Another source of pressure was that local elites would regard certain bandits as serious threats to their lives and property and to local society in general, and demand the death penalty for such bandits, even when their offenses did not entail capital punishment under the criminal code.

In the final analysis, banditry was rooted primarily in poverty (with other contributing factors particular to local societies), and punishing robbers and bandits with "quick justice" was a response by the state to the social disorder manifested in banditry, as the state had no solution to the problem of poverty. The priority of providing public security as an issue of state legitimacy prevailed over the legal-judicial reform, which also had implications for state legitimacy. While contradictory to the newly adopted principles of judicial independence and due process, the Banditry Law was consistent with Chinese legal tradition in which procedural justice was of secondary importance. That is why there was little or no backlash against "quick justice" from the public at large, except certain judicial officials and legal scholars who did not face such issues as how to provide public security at a lower cost (in terms of resources) and how to deal with banditry effectively.[4]

Defining and Punishing Chinese Collaborators, 1937–1949

During the Second Sino-Japanese War (1937–1945), the Japanese occupied a large part of Chinese territory, while the GMD government relocated to Chongqing, Sichuan province. When the war ended, the GMD state prosecuted collaborators in the former occupied territories, similar to the prosecutions in postwar European countries once occupied by the Nazis during World War II.[5] The "purge of traitors" movement (1945–1949) would show to what degree due process had taken root in criminal justice and how it was practiced in those politically sensitive cases.

Defining "Chinese Traitors" in Wartime

The first issue in prosecuting collaborators was to define a punishable offense. In August 1937, soon after the war broke out, the Central Military Commission of the National government issued the Regulations on Punishing Chinese Traitors, which was amended one year later. The regulations specified, "Those who commit the following acts in conspiring or assisting with the enemy state or its officials and people are Chinese traitors [*Hanjian*], to be sentenced to death." The listed acts included attempting to associate with the enemy state to fight one's own nation, serving in the enemy forces, recruiting soldiers and laborers for the enemy state, supplying the enemy, collecting or stealing military secrets for the enemy state, shipping or selling war materials to the enemy, and sabotaging or blocking transportation and communications. Those who had intention to commit the said acts were liable for serving at least seven years in prison. Cases of Chinese traitors were to be tried by military institutions authorized to conduct courts-martial. Thus this legal instrument was designed to deal with those Chinese who directly aided the Japanese military operations as a matter of military security. The 1938 version of the law mainly added life imprisonment as a penalty for Chinese traitors. In addition, on October 15, 1937, the Central Military Commission issued the Regulations on Voluntary Surrender of Chinese Traitors, which exempted from penalty those traitors who voluntarily surrendered to the authorities.[6]

In short, the regulations on punishing Chinese traitors in wartime targeted primarily those who acted as operatives for the Japanese military, not necessarily collaborators who had joined the collaboration regimes. Collaborators working for the Japanese occupation were typically in the occupied territories, beyond the reach of the GMD judicial arm, though not beyond the reach of assassins from the GMD special services; hundreds were killed by such assassins.[7]

Defining "Chinese Traitors" after the War

When the war ended, the Nationalist government turned its attention to high-profile leaders of the collaboration regimes and their underlings, typically civilian officials. Accordingly, the Regulations on Dealing with Chinese Traitor Cases was issued in November 1945, and the Regulations on Punishing Chinese Traitors was amended and reissued in early December 1945.[8] These special laws, as well as the Criminal Code, were the legal instruments used to prosecute collaborators.

Significantly, these 1945 special laws did not require special courts. Provincial high courts, instead of military courts, would prosecute collaborators, except for those who were military personnel and served in the puppet forces for the enemy state. This implied a shift from targeting those who served as field agents for the Japanese military to those who worked as civilian officials in the collaboration regimes. More to the point, Article 2 of the Regulations on Dealing with Chinese Traitor Cases defined collaborators by their positions or offices in the collaboration regimes. It provided that ten categories of people should be reported as collaborators. These covered essentially those who worked in the collaboration regimes and beyond, including leaders and members of various organizations and professions in the occupied territories who "relied on the power of the enemy and its puppet to harm other people." Under Article 3, however, if solid evidence existed that the said collaborators once took action to assist in the anti-Japanese resistance or benefit the people, their penalties would be reduced, but they would still be deprived of civil rights.[9]

The 1945 Regulations on Punishing Chinese Traitors largely mirrored the wartime versions but provided more grades of lesser penalties for minor offenses, which again implied that envisioned targets were mainly civilians, not military personnel. Article 2 states, "Chinese traitors who conspired with the enemy state and committed one of the following acts would be punished by the death penalty or life imprisonment." The first of these acts was Subarticle 1: "Seek to resist one's own nation."[10] These acts were so broad and vague that they could be and were indeed used to prosecute and punish any collaborators that the GMD state wanted to, but also to go easier on any it saw fit. While the number-one collaborator, Wang Jingwei, had died in 1944, other high-profile collaborators were convicted of the offenses under Article 2 and its Subarticle 1, with penalties ranging from death to life imprisonment and varying prison terms.

Notably, the convictions and sentences were rendered according to due process. The defendants were provided with public defenders or given the opportunity to hire their own lawyers; some of the accused used both. Testimony in support of their defense was submitted to the court and entered trial records, and appeals of their convictions or sentences to the Supreme Court (after trials by high courts) were submitted and responded to. On the other hand, not surprisingly, from the perspective of the defendants these trials were unfair. The wife of Chen Gongbo, who had been the number-two man in Wang Jingwei's regime and the leading man after Wang's death in 1944, made an appeal to the Supreme Court against Chen's death sentence. She argued, among other things, that the public defender designated by the court was a useless formality, since the lawyer did not have an opportunity to meet the defendant and did not have access to indictment documents, evidence, and witnesses before the trial. Her appeal was rejected, and Chen was executed.[11]

Petty Collaborators

In prosecuting collaborators, a more complicated issue was how to deal with so-called petty collaborators in local society where the guilt of being a traitor was even more ambiguous to define morally and difficult to prove in court legally, since many petty collaborators found employment in local offices of the collaboration regimes just to survive the war and occupation. The issue was raised in the prosecution of high-profile collaborators. Chu Mingyi was a brother-in-law of Wang Jingwei. With a doctoral degree in medicine earned in France in 1926, he was a member of the Medical Practitioners' Association of Shanghai and of the GMD party Central Committee before the war. When Wang formed the collaboration regime in Nanjing in 1940, Chu served as the vice chairman of its Executive Council and as foreign minister (and ambassador to Japan for one year). In April 1946 he was tried and convicted of the offenses under Article 2 and Subarticle 1 and was executed in August. During his trial he wrote his own self-defense statement. In an appendix he asked the GMD state to be lenient on all those who had served in the puppet regimes. In the postwar years the nation would need capable people, said Chu, and if the state would treat all those experienced people by judging whether they had served in the puppet regime and not considering whether they had committed any traitorous acts, then all those talented people would be wasted, which would be a great loss to the nation. He also argued that because the Regulations on Punishing Chinese Traitors were issued and amended during wartime it was anachronistic to apply them in peacetime.

Wu Chengyu was another veteran GMD member who had once studied in Japan. From 1925 onward he stayed out of politics and practiced law in Shanghai. When the Reformed government was formed in 1938 (preceding Wang Jingwei's regime), Wu was invited to be a member of the Legislative Council, and then continued in this role in Wang's regime. Wu was tried and convicted of the offenses under Article 2 and Subarticle 1 in June 1946 and sentenced to twelve years in prison. Upon his appeal the sentence was reduced to eight years in April 1947 because evidence showed that at one time he had rescued eighty people arrested by the collaboration regime. In his own self-defense statement, Wu wrote his "reflections" on the prosecutions of collaborators. Those who had allowed the Japanese force to land at Jinshan (which led to the collapse of the Chinese defenses in the Battle of Shanghai in 1937) and those who had signed various agreements with the Japanese, he wrote, should be pursued but were not; aiding the enemy did not depend on what position one held; local officials and merchants, who had directly aided the enemy more than someone like himself should not be overlooked; those who had participated in the Japanese "mopping-up campaigns" might have committed serious crimes and should be closely examined; all those who had served in collaboration regimes faced varied circumstances that should be carefully differentiated; in all Chinese traitor cases only one's official position mattered, not the facts, and *evidence of offenses (based on which collaborators were convicted) contradicted legal interpretations*, which caused the law to lose credibility; when every allegation led to prosecution and every prosecution to conviction, it made people think there was no law to speak of in Chinese traitor cases and doubt the spirit of judicial independence.[12] Chu and Wu were self-serving in making these comments, but that did not render invalid their legal argument that one should be convicted on the facts of traitorous acts rather than by one's office in or association with collaboration regimes.

Indeed the GMD judicial officials were not unaware of this critical issue. What Wu said of the contradiction between evidence of offenses and "legal interpretations" referred to the two documents that had been issued by the Judicial Council that supervised the Ministry of Justice and the Supreme Court. On March 12, 1946, the Council issued Legal Interpretation No. 3101 and made three points. It clarified that the ten categories of people in the Regulations on Dealing with Chinese Traitor Cases did not define traitors, but only suggested that such people might be suspects to be reported on by citizens; serving in the puppet organizations and institutions alone did not define the offense of being a traitor, and only actual acts of conspiring with the enemy and betraying the nation would; "serving in the puppet organizations and relying on the power of the enemy and its puppet to harm the nation and the people" was not defined by whether one carried out any tasks but by what one actually did and under what circumstances.[13] One major newspaper's editorial in September 1947 summarized the legal interpretation's message as follows: in prosecuting collaborators, what was emphasized was action, not position and office, that is, considering only whether one had committed traitorous acts and not considering whether one had served in collaboration regimes; those who were only puppets but were not traitorous (*wei er bujian*) would still be deprived of civil rights, but such treatment was a civil and political sanction, not a criminal penalty.[14]

Legal Interpretation No. 3098 (also dated March 12, 1946) conveyed the same spirit. Answering an inquiry from a state agency, the Judicial Council clarified that whether leaders of trade associations in the occupied territories were considered traitors would depend on whether they committed acts listed under Article 2 of the Regulations on Punishing Chinese Traitors, and they must not be categorically labeled traitors.[15]

With these legal interpretations the Judicial Council cleared up the confusions and contradictions in the two special laws on dealing with collaborators, making the treatment of collaborators at provincial and lower levels a matter to be handled in a better-defined legal fashion. Both the difficulty of drawing a line between the innocent and the guilty and the intention of raising the bar for prosecution and conviction in collaboration cases were discernible in the interpretations, and that is why Wu Chengyu felt the trial of high-profile collaborators did not follow the spirit.

In January 1948 the Ministry of Justice announced that all provincial high courts together had processed 25,155 *Hanjian* cases, in which 369 persons received the death penalty, 979 were sentenced to life imprisonment, 13,570 to various prison terms, and 14 were only fined. An unwritten rule emerged from all *Hanjian* prosecutions that those who served as ministers in the collaboration regimes would received the death penalty; those as provincial governors, life imprisonment; those as deputy ministers, seven to ten years; those as bureau chiefs, two to five years; and the rest of those who were prosecuted would receive no more than thirty months.[16]

Hanjian Cases in Local Society

In local society the "purge of traitors" movement transpired in a complicated way. There were floods of accusations against collaborators arriving at the local governments, many of them false accusations designed to settle private scores or extort money from the accused.[17] The responses of local governments to the purge might have varied from locale to locale, but sources show that county governments in Jiangsu province did not appear enthusiastic to pursue those who were accused of being traitors. Here is one example: In early March 1947, the Jiangsu High Court Procurator's Office ordered the Baoshan County Judicial Section (forerunner of a county court) to investigate Chen Zhuo'an. The people (*renmin*) from Baoshan reported that Chen was the land tax collection office chief in the puppet county government and helped the Japanese seek economic resources and squeeze the people of their property. The Procurator's Office ordered that the judicial section summon Chen and the neighborhood headman for questioning. The procurator was acting in accordance with the Regulations on Dealing with Chinese Traitor Cases, investigating someone reported to be a traitor. After receiving the order from the county government, Mr. Zhang, the judicial section trial officer, sent a reply to the magistrate, saying that Chen was a clerk in the second section of the puppet county office from August 1938 to the end of the war, but he (Zhang) had no way to verify the charge that Chen helped the enemy seek resources and squeeze the people. The magistrate then asked the county GMD party office to investigate. On March 20 the party office confirmed that Chen was the land tax collection office chief, and said nothing more. Presumably these reports were forwarded to the High Court and ended the case.[18] It is clear that the powers that be in Baoshan county in 1947—the magistrate, the judicial section officer, and the GMD party office—were not keen on pursuing this case or any other local *Hanjian* cases. The half-hearted investigation produced reports that in effect shielded Chen from prosecution, let alone conviction and punishment, since he emerged from the reports as someone who only served in the puppet regime but did not commit traitorous acts (*wei er bujian*).

Due to its status in the judicial system, the Jiangsu Provincial High Court pursued all reported Chinese traitor cases seriously or matter-of-factly, but it did so within the legal means and judicial procedures. Here is a case handled directly by the high court: In March 1948 Mr. Zheng accused Mr. Li of being a traitor, which led to the arrest of Li on June 28. The charges against Li were that he helped the Japanese to retrieve weapons hidden by resistance workers, arrested a person named Lu who was then killed by the Japanese, and helped the Japanese find another hidden cache of weapons. Two named witnesses, Ma and Wu, were not available to the court, however, and there was no other evidence. Nevertheless the procurator chose to move the case to trial. Li's wife secured a lawyer, Yang, for her husband and informed the court of the fact. Li handed over the hearing transcripts and his self-defense statement to Yang. In turn Yang received a notice from the court informing him of the trial date.

In his self-defense statement, Li argued that, per a National government order from December 1946, the deadline for citizens to report on Chinese traitors was the end of that month, and since Zheng's report was well past that date, it should not be accepted. Moreover, he said, Zheng's accusations were fabricated, without physical evidence and eyewitnesses, and even if the three events did occur, no evidence connected them with Li. The complaint should have no standing in court under the Criminal Procedural Law. And finally, the alleged events occurred from 1938 to 1941, a time when Li was in Suzhou; his alibi could be verified by the household registration record at the police precinct in Suzhou where he stayed.

In another statement, Li revealed that in January 1947 Zheng went to Suzhou and tried to borrow a large sum of money from Li, but Li refused. Two months later Zheng showed up again. Brandishing a court summons purportedly for Li on charges of being a traitor, Zheng told Li that this serious matter could be made to go away with several gold bars. Seeing it as an extortion scheme, Li ignored him and did not realize until his arrest that the case was indeed being pursued by the high court. Li also provided the addresses of two supposed witnesses, Ma and Wu, that he (or his lawyer) had found, and asked the court to summon the two men to testify.[19] The case file ends there, which might mean that the case was dismissed.

The Li case shows that in the prosecution of collaborators at the provincial high court, due process was followed, and such rules as appointment of lawyers, requirement for evidence to prosecute and convict, communication between the accused and his lawyer, access to case files by lawyers, and so on, continued to work for the accused even in collaboration cases. All this was possible because the institutions and procedures had been established before 1937 and because the provincial high courts had replaced military organs as the institutions to prosecute collaborators under the 1945 special laws. The change of venue for prosecuting collaborators under these laws and the legal interpretations of 1946 signaled an effort on the part of Nanjing to adhere to due process as much as politically feasible so as to make prosecutions of collaborators credible and legitimate and to minimize chaos and disruptions of state functions in local society. This also makes a sharp contrast with the way robbers-bandits were dealt with, suggesting that they were deemed far more dangerous to peace and security in local society and accordingly procedural justice in their prosecutions was less important.

Toward Gender Equality before the Law, 1912–1949

The Republican era saw important progress in the legal realm with regard to gender equality and liberation of women from the patriarchal family system. After the Civil Code of 1929–1930 and the Criminal Code of 1935 were enacted, more and more women, often victims of traditional marriage practices, learned to use the law and the courts to fight for their own well-being in relation to their husband and his relatives. Both women and men would launch a lawsuit over marriage and divorce as a negotiating tool in settling marital matters in or outside the court. This was a growing arena where gradual but profound transformations of social and family structures occurred through everyday practices.

Law on Marriage and Divorce, 1912–1927

Under the Qing code, marriage was arranged by parents or grandparents and the man and the woman to be married had no say in the matter. This remained the case after the PNCC was enacted in 1912; the Supreme Court repeatedly confirmed parents' (and grandparents') consent as necessary for children's marriage.[20] The 1911 and 1925 draft civil codes contained similar provisions.[21] This was the legal framework for marriage and divorce prior to the Civil Code of 1929–1930.

One of the legal issues was how to establish a marriage. In 1913 two local procuracies in Beijing separately sent the Supreme Court an inquiry on the very question in order to determine whether they had cause to prosecute alleged bigamy and adultery cases. The Court replied that a marriage was established on the day an old- or new-style wedding was held, a concession to tradition and defying the 1911 and 1925 draft civil codes requiring registration of marriage with local officials.[22] Thus the customary practice was legal, and it would eventually enter the Civil Code of 1929–1930.

However, not all local customs in marriage were accepted as legal. In 1916 the Supreme Court upheld the Qing law penalizing a man marrying the wife of a deceased brother, a practice called "evil custom" by the Hubei Provincial High Procuracy but often tolerated by Qing magistrates for being a survival strategy of the poor. In 1917 the Supreme Court again ruled that such a marriage was unlawful.[23]

The legal ambiguity created by the absence of a civil code and the continuing effect of the Qing law regarding marriage is illustrated by a case from Sichuan province in 1916. Under a marriage agreement made by her father, Ms. Jiang was to marry Mr. Yin, but she refused. After the local court upheld the legality of the agreement per the Qing law and ruled for Yin, Jiang shaved off her hair and, claiming to have become a Buddhist nun, vowed to never marry. The Sichuan Provincial High Court asked the Supreme Court for direction. After deliberation, the Supreme Court replied that while the Qing law on marriage was in effect, the related penalties it prescribed had lost effect after the enactment of the PNCC; in view of foreign legal principles and China's national conditions, there was no way to enforce the court ruling on the marriage agreement, since marriage obligation could only be fulfilled personally by Jiang and an enforcement order might induce Yin to commit such criminal offenses as interference with personal liberty or violence.[24] The reply indicates that although the Qing law on marriage was still in effect, the separation of civil and criminal laws made it unenforceable.

As for divorce, Article 1359 of the 1911 draft civil code allowed a couple to divorce if both parties desired it, and Article 1360 required parents' permission for divorce if the husband was under thirty and wife under twenty-five.[25] Although the draft code was not enacted, it was applied in courts and even by some county magistrates, but other magistrates would apply the

Qing law. In 1917 the Supreme Court acknowledged that the Qing law on divorce—seven causes and three qualifying conditions, and *yijue* (moral betrayal, or breaking righteous bond)—was still in effect in the absence of a civil code, and the Tang Code and Annotations where the concept *yijue* came from was also relevant. But the Court admonished that in applying the law, judges should "balance law and human relations in order to achieve fairness" (*quanheng qingfa, yi ji qiping*) by "considering the situation of social progress, and not getting so entangled in semantics as to make [life] worse [for the parties involved]."[26]

While the "social progress" that the Supreme Court spoke of most likely referred to a growing public voice for gender equality, the opinion clearly reflected a legal mind conscious of aligning Heavenly reason (as fairness), state law, and human relations in the changing society. In one 1918 case, for instance, a husband refused to have sex with his wife, who had been betrothed to him at a young age, and planned to get a concubine to produce an heir. The Supreme Court ruled that if the husband's refusal of sex was to such a degree as to make life intolerable for the wife, then it was *yijue* and a cause for divorce.[27] The Supreme Court also ruled in 1920 that unlike a divorce between husband and wife, if a man and his concubine had irresolvable problems, either could declare a separation.[28] Consideration of social reality and human relations is again seen in the rulings by the Court in 1915 and 1918 that a husband selling a wife due to poverty could be a cause for divorce, and the man who bought her out of charity did not commit a crime—presumably neither did the husband, whereas both would have committed a punishable offense under the Qing law.[29]

One divorce case from Songjiang county, Jiangsu province, in 1922 shows that at least in certain jurisdictions multiple legal sources—the Qing law, the 1911 draft civil code, and the Supreme Court rulings—were invoked alternatively or together by the county magistrate. Mr. Wang's daughter Shuzhen, age twenty-one, was engaged to marry Mr. Shen, nineteen. One day Shuzhen was walking from her godfather's home and passing through a quiet area, when Shen, who had gathered a few helpers, sneaked upon her and took her by force to his home to "consummate the marriage" (*wanhun*). Shuzhen had heard that Shen had a debilitating disease, and on that day he happened to have a swollen face due to illness, which she believed was proof of the rumored disease. After she returned home and informed her father of what she thought, Wang and Shuzhen filed for her divorce at the county government office.

While the magistrate was issuing summons for the case, Shen filed a criminal lawsuit charging that his wife, Shuzhen, had adulterous affairs with her godfather's son Zhang and that his father-in-law, Wang, had agreed to sell Shuzhen to Zhang as a concubine for ¥400. In return Wang charged that Shen made false accusations. At a criminal trial after a hearing, the magistrate found Shen guilty of making false accusations and sentenced him for the offense according to the PNCC. Notably, Shen's act of "consummating the marriage" by force was not deemed criminal by either the magistrate or Shuzhen and her father. The Wangs only wanted to dissolve the marriage.

In a separate civil trial, Shuzhen insisted on her request for divorce because Shen had a disease previously unknown to her and because he committed *yijue* by making the false accusations against her and her father. Based on the facts and the available legal sources, the magistrate ruled that the original cause for divorce—the defendant having a debilitating disease—was invalid since it was untrue; the defendant falsely accusing his wife of adultery, and his father-in-law of selling his daughter, constituted serious insults and *yijue*, which met the condition for divorce, and the Supreme Court precedents would also apply. So Shuzhen was permitted to divorce Shen, and Shen was responsible for the litigation fee.[30] Both Shuzhen and the magistrate cited *yijue* from the Qing code, while one of the causes for divorce in the 1911 draft civil code was that "one of the parties is ill-treated or gravely insulted by the other, thereby making it intolerable for them to live together."[31] Thus the Wang family cited the Qing code to pursue a lawsuit for divorce, and the magistrate relied on both the Qing code and the draft civil code, plus the Supreme Court precedents, to make his ruling. Shen used a familiar litigation strategy, filing a criminal lawsuit to counter Shuzhen's civil lawsuit, but it backfired in this case because the false accusations became the cause for divorce.

Impact of the Civil Code, 1930–1949

For the first time in Chinese history the Civil Code of 1929–1930 offered the right for both women and men to freely marry and divorce. A man of eighteen and a woman of sixteen could enter a marriage agreement and get married of their own accord, without interference from parents or anyone else. Consistent with the tradition upheld by the Supreme Court since the founding of the Republic, the law did not require registration of marriage with a government office or any institution, but did require a public ceremony—normally a wedding ceremony or banquet—with at least two witnesses. As for divorce, a mutual agreement between a husband and a wife could dissolve a marriage. Importantly, either a husband or a wife could sue for divorce by invoking one of the ten causes: bigamy, adultery, spousal mistreatment, mistreatment of or by parents-in-law, abandonment with ill intent, attempted murder, having an incurable disease, having a serious incurable mental illness, disappearance for more than three years, and imprisonment of more than three years or imprisonment for disgraceful offenses. The first and second causes—bigamy and adultery—were qualified by a statute of limitation of six months after the discovery or two years after the fact of bigamy or adultery. The sixth and tenth causes—attempted murder and imprisonment—were qualified by a statute of limitation of one year after knowledge of the attempt and five years after the prison sentence.[32] Notably, the seventh cause was a return to the Qing statute that had been rejected by the 1911 and 1925 draft civil codes and by the Supreme Court in 1920.[33] No rationale was given for its inclusion in the code.

The Qing law and the Republican Civil Code were based on different ideological constructions about marriage, divorce, and illicit sex. The Qing law offered women both protection and punishment in such matters, on the assumption that women are virtuous and have limited or passive agency (in resisting or consenting to acts of men) in matters of illicit sex, abduction for sale of women, and so forth. In contrast, the Republican lawmakers assumed that women have free will and personal autonomy and therefore are responsible for their own actions. Accordingly, as the Civil Code made women free in matters of marriage and divorce, it provided neither protection nor punishment in such matters as illicit sex, abduction, and sale of women. But the social reality often departed from both ideological constructions, and the legal frameworks in both periods led to paradoxes in women's lives.[34]

A salient issue was concubinage. The lawmakers in the Beijing government refused to criminalize concubinage, a time-honored social custom, by treating it as a minor form of marriage, as was the case under the Qing law. The GMD upheld the principle of gender equality and monogamy, but GMD lawmakers did not consider concubinage a form of marriage and therefore it was not bigamy. Taking the GMD legal position to its logical conclusion, however, concubinage had to be considered adultery. After the enactment of the civil code, the inconsistencies between the principle of gender equality and the law, and between the criminal code and the civil code, were obvious.

The Criminal Code of 1928 provided a penalty (a prison term of no more than two years) for adultery only for married women (Article 256), and neither the Criminal Code nor the Civil Code mentioned concubinage, which women regarded as adultery committed by married men.

While a debate over whether concubinage should be abolished was ongoing in the print media, the definition of concubinage as adultery led to a vigorous campaign by educated women to demand a revision of Article 256 of the Criminal Code. In 1932 the Judicial Council issued this legal opinion: "After the enactment of 'Book IV: Kinship' of the Civil Code, taking a concubine could not be the purpose of a contract; if such an act occurs, it belongs to adultery and can be the ground for divorce."[35] This opinion added to the momentum for the demand to change Article 256. The movement resulted in a revision of the code in 1933; Article 256 was changed to Article 228: "Married *persons* convicted of committing adultery shall be punished by imprisonment for no more than two years, and the other party [of the adultery] shall be subject to the same penalty." Such cases would be prosecuted only if a spouse sued. After another round of social protests and political maneuvering over the issue, the revised article became Article 239 in the Criminal Code of 1935, and the penalty for adultery by men or women was reduced to one year in prison.[36]

The actual effect of Article 239 on concubinage was limited, however. First, if a wife wanted to sue her husband for divorce on the ground of his adultery in the form of having a concubine, she would be restricted by the statute of limitation. And the relevant laws—Book IV of the Civil Code, effective on May 5, 1931, and the revised Criminal Code, effective on July 1, 1935—were not retroactive. Moreover Article 9 of the Enforcement Law of the Criminal Code explicitly excluded applying Article 239 to men who had taken concubines before the Criminal Code of 1935 took effect.[37] One foreign observer noted as late as 1945 that as long as the wife did not object, concubinage could continue in China.[38] On the other hand, if a concubine had a sexual affair with someone other than her master, her master could not sue her for adultery and could only ask for separation.[39]

One more issue made the legal change problematic. The Qing law, the early Republican legal interpretations, and the Civil Code all accepted that a marriage was established by a wedding ceremony in public. This allowed some concubines to claim in lawsuits that they were actually wives because they married in open ceremonies with witnesses. They would also claim that they did not know their husband already had a wife. In one scenario, a man could be sued for bigamy because he married a second wife without telling her that she was merely a concubine. In another scenario, a woman could be sued for bigamy for willingly marrying a married man. Both kinds of lawsuits show that the ceremonies for marrying a main wife and a concubine were often similar in appearance, but the social distinction between the two roles was well understood. Yet this did not stop some concubines from trying to argue their cases one way or the other to escape from or stay with their masters, nor did it stop men from trying to keep or reject concubines through lawsuits.[40]

Judging Adultery Cases

The Civil Code of 1930 and the Criminal Code of 1935 set up a legal framework more favorable than before for women in matters of marriage and divorce. A criminal case in 1936 shows the force of law that was bearing on the county magistrate, even though he had strong opinions on what he deemed to be immoral conduct. Wenqin, twenty-nine, was a single woman who lived with her mother; they made a living by weaving towels to sale. Wenqin began an affair with a married man, Maosheng, in August 1935. One night in March 1936, the man sneaked into Wenqin's home to have sex with her and died of a heart attack during sex. Frightened by the man's sudden death, Wenqin went to another room to tell her mother about the incident. After failing to revive the man by stabbing his legs with a needle, the mother and the daughter moved his dead body to the side of a public toilet in a nearby street, hoping they would not to be connected with his death. Maosheng's wife, however, upon learning of her husband's death, accused Wenqin, her mother, and their relatives of murdering Maosheng for money and hiding his corpse; it appears that the wife was aware or suspicious of her husband's affair with Wenqin. The county magistrate sent the dead man's body to the Ministry of Justice Forensic Research Institute for autopsy, while issuing summonses for the accused.[41] Wenqin and her mother went into hiding before being caught in late July.

With Maosheng's autopsy report and the testimony of the accused, the trial established that Maosheng died an accidental death due to a heart attack rather than being murdered, and that Wenqin and her mother committed the offense of abandoning a corpse, for which Wenqin was sentenced to eighteen months in prison and her mother twelve months. Two people who sheltered them while they were on the run from law enforcement were sentenced to pay fines of ¥60 each (exchangeable to sixty days of labor if they were financially unable to pay). The magistrate strongly disapproved Wenqin's behavior on moral grounds. In the conviction and sentence document, the magistrate confirmed that Maosheng's death was not to be blamed on anyone. In flowery language he wrote, "Wenqin is as loose as a peach flower, with licentious behavior, putting shame on her bed and adding stains to her family, ruining her own personal standing and reputation, which is really shameless to the extreme." And the dead man was not spared: "Maosheng seeks sexual affairs like a wild butterfly chasing flowers, greedy with indecent desires, entering a woman's chamber in the quietness of night and going abandoned for a fleeting moment, resulting in his sudden death during sex, and bringing sin and misfortune to himself."[42]

In spite of such strong opinions, the magistrate adhered to the law and did not try to punish Wenqin outside the law for having a sexual affair with a married man. Ironically, if Maosheng had been alive and his wife had sued him for adultery, both Maosheng and Wenqin could have been sentenced to imprisonment (no more than one year) under Article 239 of the Criminal Code of 1935. Now that Maosheng was dead, the wife could only sue Wenqin and her mother for murder, and when they were acquitted by the forensic evidence, there was no way under the law to punish Wenqin for the affair.

Another case shows how the Republican criminal and civil codes helped women in a way that was inconceivable under the Qing law. A woman named Jin, who was nineteen in 1940, was engaged to marry Xu, twenty-six, but did not get to marry him before her family had to flee from their hometown when the Japanese forces arrived for the Battle of Shanghai in 1937. Later her father married her to Bao, but Jin left her husband in December 1939 to move in with Xu. Unable to find Jin, Bao requested assistance from the county Self-Defense Corps (SDC), a local security force. One day in July 1940 Gu and Wang of the SDC found Xu and Jin in a teahouse and arrested them. Gu and Wang intended to take the couple to the SDC, but when the latter refused to go there, Gu and Wang took them to the county police station and reported the case to the Songjiang District Court. To the surprise of Gu and Wang, however, the procurator charged them with "interfering with personal liberty," while charging Xu and Jin with adultery.

The trial by the criminal chamber of the district court found Gu guilty as charged, and he was sentenced to pay a fine of ¥40 suspended for two years, while Wang was still at large. The charge of adultery against Xu and Jin was dropped, however. The court reasoned that, as a member of the SDC, Gu had no power to conduct criminal investigations and execute arrests in common criminal cases, and therefore detaining Xu and Jin constituted the offense of interfering with personal liberty. As for the charge of adultery against Xu and Jin, under the law it was an offense the court would not prosecute unless the husband filed a criminal lawsuit. Bao had since stated that he would withdraw all charges against his wife, so the court would not proceed with the case.[43] Indeed, under the Criminal Code of 1935 Xu could not be punished for an extramarital affair with a married woman unless the woman was punished after being sued by her husband. The case ended up in the court simply because Gu and Wang executed an arrest they had no authority to make. It would appear that the court's rulings aimed at an alignment of Heavenly reason, state law, and human relations. One is also reminded that Songjiang county, Jiangsu province, was under Japanese occupation from 1938 to 1945.

Legal Games in Marriage and Divorce

To understand the impact of the criminal and civil codes on marriage and divorce cases and on legal culture, it is useful to see how litigants would use the law and courts and find new leverage to advance or protect their personal interests, regardless of legal merits of their lawsuits.

A typical strategy in such legal games in the Republican era, especially after the criminal and civil codes were enacted, was to conflate civil disputes with criminal lawsuits. In December 1940 a woman named Wang, age thirty-three, brought a criminal charge at the Songjiang District Court, accusing her husband of bigamy and his illegal wife of harassing her. According to Wang, she and her husband, Lu, had been embroiled in a divorce suit for more than ten years without resolution, and she had been living with her natal family all those years. Wang discovered that Lu had been living with Qian, another woman, after Lu died on September 6 in Qian's home. Furthermore Qian and her mother went to Wang's home to harass her.[44] An unhappy or mistreated wife leaving her husband for her birth family was a common practice because it was the only recourse legally available to the wife in the Qing era. Under the Civil Code, husband and wife had a mutual obligation to live together, or one of them could sue the other for not doing so (even though a court ruling would be unenforceable). But that was not what Wang wanted. Her objective was to claim that she was still the legal wife of Lu and therefore was entitled to some of his property.

After interviewing witnesses, the procurator dismissed the case for lack of merit. The witnesses testified that Lu formally married Qian with a wedding banquet after his divorce from Wang. The procurator concluded that whether Lu committed bigamy depended on whether Lu and Wang were still married under the law, which was to be determined by the civil chamber.[45] Legally, even if Lu committed bigamy, he was already dead; however, if he had been alive, Wang could not have sued him due to the statute of limitation. In other words, there was no case. Wang's intention was to share Lu's property, which was why she refused to accept the divorce in the first place and tried to preempt Qian's claim to the same property by launching a criminal suit. If the procurator had proceeded with the case, he would have accepted her claim that she and Lu were still married. But the procurator was clear-headed enough to prevent Wang from succeeding in this legal maneuvering.

Litigants would also use the law and courts as negotiating tools to settle their marital and family problems. A woman named Gu was married to Sun Guanyi in 1939. This was a marriage between two comfortable families—Sun worked in a seafood store owned by his family, and Gu, in her lawsuit documents, provided a long list of her personal property, including over sixty pieces of fine clothing, eight pieces of jewelry, and nine pieces of furniture. According to Gu's criminal complaint filed in December 1947, she gave birth to a boy who died early and a girl who was eight in 1947. Because her father-in-law, Sun Daokui, a powerful man in the area, was eager to have a grandson, Sun Guanyi married another woman, named Wu. On the evening of July 21 Sun Daokui and three men forced their way into the house, tied up Gu and Huang, a neighbor's cattle herder. Their intention was to accuse Gu of committing adultery in order to force her to sign an agreement to divorce Sun Guanyi. When she refused, she and Huang were taken to the police station. Lu, a police officer, tried to persuade her to agree to the divorce, but she again refused. After she was bailed out by Shi, a neighbor and shop owner, she was again pressured to sign the agreement. On July 28 she escaped to her natal family in Chongming county.

Gu filed a complaint charging her husband, her father-in-law, and Wu of committing bigamy and interfering with her personal liberty and requesting the return of her personal property and her share of the income from the family's farm. She named the neighbor Shi and the police officer Lu as witnesses.

Within two days Sun Guanyi filed a civil lawsuit for divorce, claiming that Gu had committed adultery with Huang. Asserting that he had captured them in the act, he referenced the same event on July 21 that Gu had described. He named a family helper and a neighbor as witnesses. Hearings for the criminal case filed by Gu and for the civil case filed by Sun proceeded in parallel from December 1947 to January 1948.

Sun Daokui, Wu, and Huang never showed up at the pretrial hearings, despite summonses, but the court established two facts: First, Sun Guanyi had *cohabited* with Wu since 1945, which Sun claimed Gu knew about all along. That is to say, since Sun did not formally marry Wu, he did not commit bigamy. (Although neighbors considered Sun and Wu married, "common law husband and wife," as it were, they could still argue they were just cohabiting if they never had a public wedding ritual.) Second, Officer Lu testified that Sun Guanyi reported the adultery of his wife on the night of July 21, that he went with two other policemen to Sun's home, saw that Gu and Huang were being held in Gu's room, and took the two to the police station. These facts did not confirm whether or not Gu and Huang committed adultery. Yet a revealing fact came to light during the hearings, to which Gu, Sun Guanyi, and another witness all attested. After the confrontation on July 21, a monetary settlement was offered to Gu; if she agreed to divorce Sun, he would paid her a sum of money as compensation, but the negotiations on the exact amount to be paid broke down before Gu left for her natal family on July 28. It seems reasonable to assume that if Gu did commit adultery, Sun would not have offered her compensation; only because the adultery charge was false and would probably not stand serious scrutiny in court would Sun try to persuade Gu to agree to a divorce by making the offer.

On January 10, 1948, Gu asked to have the civil trial moved to the district court of Chongming, where she was staying with her natal family. Invoking the principle of gender equality, she cited the financial cost of traveling to and staying in Baoshan to attend the hearings and trial and claimed that the civil case was a ploy by her opponents to interfere with the criminal case that she had filed. The court rejected the request on the ground that the criminal case did not seem to have merit anyway, and even if it would stand, it had no bearing on the civil case. On January 26, 1948, the procurator dismissed Gu's case. The trial of the civil case was postponed twice during January 8–27 and then put on hold because no one showed up in the court despite several summonses sent to the two parties and witnesses.

What happened was that both the criminal and civil cases only served to push the two sides to negotiate outside the court more intensely than before. Finally, on January 30, Gu moved to withdraw her criminal complaint, which had already been dismissed, saying that the two parties had cleared up all misunderstandings through mediation by relatives. On January 31 Sun Guanyi withdrew his civil complaint for divorce, citing the same reason in almost the same words.[46]

This case was typical of the way litigants used the law and court system in dealing with their marital and family disputes. The strategy used by both Sun and Gu was nothing new, but it was a response to the development of civil law in the Republican era. As one legal expert observed in the 1920s, "Under current provisions of the law if a husband and a wife are not in harmony and both parties are willing to divorce, they can do so without committing any offense.... It often happens that when one party wants to divorce but the other party disagrees, one would fabricate conditions that meet the causes for divorce in order to sue for a court judgment."[47] The Civil Code did not change that scenario. Sun apparently knew that under the civil law cohabitation had no legal consequences, so he insisted that he was cohabiting with Wu without marrying her. Sun wanted to have an official divorce from Gu, either through mutual agreement after a financial settlement or, failing that, through a court judgment, so that he could officially marry Wu, which might have been what Wu demanded. But legal action was used only as a negotiating tool or to pressure Gu because he did not have a real case to sue for divorce; he only demonstrated that he could mobilize resources (making people testify for his case) to accuse Gu of committing adultery, which was enough to pressure her to accept his offer of financial settlement. Gu did not have a real case either, but she filed the criminal lawsuit to pressure Sun to make financial concessions. All these maneuverings were possible, of course, because the Civil Code advanced the rights of women far more than under the Qing law.[48]

The first half of the twentieth century saw a profound transformation in Chinese law and justice. The reforms in the final decade of the Qing dynasty set in motion the establishment of institutions and procedures designed to support as much as feasible the rule of law, judicial independence, and due process. The significance of the New Policy initiatives is seen in the way the Beijing government and the National government continued and expanded the reform agendas outlined between 1901 and 1911. The GMD government differed from the Beijing government in two characteristics that were absent before. First, it held a political ideology, which entailed the conceptions and practices of political offenses defined by ideology and politics. Second, it embraced a stronger nationalist sentiment and questioned the suitability to Chinese social conditions of total Westernization of law and justice. Both characteristics were reflected in lawmaking, institution-building, and judicial practices between 1928 and 1949.

The changes in criminal and civil justice during the Republican era had both positive and negative impacts on the lives of ordinary people. Robbers and bandits were punished harshly without due process, probably resulting in some wrongful cases. This phenomenon points to the influence, especially on provincial and county administrative officials, of the legal tradition that emphasized substantive justice at the expense of procedural justice. It also speaks to the different job descriptions and therefore different concerns and priorities of judicial officials and administrative officials, ironically resulting from the separation of the judicial and executive fields of the state system.

On the other hand, Chinese collaborators with the Japanese occupiers in local society during the wartime were treated more leniently and with due process after the war, also with an eye on substantive justice. Petty collaborators were forgiven for their deeds under circumstances that were morally ambiguous and for the larger public good, that is, postwar social stability.

In civil justice, women in the Republican era gained increasingly more gender and marital equality before the law and more rights in their life choices, in stark contrast to the late imperial era. By the same token, both women and men adapted to the legal arena that was being reshaped by the enactment of the criminal and civil codes, and they were able to use law and the courts tactically and strategically for settling their marital problems.

In a larger context, the traditional notion of justice as the alignment of Heavenly reason, state law, and human relations was not articulated as such, nor was it completely absent from the minds of lawmakers, judges, and county magistrates. The goals of national sovereignty, nationalist revolution, and resistance against the Japanese invasion as well as modernization of law and justice—the rule of law, judicial independence, and due process—became "Heavenly reason" or ultimate morality. And the acceptance of local customs as legal grounds in civil adjudications since 1912 and eventually in the Civil Code of 1930, as well as instances of lighter penalties for certain criminal offenses in law and in court decisions, points to an unspoken (and sometimes spoken) appreciation of "human relations" in lawmaking by the state and in applying the law by judges and county magistrates. All this enriches and complicates the long-term significance of the legal-judicial reforms since the turn of the twentieth century. The trajectory of the reforms, however, was to be interrupted after the National government was driven from the mainland in 1949.

PART III
LAW AND JUSTICE IN MAOIST CHINA, 1949–1976

7
"Contradictions between the People and the Enemy"
Criminal Justice as the Proletarian Dictatorship

The Chinese Communist Party led by Mao Zedong defeated the Nationalist government and founded the People's Republic of China on the mainland on October 1, 1949. As a matter of course, the new state would assume judicial functions. In the PRC such functions were performed in a different conceptual and institutional framework from that of the previous states, but similar in many respects to what was practiced in the CCP base areas prior to 1949. The CCP had one thing in common with the GMD: both upheld the leading role of their respective party in the state system, including the judiciary. A key difference, however, was that the CCP under Mao was even less appreciative of Western models in the legal realm than the GMD. (And the GMD had been less so than the late Qing and early Republican reformers.) Both the Revolution that Mao had led and the future of a new China that he envisioned in 1949 were predicated on a complete break, in Mao's mind, with the past—not only with Chinese tradition but also with Western-derived precedents.

Conceptually, with the founding of the PRC a profound and consequential shift occurred in the functioning of law and justice: modernity was replaced with proletarian revolution, and capitalism with Socialism, as the Heavenly reason or ultimate morality to judge right and wrong or guilt and innocence. Starting from the Marxist-Leninist theory that the state was a tool for the ruling class to oppress and control the ruled, Mao opined that the Socialist state was for the working class or proletariats, represented and led by the CCP, to exercise the people's democratic dictatorship or the proletarian dictatorship over the former ruling class of capitalists and landlords. In this formulation, there was no room or need for the rule of law, judicial independence, and due process.

Heaven Has Eyes. Xiaoqun Xu, Oxford University Press (2020). © Oxford University Press.
DOI: 10.1093/oso/9780190060046.001.0001

More critically, in the early 1960s Mao predicted that class struggle would not cease during the entire Socialist period that was a transitional phase into a Communist society, and the CCP-led state had to exercise its power—the proletarian dictatorship—to forestall a possible bourgeois-capitalist comeback. In Mao's vision, China was to become a historically unprecedented Socialist society created by "a Socialist new people" and reenergized constantly through a "continuous revolution." In essence, Mao's endeavor from 1949 to 1976 was to realize his vision, which effected peculiar practices of law and justice in Chinese history.

Legacies of the Revolutionary Years, 1924–1949

Judicial Institutions in Base Areas

From 1924 to 1927, when the CCP partnered with the GMD in the Nationalist Revolution against warlords and imperialism, the Communists contributed to the creation of political offenses (and their punishments), called "local bully and evil gentry" and "counterrevolutionaries." The Anhui Provincial Regulations on Punishing Local Bully and Evil Gentry was not an isolated document. Similar quasi-legal documents were issued in Hunan, Hubei, and Jiangxi provinces, where the Communists were active in mobilizing peasants in the mid-1920s.[1] After Chiang Kai-shek's about-face in 1927 and the GMD and the CCP became sworn enemies, the term "counterrevolutionaries" (and the term "bandits" too) became a label used by both sides to name the enemy. Anyone who was identified as such would suffer deadly consequences in the form of summary trial and execution, reminiscent of the Reign of Terror of the French Revolution (1789–1799) and the Red Terror of the Russian Revolution (1917–1921).

During the civil war of 1927–1937, the Second Sino-Japanese War of 1937–1945, and the civil war of 1946–1949, the Communists were able to create and maintain their "base areas" in different locales around the country where they set up quasi-state systems to organize peasants and administer those territories for tax revenues, logistic support, and recruitment of soldiers. In the early 1930s the fifteen base areas under Communist control amounted to more than three hundred counties, with a combined population of 2.5 million. By June 1949 the base areas, now known as the "liberated regions," had expanded to 2.3 million square kilometers, with a population of 125 million.

(China's total population was about 450 million at the time.)² Not surprisingly, such a quasi-state required rudimentary legal instruments and judicial functions for maintaining public security and social order.

From the beginning the base areas had ad hoc revolutionary courts to try and punish counterrevolutionaries. In November 1931 the CCP established the Chinese Soviet Republic in the central base area in Jiangxi province, as a rival to the National government. The regime included a set of judicial organs modeled after the Soviet Union. At the top level, the supreme court would try cases, review appeal cases, and offer legal interpretations, while the people's judicial commission (a Soviet term) would run judicial administration. At the lower levels of province, county, and ward a trial organ with procurators and judges would try cases and double as a judicial administrative body. In reality, however, such organs failed to materialize in many locales, and summary justice took place as a result. The Red Army had its separate court-martial bodies. All these institutions were supervised by their superior institutions and the Party committees at the same levels, and judges and procurators were Party members.³

During the Second Sino-Japanese War, the GMD and the CCP reached a truce and formed a united front to fight the Japanese. In 1943 the Communists reorganized the judicial institutions in their base areas in a fashion similar to those of the National government—high courts (and their branches), district courts, and county judicial sections, each with procurators—to be nominally under one government. Penalties in serious criminal cases that occurred at the county level would be decided by the county government commission instead of the county judicial division itself. From August 1942 to February 1944 the Border Region Government (the new name of the CCP base area government) established the Adjudication Committee to hear appeal cases from the high courts, administrative lawsuits, and civil cases over marriage; to review capital cases; and to provide legal interpretations.⁴

After the civil war resumed in 1946, the CCP launched land reform in its base areas. For that purpose, special courts were formed to punish anyone who would resist or sabotage the land reform. As the Communist forces seized one major city after another from the Nationalists during 1947–1949, they imposed martial law and set up special courts to try counterrevolutionaries. Special courts' sentences were to be approved by the authorities of the base areas. In 1948 land reform came to an end in the old base areas (held by the CCP prior to 1946), and judicial institutions were reorganized into the people's courts at three levels, with the base area on top, the province in the middle, and the county at the bottom. (A base area often cut across parts of two or more provinces.) The people's courts were also established in major cities newly seized by the Communist forces.

Legal Instruments and Judicial Practices

Throughout the revolutionary years (1924–1949) neither substantive nor procedural laws in criminal and civil justice were enacted by the Communist quasi-state. Instead individual ad hoc statutes or regulations in various criminal and civil matters were issued from time to time. The Hubei Province Provisional Regulations on Punishing Local Bully and Evil Gentry (January 1927) defined the offenses in the same way as did the Anhui regulations and provided penalties ranging from death to life imprisonment, lesser prison terms, fines, deprivation of civil rights, and confiscation of property. The Regulations on Punishing Counterrevolutionaries of the Chinese Soviet Republic (April 1934) defined counterrevolutionary acts as "any attempts to overthrow or subvert Soviet governments, and also to deprive workers and peasants of rights attained in the democratic revolution, and any attempts to support or restore the class domination of local magnates, landowners, and capitalists, irrespective of means." Twenty-eight specific offenses were listed and were punishable by the death penalty or prison terms. The statute did not provide life imprisonment, and Article 40 stated that prison terms should not exceed ten years, which meant that the penalty above a ten-year term was death.[5] These provisions may have resulted from a lack of resources to maintain confinement facilities in the base areas and a lack of stability of the base areas themselves in wartime conditions; the Communists often had to retreat from or abandon parts or the whole of a base area. Under Article 37, offenders age sixteen and under would receive lighter sentences, and those age fourteen and under would be sent to educational facilities for reeducation.[6]

The Second Sino-Japanese War saw ad hoc statutes on Chinese collaborators, similar to those issued by the National government in 1937 and 1938. The Shaanxi-Gansu-Ningxia Border Region Regulations on Punishing Chinese Traitors issued in 1939 largely mirrored similar instruments of the National government. In August 1945 the Shandong Province Provisional Regulations on Punishing War Criminals and Chinese Traitors marked the settling of scores with Chinese collaborators, which again paralleled Nanjing's prosecution and punishment of collaborators.[7]

The civil war of 1946–1949 brought back ad hoc statutes on political offenses. In October 1947, in anticipation of the victory over the National government, the People's Liberation Army issued a declaration announcing the intention to "arrest, try, and punish civil war criminals headed by Chiang Kai-shek." The message was repeated in the People's Liberation Army Headquarters Directive on punishing war criminals (November 1948). When land reform began in 1948 in the base areas, the Provisional Regulations on Punishing Sabotage of Land Reform was issued by the Shanxi-Hebei-Shandong-Henan Border Region Government. It provided the death penalty for anyone who would murder peasants and party cadres to resist the land reform. In the meantime the Liaoning Province Provisional Measures of Punishing Bandit Criminals provided punishments, including the death penalty, for offenses of armed robbery, arson, rape, and so on, and offered reduced penalties for those who turned themselves in.[8]

As for judicial procedures, the Communist quasi-state in the base areas issued various policy documents or regulations between 1927 and 1949. These measures hinted at the principles of judicial independence (the court was supposed to try cases independently) and due process (open trial, jury trial, no corporal punishment, and no torture to obtain confessions). In 1942, for example, the Border Region Government issued the Draft Regulations on Criminal Lawsuits and Draft Regulations on Civil Lawsuits. These instruments established several principles of judicial procedures: judicial organs as sole authorities to perform judicial functions; protection of human rights, including citizens' personal freedom, property rights, and litigation rights; equality before the law; deciding cases based on evidence, not confession; and the judiciary relying on and serving the masses.[9] These principles were hardly followed in practice, however. Moreover, under the 1943 regulations on judicial procedures, the county government commissions would decide important cases, which did not square with the principle of judicial independence. Corporal punishment and torture to obtain confessions would still occur in various judicial institutions. Legal representation and defense did not exist; both the concept and lawyers were lacking.

In legal instruments and in practice, equality before the law was negated by expressed considerations of class identity or family background of the accused, along with motives and circumstances of offenses; on the other hand, voluntary surrender and confession before or after discovery of offenses would lead to reduced punishment.[10] Open trials were not court trials being open to the public, but trials held at mass rallies, followed by parades of the convicted. As for appeals and death sentence reviews by the highest authorities, they rarely took place.[11]

Criminal Cases in Base Areas

During those revolutionary years, the Communist judiciary in the base areas spent much energy on fighting real and imaged counterrevolutionaries. When the Chinese Soviet Republic was set up in Jiangxi province in 1931, the Political Security Bureau was an arm of the quasi-state responsible for internal security. Its initial charge was only to investigate and arrest suspects of counterrevolutionary offenses, but soon it would also prosecute, try, and even execute such offenders. In a three-month period in 1932, 70 percent of 1,641 cases dealt with by all judicial organs in the Chinese Soviet Republic were political offenses.[12] The Chinese Soviet Republic Regulations on Punishing Counterrevolutionaries (1934) defined "counterrevolutionaries," but due to intraparty politics, and sometimes paranoia, Communist cadres and the rank and file were often accused, convicted, and executed as counterrevolutionaries, especially during the civil war of 1927–1937 and the Sino-Japanese War of 1937–1945.[13]

Communist cadres or soldiers would be prosecuted and punished for common crimes as well, even though such cases were fewer. Huang Kegong's was the best-known case. Huang joined the Red Army and the CCP in 1930, when he was nineteen. He was in the fight defending the central base area against Chiang Kai-shek's forces (1930–1934) and then in the Long March. (The CCP quit its base areas in central and southern China to retreat to Shaanxi province in 1934–1935). Huang rose through the ranks and at the age of twenty-six became one of the directors at the CCP cadre-training institution, the Military-Political University for Anti-Japanese Resistance, in Yan'an, Shaanxi, where the CCP set up its central base area after the Long March. In the fall of 1937 Huang dated Liu Xi, twenty, a female student, for a short while before Liu wanted to break up. One morning, having failed to persuade Liu to marry him, Huang shot and killed her. When Liu's body was found, Huang was an immediate suspect in the murder, and when questioned, he confessed. He was tried at a mass rally and convicted of murder by the Border Region High Court and sentenced to death. Since Huang's case involved a senior party cadre and officer (an exemplary one otherwise), it was reviewed, and his death sentence approved, by Mao and other top CCP leaders before his open trial and execution.[14]

The Huang case shows how justice was administered by the CCP: substantive justice was achieved (in this case Huang would have been convicted of murder or manslaughter under any legal-judicial system) at the expense of procedural justice or due process. Huang was tried, convicted, and executed, not under any criminal code and criminal procedural law, since none had been enacted in the base areas, but under the party leaders' decision and in an ad hoc fashion. Other criminal cases in which CCP cadres received the death penalty in a similar fashion, with Mao's and other top leaders' approval, involved crimes of embezzlement of public funds.

Besides the cases of political offenses and official corruption, the Communist judiciary in the base areas dealt with common crimes and civil disputes occurring in the population. In the early 1940s one senior judicial officer, Ma Xiwu, became a celebrated judge for his careful approaches to criminal and civil cases. He would go to villages to conduct thorough investigations and solve crimes and disputes on the spot. In one murder case, the Su brothers were convicted by the county judicial section on the grounds that they were seen walking with the victim on a road and that blood stains were found in their home. When the case was reviewed at the branch high court, of which Ma was the head, he found the evidence insufficient. Investigating the case personally, Ma learned that witnesses saw the Su brothers walking with, but then parting from, the victim. As for blood stains in the Su home, the blood in bed was from the wife of one of the brothers, the blood on the floor was from a family member's nosebleed due to illness, and the blood on an ax was from slaughtering a goat. (These findings tell us that tests of blood types, let alone DNA and other kinds of forensic evidence, did not exist.) Based on new evidence, Ma cleared the Su brothers, and he then discovered the real murderer with evidence found in further investigations.[15]

Penal Practices in the Base Areas

As early as the Soviet Republic years, detention houses were set up under three different agencies: those of the Adjudication Department (*Caipanbu*) held common criminal defendants; those of the Committee on Purging Counterrevolutionaries (*sufan weiyuanhui*) held counterrevolutionaries waiting for trial and common criminal defendants or convicts of short prison terms; and those of the State Political Protection Bureau (*Guojia zhengzhi baoweiju*) also held counterrevolutionaries waiting for trial. In 1936, after the CCP moved to Shaanxi following the Long March, county-level revolutionary courts had "trial waiting rooms" (*daishenshi*).

One similarity to the National government, and earlier states for that matter, was that the CCP also believed in the necessity and possibility of reforming criminal offenders into better persons through moral education and physical labor.[16] The Party defined a prison's three functions as control of criminal elements, production to help penal institutions be self-sufficient, and education to reform prisoners. A slogan at the time was "Education is primary and punishment is secondary."[17] As early as November 1931 the CCP established Institutes for Reformation through Labor (*laodong ganhua yuan*) at provincial and county levels for convicts sentenced to long prison terms. Regulations on such institutions were issued in 1933 and relevant administrative agencies were set up. Prisons were also built, and their organization and administration were similar to those for the Institutes for Reformation through Labor, but on a smaller scale and with more restrictions on inmates' activities. A further practice was that in 1932 the Chinese Soviet Republic decided to organize convicts with lesser offenses and sentences into "hard labor teams" (*kugongdui*).

All these practices were guided by what Mao said in his report to the Second Soviet National Congress in January 1934: the Chinese Soviet prisons treat criminals, except those who committed capital crimes, with reformism (*ganhua zhuyi*), that is, to use Communist spirit and labor discipline to educate prisoners and change their criminal nature. The same message was conveyed in the Chinese Soviet Republic Provisional Regulations on the Institutes for Reformation through Labor. Other regulations and directives on prisons and reformation institutes prohibited inhumane treatment of prisoners such as torture and physical abuse and emphasized a proper balance of prisoners' time for labor, study, rest, and recreation.[18]

Just as under earlier states, however, regulations on paper were not seriously followed in practice for a variety of reasons. Two reasons were particular to the Communist base areas: there were no secure confinement facilities nor legally trained prison staff; prison guards were often just locally recruited peasants. The base areas were constantly or frequently on a war footing, and there were constant shortages of material supplies, from food to everything else, for the CCP cadres, the Red Army soldiers, and the civilian population, so that prisoners' fate would inevitably drop to the lowest priority.

In sum, the CCP legal-judicial practices in the revolutionary years may be characterized as follows. A criminal code and a criminal procedural law did not exist, nor were judicial organs systematically established; both were ad hoc and decentralized, partly because the base areas were not geographically congruous to one another and were often on a war footing. Judicial functions were supervised and important cases were decided by the Party organizations, even though the notion of judicial independence was conveyed in Party documents and various regulations. Similarly protection of human rights and rights of the accused were expressed but rarely followed in practice. Judicial personnel were not legally trained and were politically selected. Finally, law and justice, and indeed the Communist quasi-state itself, were deemed and used as tools of class struggle in a nationalist and Socialist revolution, which justified all of the above.

Despite these characteristics, there was a search for substantive justice (even if at the expense of procedural justice), which was motivated not only by a commonsense understanding of right and wrong (or Heavenly reason) but also by the need for political legitimacy of the emerging state under the CCP. That is why Party cadres such as Huang Kegong were punished for common crimes and corruption. The overriding objective and primary work of law and justice in the CCP base areas, however, was the suppression of real and perceived counterrevolutionaries, which often led to harsh punishment of the guilty and wrongful punishment of the innocent. All these aspects of the pre-1949 experiences, and the ideology that guided them, would shape to a large degree the way justice was administered in the Mao era.

Contradictions between the People and Enemies, 1949–1976

Transition to the PRC Judiciary

When CCP leaders began to imagine a Socialist state, their vision was framed by Marxist-Leninist theory, reinforced by the precedent of the Russian Revolution and civil war (1917–1921), that the state was an instrument of class struggle. Guided by such an ideology, the CCP considered the laws and the judiciary established by previous states as instruments for suppressing the people, and therefore proceeded to abolish those instruments completely as the Party was on its way to take over the country in the late 1940s. With that clean slate, the CCP would establish a new state that was supposed to represent and exercise power on behalf of the working class and the people at large. To a great degree, the new state was a transplantation and enlargement of the pre-1949 quasi-state in the base areas.

The demolition of the previous legal-judicial system began as early as February 1949. The CCP Center issued a directive on abolishing the six laws of the National government (the Constitution, criminal and civil codes, criminal and civil procedural laws, and Company Law):

> Just as any bourgeois laws, the six laws appear in the guise of the so-called equality of everyone before the law, but in reality there is no true common interest and therefore no true equality between the ruling class and the ruled, between the exploiting class and the exploited, and the propertied class and proletariats. Thus, all the GMD laws can only be the tools of protecting the reactionary rule of landlords and comprador bureaucratic bourgeoisie, and the weapons of suppressing and restricting the vast masses of the people.[19]

In one stroke, the monumental work of two generations of legal reformers since 1901 was swept aside.

The demolition shifted from laws to institutions. In October 1948 the administrations of two Communist base areas in northern China had merged into the People's Government of North China (PGNC), with a Ministry of Justice. From then to July 1949 several liberated provinces established the people's provincial governments, all having departments of justice. In early 1949 the CCP took control of Beijing after the Nationalist garrison forces had surrendered. The PGNC immediately moved into Beijing and put the city under martial law. In March 1949 the Beijing Martial Law Commission announced four policies regarding the judiciary: the GMD judiciary was abolished, and a new judiciary was to be established; former senior judicial officials (court presidents, chief procurators, chief judges, and judges) were dismissed and lower-level personnel were to be screened; former judicial personnel who did not harm the people would be selected for new appointments; and all laws enacted by the GMD state were voided and not to be applied in criminal and civil cases. The policies took effect first in the liberated regions and then nationwide after the PRC was proclaimed on October 1, 1949.

In October 1949 the People's Central Government appointed Shen Junru as the president of the People's Supreme Court, Luo Ronghuan as the head of the People's Supreme Procuracy, and Shi Liang as the Minister of Justice.

Of the three, Luo was a veteran Communist, but Shen and Shi were not Communists. Both former lawyers, Shen and Shi rose to national fame in 1936 as part of the "seven gentlemen" case: as members of the Shanghai National Salvation Society, they were prosecuted by the National government for advocating resistance against the Japanese aggression and were released after the Sino-Japanese War broke out in July 1937. That Shen and Shi were appointed to leading judicial posts was part of the CCP's "united-front" policy to co-opt non-Communist experts to be technocrats of the People's Republic, but they would not have decisive roles in policymaking.

In December 1949 the People's Supreme Court was formally established in Beijing, with branches in six administrative regions, into which the country was organized. In early 1950 the central government authorized county- and municipal-level governments to form the People's Courts to prosecute and punish "vicious strongmen," bandits, spies, counterrevolutionaries, and anyone who sabotaged the land reforms. This was an extension of the movement in the liberated areas in the late 1940s.

In September 1952 the central government began to establish courts at provincial, subprovincial district, and county levels to move beyond previous ad hoc judicial organs. It was a three-level and two-trial system whereby criminal and civil cases tried at a lower court would be reviewed by or appealed to a higher court. These courts were under dual supervision, by their superior courts and by the administrative office and the Party committee at the same level. Within each court there was an adjudicating committee made up of Party cadres and chief judges in the court. The committee would discuss and review important or difficult cases to ensure the Party's policies and judicial principles were not compromised. In other words, an individual judge could not make rulings in such cases but had to follow the decisions of the committee. The regulations that enabled these courts provided for some minimal measures of due process, such as open trials, appeals, and the use of the language of defendants or litigants in the court.

In September 1954 the first Constitution of the PRC was adopted at the National People's Congress. The Constitution provided that "all citizens are equal before the law" and "the people's courts adjudicate independently, only subject to the law." The Congress enacted the Organic Law of the People's Courts. A four-level court and two trial system was set up, which allowed a second trial at a higher level after appeal for a case tried at a lower level. With six administrative regions having been dissolved and the six supreme court branches abolished, provinces were now directly under the central government. Under the Supreme Court were superior courts at the provincial level, intermediate courts at the subprovincial district level, and local courts at county and municipal levels. Each court had an adjudicating committee.

A system of procuracies was also established, modeled on the systems in the early Republic (1912–1927) and in the Soviet Union. Parallel to the courts, the People's Procuracies had four levels: the Supreme Procuracy in Beijing and its counterparts at provincial, intermediate, and local levels. In theory, under the Constitution of 1954 the people's procuracies were to "carry out their duties independently, not subject to interference from local state agencies." Just as the court system, however, all procuracies were under dual supervision by their superior institutions and by the Party committees and administrative offices of the same level.

The Ministry of Public Security in Beijing and its counterparts at provincial and lower levels were to investigate and arrest common criminal suspects as well as enemy spies, robbers-bandits, and counterrevolutionaries. The Regulations on Arrest and Detention (1954) legally authorized such functions of the public security apparatus. Thus the public security agencies, procuracies, and courts (*gongjianfa*) constituted the tripartite system of law enforcement and judiciary.

The principle or the mere language of judicial independence enshrined in the 1954 Constitution may have reflected, and certainly led to, a tension between the judicial personnel and the Party leaders over whether the principle was to be taken seriously. In practice, some judges were not inclined to consult with Party leaders in adjudicating criminal cases. As a legal scholar observed long ago, from 1949 to 1959 the CCP was seeking "institutional arrangements that would maximize the advantages of resort to legal procedures while minimizing disadvantages." The search began with the party-state controlling adjudication; after the 1954 Constitution, court decisions were insulated from direct interference from other state agencies, leaving the question of the Party's interference unsettled; and finally, the Anti-Rightist Movement of 1957 "ended all uncertainty, as the Party openly preached and practiced interference in important cases, and as it also revised the organization of the government to permit the police and procuracy to exert direct influence over judicial decision making."[20]

The institutional history of the Ministry of Justice is illustrative of that trend. Built in late October 1949, the Ministry was responsible for judicial administration, such as demarcation of jurisdictions, collection of judicial statistics, training and appointment of judicial officers and personnel, and so on. Its subordinate agencies were housed at provincial, subprovincial district, and county or municipal governments. In the wake of the Anti-Rightist Movement (1957), the leaders of the Ministry of Justice came under attack for politically incorrect viewpoints, such as the following: counterrevolutionaries had largely been cleared from society and most criminals were not class enemies; the Party committees in the local governments should give their opinions on criminal cases after, not before, prosecutions and trials were completed; and the practice of collapsing the public security bureau, the procuracy, and the court under one leadership weakened the checks and balances among the three functions. In addition, these leaders were accused of not being active in hunting the rightists within the Ministry of Justice. In mid-1958 the nine top leaders of the Ministry were denounced as an anti-Party clique and removed from their posts. In April 1959 the Ministry was abolished, along with its counterparts at lower levels of the state system. The work of judicial administration was taken over by the courts of all levels.[21]

The Fate of the Legal Profession

After the laws and the judiciary of the National government were abolished in 1949, the Ministry of Justice issued a document, "A Circular on the Abolition of Black Lawyers and Litigation Sticks," in December 1950. It stated, "The old lawyer system as part of the old judicial system has ceased to exist. If any old lawyers are still active illegally, they will harm the court's authority and credibility and the people's interest, and must be stopped."[22] Logically such a position did not reject the lawyer system as such, but only regarded old lawyers as part of the old judicial institutions and practices to be abolished.

A new lawyer system was in the making in the early 1950s. In 1952 the Shanghai People's Court set up the Office of Public Defenders. Public defenders were soon to be called lawyers and their job was to defend criminal defendants. In July 1954 the Ministry of Justice (recall that Minister Shi Liang was a former lawyer) authorized the courts in Beijing, Shanghai, Tianjin, Chongqing, Wuhan, and Shenyang to experiment with a lawyer system. Furthermore, the Constitution of 1954 (adopted in September) provided that criminal defendants had the right to legal defense. Under the Organic Law of the People's Courts that was enacted at the same time, a defendant could defend himself or entrust a lawyer or his close relatives or guardians to defend him; if a court deemed it necessary, the court could appoint a defender to defend him. These tentative measures between 1950 and 1954 led to the final step: in January 1956 the Ministry of Justice submitted, and the State Council approved, a plan to establish the lawyer system. Thus the lawyer system was officially restored, but on a much smaller scale than in the Republican era. Instead of forming an independent profession, lawyers were state employees working in the Legal Consulting Offices of the People's Courts. In mid-1957 there were 820 legal consulting offices nationwide, with a total of 2,572 full-time and 350 part-time lawyers.[23]

Yet even this limited lawyer system was short-lived, a casualty of the Anti-Rightist Movement of 1957. During that campaign political attacks were mounted against the lawyer system, as well as the entire judiciary. The lawyer system was said to be a bourgeois element, and legal defense was said to be "losing [the] proletarian class position" and "defending bad guys." Many lawyers were among the rightists who fell victim to persecution. As a result, by 1959 the position of lawyer had ceased to exist in China, until its revival in the post-Mao era.[24]

The Judiciary under the Party

After the new judicial system was established, no criminal and civil codes, nor procedural laws, were enacted to replace their Republican predecessors. Even before the complete demise of the legal profession, the judiciary had to face interference into court cases from political players using ideological language. The absence of a criminal code and a procedural law made it more imperative that when something happened, the judiciary try to persuade Party leaders to support its opinions in matters of whom to prosecute, what to be prosecuted for, and how to punish the guilty. Two cases in the 1950s are illustrative.

Wang Guangying was the brother of Wang Guangmei, who was the wife of Liu Shaoqi, the president of the PRC in 1954–1966. Wang Guangying owned a chemical plant in Tianjin, but in early 1954 he voluntarily agreed to make the plant jointly owned with the state (*gongsi heying*), in response to the Party's call for transition to Socialism. A few months later an industrial explosion occurred in the plant, killing six workers and injuring five. The Tianjin Municipal Labor Union wanted to have Wang prosecuted for the accident, but the Tianjin Municipal Procuracy disagreed, arguing that to prosecute Wang would harm the united-front policy for the CCP to unite the "nationalist bourgeoisie." A complaint emerged that Wang was protected by the judiciary because he was Liu Shaoqi's brother-in-law. The controversy prompted the Supreme Procuracy in Beijing to send Zhao Wenlong, the deputy head of the Supreme Procuracy First Chamber, to investigate the incident. Zhao concluded that the direct cause of the accident was the violation of safety regulations by some workers, and since the plant was jointly owned, Wang had only indirect leadership responsibility shared with Mr. Wei, the state representative, and should not be prosecuted. This view was accepted by the Supreme Procuracy and the matter was closed, but Zhao would suffer for this in the Cultural Revolution, when Liu Shaoqi was a main target of Mao's political campaign (discussed later).[25]

Another case similarly divided the Party-led labor union and the judiciary and caused Premier Zhou Enlai to intervene. Mr. Wang was the captain and Mr. Li the second mast of a ship that was towing a dredger, with a few dozen sailors' family members onboard, from Yantai to the Tanggu harbor in Tianjin. They started the journey knowing that the ship did not carry sufficient fuel. At the midpoint of the journey, they ran into a storm. Wang and Li simply abandoned the dredger and steamed their ship alone to the Tanggu harbor. Without telling the authorities about the abandoned dredger and people onboard, they went to sleep. The dredger sank, but all the people onboard were rescued by a passing British ship. The outraged public demanded that Wang and Li be prosecuted, and the Tianjin Municipal Procuracy began to proceed, but the General Labor Union of Sailors disagreed, arguing that officials at Yantai and Tanggu were responsible and accusing the procuracy of punishing workers to protect officials. The dispute found its way to Zhou Enlai, who then asked Luo Ruiqing, minister of public security, to look into the matter. After listening to the report from Zhao Wenlong, who again did the investigation for the Supreme Procuracy, Luo agreed that Wang and Li should be prosecuted. Zhou also agreed, observing that while Wang and Li were of the working class, those people they abandoned at sea were of the working class too. Wang was sentenced to eight years in prison and Li, three years, and one low-level official who had allowed Wang's ship to leave Yantai without sufficient fuel received a one-year prison term suspended for one year.[26] In these instances, the labor unions defended workers against criminal liability by using the rhetoric of class to blame managers; similarly the judicial officials (and even Zhou Enlai) had to use the ideologically correct language to make their case.

Just as in the imperial and the Republican eras, the principal-agent relationship remained a challenge to the proper functioning of the state. Corruption by officials was also a grave concern to the Party and therefore an offense punished by both the Party and the judiciary. A well-publicized case of official corruption took place in the early 1950s. Liu Qingshan and Zhang Zishan were CCP cadres. Liu joined the CCP in 1931 and Zhang in 1933. After 1949 Liu became the deputy Party head of Shijiazhuang, the provincial capital of Hebei province, and Zhang became the Party head of the Tianjin subprovincial district, also in Hebei province. In November 1951, when the Three-Anti movement (against corruption, waste, and bureaucratism among Party and government officials) was taking place, Liu and Zhang were found to have embezzled huge sums from the natural disaster relief funds; Liu was also addicted to narcotics. They were expelled from the Party in December 1951 and tried and sentenced to death at a mass rally in February 1952. Like Huang Kegong's case in 1937, their sentences were decided by the Party. The CCP Hebei provincial committee recommended the death penalty for Liu and Zhang to the CCP North China Bureau, which, after conducting an opinion survey among Party cadres, recommended the death penalty with execution suspended for two years (normally commuted to life imprisonment) to the Party center. Having reviewed these opinions and also invited opinions from non-Communist officials, Mao and other top Party leaders finally decided on the death penalty with immediate execution.[27] This would be the way all such cases were decided: the judiciary processed these cases, and Party leaders made the decisions on the nature and severity of offenses and corresponding punishments, based on the policies and the political situation of the time. During the Anti-Three movement, over 100,000 cadres were found guilty of embezzlement; nearly 10,000 cadres were sentenced to prison terms; 67 to life imprisonment; 42 (including Liu and Zhang) received the death penalty; and 9 received the death penalty with execution suspended.[28]

Political Campaigns and Criminal Justice

Along with the CCP's theory that the state and its laws were instruments of class struggle and justice was a matter of the state suppressing the enemies of the people, the human rights protections and equality before the law that had been enshrined in CCP documents before 1949 were now gone. Since the CCP would define who were the enemies, a definition that could and did change over time, and how to deal with them, the Maoist state did not see a need for a criminal code or criminal procedural law.

In practice, common crimes were prosecuted based on the pre-1949 revolutionary precedents and under a number of individual statutes pertaining to criminal offenses, such as the Regulations on Punishing Counterrevolutionaries, the Regulations on Punishing Corruption, the Provisional Regulations on Punishing the Crime of Harming National Currency, and the Circular Directive on Prohibition of Opium and Narcotics. More mundane common crimes, such as theft, robbery, murder, and rape, were simply tried and punished with common sense and precedents. Essentially the adjudicating committees in the court, and in serious cases the Party committees in the government, at various levels would decide which punishments fit which crimes by following and interpreting relevant policy documents, regulations, and statutes issued by the Party and the government.

The offense of being counterrevolutionary was defined by the party-state, depending on the Party's policies of the day. Actions and speeches against a particular policy at a given time, as well as those against the CCP and Socialism in general, would constitute the offense. That is why the adjudicating committees in the courts were responsible for deciding the guilt and penalty for such offenders. Political campaigns launched by Mao or the CCP would result in situations where people were charged as "enemies of the people" or "class enemies" and punished, not necessarily through the judiciary but often through extrajudicial actions taken by Party organizations or administrative offices or work units.

One crucial area of political offense was deviation from the CCP's ideology; offenders would be identified as counterrevolutionaries for their words and ideas. This stemmed from Mao's agenda to compel independent-minded intellectuals to toe the Party lines and serve its Socialist programs. In Mao's theory, intellectuals were bourgeois or petit bourgeois elements who must be reformed to become part of "the people"; logically, those who would resist such "thought reform" were "enemies of the people." In other words, no one was safe even within the category of "the people"; all were to reform themselves, to different degrees and in different ways, for the cause of Socialism and Communism, and any person who resisted the reform was in danger of becoming the enemy and being forced to reform under penal confinement.

This logic and its consequences may be glimpsed in the Hu Feng affair in the mid-1950s, which set a chilling example and cast a long shadow all the way to the end of the Mao era.[29] Hu Feng was a writer. In the 1930s and 1940s he associated with left-leaning writers such as Lu Xun and engaged in literary-intellectual debates with certain writers who were underground CCP members. After the founding of the PRC, those CCP writers became the Party cadres in literary-cultural circles. As their personal and intellectual disagreements with Hu fermented, they used the Party-controlled print media to launch a campaign in 1954 to criticize Hu's ideas about what literature should be. In the midst of the movement to "purge hidden counterrevolutionaries" and in the wake of criticizing two artistic works in the early 1950s (a historical movie about a beggar-turned–private teacher and a book of literary criticism on the Qing novel *A Dream of Red Mansions*), Mao personally intervened in the Hu Feng affair in 1955. Hu was labeled the head of a counterrevolutionary clique, which sealed his fate and impacted many more intellectuals who were his friends, students, or mere acquaintances. In total, this "counterrevolutionary" case netted 2,100 suspects, of whom 92 were arrested by the public security bureaus and another 73 were fired from their jobs; by late 1956 78 men and women were labeled Hu Feng clique members, 23 of them core members sentenced to prison terms.[30]

The Hu Feng affair shows a pattern: it was semijudicial (people were arrested by the public security bureaus and confined in detention houses or prisons), not legal (no criminal code to invoke), and entirely political (guilt was decided by Party leaders). Jia Zhifang, for instance, was a writer and a friend of Hu. Working to resist the Japanese invasion and writing for left-leaning journals, he had been imprisoned once by the collaboration regime and twice by the National government before 1949. On May 15, 1955, he was arrested by the Shanghai Public Security Bureau at Fudan University, where he was teaching. Imprisoned as a "Hu Feng clique core member" without trial for nearly eleven years, he was finally given a sentence (in private, not in a court) of twelve years in prison in March 1966. He did "supervised labor" at his former work unit, Fudan University, for the remainder of his prison term, only to suffer further extrajudicial physical and mental torment in the Cultural Revolution. He was not fully exonerated until 1980.[31] Ironically, and characteristic of the system, those CCP cadres who persecuted the Hu Feng group would themselves be persecuted in subsequent political campaigns—the Anti-Rightist Movement and the Cultural Revolution—based on the same logic and process of how political offenses were defined and dealt with.

The Anti-Rightist Movement was preceded by Mao's initiative in 1956 to rectify the work style of CCP cadres and to rid the Party of what was called bureaucratism (being out of touch with the common people), factionalism (following certain superiors instead of the Party's policies), and subjectivism (making decisions without investigating objective conditions). After the Party newspapers issued calls to allow "one hundred schools to contend and one hundred flowers to bloom" and invited the public to expose the three "isms," a flood of sharp criticisms of the CCP and its policies surged up from among intellectuals, non-Communist officials, and even some Party cadres. Many of the criticisms were published in the news media or communicated to the Party center via internal reports by Party newspaper reporters. Other Party leaders who had been reluctant to invite criticism were shocked and alarmed by the unexpected animosity expressed in the criticisms and perceived it as a hostile anti-Party force.

Mao then made a U-turn in mid-1957, launching a crackdown on those outspoken critics as "rightists."[32] In short order, over half a million intellectuals and officials were persecuted. They were denounced in mass rallies, dismissed from jobs, relocated to rural areas, sent to labor camps or prisons, or all of the above. Critically, in most cases the punishments were carried out not by the judiciary but by administrative actions of local governments and work units, state employers such as hospitals, schools and universities, research institutes, factories, government offices, publishing houses, and newspaper headquarters. CCP leaders conceded in the post-Mao era that out of 550,000 people labeled "rightists," only 1 percent might have been really opposed to the Party and Socialism, and the remaining 99 percent had been wrongfully persecuted by a mass movement instead of a judicial process.[33]

One of the victims was Xu Zhangben. He had earned a Ph.D. in physics at the California Institute of Technology in 1940 and returned to China in the early 1950s to work at Tsinghua University. In July 1957, when the "strike-back at rightists" had already started, Xu openly issued his "Declaration of Founding the Labor Party" and criticized Marxism at his university. He was promptly arrested as an "active counterrevolutionary" and imprisoned in the Beijing First Prison. He was better treated there than most "rightists," but in 1969 he was sent to a labor reform farm where other rightists were usually sent. He would remain there until 1975 and was not fully exonerated until 1979.[34]

Urban Residence Registration and Work Units

During the Mao era, the law and judicial system were less developed than in the Republican era, but that fact did not seem to cause social problems, and the rate of common crimes was low. This was partly due to the social engineering that the CCP designed and carried out for the sake of building a Socialist system. A crucial dimension of the project was the segregation and regimentation of urban and rural populations accomplished by the system of urban residence registration, a first in Chinese history.

The system came about in 1958 as a requirement and a result of the transition from the "New Democracy" (Mao's term) to Socialism. Under the New Democracy of 1949–1956, private enterprises owned by nationalist bourgeoisie, private land owned by peasants after land reform, and the free market for privately produced goods were allowed, alongside the state-owned enterprises. The policy ended in 1956, when Mao decided to eliminate private enterprises to implement a thoroughly Socialist state-planned economy. To allocate resources, the state needed to know and control the size of the urban population whose food supply was supported by the agricultural sector and the rural population. That was the primary reason for the urban residence registration, which negated the provision for freedom of movement in the 1954 Constitution.

Under the system all urban residents had to register with the government through their local police precinct. When a child was born in an urban family, he or she was added to the family's registration book and the government registry. All urban households would receive ration coupons for grain, cooking oil, sugar, cotton cloth, and fuel (for stoves), according to the number of people in the household registered with the government. This in effect segregated the urban and rural populations because people from rural areas were not allowed to move to the city without permission from and registration with the government.

The regimentation of the urban and rural populations further augmented the effect of the registration system as a social control mechanism. City administration was organized in a hierarchy from the municipal government down to district-level governments, precinct-level offices, and finally to residents committees in neighborhoods. To absorb unemployed people, precinct offices in certain cities would sponsor small, collectively owned businesses in neighborhoods, such as day care facilities, book-renting stalls, barber shops, repair stores for household items, handicrafts workshops, and the like.

Staff of residents committees often included retired or otherwise unemployed people. The committees would provide social services such as public sanitation and neighborhood watch, and organize social activities such as entertainment for the elderly and the retired. One of their functions was crime prevention, in coordination with local police precincts, such as making sure newborn children were promptly registered with the government, watching out for strangers in the neighborhood, and checking on people under "supervised labor" or "supervised living." Another function was to mediate and arbitrate disputes in families and between neighbors.[35] In rural areas the people's communes were similarly regimented, even though no formal residence registration was required. A commune was composed of several "production brigades," and each brigade was composed of several "production teams," usually based on natural villages (spontaneously and historically formed by land features or natural environment).[36]

For urban residents who had jobs, their life was further regimented in their "work units"—whatever entity that employed them.[37] First of all, under the Socialist system, employers could not fire or lay off workers, but workers could not find jobs on their own either, because they were assigned to their jobs upon graduating from college or high or vocational or middle schools. The work unit would pay employees salaries or wages, rent housing to them, and give bonuses for good work or mete out discipline for bad behavior. Investigation of an employee for common crimes or political offenses would usually start with their work unit. When political campaigns were launched, work units were the places where the majority of the urban population would experience (or suffer from) them first and foremost. Work units were also the first places to go to seek redress when working women or men had marital problems or wanted a divorce.

These administrative and social arrangements and practices had important implications for law and justice in the Mao era. Their effects included implementing state policies, controlling society, mediating civil disputes, preventing crimes, and capturing offenders when crimes did occur. In such a regimented society, even without the surveillance technologies of the twenty-first century, running away from the law or the state was quite difficult because fugitives would have fewer places to hide than ever before. This explains why prison and labor camp inmates (discussed later) would not be able to escape easily.

Reform through Labor

In the absence of a criminal code, punishments for common crimes and political offenses were meted out according to various individual laws, ordinances, regulations, or Party policy documents issued at different times. Therefore one offense would result in different penalties at different times. As for deprivation of freedom before (or without) trial, besides formal arrest by the public security bureaus, one could be taken into administrative detention; for instance, vagabonds were "taken into custody" (*shourong*), and political suspects were "taken into custody to be investigated" (*shourong shencha*). As for penalties, there were in theory ten categories: reprimand, fine, confiscation of property, deprivation of political rights, suspension of sentence; supervised labor, detention, prison term, life imprisonment, and death. A death sentence could be ordered in one of two grades: immediate execution or suspended execution for two years, the latter leading to commutation to life imprisonment. Another penalty was "supervised living" (*jianshi juzhu*), which was often a halfway measure between confinement and freedom.

In practice, the most widely used penalty was reform through physical labor. The idea and practice of reforming convicts through physical labor and moral education in penal institutions began with the late Qing legal reforms, inspired by both modern Western penology and Chinese Neo-Confucian tradition.[38] The reform agenda of the late Qing New Policy decade included plans to establish workshops inside prisons as part of prison reform. Carried into the Republican period, such a reformist principle in penal practices resonated with a notion widely shared by Chinese elites, that reforming Chinese minds was the prerequisite for transforming China from an ancient civilization into a modern nation. It went hand in hand with various movements launched by reformers of different types, as well as Nationalist and Communist activists, to spread literacy among the common people, promote civic education, and train politically conscious cadres and citizens. That is why the National government established "institutes for repentance" for arrested Communists, as well as provided moral education classes to common criminals in regular prisons.

The CCP shared the same belief in the power of moral-political education, or thought reform, and experimented with labor reform camps or teams before 1949. In November 1950 Beijing authorized the public security apparatus to assume responsibility for administering all penal institutions, supervised by the Ministry of Justice and the provincial governments. In May 1951, with Mao's blessing, the Third National Conference on Public Security Work adopted a resolution on organizing all convicts into a system of reform through labor (*laodong gaizhao* or *laogai*). In August 1954 the Political Affairs Council (later the State Council) issued the PRC Regulations on Reform through Labor. In December 1962 the Ministry of Public Security issued the Work Rules of Reform through Labor Disciplinary Education Teams.[39] Step by step, these documents formed the legal framework for the entire penal labor system.

Under the 1954 regulations, penal institutions were classified into four categories: detention houses, prisons, reform through labor disciplinary education teams, and juvenile disciplinary education institutes. Under the Ministry of Public Security, the Bureau of Reform through Labor Work had subordinate agencies at the provincial level. Public security agencies at all administrative levels had offices in charge of the matter. While doing manual labor, convicts were provided with vocational and political education and medical care. Depending on their performance, they would receive reward or punishment in the form of their terms being shortened or lengthened. *Laogai* inmates who served out their terms were mostly retained on the same jobs where they had worked as inmates or employed by different entities in the same locale. Those who had come from cities were not allowed to return to their original residence.

The official policy for the *laogai* system was "reformation first, and production second." The fact that the policy was reiterated repeatedly, even by Mao personally on several occasions, suggests that it was not faithfully followed by officials in charge of the system.[40] At different times there were also attempts by some central government officials to increase production output from the penal-labor system.[41]

As for material conditions of the system, like the penal system of the Republican era there was always a gap, to varying degrees in different locales, between the regulations and policies on paper and the harsh realities that did not measure up to the official prescriptions. Hunger, exhaustion, abuse, squalid living conditions, disease, and unnatural death were the running themes of many horror stories reported by former labor camp inmates.[42] In contrast, government reports and certain former inmates' memoirs pointed to successful examples of criminals being reformed into normal citizens. Li Baiying was a GMD provincial-level official in Sichuan. He turned himself in after the Communists took control of Sichuan in 1949. As one of the "GMD war criminals" undergoing reform through labor, he was among a few hundred fellow war criminals pardoned by the government in March 1975. His positive account of his experience of *laogai* was published in 1984, so it did not seem to be motivated by a desire to conform to the official line.[43] Yet "war criminals" who were treated much better than common criminals and political offenders in the *laogai* system—another irony—were hardly typical.

Mao's vision of a new China built by "a new Socialist people" was predicated on his belief in the reforming power of labor and education. Not surprisingly, penal practices in the Mao era (and after) were characterized by the use of reform (and reeducation) through labor as the most common penalty for common crimes, social delinquency, and political offenses. In the larger scheme of thought reform for the entire population, the *laogai* system that criminals and political offenders experienced was at one end of a continuum (in terms of material conditions and physical hardship) that extended to the other end (in terms of the fundamental principle) the endless political movements that average citizens experienced during the Mao era.

Reeducation through Labor

It is important to note that there was a system of "reeducation through labor" (*laodong jiaoyang,* or *laojiao*) parallel to but separate from the "reform through labor" (*laodong gaizhao,* or *laogai*) system, even though both types were underpinned by the same belief in transforming human minds and behavior through physical labor and moral suasion. Both *laogai* and *laojiao* facilities may be conveniently called "labor camps," but those facilities actually included not only outdoor camps such as rural farms or construction sites, but also indoor factories and workshops where living and working conditions were less harsh than outdoor work sites. Conceptually and institutionally, the *laogai* system was part of the judiciary (run by the public security apparatus), and its facilities were penitentiaries for criminal convicts. By comparison, the *laojiao* system was run by state administrative offices at all levels, and its facilities were set up as a way to educate (and transform) wayward people who were not convicts sentenced by courts. In that sense, *laojiao* was an extrajudicial practice to confine nonconvicts and put them to work. The state believed the practice filled a gap: it was a useful way to transform those who were not state enemies but were in need of correction of their minds and behavior.

The *laojiao* system originated in 1955. In the wake of a movement to "purge hidden counterrevolutionaries" in state agencies, state-owned enterprises, and educational and research institutions, a large number of people were fired, not because they were identified as counterrevolutionaries but because they were found politically unfit to stay on their jobs or were guilty of undesirable conduct (hooliganism, absenteeism, alcoholism, etc.) that was not serious enough to be prosecuted under the law enforcement policies. In August 1955 the Party center issued a directive to the effect that those who did not deserve criminal penalties but were unfit to stay on their jobs should go through *laojiao*, so that a large number of unemployed people would not idle in society but could reform their minds through labor to become contributing members of society. In January 1956 the Party center issued another directive, prescribing the nature, principle, task, management, and leadership of the *laojiao* system. In August 1957 the State Council published the "Decision on the Issue of Reeducation through Labor," further laying out details of the system's operation. By the end of 1958 several hundred *laojiao* facilities or sites had been set up across the country. In October 1960 a directive from the Party center ordered that *laojiao* facilities at the county level and below be dissolved and consolidated at the provincial level. It stressed the principle of "reformation first and production second" and provided the ways in which moral education, labor activity, and wellness were to be taken care of at the same time.[44] Again, official regulations were not seriously followed and implemented. Moreover, practically, if not conceptually, *laojiao* as an administrative measure was indistinguishable from *laogai* as a legal penalty in their actual implementation and in physical, mental, and social consequences for inmates of both systems—hence the conflation of the two in many survivor reports and scholarly studies.

Lawlessness in the Cultural Revolution, 1966–1976

Why the Cultural Revolution

Any semblance of law and justice established between 1949 and 1966 utterly collapsed during the Cultural Revolution when, by Mao's design, the entire party-state system was paralyzed and then reshuffled. Mao's agenda to push China into a Communist society as fast as possible was not shared by other Party leaders. After the economic mass campaign known as the Great Leap

Forward (1958–1961) failed with disastrous consequences, Mao reluctantly took some responsibility and retreated to what he called "the second line" (away from day-to-day decision-making) to let other Party leaders devise ways to recover the economy. By the mid-1960s Mao believed other leaders' policies had strayed too far from his vision of Socialism, but he had lost the ability to guide the Party's direction. This was essentially what motivated him to launch the Great Proletarian Cultural Revolution in 1966.

To take back the party-state apparatus that seemed to be slipping away from him, Mao worked from a theory of "continuous revolution" that he had been floating within the Party since the early 1960s. In one speech given at a Party center work conference in January 1962, for instance, Mao stated:

> Among both old and new Party members—especially among the new members—there are always some people whose character and working styles are impure. Those people are individualists, bureaucrats, subjectivists: some even become degenerate elements. There are some people who adopt the guise of Communist Party members, but they in no way represent the working class; instead they represent bourgeoisie. All is not pure within the Party. We must see this point, otherwise we shall suffer.[45]

Mao theorized that during the entire transitional period from a Socialist to a Communist society there would always be a danger that the country would slide back into capitalism, because the old bourgeois class would not sit quietly and new bourgeois elements would emerge from within the Communist Party itself, who would betray the Party's historical mission. For that reason, constant and continuous revolution would be needed to uncover and eradicate such bourgeois elements, and class struggles would not cease during the Socialist period. In articulating this theory, Mao was both prophetic and utopian—prophetic in that after Mao's death the CCP was to pursue economic development by way of capitalism under the Party's rule, and utopian in that such a development was inevitable, even according to Marxism, given the reality of China's economic conditions in the mid-twentieth century. (The post-Mao economic reforms would indeed be justified by Party theoreticians citing Marxism on the relationship between capitalism and Socialism.)[46] By "developing" or revising Marxism into his theory of "continuous revolution," Mao tried to transcend that reality and inevitability by sheer human will, which explains both why the Cultural Revolution would happen, with disastrous consequences, and why it would fail to achieve Mao's goal.

Starting with articles criticizing bourgeois thoughts in the cultural field, including movies, theater, and literary works (hence the term "Cultural Revolution") in 1965, by the summer of 1966 Mao had set up a Cultural Revolution Group headed by his wife, Jiang Qing, and a few other confidants, a body that in effect replaced the function of the Party center. He called on college students and then ordinary Chinese in all walks of life to rebel against their bosses and to "bombard" a "bourgeois headquarters" within the CCP that had deviated from the Party's goal of Socialism and Communism. This so-called bourgeois headquarters meant the top Party leaders other than Mao. Average Chinese responded, out of a variety of personal and social discontent against the status quo. Students self-styled as the Red Guards of Mao, and state employees, especially factory workers, became "revolutionary rebels." All went about their revolutionary activities by roughing up their bosses and throwing them out of offices. They also engaged in destroying symbols, objects, and sites of Chinese cultural tradition, from Daoist and Buddhist temples to university libraries. In the face of such an unprecedented mass rebellion in the name of supporting Mao, the party-state apparatus was paralyzed, and Party and government officials and intellectuals, such as professors, scientists, writers, actors, and entertainers, were forced out of their offices and jobs, even though most of them were still paid salaries as state employees. Out of the nationwide anarchy Mao was able to install a new crop of cadres that he chose—recent activists as well as some former officials—to reestablish the party-state apparatus, officiated at the CCP Ninth National Congress in April 1969. Yet intra-Party political struggles, cultural-historical nihilism, and economic slowdown continued. The Cultural Revolution did not officially end until Mao's death in September 1976.[47]

Breakdown of Law and Justice

The public security apparatus, the procuracies, and the courts (*gongjianfa*) were among the state agencies that were paralyzed early in the Cultural Revolution. Any persons or groups could claim to be followers of Mao's call and attack any people they identified as enemies of Mao. No law and order could be enforced by anyone, since any such efforts would be denounced as suppressing the revolution or acting against Mao. Consequently everywhere "revolutionary rebels" stormed the courts, the procuracies, and the public security bureaus. They would attack personnel and destroy files or search through files to find "hidden class enemies," people who had served under the National government before 1949. In some locales even prisons were similarly attacked and inmates were set free. Judicial officials were detained, beaten, and even killed by rebels.[48]

While the judiciary and law enforcement apparatus collapsed, extralegal and extrajudicial practices flourished, and the number of victims of political violence dramatically increased. Although the rate of common crimes decreased greatly in 1966–1969, many citizens faced terrifying accusations of political offenses. Former officials, professors, writers, artists, and others were labeled bourgeois elements or capitalist-roaders or counterrevolutionaries and were detained and abused; their homes were searched and ransacked without cause; many people were publicly humiliated, physically assaulted and even murdered, or driven to commit suicide.[49] One ironic case was that Luo Ruiqing, minister of public security, who was driven to jump off a building in 1966, but survived with broken ankles. Another was that of Liu Shaoqi, the former president of the PRC and the main target of Mao's campaign, who died a lonely death from illness without medical care after being detained by Red Guards and revolutionary rebels and physically abused for two years. Citizens' private writings such as diaries and personal letters would be seized from their homes and used as evidence of their counterrevolutionary thought.[50]

Rival rebel factions engaged in power struggles, accusing one another of being Mao's enemies, and fought each other with knives, clubs, rifles, even machine guns. Many locales across the country experienced rising death tolls. These unnatural deaths can never be accurately counted. Many were never investigated, and very few were prosecuted later on. Most were forgotten.[51]

The breakdown of law and order and the spread of social chaos reached such a height that Mao, and the Cultural Revolution Group, decided to use the People's Liberation Army to intervene and restore order, starting in Beijing in February 1967. In December 1967 the Party center, the State Council, the Central Military Commission, and the Cultural Revolution Group jointly issued the Decision on Exercising Military Control in Public Security Agencies. In March 1968 they extended military control into the procuracies, and by mid-1968 all judicial organs and public security agencies had come under military control.

By the early 1970s the judiciary and law enforcement agencies had supposedly returned from anarchy to normalcy. After Mao reshuffled the party-state apparatus at the CCP Ninth National Congress in 1969, with Lin Biao named Mao's successor, Party leaders worked to consolidate the existing political structure while trying to return to some semblance of law and order. In 1971 Premier Zhou Enlai spoke positively of the law enforcement agencies' work during 1949–1966, which, he implied, should not be negated by the claim that there was a bourgeois headquarters within the CCP. From 1972 onward, the people's courts were gradually restored and former judicial personnel returned to their jobs, and military control was withdrawn. In January 1975 the Fourth National People's Congress was convened and a new Constitution was adopted, under which the people's procuracies were abolished and the public security agencies would assume the prosecuting function; the presidents of the people's courts were to be appointed by the governments at the same level.[52] These institutional changes conflated the state's judicial and administrative powers. Most critically, still no criminal code or civil code or procedural law was enacted. Such a state of affairs would linger into the early years of the post-Mao era.

These developments did not mean that people could escape from political offenses more easily. The death of Lin Biao in September 1971 and the purge of his followers thereafter gave a boost to Jiang Qing and her group (known as the Gang of Four) in seeking more power.[53] Any criticism of Jiang was considered a counterrevolutionary act to be severely punished.

One of many who thus suffered was Wang Xuetai, a college graduate and middle school teacher in the suburb of Beijing. When his private conversation with a friend that vaguely criticized Jiang was exposed in March 1975, they were both arrested as counterrevolutionaries. He was taken from his workplace and interrogated, but was not formally tried in a court. His family learned only later what had happened to him, and only from a person who happened to be in the same interrogation room where Wang was taken. In May 1976, fourteen months after his arrest, a sentence of thirteen years in prison was announced to him in private. He was moved from the detention house to the Beijing First Prison (the former model prison of the late Qing), where food was adequate, better than the detention house and better than many peasants would have at that time, and inmates did "reform through labor" at a plastic shoe factory attached to the prison. Wang was not exonerated and released until late 1978, even though the Gang of Four had been arrested as counterrevolutionaries—another irony—two years earlier.[54]

Wang's case was far from an isolated one. Even in the mid-1970s many people became "counterrevolutionaries" unknowingly and accidentally, for trivial things they said or did that were politically incorrect. After Zhou Enlai's death in January 1976, a low-level Party cadre in Miyun county near Beijing had a chat with a former entertainer in the presence of a pre-1949 "rich peasant." Fond of a prophecy type of gossip, the cadre said that, 1976 being a year of misfortune in the Lunar calendar, after Zhou's demise something might also happen to Zhu De, chairman of the National People's Congress Standing Committee, and to Mao. (Zhu and Mao would indeed die in July and September, respectively.) When these words were revealed by the rich peasant under duress, the Party cadre was arrested as a counterrevolutionary and sentenced to twenty years in prison; the former entertainer, fifteen years; and the rich peasant, four years. No less incredible, one peasant was arrested as a counterrevolutionary when he made noise eating fried peanuts in the midst of an organized group-watching of Mao's funeral on TV in September 1976; another peasant was arrested for not buying a piece of black clothing to make an armband to mourn Mao's death and saying it was a waste of money. (His adopted daughter reported him.) The two peasants each received eight years in prison. Yet another man was sentenced to twenty years in prison for being a counterrevolutionary, because having no newspapers or radio or TV set or friends and not knowing Mao had died that day, he was singing songs aloud to himself while he worked. Singing aloud was his daily routine, but it annoyed some young women working nearby so that, to get rid of him, they reported to the authorities that the man had "celebrated" Mao's death.[55] The absurdity of these and countless similar cases illustrates the arbitrariness and lawlessness with which people were accused of and punished for political offenses during the Cultural Revolution and beyond.

Besides political offenses, common crimes in the 1970s were dealt with harshly as well. Those who committed homicide, rape, and robbery tended to get the death penalty, even though there was no statute to guide sentencing. Since antisocial behavior could be broadly construed as anti-Party and anti-Socialism, offenders of violent crimes were considered enemies of the people and punished as such. A murderer would be executed as a "counterrevolutionary murderer," and a rapist as a "counterrevolutionary rapist," and so on. Offenders of lesser crimes tended to be sent to *laogai* or *laojiao* institutions, with or without prison terms. Many offenders of violent crimes were sentenced, or rather their sentences were announced, at mass rallies; they were then paraded on trucks through the streets on their way to execution sites or penitentiary destinations; some executions were carried out in front of a crowd. All this was a return to the pre-1949 Nationalist and Communist practices or the imperial ones that were supposed to serve didactic purposes.

One ambiguous but catch-all category of criminal offenses was "hooliganism," which was somewhat similar to the "bare sticks" substatute in the Qing code, but even broader in coverage. Hooliganism covered brawling, bullying, damaging public property, disorderly conduct, sexual harassment, sexual promiscuity, and male homosexual acts. These offenses were not always handled by the police or the judiciary, but often by work units. Less serious offenders were disciplined, and more serious offenders were sent to the *laojiao* system.

Criminal justice in the Mao era was a carryover of legal practices from the revolutionary years, with several characteristics. First, no institutional forms and procedural norms for judicial independence and due process existed, even though these were mentioned in the 1954 Constitution and in some Party policy statements, which were merely residual influences from the Republican-era reforms. The absence of a criminal code and criminal procedural law was never a concern to the CCP, since justice was treated as part of the party-state administration. "The courts were not considered to be different from other hierarchically organized government organizations because of their functional specialization but were viewed as a constituent part of a larger sanctioning bureaucracy."[56]

Second, instead of the rule of law, the proletarian dictatorship was emphasized as the primary function of criminal justice. Without a criminal code, being a counterrevolutionary as the most serious offense was defined by the party-state, case by case, with changing political situations, recurring political campaigns, and shifting political winds (e.g., criticizing Lin Biao or Jiang Qing was a counterrevolutionary act before their respective fall from power but was not so after). Punishments were not guided by any law either, but by Party policy documents or ad hoc statutes; more serious cases were determined by Party leaders within and outside the judiciary. A large number of Party cadres, from Liu Shaoqi at the highest level to many more at lower levels, fell victim to such practices, even though some of them might have victimized others in the same way.

Third, common criminals were categorized by their offenses and class identities. Those committing violent crimes such as homicide, rape, and robbery tended to be viewed as enemies of the people, and their punishment would be severe, including death and life imprisonment; nonviolent crimes such as petty theft and swindling would lead to the judgment of offenders as bad elements, though "curable" enough to rejoin society, and their punishment would be prison terms sentenced by the court or reeducation through labor (*laojiao*), which did not require court actions. Juvenile delinquents or "hooligans" of any age would also be sent to *laojiao*, which in practice was no less severe a penalty than a prison term of two or three years.

Finally, legal practices in the Mao era were part of a grand scheme of thought reform for the entire population and had a supposed moral purpose of seeking justice or righting wrongs. The traditional notion of justice as an alignment of Heavenly reason, state law, and human relations was abandoned, as were the rule of law, judicial independence, and due process, since Mao intended to break with both legacies. Instead "serving the people" and "Socialist revolution" became the Heavenly reason or ultimate morality to guide and justify state actions, but actual state policies and actions could and did easily exclude any individual citizens from "the people" and turn them into targets of the "revolution." In reality, therefore, the way in which right and wrong or guilt and innocence was defined in regard to political offenses often resulted in gross injustice committed against citizens. These problems existed from 1949 to 1966, and reached the most appalling extent and produced the worst abuses during the Cultural Revolution.

8
"Contradictions among the People"
Mediation and Adjudication of Civil Disputes

As early as 1922 the CCP expressed its concern in various Party documents on certain civil matters such as labor rights and gender equality. These expressions would remain political rhetoric until the emergence of the Communist quasi-state. When the Chinese Soviet Republic was formed in 1931, it issued the Labor Law. Among other labor protection measures, the law provided that "workers must be hired through collective contracts through union and labor exchanges"; working time for adults could not exceed eight hours; and worker's earnings "should not be lower than the real minimum wages established by the Commissariat of Labor."[1] In November 1931 the Soviet Republic also issued the Statute on Marriage, which was updated as the Law on Marriage in April 1934. The law guaranteed freedom of marriage and divorce for both men and women and outlawed concubinage as well as all forms of arranged or coerced marriage. In cases of divorce, young children would stay with the mother, and the father would provide "two-thirds of the means needed for their support."[2] The CCP's ideological and legal commitment to gender equality and protection of women was evident in the law.

After the founding of the PRC, during the New Democracy period (1949–1956), private enterprises and private property were curtailed to a much smaller degree than before. After the transition to Socialism between 1956 and 1958, private enterprises were nationalized and private property was limited to peasants' houses and small plots of land on which the houses stood. One result of this Socialist economy was that civil disputes over commercial transactions, purchase and rental of land and houses, large amounts of debt, inheritance, and household divisions, among other things, became rare. Typical disputes included "children fight; neighbors argue about noise, communal sanitary conditions, insults fancied or real, minor debts and sales, and alleged damage to property; husband and wife argue over money, the children, innumerable domestic concerns, and divorce."[3] Thus the primary category of civil disputes in the Mao era was marriage and divorce.

In the absence of a civil code, the PRC issued the Marriage Law in 1950 as the guide to resolving disputes over marriage and divorce, with significant social consequences. The way the state implemented marriage law and handled disputes over marriage and divorce illustrates the particularity of legal practices in the Mao era. Fundamentally, civil disputes over marriage and divorce were conceptualized as "contradictions among the people," to be resolved as amicably as possible, through mediation as well as adjudication, so as to promote gender equality and protect women and children.

Marriage Laws of the Revolutionary Years

Just like Maoist legal practices in criminal justice, the Marriage Law of 1950 was based on the experiences of implementing similar laws during the revolutionary years. The Chinese Soviet Republic issued statutes on marriage in November 1931 and April 1934. Expressing an agenda to liberate women from oppression by the patriarchal family system and realize gender and marital equality, these early laws provided freedom of marriage and divorce initiated by either men or women or both and outlawed marriages that were arranged, coerced, purchased, and betrothed. The laws prohibited marriage between blood relatives and people with mental disease or certain contagious diseases. They required registration with the government for the marriage to be valid, which was a clear break from the century-old tradition and the Civil Code of 1929–1930.[4] Owing to the lack of sources (the archives of the base areas were destroyed when the CCP started the Long March in October 1934), information is sketchy at best on whether and how those laws were implemented and what their actual impact was on marriages and gender relations in the Jiangxi base area in the early 1930s.

In 1939 a new statute on marriage was enacted in the CCP base areas, including the Shanxi-Hebei-Shandong-Henan (*Jin-Ji-Lu-Yu*) Border Region and the Shaanxi-Gansu-Ningxia (*Shan-Gan-Ning*) Border Region, to be enforced by a court system that had been established. One set of case files published in 2011 shed precious light on how marriage and divorce cases (among other civil cases) were dealt with, under what ideological and legal guidelines, in the Jin-Ji-Lu-Yu Board Region. Of the sixty-three cases from She county in Hebei province, twenty-five (40 percent) were marriage and divorce cases between 1941 and 1948.[5] The case files show the process by which divorce cases were handled. A woman would make a request for divorce to village cadres; an effort at mediation would be made, and then a decision was reached as to whether to allow the divorce case to move forward. Next stop was the ward (*qu*, a level between village and county), where the ward leader would investigate by asking for factual information in writing regarding the case from various sources, including the Women's National Salvation Society, the village head, neighbors, and colleagues or superiors of the man or the woman or both, and so on. If the case was found to have merit, it would then be forwarded to the judicial section of the county government. The trial officer of the judicial section would summon the two parties to the county seat to question them separately, or sometimes in the same room. Based on the testimonies of the two parties as well as factual information and opinions from other investigative sources, the trial officer would reach a verdict, granting or rejecting the divorce.

Two typical reasons for divorce were physical abuse of wives by husbands (and some abused wives had extramarital affairs), and husbands being absent from home for many years without contact. In twenty-one divorce cases under study, the county judicial section granted divorce at the request of the wife for these reasons. In another case, after a divorce was granted, the estranged couple reconciled through mediations by village members, and the county government officially approved the settlement. The legal guidelines for decisions in these cases were Articles 16 and 17 of the 1939 Marriage Regulations, under which divorce was warranted when a couple lost mutual feelings, making cohabitation impossible (which was essentially similar to the provisions in the draft civil code and the Civil Code of 1930), or when the husband was absent for more than three years without contact (which was similar to the Civil Code and the Qing law).

In one case, however, the wife requested a divorce because her husband was serving in the military and had not been in contact for five years; the county granted the divorce, but the ward and village leaders obstructed the decision, suggesting that the husband might show up one day. Two county cadres had to write separate letters to the ward leader asking him to faithfully implement the government's marriage policy, "otherwise the masses would say that the policy was made only for men's benefit."[6]

A litigant could appeal the county decision to the district (*qu*) government above the county government, which happened in two of the divorce cases in She County. Mr. Cheng frequently beat his wife, Fan, and interventions from the village and the ward leaders did not change his behavior. Fan requested a divorce. After investigation, the county government granted her divorce. Cheng appealed to the district government against the decision and lost. A similar outcome resulted in another divorce case.[7]

Premised on the notion of romantic love and free will of a man and a woman leading to marriage, the 1939 Marriage Regulations provided freedom of marriage and banned concubines and other forms of marriages that were against women's free will, as the 1931 and 1934 versions did. Yet the social reality in the Shan-Gan-Ning border region, which was west of the Jin-Ji-Lu-Yu border region, gave rise to marriage practices that were very different from those typical of Chinese urban society informed by Confucian norms. Big families with multiple generations were rare, and so was female infanticide; widows would often remarry, or stay in the family of the deceased husband while selecting a new husband to marry; an indebted husband would rent out his wife to pay off the debt; a poor man had an option to be a temporary or substitute husband for a woman whose husband was absent for a long time; a rich man might have a concubine, but a woman might also have more than one husband, as polyandry living arrangements were accepted; not only young girls but also young boys would betroth to the family of a future husband or wife; and the custom of marriage by kidnapping offered women some ways to escape a father's power and for men to avoid paying bridal prices, while sexual relations outside marriage were quite common. All these unorthodox marriage practices defied the Marriage Law, but they did not necessarily function as gender oppression but as strategies for economic survival among poor peasants.[8] Some variations of the practices were also seen in the Qing dynasty, if not earlier.

In all these scenarios patriarchal power was still dominant, however. In such a context the shorthand term "freedom of marriage" in the law offered a convenient excuse for a father to break a previous marriage agreement concerning his daughter in order to marry her to another man for a higher bride price, which led to an increase in divorces and broken marriage agreements. An unintended consequence was that poor male peasants who had paid a bride price for such marriage agreements ended up losing both wife and money. In 1944 the Marriage Law was revised to require that the bride price be returned to the groom's family when the court supported nullifying a marriage agreement. In 1946, however, the law was again revised so that the bride price would not be returned if it was a token gift (a small amount), and if it was a purchase price (a large amount), which was banned by the Marriage

Law, a major part of it would be confiscated by the local authorities and a minor portion returned to the groom. The legal intent was to legitimate a local marriage custom while restricting the purchased marriages that would benefit girls' parents only. More important, in response to parents gaming the system, the courts began to deny a woman's request for divorce if it was found to be instigated by her parents. Knowing that a woman who escaped an abusive husband would only fall into the hands of her parents to become the object of the next arranged marriage, CCP cadres spoke of the need for women's economic independence, though that was difficult to realize.[9] These legal experiences in dealing with marriage and divorce in the revolutionary years would have immediate relevance to the post-1949 era.

Under the CCP quasi-state, one similarity to the National government was a strong emphasis on the role of mediation in civil disputes. In historian Philip Huang's analysis, this continuity may be traced to the "centralized minimalism" of the imperial era, when the Qing dynasty operated a limited governmental apparatus, with county magistrates as its lowest level, which created a need for quasi-officials and dispute resolution by community mediation at the county level and below. In a similar way, the Maoist commune system in the countryside could be considered a continuation of the minimalist state, in that cadres at the village level (production brigades and teams) were not funded by the state but self-funded, which was called "eating collective grain." These cadres had a stake in the local community's well-being despite the line of control through Party organization they were subject to.[10]

Indeed the CCP's minimalist approach to governance and civil dispute resolution began long before 1949. Between 1937 and 1945 the CCP border region governments issued several sets of regulations on mediation of civil disputes (and minor criminal offenses arising from such disputes). Mediation was conducted by four possible parties: public-minded local figures with a good reputation or relatives of disputants; mass organization such as peasant associations or women's associations; government agencies; and judicial organs. The efforts at mediation led to the desired result of reducing civil lawsuits. In the Shan-Gan-Ning Border Region, settlements of civil disputes through mediation increased from 18 percent in 1942 to 40 percent in 1943, and civil cases filed at the courts dropped from 1,832 to 1,544 in the same period, and further down to 622 in the first half of 1944.[11] Mediation at multiple levels for civil dispute resolution would continue into the PRC period.

The 1950 Marriage Law and Its Implementation

The New Marriage Law

Continuing the trajectory of the revolutionary years, the PRC central government enacted a new Marriage Law on April 13, 1950. Built upon earlier versions, the new law included more comprehensive provisions covering marriage and divorce and relationships between husband and wife, and between parents and children, with an emphasis on gender and marital equality and protection of children.

Article 1 declares, "The feudal marriage system, which was based on parental arrangement and coercion, subjected women to men, and disregarded the interests of children, is abolished. The new democratic marriage system, which is based on free choice of men and women for marriage, monogamy, and protection of the lawful interests of women and children, is put into effect." Under Article 2, "bigamy, concubinage, child betrothal, interference in widow's freedom of remarriage, and exaction of money or gifts in the name of marriage, [was] prohibited." The law set the legal age of marriage at twenty for men and eighteen for women (Article 4). Marriages had to be registered with and receive a certificate from the local government to be valid (Article 6). Articles 7 through 12 guaranteed equal rights for and mutual obligations of husband and wife, including equal rights in possession and management of family property. The law also provided mutual obligations of parents and children and strictly prohibited "infanticide by drowning and similar criminal acts" (Article 13). Illegitimate children would have the same rights as legitimate children and not be subject to harm or discrimination by any persons; if identified, the birth father of an illegitimate child was obliged to bear full or part of the child's living and educational expenses until the child reached eighteen; the birth father could reclaim the child if the mother consented (Article 15). The provision on illegitimate children was essentially similar to the Qing and Republican laws.

Under Article 17, divorce was granted when both husband and wife desired it; when only one party desired it, divorce was granted *only when mediation by the local government and the judicial organ had failed to result in reconciliation*. The husband could not petition for divorce when the wife was pregnant or within one year of the birth of a child (Article 18). The wife of a military serviceman could seek divorce only if her husband agreed or if the husband had had no contact with her for two years (Article 19). After divorce the wife retained the property she owned before the marriage, and the disposal of other family property was subject to agreement between the two parties or, failing that, to the court's decision (Article 23). In case of divorce, the husband was responsible for debts incurred during the marriage if there was no or insufficient property jointly acquired by the two parties to pay them (Article 24). If one party had financial difficulties after divorce, the other party was expected to render assistance (Article 25).

Persons violating the Marriage Law would be punished in accordance with the law; persons who, by interfering with the freedom of marriage, caused death or injury criminally liable, without exception (Article 26). In regions where minority nationalities lived in clusters, the regional or provincial governments could enact modifications or supplements to this law in view of local customs regarding marriage, subject to the central government's approval (Article 27).[12] In short, the new Marriage Law moved much further toward protecting women's rights in marriage and divorce and children's rights.

The Implementation of the Marriage Law

The enactment of the Marriage Law in 1950 was accompanied and followed by a state-directed campaign to publicize and implement the law and its guiding principle of gender and marital equality.[13] The state policy toward divorce went through a change from the 1950s to 1960s. In the 1950s, if a woman claimed that she was in a feudal marriage from which she wished to be liberated, she would get her wish rather easily. In such cases, mediation would hardly be necessary and was not much used. By the 1960s feudal marriages were largely gone, and marital problems and divorce cases arose due to mundane quarrels and issues such as adultery, drinking, gambling, abuse, and unemployment. So the courts tended to discourage divorce. When a divorce was filed, two steps or mechanisms were followed: mediation by multiple levels of mediators and adjudication by the court. With the policy change in the 1960s, mediation became even more important than before in pushing estranged couples to reconcile and avoid a formal divorce.[14]

Although the Marriage Law referred to mediation by the local government and the judicial organ, based on the experience of the revolutionary years, mediators in marital problems and divorce cases actually came from four sources: well-known or reputable people in local society; the Chinese

Women's Federation and the Chinese Labor Unions, both with local and work unit branches; neighborhood mediation committees and work unit mediation committees; and the mediation office in the people's court.[15] Usually one or more of these mediators would intervene when a woman or a man reported marital problems or sought divorce. Not all mediators were trusted by people having marital problems, and both urban and rural residents often doubted the educational and moral qualifications of work unit leaders, labor unions, residents committees or village leaders, some of whom were seen to practice favoritism and mete out unfair penalties. Some plaintiffs would try to curry favor with the mediators, and others would try to avoid them. Mediators were also avoided because they were seen as ineffective and unable to offer resolutions to plaintiffs' disputes.

Marriage and Divorce in Urban Society

Urban middle-class women in Shanghai who were homemakers and did not have economic independence were less willing to seek divorce from their husbands, even if they were in an arranged marriage or were concubines or suffered from domestic abuse, so as not to lose face and financial security or social status. They were equally unwilling to speak up to mediators or investigators about marital problems, afraid of airing the family's dirty laundry in public. Two cases involving middle-class women offer some insights into the mediation process and its consequences.

In one case, Mr. Chuan, a clerk in the Bank of China, had an affair with Ms. Guo, his subordinate, not long after his marriage with Ms. Wang in 1950. As his relations with his wife deteriorated, he moved out of his home and lived in the bank's dormitory for eight months before filing for divorce. Following the Marriage Law, the local court began to mediate, starting with an investigation by court personnel into Chuan's work and personal life. His colleagues spoke well of him. Guo left Shanghai for Beijing and in a letter to Chuan expressed her loss of interest in continuing the relationship. After going through Chuan's and Wang's personal documents, the court decided that the couple still had feelings for one another and thereby denied Chuan's petition for divorce.[16] In this case it was the husband, not his wife, who tried to get a divorce but failed to persuade the court to agree with his petition.

In another case, Ms. Lu, a single woman working at the Shanghai Telephone Company, met Mr. Gu, a married man working in the same company, in the winter of 1952. They began an affair, and Lu moved into Gu's home when his wife was away for a period of time. After the wife returned and learned of the affair, she accepted it, since the alternative would likely be a divorce, which she feared. The three lived together in peace, until Gu's mother-in-law angrily reported the amoral living arrangement to the company's labor union. In response, the union put great pressure on Lu as the culprit in the matter. Lu made self-criticism, but the union found it inadequate, and the pressure on her continued. Feeling humiliated and treated as a "loose" woman, with no clear end in sight, Lu jumped off a building to her death on February 16, 1953.[17] In this case, Gu's wife accepted her husband's extramarital affair, but the living arrangement was de facto bigamy, in violation of the Marriage Law, so the union had to respond when the matter was brought forth. These cases illustrate that mediation (and related investigation and intervention) by formal and informal agents of the state were as critical and consequential as adjudication by the court.

Whereas middle-class women were reluctant to draw the state's attention to and intervention into their marital problems, working-class families were more willing and ready to draw on the state's power to settle family problems. One residents committee in Shanghai reported in the early 1950s that each day two or three incidents of marital problems were brought to it for mediation. The Women's Federation in Beijing reported in 1951 that since the promulgation of the Marriage Law in late 1950, the number of marriage cases that it handled increased by one third, most of them from laboring classes, and 80 percent were divorce cases. Unlike middle-class families that lived in relative isolation from one another, working-class families lived in more densely populated neighborhoods, and therefore their family quarrels and marital problems were often known among their neighbors: private affairs were public knowledge. In such circumstances, "losing face" was hardly a concern for working-class women. On the contrary, bringing in the state to intervene was a strategy these women used to redress their suffering. In addition, working-class men were not the only earners in their families, so married working women, albeit earning low incomes, did not fear breaking up with their husband.

In one case from Shanghai, Mr. Wang and his wife, Hai, both natives of Anhui province, got married in 1952 when Hai was twenty, a marriage arranged by their fathers. Their life was not happy. Hai wanted to be socially active and independent, but Wang disliked that. Hai reported Wang's alleged theft to the authorities and tried to get Wang's brother to corroborate her charge, but he only informed Wang of Hai's action. Wang's parents began to spread a rumor about Hai having illicit sex with a fellow worker. That was when, bypassing the residents committee, Hai went directly to the court for a divorce on the grounds that her marriage had been arranged, Wang prevented her participation in social activities, they did not share the same political views, and their marriage had no basis in love. The court sent officials to their neighborhood and convened a meeting of the family members along with neighbors. Wang's parents made a scene and had to be removed, and neighbors supported Hai's claim. The court officials orally approved the divorce. Later, in a court session to settle property issues, Wang made a scene. After the court gave its oral verdict, Wang went home and destroyed Hai's clothes, shoes, and other possessions. At her request, Hai was escorted home by Women's Federation representatives, a mediator, and court policemen to gather what was left of her belongings. She also requested that these parties pay Wang a monthly visit to collect alimony.[18]

In another case, Mr. Sun, fifty-two, hailed from Anhui province and worked in a Shanghai tobacco factory. He married Huang but went to live with another woman, named Yu, for over six years. He physically abused both women. In 1952 Yu went to the court to seek separation from Sun, and then the factory leaders intervened to push Sun to return to Huang. Sun did, but he bought a knife and threatened to kill Huang. His daughter reported the threat to the police, and the police informed the residents committee. The couple's fight and Sun's threats continued, until the Women's Federation decided to encourage the couple to divorce; it also decided to meet with the court to settle the children's custody and expenses.[19]

These cases show a pattern of state response to divorce cases that did not result from feudal marriages. When women or men went directly to the court for divorce, the court would follow the Marriage Law and either send its personnel to investigate or send the cases to one or more mediators, such as a residents committee, a labor union, the Women's Federation, or work unit leaders. Each of these mediators would investigate the circumstances, then submit to the court their conclusions of the parties' real reasons for divorce, as well as testimonies from friends, relatives, neighbors, and coworkers. In most cases these mediators and the court would intervene to promote gender equality and help victims of domestic abuse, short of divorce if possible, but would support or grant a divorce to protect women and their rights if reconciliation was impossible.

Marriage and Divorce in Rural Society

Rural society saw the same trend in divorce cases as that in urban society; that is, the easier breakup of feudal marriages initiated by women led to a rise in the divorce rate in the early 1950s and then a leveling-off in the 1960s through the end of the Mao era. Nevertheless divorce cases were the main reason for all civil disputes throughout the period.

In Songjiang county near the city of Shanghai, a young woman was married to a man who was "short and ugly." The marriage was unhappy and she returned to her natal family. During the Marriage Law campaign in the early 1950s, she was able to obtain a divorce on the ground that her marriage was feudal—that is, arranged. Another woman was betrothed at an early age and then married to one of the sons of her adoptive family. As the marriage did not go well, she petitioned and won a divorce, since hers was one of those feudal marriages that the Marriage Law prohibited.[20] Divorce cases launched by women on the ground of being in a feudal marriage were gone from the scene by the early 1960s; afterward contested divorces on other grounds were subject to the same mediation process as that in cities, before being approved by the court.

In contrast to the imperial and Republican eras, when mediators of civil disputes in rural society were elites of the local community, mediators in the Mao era were appointed cadres and thus agents of the state, even though they were still local people with some social status. Before the transition to Socialism from 1956 to 1958, these were village heads or other kind of local leaders (e.g., heads of a local militia or women's organization). After the people's commune system was established, local mediators were production team heads, CCP branch committee members, village security chairs, production brigade heads, and Party branch secretaries. Although the official documents stated that civil mediation was to be carried out by mediation committees as "mass organizations," in the countryside it was those local cadres who performed that function, without setting up separate mediation committees. Those cadres were appointed by the state, yet they lived not on state salaries but on the income of their production brigades and teams. Their dual identity as members of local society and agents of the state obliged them to consider the interests of both, but they were often pushed to attend to the interests of state law and policy as a priority.

In the 1960s through 1970s the state discouraged divorce by vigorously pushing "mediated reconciliations." Mediation in divorce cases tended to be administrative resolutions achieved through coercive methods rather than voluntary compromises mediated by third parties and reached by disputants. The process would typically end up in one of four categories. Mediated reconciliation was most common. In adjudicated reconciliation, when one party had an extramarital affair and sought divorce, the court tended to deny the petition. In mediated and adjudicated divorce, when the marriage was not salvageable and one party was only seeking to frustrate the other by not agreeing to divorce, the court tended to rule for divorce.

In dealing with divorce cases, the courts used two methods characteristic of the Maoist approach. One was spending time and effort to investigate the circumstances of the estranged couple by visiting their kin, coworkers, and neighbors, as in urban divorce cases; this was considered a "mass line" approach. The other was an emphasis on the couple's emotional relationship as the most important basis for marriage and divorce and as the guide for court decisions. These approaches stemmed from Mao's ideological formulation of "non-antagonistic contradictions among the people." In practice, mediation was not an entirely voluntary process. It "involved a mixture of coercion from the court and voluntary compliance from the couple. The judges used moral-ideological suasion as well as material inducements, exerting their own pressure and calling on that of the community and family to produce the results they sought from the couple and their relatives. They drew freely on the special ideological authority of the party-state and the powers of the local village leadership to effect a reconciliation."[21] This explains the lower divorce rate in the 1960s and 1970s.

Mao's formulation of "contradictions among the people" covered civil disputes among citizens. An emphasis on mediation and settlement of disputes, especially marital and familial disputes, helped reduce the number of such disputes to be adjudicated by courts. At the same time, the political environment, administrative arrangement, and social ethos—a lack of private property, social regimentation through residence registration and work units, the notion of the people versus enemies, and so on—also made civil disputes less prevalent than at other times in Chinese history. That is why civil law and justice again became de facto "minor matters" (the term used by imperial-era lawmakers). The relatively low incidence of civil disputes helped the state function normally, even in "the minimalist state," with sparsely located judicial institutions, a small body of judicial personnel, and the absence of a civil code.

Criminal and civil matters during the Mao era constituted two contrasting dimensions of law and justice. On the one hand, the ideological constructs and political-legal framework of criminal justice as a matter of eliminating enemies of the people resulted in wrongful rulings, harsh punishments, physical and mental abuse, and denial of rights of the accused—in short, a negation of the rule of law, judicial independence, and due process that had guided the legal-judicial reform in the first half of the twentieth century. On the other hand, the ideological and legal mindset about civil justice as a matter of reconciling nonantagonistic contradictions among the people led to much more humane and reasonable approaches to settling civil disputes, with an emphasis on mediation, despite limited choices available to citizens in their regimented life.

One outstanding feature of civil dispute resolution in the Mao era was a commitment to promoting gender equality and protecting the rights of women and children, as shown in the Marriage Law and its enforcement through mediation and adjudication. In both criminal and civil justice, substantive justice (defined by Mao or the party-state) was pursued to the neglect of procedural justice, especially in criminal justice. At the same time both criminal and civil matters were dealt with as part of a larger project of reforming the minds of the entire population. Between the state agenda (or Mao's vision and action) and all kinds of reactions to it from individuals (Party officials and average citizens alike) transpired what was called justice in the Mao era.

PART IV
LAW AND JUSTICE IN POST-MAO CHINA, 1977–2018

9
The Legal System and the Rule of Law
Changes in Criminal Justice, 1977–1996

After Mao's death in September 1976, China experienced profound transformation under the "reform and opening" policies initiated by Deng Xiaoping. The development in law and justice in the post-Mao era has been both a component and a result of these policies. In a broad sense, the legal-judicial reforms are a return to, and a move beyond, the trajectory from the late Qing through the Republican era that was interrupted by the Mao era. From the late 1970s onward, under Deng, the CCP moved away from the rhetoric and practice of Maoist "class struggle." Since the mid-1990s, the CCP has gradually accepted and co-opted the international discourse on human rights, which to a significant degree has influenced the ongoing reforms.[1] In the process "class interest" and "proletarian revolution" were jettisoned as the moral ground (or Heavenly reason) for judging right and wrong, while the rule of law, judicial independence, and due process were reinstated as the principles to guide legal-judicial reforms. These principles have created a contradiction between the rule of the Party and the rule of law, as was the case under the GMD state before 1949. To date no change in the CCP being the country's political leadership has been hinted at in official discourse, and whether it is possible to work out a theoretical and institutional formula to reconcile the rule of the Party and the rule of law remains to be seen.

How should one assess laws and judicial practices in post-Mao China, given this contradiction? Legal scholar Randall Peerenboom argues for using a thin theory of the rule of law instead of the thick "rule of law" of Western liberal democracies to analyze the legal reforms in post-Mao China. A thin rule of law means "the formal or instrumental aspects of rule of law—those features that any legal system allegedly must possess to function effectively as a system of laws, regardless of whether the legal system is part of a democratic or nondemocratic society, capitalist or socialist, liberal or theocratic."[2]

Examined from the perspective advised by Peerenboom, what has been pronounced and delivered in the legal-judicial reforms under the existing

Heaven Has Eyes. Xiaoqun Xu, Oxford University Press (2020). © Oxford University Press.
DOI: 10.1093/oso/9780190060046.001.0001

political system in China are significant. For the sake of governability, any form of government or state needs legitimacy (or the Mandate of Heaven, as it were)—at least a tacit acceptance of the state authority by a majority of the people. At a deeper level, the post-Mao Chinese state's agenda to strengthen the functions of criminal and civil justice as part of good governance echoes the Confucian ideal of benevolent rule that would help build legitimacy among the people, who were conceived as the water that supports or sinks the ship of state. The conception is compatible with the Maoist moral command "Serve the people." In fact, more recent official discourses have reaffirmed the intellectual-moral tenets from the Confucian legacy as pertinent to practicing good governance in the "new era of Socialism with Chinese characteristics."

Another angle from which to analyze the legal practices in post-Mao China is a schematic model to study the functions of courts in various authoritarian regimes, as proposed by legal scholars Tom Ginsburg and Tamir Moustafa. These functions include establishing social control and sidelining political opponents; bolstering the regime's claim to legal legitimacy; strengthening administrative compliance within the state bureaucracy and reconciling competing factions within the regime; facilitating trade and investment; and implementing controversial policies so as to allow political distance from core elements of the regime.[3] It would require comparative studies to show how these functions of the courts in authoritarian countries are different from or similar to those in nonauthoritarian countries, but the model is useful in alerting us to the complex ways in which laws and courts functioned in post-Mao China. One critical dimension of the complexity is that the intention of the state in using laws and courts for multiple purposes does not always lead straight to what is intended; often the state moves in a convoluted way to an intended outcome and also to side effects and unintended consequences that tend to subvert or defeat the intent.

The underlying twin agendas of the Chinese state—maintaining its legitimacy and delivering good governance—have faced a universal and ubiquitous challenge: the dynamics of the principal-agent relationship (state agents failing the state agendas). In the meantime, the state agendas have invited both resistance and adaptation from all social actors for their legitimate or illegitimate pursuits, with more diverse individual and group interests than ever before. For all these reasons, subversions of progress toward the rule of law, judicial independence, and due process, including widespread official corruption at all levels, have been serious concerns to the state. Legal-judicial actions to address these problems, on top of dealing with newly emerging and proliferating crime and civil disputes, have become increasingly salient features in post-Mao China.

The Post-Mao Political Transition

Deng's Return to Power

After Mao's death in September 1976, his designated successor, Hua Guofeng, became the top leader of the Chinese Communist Party. Facing fierce opposition from Mao's wife, Jiang Qing, and her three close associates (together they were called the Gang of Four), Hua made an alliance with veteran Party officials who had suffered during the Cultural Revolution. They were able to have the Gang of Four arrested in early October 1976, within a month of Mao's death. Indebted to the support of these Party veterans, however, Hua was compelled to meet their demand that Deng Xiaoping be brought back to the leadership. Deng had been banished from the Party center early in the Cultural Revolution and brought back in 1974, only to be sacked again in early 1976, all by Mao. Having returned as the vice premier of the government and the vice chairman of the Party in 1977, very soon Deng emerged as the de facto leader. Hua became a figurehead with three official titles, until he was formally replaced by Zhao Ziyang as the premier in 1980, and then by Hu Yaobang as the CCP secretary general (the title that replaced "chairman") and by Deng as the chairman of the Central Military Commission in 1981. Deng became the top leader, who actually selected Zhao as the premier and Hu as the secretary general.

One key difference between Hua and Deng was that Hua intended to continue Mao's policies, but Deng wanted to reject them and chart a new course for China. After Hua succeeded Mao, he immediately put forward the slogans "Resolutely support whatever policy decisions were made by Chairman Mao" and "Follow whatever instructions were given by Chairman Mao."[4] Of course, the "Two Whatevers" conveniently included Mao's choice of Hua as the successor. To counter Hua's slogans, Deng launched a campaign to publicize the idea that "practice was the sole criteria for testing truth," which was another way to express his famous colloquial saying, "No matter whether a white cat or a black cat, a cat that catches mice is a good cat." The message was simply that some of Mao's policies, and the Cultural Revolution in particular, had been proven by experience to be disastrous for China and therefore must be rejected. Deng advocated that the CCP set aside Mao's theory of class struggle and make China's economic development and modernization the central focus of the Party's work. This policy was adopted by the CCP Third Plenum of the Eleventh Central Committee in December 1978, a turning point in the history of the CCP and the PRC.

Deng's Vision of Post-Mao China

Deng Xiaoping's rejection of the class struggle theory and the Cultural Revolution did not mean that he was rejecting the role of the CCP as the leading force of the country and the role of the state's coercive power. Quite the contrary, Deng wanted to make the Party more effective as the leading force and make the Party and the state more legitimate by delivering economic growth as good governance. In 1979 Deng announced the "four cardinal principles" as the Party's bottom line: the CCP must insist on the Socialist road, the proletarian dictatorship, the Party's leadership, and Marxism-Leninism-Maoism.[5]

These four points were theoretically and politically interconnected. According to Marxism-Leninism, the Communist Party would be the only political force to lead the country toward a Socialist society transitioning to Communism. To argue for the CCP's leading role, it was necessary to insist that whatever reform policies might bring about would still be Socialism, not capitalism, since practicing capitalism would not require a Communist Party in power. Although class struggle was no longer the main task the country faced (and economic development was), the state would still have to use coercive power to deal with what was called "internal and external hostile forces." In all this, the CCP's control of state power was key. In short, what Deng envisioned was that China's economic development would be realized in capitalist fashion (with free enterprise and a market economy) but under the Party's leadership, which was in essence a return to, and a move beyond, the New Democracy of 1949–1956.

It is in the context of the four cardinal principles and the debate within the Party over what path the country should take—a transformation into the Western-style state and society or a return to the Maoist state and society, or a sort of hybrid between the two—that the Tiananmen Incident of 1989 took place. Initially set off by resentment against official corruption that arose in the economic-social changes resulting from the reform and opening, in due course the Tiananmen movement signaled more meanings, as protesters began to imagine and push for the possibility of a political change inspired by the Western democracies. Precisely for that reason—a Western-style political system would mean negation of the CCP's power—Deng decided to crush the movement by force, intra-Party politics notwithstanding.[6]

After the strong international backlash against the Tiananmen crackdown and a period of uncertainty within the CCP and among the public as to where the Party and the country would be heading, Deng surprised everyone, including those who wanted to slow down or reverse the reform-opening policies and those who wanted to stay the course of these policies. He called for more rapidly expanding and deepening the reform and opening. He did so during a tour of southern China in January and February 1992. Deng made several key points during the tour: Planned economy and market economy are two approaches to economic growth, not the essential features defining Socialism and capitalism. To judge whether the reform and opening policies belong to Socialism or capitalism, the criteria should be whether they are beneficial to the development of Socialist productive force, the increase of the Socialist country's overall strength, and the rise of the people's living standards. For Socialism to be advantageous over capitalism, China must absorb and borrow achievements from all civilizations throughout human history, including the advanced managerial methods in developed capitalist countries that reflected the law of modern Socialized production.[7] In short, with his pragmatism and willingness to break away from Maoism and experiment with new approaches in a search for China's path toward economic growth and modernization, Deng's speeches in 1992 ended the debate and uncertainty within the CCP and marked the start of a new phase of the post-Mao reforms.

Reform and Opening to the World

Reforms in Rural Society

The first phase of the reforms had officially begun in rural China in the early 1980s to dismantle the people's commune system. It originated in an initiative taken by eighteen peasant households in a village in Fengyang county, Anhui province. They signed an oath of secrecy, under which each family took over a portion of the land that belonged to the production team (composed of the households in the village under the commune system) to individually grow crops. After meeting a certain quota owed to the state as taxes, any surplus harvest would be each family's income instead of being shared among all members of the production team, as was the rule under the commune system. This experiment of an incentive system proved a great success in the fall of 1979, with a bumper harvest of sixty-six tons of grain from the eighteen households, equaling the total of six harvests in 1965–1970. When informed of the experiment in May 1980, Deng confirmed it as a good practice. In January 1982 the Party center issued a policy document to establish throughout the country the practice known as "the family contract responsibility system."

The new system was a profound change in how land was used in China. The system separated landownership and management, in that the land was still owned by a collective (the production team and then the village), but was contracted to and managed and worked on by individual peasant households. It allowed peasants to transform their roles from mere laborers to both private entrepreneurs and laborers, thus unleashing great potentials of productivity. By early 1983 93 percent of all former production teams had shifted to the new system, and by 1984 100 percent had done so. Other state policies encouraged peasants to diversify their agricultural products and even start nonagricultural businesses while subcontracting their land to those households specializing in agricultural products. These developments led to the spread of free markets, private enterprise, and a diversified economy in rural society. Within a few years the changes dramatically increased agricultural productivity and output and rapidly transformed the social-economic landscape of China's countryside.

The responsibility system showed its downside as well. First of all, it was directed by state policies, not by legislation, and therefore peasants did not have legal protection when local officials arbitrarily changed the terms of contracts, or even voided contracts, that were signed with individual households, or otherwise harmed peasants' interests. It is in these and other areas that civil disputes have mushroomed in the past three decades. Second, there were conflicts between peasant households and collectives (production teams or villages) regarding what public or collectively owned resources individual households could use for their contracted land, and between individual households in using such resources (e.g., conflict between one family on the upstream and the other on the downstream of an irrigation canal).

These conflicts also contributed to civil disputes. Third, there was increasing tension between the labor-intensive family-managed agriculture under the responsibility system and the prospect of technology-intensive large-scale corporate farming.[8]

Partly in response to these problems, in 2014 the state issued a policy document to establish and protect separate rights to land by the owner (the collective), the contractor (a household), and the manager (another household), a practice known as *sanquan fenzhi*. The goal was both to preserve the nation's farm land at a minimum of 1.8 billion *mu* and to allow more flexible use of land for economic development.[9] The long-term prospect of agricultural production and economic growth in rural society is still an unfinished story.

Reforms in Urban Society

The second phase of the reform and opening policies that began in 1992 involved changing the way industries, especially state-owned enterprises (SOEs), were operated and managed. Along with the commune system being replaced by the responsibility system and private entrepreneurship in the countryside, privately owned small businesses (mostly in retail, services, and small household products) emerged and flourished in cities as well. In 1984 4 million people were employed or self-employed in the private sector of the urban economy, and 30 million were in urban "collective" enterprises.[10] Many urban families broke through a wall of their house to open storefronts facing the street.

Yet the mainstay of the national economy, the SOEs, remained unchanged and became the bottleneck blocking the realization of economic benefits from the reforms in agriculture. For one thing, as peasants' purchasing power increased due to the responsibility system, the inadequate supply of goods and services demanded by peasants became obvious. More problematic was the long-term stagnation of the SOEs due to low efficiency and low productivity on the one hand and rigid state planning and endless red tape on the other hand. The SOEs were state employers of workers; as such, they had to follow the commands of the government and could not respond to the demands of the market nor lay off workers nor go bankrupt. Some successful SOEs that were profitable and contributed more to the national economy did not see any benefit for their leaders and workers, while those SOEs that were economic failures remained in operation and their leaders faced no consequences because they were propped up by state finances. All these problems cried out for reform.

By the mid-1980s the CCP leaders had accepted the notion of the "planned market economy" (combining market and state planning) and begun to transform the state-planned economy and the SOEs. But it was slow going since no one knew how it would work; in Deng's words, the reform was like "feeling stones under water to cross a river." Only in October 1992, after Deng's southern tour, did the CCP officially jettison the term "planned economy" to formulate and publicize a "Socialist market economy," following Deng's comment that a planned economy did not define Socialism. More radical reforms in the SOEs and in most industrial sectors began.

The key to the reform of the SOEs was to allow them to operate as self-reliant economic enterprises responding to market forces. They would be allowed to earn profits that they could keep (after paying taxes to the state) and absorb losses, to hire and lay off workers, and to use innovations and incentive schemes to improve productivity. They could also issue stock to employees and eventually to the public—hence the reemergence of the stock market that was abolished in 1949. The SOEs that failed had to go bankrupt. (Their employees had to either retire or seek reemployment.) Critically, amid flourishing private enterprises the state has maintained control of certain SOEs in essential industries through financial and administrative means. These SOEs have remained vital to the state's economic development plans, a fact that the CCP calls "Socialism with Chinese characteristics" and foreign observers call "state capitalism."

The urban reforms had many intended and unintended consequences. The 1995 Labor Law changed SOE workers' lifetime employment to contractual labor. In 2007 the state enacted the Labor Contract Law (amended in 2012) to give workers (especially migrant workers) more protection of their rights and benefits. A majority of employers complied with the law, but they complained about rising labor costs and other difficulties caused by workers gaming the law; other employers failed to comply with the law, and some local governments failed to enforce the law, leading to lawsuits and public protests from workers.[11]

Also, SOEs as work units began to shed their responsibility for providing housing to employees. In conjunction with the housing reforms introduced in the early 1990s, SOE workers were offered opportunities to buy at a discount the housing units they used to rent from their employers, and such units then became salable commodities. In parallel, a real estate market and a housing development industry boomed, creating another arena where civil disputes as well as corruption would proliferate. One related complication, for instance, is that state policy officially prohibited rural land (and residential housing on it) to be sold to urban residents, but such sales have actually existed and proliferated as "urban sprawl" has followed economic growth; thus multiple-level negotiations between the policy and the reality have been occurring in both legal and social arenas.[12]

Another unintended consequence has been environmental degradation, to which the central and local governments, businesses, nongovernmental organizations, ordinary citizens, and courts have responded in a variety of ways.[13]

Opening to the World

The reform of the SOEs was preceded and then accompanied by China's opening to the world—opening to foreign trade, foreign technology, foreign experts, foreign education, and foreign investments. Thus competition with foreign businesses inside and outside China became one of the driving forces for the reform of the SOEs. Zhuhai, Shenzhen, Shantou, and Xiamen in Guangdong and Fujian provinces had been set up in the 1980s as "special economic zones" open to foreign investment, with tax and other benefits. After 1992 more regions opened to foreign investment, the most important among them being the Pudong New District on the eastern outskirts of Shanghai. By 2014 twelve greater metropolises or regions had been opened to foreign investments. Practically, beyond officially opened regions, individual foreigners have been able to start small businesses nearly anywhere in China. Initially foreign investment took the form of joint ventures with Chinese business entities (a statute for that purpose was enacted in July 1979), and later entirely foreign-owned businesses were allowed to establish themselves (a statute to that effect was enacted in April 1986). In the 1980s and 1990s foreign investments were limited to the sectors of manufacturing and food-beverage services. After China joined the World Trade Organization in 2001, financial services (banking, insurance, and equity investment), pharmaceutical companies and hospitals, and telecommunication services and information technology were also opened to foreign investment. Foreign capital entered most of the major sectors of the Chinese economy, and foreign goods (from luxury to common consumer goods) and services took a large share of China's market.

Cheaper Chinese labor made producing goods in China to be sold in the United States and other countries more profitable for foreign companies, which contributed to world trade (and to the U.S. trade deficit). In short, China's opening to the world was an important part of globalization in the late twentieth and early twenty-first centuries. The constant and enormous movements of people, goods, services, technologies, ideas, and cultures between China and the world have had important implications for the reform in Chinese law and justice.

Laws and Institutions of Criminal Justice

Legal System and Rule of Law

In the wake of the Cultural Revolution, CCP leaders shared a consensus that the kind of lawlessness seen during the Cultural Revolution should not be allowed to happen ever again and that both political life within the Party and the social and economic life of ordinary people should be protected by law. The consensus was reflected in Deng's emphasis on making and enforcing laws at a Party center work conference in December 1978:

> At the present our problem is that laws are not complete and many laws have not been made yet. Frequently words said by leaders are treated as "law" and disagreement with leaders' words are called "violation of law"; when leaders' words change, "law" also changes. Therefore, we must concentrate our efforts on making the criminal code, the civil code, the procedural laws, and various other laws that are necessary, such as factory law, the people's commune law, forest law, prairie law, environmental protection law, foreign investment law, and enacting them after discussions through certain democratic procedures, and strengthening the procuracies and the courts, so that laws are available, laws are always followed, and laws are strictly enforced, and violation of laws is prosecuted.[14]

In the political parlance of the late 1970s and 1980s, the key words were "building up the legal system" (*jianquan fazhi*) and "practicing the rule of law" (*shixing fazhi*), or "governing the country according to law" (*yifa zhiguo*), the latter becoming more regular usage in the 1990s and after. In reality, both institutional forms and procedural norms needed to be established for the rule of law.

One symbolic move in the direction of practicing the rule of law was the televised trial of the Gang of Four in 1980–1981. Jiang Qing, Zhang Chunqiao, Yao Wenyuan, and Wang Hongwen rose to high positions close to Mao in the Cultural Revolution and played key roles in pushing radical policies with disastrous results, including countless deaths. Four years after their arrest, Deng Xiaoping and other leaders decided to put the Gang of Four (along with five other officials) on trial, which essentially put the Cultural Revolution on trial without directly indicting Mao. At the same time, the trial was meant to send the message that legal procedures had been restored and the lawlessness in political life had ended. Of course, the guilty verdict for the Gang of Four was a foregone conclusion. Jiang and Zhang each received the death penalty with execution suspended for two years (to be commuted to life imprisonment), and the others received prison terms.[15]

In retrospect, the trial was not a model for the rule of law or judicial independence or due process. The defendants were not allowed to speak freely, nor could they choose their own defense lawyers; some on the prosecuting team were victims of the defendants' persecution during the Cultural Revolution, but they did not recuse themselves to avoid the appearance of conflict of interest; and the defendants were indicted under a criminal code enacted in 1979, but their alleged crimes had been committed prior to October 1976— in other words, the law was retroactively applied to them. Although even without a criminal code, being a counterrevolutionary was a standing criminal offense under various policy documents and individual statutes before and since the founding of the PRC, it is precisely the politically defined offense that was problematic in the first place. The fact that what the Gang of Four said and did was not a crime when Mao was alive and then became a crime after he died points to the shaky legal ground of the entire prosecution.[16]

Nevertheless, at that time the trial was popular among the Chinese public; the defendants were viewed as guilty of wrongdoing. Indeed many people said "Heaven has eyes" when referring approvingly to the fall of the Gang of Four. The trial was also deemed a positive development because the high-level Party officials fell from grace through a judicial process, even if a flawed one. Both the positive and negative aspects of the trial may be traced to the legal instrument used at the time: the 1979 Criminal Code.

The 1979 Criminal Code

The first ever criminal code of the PRC was enacted by the National People's Congress in July 1979.[17] The code featured eighty-nine articles under "general principles" and 103 articles under "special provisions" covering 129 offenses. The law provided five main categories of penalties: supervised residence, detention (one to six months), prison terms, life in prison, and the death penalty (immediate or suspended execution), not applicable to pregnant women or persons under eighteen. Three supplementary penalties were fines, deprivation of political rights, and confiscation of property. Turning oneself in after committing a crime would be a cause for reduced penalty. Commuting of penalties and parole were provided for remorse and good behavior after serving half a prison term or ten years of a life sentence.

Article 79 under general principles states that offenses not specified in the special provisions may be convicted and sentenced by analogy to the most similar articles, subject to the approval of the Supreme Court.[18] In other words, conviction and punishment of criminal offenses by analogy, one of the imperial legal practices abolished by the late Qing and Republican reformers, was revived as the law of the land until 1997.

The special provisions were grouped under eight chapters. In chapter 1, "Counterrevolutionary Crimes," Article 90 provided that all acts intended to overthrow the government of the proletarian dictatorship and the Socialist system and harm the People's Republic of China were crimes of a counterrevolutionary nature. Articles 91–102 listed some of these acts, such as conspiring with foreign countries to harm China's sovereignty or territorial integrity or security, intending to subvert the state and split the nation, spying for foreign nations, defecting to enemies, organizing rebellions, forming counterrevolutionary organizations, engaging in violent sabotage, and inciting the masses to resist or break state laws. Penalties for such offenses ranged from prison terms of three years to life up to the death penalty.

Chapter 2, "Endangering Public Security," covered acts of harming infrastructure, public utilities, public transportation, facilities for toxic materials, and state property. Chapter 3, "Disrupting Socialist Economic Order," covered economic crimes, such as fraud, tax evasion, counterfeiting, using public offices for private gain, price gouging, and violation of trademark law and other commercial laws.

Chapter 4, "Infringement on Personal Rights and Democratic Rights of Citizens," dealt with such crimes as murder (intentional homicide), manslaughter, assault, rape, framing innocent persons, using torture for confession, illegal detention, kidnapping and selling persons, forcing women to prostitute, state personnel abusing power, and state personnel illegally depriving citizens of their right of religious beliefs or infringing on social customs of ethnic minorities. Chapter 5, "Infringement on Property," covered such crimes as robbery, theft, extortion, embezzlement, and willful destruction of public property. To some of the offenses in these two chapters (e.g., homicide, rape, assault, robbery, and kidnapping), the death penalty, life imprisonment, and prison terms would apply, depending on the severity of the crime.

Chapter 6, "Disrupting the Social Administrative Order," covered offenses such as using violence or threats to prevent state personnel from carrying out their duties; refusing to accept court rulings; impeding work, production, business, teaching, or scientific research; disrupting public places and transportation; brawling or molesting women or "other hooligan activities"; shielding counterrevolutionaries; possessing firearms and munitions; manufacturing and selling fake medicine; using superstition to swindle money; impersonating state personnel; counterfeiting, forging, stealing, robbing, or destroying personal identifications or public documents or seals; organizing gambling; running a prostitution ring; making and selling pornography; and making and selling narcotics. These offenses would entail prison terms of no more than three, five, or seven years, but leaders of hooligan rings would get more than seven years. (This reminds one of the Qing substatute on "bare sticks.")

Chapter 7, "Disrupting Marriage and Family," covered offenses such as interfering with other people's freedom of marriage; committing bigamy; having sex with the wife of a military serviceman; abusing family members; viciously treating the old, the young, or the sick who need support; and kidnapping boys or girls of fourteen and under. Penalties for such offenses ranged from no more than three years to no more than seven years. Chapter 8, "Dereliction of Duties," dealt with state personnel who failed their duties or abused power or committed corruption. Penalties ranged from three to ten years.

Overall the 1979 Criminal Code was an achievement since it was the first criminal code of the PRC, but because of that it was also rudimentary and unsophisticated, lumping together many diverse acts into one broad criminal category. It also exhibited both the efforts to deal with common crimes as the main task of criminal justice and the lingering influence of Maoist concepts and vocabulary in adopting the broadly defined "counterrevolutionary" as a criminal category.

The 1979 Criminal Procedural Law

The Regulations on Arrest and Detention of February 1979 provided that only the public security apparatus was permitted to make arrests, and only after approval by the courts or the procuracies, thus making lawless detention of the Cultural Revolution era a thing of the past.[19] A more significant milestone was the Criminal Procedural Law enacted in July 1979 (along with the Criminal Code), which established the norms for procedural justice, although it was flawed in some respects.[20] The law had 164 articles in four sections. Some key points in "Section I, General Principles" explained procedural norms.

In Chapter 1, "Guiding Ideas, Tasks and Basic Principles," Article 3 stated that the public security organs were responsible for investigation, detention of suspects, and preliminary hearing of criminal cases; the People's Procuracies, for permission of arrest and prosecution; and the People's Courts, for trials. "No other institutions, organizations or individuals are permitted to exercise these powers."

Under Chapter 2, "Jurisdictions," all cases went through two trials, in contrast to the three-trial procedure of the Republic from 1912 to 1949 but consistent with the CCP practices in the base areas from 1927 to 1949. Ordinary criminal cases would be first tried at the district courts. Counterrevolutionary cases and cases entailing the death penalty or life imprisonment would be first tried at the intermediate courts. Serious provincial-level cases would be first tried at the superior courts, and serious national-level cases would be first tried at the Supreme Court.

Chapter 3 is about avoidance. Under Articles 23–25, judges, prosecutors, investigators, clerks, translators, and expert witnesses of criminal cases were required to recuse themselves if they were parties to a case or had anything to do with it.

Chapter 4 covers the legal defense. Defendants could defend themselves or entrust lawyers or other legal representatives to defend them. When a defendant did not have a defender, the court *was permitted to* appoint one for the defendant. If the defendant was impaired in speaking or hearing or was a minor, the court *was required to* appoint a defender. This was a critical change in PRC judicial procedures, a transition from inquisitorial trials to quasi-adversarial trials. Judges and prosecutors would struggle to adapt to it, while lawyers would have an increasingly important role to play in the process.

Chapter 5 provided the rule of evidence. All cases had to be decided on the basis of evidence, including material and documentary evidence, witness testimonies, victim's statement, defendant's statement and argument, expert testimonies, conclusions of (medical and other) examinations, and investigation and examination records. "*A defendant's statement, without other evidence to corroborate, cannot be used to convict and punish the defendant.* All persons who have knowledge of a case are obligated to testify" (emphasis added). The provision in italics was another significant departure, at least in normative terms, from the previous judicial practices in the PRC (and in the imperial era), when making defendants confess was emphasized and prized in the criminal procedures. Yet in reality torture and physical abuse would still take place, as some public security officers relied on obtaining confessions as the easiest way to score high on job performance.[21]

Security Administrative Penalty Regulations

In dealing with a spectrum of criminality, the PRC adopted another legal instrument, the Security Administrative Penalty Regulations (SAPR; Zhi'an guanli chufa tiaoli). Originally issued in 1957 and revised in 1986 and 1994, the SAPR was designed to punish offenders who had delinquent behavior or committed minor offenses but were not yet criminal suspects. The offenses were broadly covered: where an act disrupted public order or interfered with public safety or infringed personal rights of citizens or damaged public or private property, for which criminal penalty was not warranted, the SAPR would apply. Such acts could include brawling, prostitution, gambling, drunk-driving, price-scalping of coupons or tickets of all kinds, and illegal drug use. The public security bureaus were to arrest offenders and mete out penalties. The penalties included a warning, a fine (up to ¥200), and detention (up to fifteen days).[22] Critically, however, it was the public security bureaus that could impose *laojiao* as a penalty for offenses covered by the SAPR, even though *laojiao* was not prescribed in the SAPR but separately authorized by policy documents. That application of the SAPR was widespread is clear: in 1992 public security bureaus nationwide processed nearly 3 million SAPR cases, while the judiciary tried 423,000 criminal cases.[23]

It is worth noting that, inspired by foreign models, a similar legal instrument, the Law on Penalties for Violating Police Orders (Weijing fafa), was enacted in the Republican era (1915, 1928, and 1943). The amended version of 1947 allowed the police to use detention (from four hours to seven days; up to fourteen days for multiple offenses), fines (¥1 to ¥50; up to ¥100), community service (two to eight hours; up to sixteen days), and oral reprimand, plus confiscation and closure of business, to punish minor offenses, such as spreading rumors; impeding air, land, or water transportation or the postal service; making a false report to the police; inconveniencing other people; and harming social mores by unlicensed prostitution, whoring, or "loitering or rogue behaviors" (the last was as vague as "hooligan activities" in the PRC laws).[24] It is unclear how the Republican-era law was enforced, but the frequent application of the SAPR in the PRC was partly due to the underdevelopment of judicial institutions and criminal law and procedures, and partly to the higher incidence of misdemeanors in a much larger population than in the Republican era, hence a need for reducing court caseloads.

Construction of Courts

With the enactment of the Criminal Code and the Criminal Procedural Law came the restoration and expansion of judicial institutions. The Organic Laws of the People's Courts of July 1979 reestablished the four-level courts: the Supreme Court, the superior courts, the intermediate courts, and the district courts (plus special courts such as the military courts, the transportation courts, and the forestry courts). The Supreme Court would review and approve all capital cases sentenced in the lower courts and would provide legal interpretations. Article 4 stated, "The People's Court adjudicates independently and only obeys the law."[25]

Parallel to courts, a hierarchy of procuracies was built under the Organic Law of the People's Procuracies of July 1979. Under the law, the procuracies supervised legal activities for the state. Within each procuracy a committee would handle and vote on important cases and issues. The chief procurator could send a separate report to the superior institution if he disagreed with the committee's majority vote. A procuracy would prosecute criminal cases, supervise public security bureaus' criminal investigations and ensure the legality thereof, issue arrest warrants, and correct wrongful sentences or enforcement by courts. Procuracies were to "apply law equally to all citizens, not allowing privileges for anyone."[26]

In September 1979 the Ministry of Justice was restored to administer judicial affairs and institutions, including supervising law schools and training judicial officers. The Ministry's lower-level counterparts were gradually established thereafter (as many as 3,279 bodies in 1988). In 1982 the Ministry withdrew from managing administrative matters of the courts. In 1983 prisons and detention houses, and institutions of reform through labor and of reeducation through labor, were moved from the purview of public security organs to that of judicial administrative bodies.[27]

Professionalization of Judges

After the founding of the PRC in 1949, judicial officers, such as judges and procurators, were state cadres selected for their political qualifications. Many were ex-military. When the agenda of building the legal system and practicing the rule of law was launched in 1979, the main source of judges and procurators remained the armed forces, and other government services were the second source. After law schools were gradually restored and established in the country from the 1980s onward, graduates from law schools became a new and increasingly important source, while some lower-level court clerks were promoted to judgeships.

The Judges Law of 1995 marked the beginning of professionalization of judges. At the time, 80 percent of judges had two years of legal training at college level; only 5 percent had bachelor's degrees in legal training and 0.25 percent had graduate degrees. Five years later bachelor's degree holders made up only 19 percent of president and vice-president judges, and 15 percent of judges and assistant judges, at the district courts. Judges' inadequate legal training and experience had a negative impact on judicial practices, for many cases were incorrectly decided. In 1999 higher-level courts reviewed 96,739 cases and corrected the rulings in 21,862 of them, or 22.6 percent of the total.[28] In short, due to the neglect of professional training of judges in the Mao era, a huge gap remained to be filled by professionally trained and qualified judges in the 1990s.

To address the issue of professional competence of judges, in 2000 the government began to require that all new judges take a national examination, and in 2001 the requirement was formally amended to the Judges Law. Other amendments required that new judges in the district courts must have a bachelor's degree in law or in some other subject combined with law, plus two years of experience in legal work. Appointments at the superior courts and the Supreme Court would require three years of work experience. All new judges, after passing the national examination, would go through three months of training before assuming their posts.

The change in criminal procedures also raised demands on judges' competence. A large and growing body of laws had been enacted and continued to grow. As adversarial trials replaced inquisitorial trials, judges had to rule on evidence in the face of challenges from increasingly better-trained defense lawyers. The procedural law required judges to write extensive judgments to explain their legal analysis and reasoning. Since most criminal trials were open to the public and widely reported by mass media and social media, judges faced public scrutiny and criticism for any failings. They would be disciplined and even demoted or dismissed for serious mistakes in legal judgment.[29]

The Ways Courts Operated

Criminal cases in China were decided by a majority vote in a collegiate panel of three or two judges, one of whom was the presiding judge. The panel would be under the supervision of an adjudicating committee composed of the court president, vice presidents, department chiefs, and senior judges. The committee would discuss and decide serious or difficult cases and address various issues regarding trials, without involving the CCP committee within the court in individual cases.[30]

The role of the adjudicating committee would help address the low level of professional competence of some judges, but it also shielded individual judges from taking responsibility for wrongful rulings. The committee would usually decide on convictions and sentences before the actual trial, which became a formality; when "those who tried the case could not make a decision, and the real decision-makers did not try the case," "litigants could succeed in affecting the judicial decision somewhere in the chain process through the 'back door.'"[31] Despite these problems, studies published in 2010 show that "judges [were] more competent and professional than in the past, and that parties [were] reasonably happy with the courts, with most parties obtaining results in line with their expectations despite problems in particular types of cases and attempts by the parties to influence the outcome in some cases."[32]

One dimension of the complexity in post-Mao legal practices was the fact that all Chinese courts were not equal in the way they were situated in the state system and therefore in the way they would operate and adjudicate.[33] There were two deal types of courts—"firms" and "work units." The former would prefer adjudication over mediation, dispense cases quickly rather than stalling, and the latter would welcome rather than shirk cases; most courts, however, situated along the continuum between the two. Courts would behave differently because they were embedded in different economic, social, and political environments. The *work unit–type court* prized tight vertical control over efficiency. It was a highly oligarchic decision-making body made up of senior judges and officials of the local party-state and would function as an integral part of the local coalition of governance. (Courts were funded by the local government.) The court would usually face an adverse environment, "a public with less knowledge and little trust of the law, a lack of quality frontline judges, an under-developed economy that leads to an outsized proportion of disputes for litigants engaged in multiplex relationship (family disputes and divorce), and in some multi-ethnic regions away from the coastal area, a community divided by languages and ethnic cultures."[34] On the other hand, the *firm-type court* was less hierarchically controlled and financially more independent, would use more law, face a bigger caseload in a less volatile or risky judging environment, have personnel with more legal knowledge and expertise, and has more mobility of employment. Not surprisingly, the firm-type courts existed in more developed urban areas, while the work unit–type courts were in rural regions.

Restoration of the Legal Profession

As a corollary to the provision of legal defense in the Criminal Procedural Law, in August 1980 the National People's Congress adopted the PRC Provisional Regulations on Lawyers, thus restoring the legal profession that was abolished in 1959.[35] The National Association of Lawyers was founded in July 1986. By 1989 more than 3,500 law firms had been in operation nationwide, with over 31,000 legal workers. Consistent with the conception in the 1950s, the 1980 regulations defined lawyers as "state legal workers," not independent professionals. In 1986 the Ministry of Justice announced further reforms of the lawyer system: bar examinations to be instituted; law consultation offices as state agencies to be changed to partnerships; instead of having salaries paid by the state, law firms were to become self-supporting and even profitable; and upgrading a system of enforcing professional ethics and moral standards in lawyers' practices. Similarly in December 1993 the Ministry issued the Professional Ethics and Practicing Disciplinary Rules for Lawyers. Finally, in May 1996, the PRC Lawyers Law was enacted (effective January 1, 1997); it redefined lawyers as "social legal workers" instead of "state legal workers," which suggested that lawyers were independent legal professionals.[36]

The transition of lawyers from state employees to independent professionals was not instant and complete, but a work in progress with mixed results. In the late 1990s, of 8,963 law firms nationwide, 27 percent were partnerships, 11 percent were cooperatives, and 59 percent were still state-funded.[37] Even state-funded law firms, however, would be increasingly relying on profit-making by serving paying clients—that is, becoming financially more independent and thus professionally more independent in their legal practices.

While the growth of the legal profession was impressive (more than forty thousand lawyers working in four thousand law firms nationwide in the early 1990s), it was plagued by several problems. First, the issue of professional competence: in the early 1990s barely 20 percent of lawyers had earned university law degrees, and many studied law under the state-planned economy that had been largely superseded. The government tried to address the issue by offering various remedial trainings to lawyers and other legal workers. Second, the issue of professional responsibility and ethics: lawyers would bribe officials and judges, while officials in charge of regulating law firms extracting payments from the latter. All sorts of conflicts of interest and other ethical dilemmas abounded between lawyers and judicial officers, clients, other firms, and colleagues within their own firms. Aware of the issue, the Ministry of Justice issued a number of documents calling for high ethical standards for the legal profession. The All China Lawyers Association also spoke on the issue, and legal scholars and other commentators published articles addressing the problem. The effects of all those efforts were limited, however.[38]

Chinese lawyers were not as independent as lawyers in Western countries. The All China Lawyers Association was not equivalent to the bar associations in the United States, but was among the so-called mass organizations (such as the All China Labor Union and All China Women's Association) under the leadership of the CCP. Under the Lawyers Law, the Ministry of Justice (and its lower-level counterparts) was to supervise the legal profession, with the authority of issuing and renewing law licenses. Besides the power to deny licenses to lawyers for political reasons, some judicial officials would abuse their power by demanding bribes or engaging in other forms of corruption. All lawyers were not equally committed to the rule of law and professional ethics. Some would engage in unethical and even illegal conduct, while others would try to perform their professional duties under difficult circumstances.[39]

According to an empirical study published in 2002, Chinese lawyers faced many difficulties in trying to perform under the Criminal Procedural Law. Public security officers and procurators resisted the actual workings of the law regarding suspect's and defendant's rights. Lawyers were often denied access to arrested suspects and to evidence held by the police or procurators against suspects. When lawyers did meet with their clients, their meeting time was limited and their conversations monitored. Lawyers rarely had opportunities to cross-exam prosecution witnesses because the witnesses were often absent from trials; besides safety concerns, prosecutors worried that witnesses would retract their statements. According to one estimate, less than 10 percent of criminal trials had witnesses present. The obstacles faced by lawyers were such that between 1997 and 2002 nearly 60 percent of criminal cases had no lawyers involved. Finally, in trying to defend their clients, lawyers risked being detained, prosecuted, and convicted under a variety of charges, such as perjury; assisting suspects in concealing, destroying, or forging evidence; helping suspects collude with one another; or corruption. Fundamentally, the police and prosecutors were resistant to an adversarial judicial process and unwilling to treat defense lawyers as equals, especially after lawyers became social legal workers instead of state legal workers—their equals.[40]

Writing in 2007, one legal scholar assessed the Chinese legal profession in the following terms:

> There are undoubtedly exceptions, but it could be argued that at least some in the Chinese bar, and perhaps most especially elite business practitioners in the capital, have struck a Faustian bargain with the party/state, willingly accepting good life materially and in terms of prestige and security in return for foregoing certain of the attributes (most notably, a considerable

measure of independence from the state) generally associated with legal professionalism in liberal democratic states and for acquiescing in the role the CCP has accorded itself in Chinese political and legal life.[41]

That Chinese lawyers should resist or oppose the role of the CCP in political and legal life might be too tall an order, since they had to work within the system in order to function at all, given the reality described in the 2002 study.

In more recent years, "activist attorneys" have appeared in the rights-claiming (*weiquan*) movement. Some were known as "diehard lawyers" or "suing to the death lawyers" (*sikepai lüshi*). Often using social media to mobilize fellow lawyers and the public, they would challenge the court or the judicial process and even the legitimacy of the state itself in a variety of ways, and they ended up being prosecuted for breaking the law.[42] At the same time, certain deficiencies in professional attributes, such as weak professional ethics or outright corruption, were due to the moral failings of individual lawyers as well as to the larger social environment, to which some activist lawyers were not immune.

The Law on State Compensation

One important development in protecting the rights of the accused was the enactment of the Law on State Compensation in May 1994 (amended in 2010 and 2012). The law allowed financial compensations to citizens, legal persons, and other organizations whose rights and interests were damaged by the actions of state institutions or their agents. While the law also covers administrative actions of state agencies, its chapter 3 is about compensation in criminal cases. Under Article 17, compensation is called for in the following situations: detention of citizens violated the Criminal Procedure Law, or a case was dropped after the suspect was detained; a case was dropped after the suspect was arrested; a retrial overruled a conviction but the penalty from the conviction was already carried out; bodily injury or death due to torture or mistreatment; bodily injury or death due to illegal use of weapons or police instruments. Under Article 18, victims would be compensated if their property was illegally sealed, seized, frozen, or collected by the public security organs, the procuracies, and the courts or by the detention houses and prisons or other state agents, or if an earlier conviction was voided by a retrial but fines were already imposed or confiscation of property due to the conviction was already carried out.[43] This law was a first, and came a long way in protecting citizens' rights and holding state agencies accountable for wrongful acts in criminal justice. Under the law, more and more victims of wrongful convictions and punishments would sue for state compensation. In the year 2003, courts in China ruled on 1,876 cases of state compensation for criminal proceedings and rewarded compensation in 853 (45.5 percent) of the cases and rejected compensation in 361 (19.2 percent) of them (143 cases were withdrawn, and the remaining 519 cases were listed as "other outcomes," the meaning of which is unclear).[44]

Strike-Hard Campaigns and Six Vices

The shift away from "class struggle" in criminal justice resulted in a relatively small number of counterrevolutionary cases, even though the offense was prominently listed as the first offense in the 1979 Criminal Code. From 1983 to 1987 only 0.28 percent of all criminal cases were in this category; in 1996 the number dropped to 0.06 percent.[45] Inversely and independently, in the wake of the economic reforms that drastically changed the Chinese economy and society, new types of crime appeared and old ones reemerged, in sharply increasing numbers, causing great anxiety for the public and the state alike. In 1980 alone 570,000 criminal offenses were recorded, compared to an annual average of 290,000 from 1950 to 1965.[46] Another disturbing development was that more and more Party and state officials colluded with or shielded such criminals for personal gain.

In response to these problems, in March 1982 the National People's Congress Standing Committee (NPCSC) adopted the Decision on Severe Punishment of Criminals Seriously Harming National Economy.[47] Targeting smuggling, illegally buying foreign currencies, speculating and profiteering, stealing public property and national treasures, and bribery, the decision upgraded penalties in the 1979 Criminal Code for these crimes. Under the code, smuggling, illegally buying foreign currencies, and speculation and profiteering were punished by prison terms of three to ten years; theft, robbery, and fraud, by five to ten years, up to life imprisonment; drug trafficking, by five years or less; and smuggling national treasures out of the country, by five to ten years, up to life imprisonment. Under the NPCSC decision, these crimes could be punished by more than ten years, life imprisonment, and death. State personnel were to be punished more severely for involvement in such crimes.

This act was followed by another NPCSC decree in September 1983, which officially launched the "strike hard" anticrime campaigns that would continue into the early 1990s. The Decision on Severe Punishment of Criminals Seriously Harming Social Order would impose, above the penalties prescribed in the Criminal Code, the death penalty for the following crimes: aggravated hooliganism; assault causing serious injury or death; leading a gang to kidnap and sell persons; making, selling, transporting, or stealing weapons and ammunition; organizing evil cults to engage in counterrevolutionary activities or seriously disrupt social order; and enticing, arranging, or forcing women into prostitution.[48] Another NPCSC Decision that accompanied the 1983 Decision waived Articles 111 and 131 of the Criminal Procedural Law about days needed for the delivery of prosecutorial documents to criminal defendants, lawyers, and witnesses, and for the defendants to submit appeals, in capital cases.[49] In short, these measures increased the severity of penalties for certain crimes in the Criminal Code and reduced the safeguards of procedural justice for suspects accused of those crimes, all of which reminds one of the Banditry Law of the Republican era. Thus, with the goal of ensuring social and political stability, law enforcement was to be carried out as "campaigns" to achieve "swift and severe" punishment of criminals.

As a result, the Criminal Procedural Law was not strictly followed, besides waiving Articles 111 and 131, and wrongful convictions and punishments occurred, let alone harsh penalties for offenses that were not very severe. According to a report dated March 14, 2007, by Xinhua News (China's state news agency), more than 1.6 million criminal cases were processed nationwide in 1983 alone: "Rapid police interrogations and hasty judgments by the courts were also blamed for widespread torture and unjust punishments for innocent parties. Many others were given penalties harsher than they deserved in accordance with the law."[50]

Here is one example of overly harsh punishment in the strike-hard campaigns. In 1984, Mr. Niu, age twenty, was convicted and sentenced to death with suspended execution for hooliganism; he was in a youth gang that used knives to engage in street brawls. In 1986 his death sentence was commuted to life imprisonment. In 1990 his term was further commuted to eighteen years. He was given bail for medical reasons for one year, extended to two years, during which time he got married and had a child. He did not return to prison voluntarily, due to miscommunication between the local police and the prison, but he was brought back twelve years later (2004) and was to serve out his time until 2022. The case caused lively discussions on the internet as to whether his punishment fit the crime, and a waiver or reduction of his remaining serving time was reported to be possible.[51]

In another case, dating from 1986, Mr. Pei, forty-two, worked in the cultural center of Wuwei city, Gansu province. Nine days after Pei gave an amateur singer a private lesson, he was accused of rape by the woman, who was pressured by Pei's boss and her fiancé to do so. Pei was convicted by the district court entirely on the accuser's words, without medical or physical or any corroborating evidence, and was sentenced to seven years in prison. Pei appealed to the intermediate court in March 1987 and lost his case. He appealed to the superior court and lost again. After he served out his prison term in 1993, he continued to appeal for an overthrow of his conviction, but to no avail. In October 2000 the original accuser wrote Pei a letter of repentance admitting that she had lied in 1986. Based on the letter, Pei appealed again to all the courts that had tried or reviewed his case. Finally, in December 2009, the Supreme Court found the case "unclear in facts and insufficient in evidence" and told the superior court to retry the case. At long last, in July 2010, the district court (with different judges from those who had tried the case twenty-four years earlier) annulled Pei's conviction.[52] These two cases show the vagaries of the judicial process in the strike-hard campaigns, and they are merely the tip of the iceberg.

In one important dimension, the strike-hard campaigns continued the practices from the pre-1949 years and the Cultural Revolution. They featured blanket coverage of the anticrime campaigns and their results in the mass media, frequent mass rallies in cities and towns where criminals' convictions and sentences were announced, and parades of the convicted on open-top trucks through major streets on their ways to executions or penitentiaries. Such practices, called by one legal scholar "displaying law," were supposed to have the didactic effects of deterring would-be criminals and reassuring the public.[53] Based on official statistics, however, the strike-hard campaigns did not seem to have an obvious effect in reducing the crime rate, which was 8.9 per 10,000 population in 1981 and 20.1 per 10,000 in 1990.[54] It may be argued, though, that the rate might have been even higher without the campaigns.

Trafficking Narcotics

From the 1980s onward several categories of newly emerging or reemerging crimes, known as "six vices," received particular attention from the state. These included trafficking narcotics, organizing prostitution, trafficking women and children, making and selling pornography, organizing gambling, and using superstition to swindle. An examination of the way four of these offenses were defined and dealt with will shed more light on the criminal justice of a changing society during this period and beyond.

After opium and other narcotics were eradicated in the early years of the PRC, illegal drugs were unknown in China for three decades. Starting in the early 1980s, however, opium, marijuana, heroin, cocaine, and other substances began to penetrate southern China from the notorious Golden Triangle—the narcotics-producing region in northern Myanmar and northern Thailand. Some Chinese cities became transit points for international drug traffickers. In 1981–1983 the Chinese authorities broke twenty-three drug-trafficking cases and confiscated five kilograms of opium and sixty kilograms of heroin; by 1991, drug cases had risen to 8,395 and confiscated drugs totaled 2,026 kilograms of opium, 1,959 kilograms of heroin, and 774 kilograms of other substances. Registered drug users more than doubled, from 70,000 in 1989 to 148,000 in 1991. As is the case in other countries, drug trafficking and drug abuse led to a public health crisis, including the spread of HIV through injections, but also other crimes such as theft, robbery, assault, murder, rape, and prostitution.[55]

To address the issue, the state enacted new laws. Under Article 171 of the Criminal Code, prison terms of five years or less and fines would be the penalty for making, selling, and transporting opium, heroin, or morphine, and more than five years for doing these in large quantities. In January 1988 the NPCSC enacted supplemental provisions to the Criminal Code, providing life imprisonment and the death penalty for smuggling narcotics in serious cases. In December 1990 the NPCSC issued the Decision on Strict Prohibition of Narcotics,[56] and the penalties were raised to fifteen years, life imprisonment, and the death penalty for making, selling, or transporting one kilogram of opium or a half-kilogram of heroin; leading a gang to smuggle, sell, transport, or make narcotics; using arms to do these; using violence to resist inspection, detention, or arrest; and participating in organized international drug trafficking. Those who smuggled, sold, transported, or made between 200 and 1,000 grams of opium or between 10 and 50 grams of heroin would receive prison terms of seven or more years. Enticing others to use drugs would receive seven years or less and fines; forcing others to use drugs, three to ten years and fines. Under Article 8 of the statute, drug users would be detained for fifteen days and fined ¥2,000, and their drug paraphernalia would be confiscated; addicts would be involuntarily rehabilitated; recidivists after rehab would be subject to *laojiao* and further rehab. While drug traffickers were punished more harshly under the statute, drug users and addicts were deemed victims, but they could still be involuntarily sent to rehab and even *laojiao* institutions.[57]

Trafficking Pornography

Along with narcotics and prostitution, pornography was eradicated in the Mao era. Any speech and writing about sex was taboo, and therefore even sex education and sexology were absent. During the Cultural Revolution any written, visual, or audio materials suggestive of love, let alone sex, were prohibited, even though in the early 1970s hand-copied fiction about love and sex spread underground in some cities (and some copiers were imprisoned).[58] With the reform and opening to the world, however, pornography came back with a vengeance beginning in the early 1980s. In the form of pictures, magazines, books, videotapes, playing cards, and small objects like lighters and pens, porn materials initially came from Hong Kong, Taiwan, Japan, and Southeast Asian and Western countries (in that order). Soon Chinese individuals, groups, and even some publishers found making porn a lucrative business. In the late 1980s the coastal city of Shishi, Fujian province, boasted more than thirty entities reproducing porn materials (mostly copying videotapes), a business worth over ¥10 million a year, reaching a national market through twenty-six licensed private shipping agencies. Another group in Zhenjiang, Jiangsu province, published over 1.7 million sets or volumes of illegal print matter, including pornography, in two years.[59]

Under Article 170 of the criminal code, making and selling porn books and pictures for the sake of making a profit was to be punished by a prison term of three years or detention or supervised residence, and fines. In view of the rise of a porn industry, the government began to crack down in 1985, with the State Council's Regulations on Strict Prohibition of Obscene Materials. In 1987 the State Council issued a notice to all local governments on "striking at illegal publications," which covered porn materials as well.[60] Finally, in

December 1990 the NPCSC issued the Decision on Severe Punishment of Criminals Smuggling, Making, Selling, and Spreading Obscene Materials.[61] The statute superseded Article 170 of the Criminal Code, per the Supreme Court's interpretation in May 1992. The new law raised the penalty for the offense from three years to life imprisonment in serious cases and added confiscation of personal property.

The crackdown on porn materials was carried out in campaigns. From August 1989 to August 1990 a major "sweeping yellow" (the word "yellow" refers to prostitution and porn) campaign confiscated 32 million copies of print porn materials and 2.4 million copies of porn video and audio tapes, and 780,000 smuggled items from overseas, catching more than 80,000 offenders. From late 1990 to early 1991, another "sweeping yellow" drive captured more than 6.8 million copies of illegal publications, over 3,000 copies of porn books and magazines, 490,000 copies of illegal audiotapes, 50,000 copies of illegal videotapes, and 4,000 copies of porn videotapes. More than 3,100 unlicensed publishers were shut down, and 83 licensed publishers were "reorganized," meaning that the leaders of such entities were fired.[62]

In dealing with porn as a law enforcement matter, two legal issues were confronted: first, it is not easy to define what porn is, and second, it is debatable whether porn should be illegal in the first place. Although the answer to the second issue was not debated in China at the time, the first issue remained. The 1990 NPCSC Decision defined porn as "specific depiction of sexual acts or explicit propagation of lust in books, magazines, films, videotapes, audiotapes, pictures, and other obscene objects" (*yinhui wupin*), excluding scientific works on human physiology and medical knowledge and literary and visual work that has artistic value. The definition did not solve the problem, however. For instance, legal scholars struggled with the question of whether sex toys were "obscene objects" or sexual health aids. A further issue was what would constitute the offense of "spreading" porn materials, while possessing porn was not an offense. Did showing a porn videotape at home to visiting friends, for example, fit the definition of "spreading," or was showing it in a public setting necessary? What would constitute a "public" setting?[63]

All these issues were up to the public security bureaus, the procuracies, and the courts to decide, and their decisions varied with time and place. In one case in 1994, Mr. Long bought 1,580 copies of nine porn fictions from an underground outlet in Wuhan, Hubei province, and sold them for retail to fifteen private bookstores in Nanchang, Jiangxi province, making a profit of

¥2,000. He was convicted of selling pornography and sentenced to four years in prison and a ¥1,000 fine.[64] Prosecutions of pornography offenses became less frequent after the mid-1990s, but in a case as recent as November 2018, a woman of thirty was convicted and sentenced by the Wuhu County People's Court, Anhui province, to ten years and six months for making ¥150,000 from selling over seven thousand print copies of an explicit porn book about homosexual men that she authored. Four co-offenders received from ten months to ten years for their roles in the illegal enterprise. The woman's harsh sentence caused some debates.[65] Typical of the twenty-first century, pornography has mostly migrated to the internet, and there have been recent reports on prosecutions of such cases.[66]

Prostituting and Whoring

Prostitution was eliminated soon after the founding of the PRC and remained absent in the Mao era. Then, in the late 1970s, prostitution returned and has since grown to be a permanent feature in China's social landscape. In 1979 the public security organs in the city of Guangzhou rounded up more than forty prostitutes and their clients; that number climbed to more than eight thousand in 1989. Nationwide, the numbers were more than 10,000 in 1984 and more than 110,000 in 1989. It was estimated that those who were caught represented only 10 to 20 percent of all prostitutes and their clients.[67]

Most prostitutes voluntarily became sex workers. Motivated by the opportunity to make easy money, they came from various occupations, such as college students, school teachers, engineers, factory workers, and even officials in state agencies. Initially their clients were lower-class men or foreign visitors, but gradually men from all walks of life were included. In one southern province in 1988, among all customers of prostitutes who were caught by the police, 37.3 percent were truck or taxi drivers, 34.5 percent were private entrepreneurs, 16.1 percent were officials, and the remaining 12.1 percent fit a variety of other categories.[68]

Over the years prostitution grew from self-employed, underground, and private-contact operations to semi-open or open and well-organized businesses, often in collusion with and under the protection of corrupt local officials and police. As was the case in the Republican era, prostitutes came in different classes, from members of high-priced clubs to street walkers and every shade in between, serving clients of different social statuses and income levels. They operated in nightclubs, Karaoke bars, dance halls, beauty salons, massage parlors, bath houses, and foot treatment stores and as call-girls. The well-connected prostitution establishments were equipped with receptionists, chauffeurs, room servers, managers, and all the bells and whistles of legitimate enterprises. Inevitably prostitution was mixed with other forms of crime, such as narcotics offenses, human trafficking, racketeering, and bribery, with official corruption at the core.

Legal responses to prostitution developed gradually. Article 169 of the 1979 Criminal Code provided that enticing or hosting women to sell sex for profit would be punished by a prison term of five years or less, detention, or supervised residence, and fines. As noted earlier, the 1983 Decision on Severe Punishments of Criminals Seriously Harming Social Order imposed the death penalty for six crimes, one of which was "enticing or arranging or forcing women into prostitution under aggravating circumstances." The 1986 Security Administrative Punishment Regulations authorized the police to deal with prostitution for disrupting social order. The relevant offenses included selling and buying sex and enticing or arranging prostitution. Punishments included detention (one to fifteen days) and fines up to ¥5,000, or *laojiao*.[69] In September 1991 the NPCSC issued the Decision on Strict Prohibition of Prostitution, targeting those who organized, forced, enticed, arranged, or introduced others to prostitution. It provided security administrative penalties (warnings, fines, and detention for one to fifteen days), involuntary education, *laojiao*, and involuntary examination and treatment for sexually transmitted diseases. The Decision provided that state personnel who colluded with prostitution rings would be prosecuted for malfeasance under the Criminal Code.[70] All the named offenses and their penalties would eventually be revamped into the 1997 Criminal Code as Articles 358–362.

Like drug addicts, prostitutes were generally considered victims instead of criminals, but during the strike-hard campaigns of the 1980s, prostitutes in some locales would typically be sent to *laojiao* institutions. In 1988, 94.89 percent of women in *laojiao* institutions in Zhejiang province were prostitutes; at the same time, customers of prostitutes were rarely punished beyond being fined and/or detained (for one to fifteen days).[71] Despite the strikes at prostitution over the years, the phenomenon has shown no sign of going away, and the enforcement of the law against prostitution has been an intermittent and half-hearted effort, just as in other countries where prostitution is officially illegal.

Trafficking Women and Children

Starting in the early 1970s, before the end of the Mao era, the crime of trafficking women and children returned and grew in the country. The 1983 strike-hard campaign included the offense as one of the targets, but the crime continued to occur in increasing numbers. During 1983–1990 the courts tried a total of 51,777 cases and 72,620 offenders for the crime. The numbers of victims were staggering: In Sichuan province alone, during 1974–1991, trafficked women and children numbered 176,000. In Guangxi province during 1985–1991, such victims numbered 24,678. In Shandong province during 1980–1990, over 50,000 women and more than 1,300 children were trafficked in from other provinces.[72]

Under Article 141 of the 1979 Criminal Code, a prison term of five years or less was the penalty for "abducting [by deception] and selling [*guaimai*] people," and more than five years for committing the offense under aggravated circumstances. Because the penalty was considered too light for this growing crime, the 1983 Decision on Severe Punishment of Criminals Seriously Harming Social Order provided punishment up to the death penalty for leaders of trafficking rings. The crime was such a menace that during the 1980s separate notices were issued by the state agencies, such as a notice from the Ministry of Public Security (1982); a joint notice from the Supreme Court, the Supreme Procuracy, the Ministry of Public Security, the Ministry of Civil Affairs, the Ministry of Justice, and the All China Women's Federation (1986); and a notice from the State Council (1989). All called for vigilant efforts to deal with the crime.[73]

Human trafficking was complicated and imbedded in the fabric of the social-economic environment: poverty, lack of education, and the extremely uneven male-female ratio in certain parts of the country. In fighting the crime, the state faced some legal issues as well. Some women were willingly led away from their homes and hometowns in order to get out of undesirable circumstances, such as an abusive husband or extreme poverty, or simply out of a desire on the part of some women from isolated locales to "see the world." Some trafficked women made a comfortable living and had families with men who purchased them. In other words, there is ambiguity in defining who is a victim and therefore where the crime is in such cases. An investigation of 2,256 women who had been trafficked and rescued by the police found that 38 percent of them went with their abductors in order to obtain new jobs; 42 percent to find marriage partners; 9 percent to get out of familial conflicts; and 5 percent to join tourist groups; altogether these constituted 94 percent of the victims.[74]

Another issue involved the legal liabilities and penalties for some offenders. For example, some traffickers only abducted but did not sell their victims, and others only sold but did not abduct, which made application of Article 141 and the 1983 Decision problematic. Some traffickers transported and sheltered women for abductors and sellers, but they themselves did not abduct nor sell victims. Some men voluntarily sold their own children and family members. Some people knowingly bought abducted women and children, thinking they were offering a good outcome to the victims. Some women had been victims but then became victimizers; they went into the business of abducting and selling women and children.

To address all these issues, in September 1991 the NPCSC enacted the Decision on Severe Punishment of Criminals Abducting-Selling and Kidnapping Women and Children. The statute listed separately the following offenses: abducting-selling women or children; kidnapping women or children; kidnapping women or children for ransom; purchasing abducted or kidnapped women or children; gathering people to obstruct the rescue of abducted or kidnapped women or children; and using offices to obstruct the rescue of abducted or kidnapped women or children. Under the statute, persons who abduct-sell women and children were punished by five to ten years in prison and a fine under ¥50,000; those who met one of six conditions, by ten years to life, and a fine under ¥50,000 or confiscation of property; with especially aggravating circumstances, by the death penalty and confiscation of property. The six conditions were being a ringleader, having three or more victims, raping victims, deceiving or forcing abducted women into prostitution or selling them to others to do so, causing serious injury or death to victims or their kin, and selling victims out of the country. Importantly, the statute defined the offense of abducting-selling as *"for the purpose of selling,* committing one of the acts of abducting, buying, selling, transporting, and transferring women and children."

Furthermore, the statue separated kidnapping from abducting-selling: *"for the purpose of selling,* using violence, threats, or drugging to kidnap women and children" was punished by ten years to life in prison and a fine of under ¥50,000 or confiscation of property; with especially egregious acts, by the death penalty. Stealing infants was equivalent to kidnapping. As for buying abducted or kidnapped women and children, the penalty was a prison term of three years or detention (one to six months) or supervised residence.

Buying and then selling abducted or kidnapped victims was punished the same as initially abducting-selling them. In short, the 1991 statute addressed the entangled legal issues; its provisions would later enter the 1997 Criminal Code as Articles 240–242.[75] This was a conscientious effort on the part of lawmakers to deal with a complicated criminal and social phenomenon.

The two decades from 1977 to 1996 were a time of rapid changes in China in all spheres of life: political, economic, social, cultural, and, not least, legal-judicial. The development of law and justice responded to, but was barely keeping up with, an unprecedented rise in the crime rate and reemerging as well as new crimes characteristic of an ever more complex society in the era of economic reforms and globalization. The regimented society under Mao, with many fewer common crimes, was loosened up. In the Mao era the minimalist approach to law and justice had been adequate in dealing with counterrevolutionaries as enemies, even though it offered little protection of the rights of the accused.

The reform and opening policies launched under Deng Xiaoping changed China forever; the most profound change was that now all citizens could pursue their life goals and lifestyle with few restrictions. This also meant pursuit of money, sex, and power in any way one could, even illegally if one could get away with it. In other words, crime flourished along with economic growth and rising living standards. The state responded by enacting the Criminal Code and individual statutes. At the same time, lessons learned from the lawlessness of the Cultural Revolution compelled lawmakers to come up with more legal protections for the accused, hence the Criminal Procedural Law.

One aspect of the rapidly changing society was the rise of official corruption at all levels of the state system and in social, economic, and cultural transactions, and even in political life (such as buying and selling offices among cadres and buying and selling votes in village leadership elections). These were the challenges that the Chinese, both the state and the public, had to confront.

10
"Naked Officials" and "Heavenly Net"
Changes in Criminal Justice, 1997–2018

At least three noteworthy events transpired in the year 1997. First, Hong Kong was returned to China on July 1, 1997, by the United Kingdom, which had obtained it at the end of the Opium War in 1842.[1] Second, Deng Xiaoping died in February 1997, not seeing Hong Kong's return, which he had negotiated and signed the agreement for with British prime minister Margaret Thatcher back in 1984. Third, a new criminal code that revamped the 1979 code was enacted in March 1997. The passing of Deng and the enactment of the new criminal code in the same year, albeit coincidental, may be taken as a signal that the reform and opening policies that Deng had charted, including legal-judicial reforms, would outlive him and guide China's path of development in the twenty-first century.

The changes in criminal justice after 1996 extended the earlier trajectory. New forms and norms for the rule of law, judicial independence, and due process had been continuously developed, though they were far from being completed and fully delivered in practice. In the Criminal Code of 1997 class struggle as a guide to criminal justice and "counterrevolutionary" as a criminal category were jettisoned, and the category of "harming national security," a term learned from the West, was introduced instead. Article 3 revived the principle "No crime unless the law says so," another change from the 1979 Code. Over the years, the number of capital crimes were gradually reduced by a series of amendments to the 1997 Criminal Code. At the same time, safeguards for the rights of criminal defendants were strengthened by changes made to the Criminal Procedural Law. At long last, a Chinese rendering of the "due process" principle was coined as *zhengdang chengxu*, as discussions and debates on due process in the public domain became common, and the term "procedural justice" (rendered as *chengxu zhengyi*) also entered legal parlance, at least among legal scholars. In 2013 the system of "reeducation through labor" (*laojiao*) came to an end.

Heaven Has Eyes. Xiaoqun Xu, Oxford University Press (2020). © Oxford University Press.
DOI: 10.1093/oso/9780190060046.001.0001

Changes in criminal justice also included legal responses to official corruption and to new crimes, such as financial and securities fraud, intellectual property theft, and cyber crimes. Yet after four decades, the legal-judicial reforms are still an ongoing project with no end in sight. In both criminal and civil justice many problems remain to be addressed, and more substantive and procedural laws need to be enacted and, more important, enforced and practiced. In short, new chapters of continued changes in the legal-judicial realm have yet to be written.

Political Transitions after Deng Xiaoping

Jiang Zemin in Charge, 1997–2003

In 1989 Deng Xiaoping picked Jiang Zemin to be general secretary of the CCP and chairman of the Central Military Commission (CMC) in the aftermath of the Tiananmen Incident. Jiang assumed the presidency of the PRC in 1993. Although Deng had nominally retired in 1989, he remained the paramount leader whom Jiang and other leaders would consult on important policy decisions. After Deng's death, Jiang made efforts to establish his own authority, including his exposition of how the CCP should stay relevant in the twenty-first century. In 2000 he put forward a formula to achieve this: the CCP should represent the requirements for developing China's advanced productive forces, the orientation of China's advanced culture, and the fundamental interests of the overwhelming majority of the Chinese people. The formulation was adopted by the CCP Sixteenth National Congress in 2002.

Aside from Jiang's agenda to solidify his own position and leave an imprint on the CCP alongside that of Deng, the "three represents" theory had crucial ideological implications for the Party and its policies. As the result of the reform and opening, the CCP in effect became a party of Chinese elites that included technocrats, entrepreneurs, property owners, investors, mangers, and professionals, as well as Party officials, above average workers and peasants, even if the latter were Party members. In a sense, CCP cadres running SOEs in a market economy may be considered state capitalists, while private entrepreneurs of all stripes also joined the Party as members, which was exactly what Mao had warned would happen and tried in vain to prevent with his continuous revolution. The "three represents" was an ideological justification of the CCP's transformation; it was required by China's economic-social development known as "Socialism with Chinese characteristics" and was therefore in line with the fundamental interests of the Chinese people. The theory allowed the CCP to officially shift from "the Party of proletariats" (per the 1969 CCP Constitution) to "the vanguard of Chinese working class, . . . the Chinese people and Chinese nation" (per the 2002 CCP Constitution) to include the elites. This redefinition of the CCP stemmed logically from Deng's reform and opening policies and his four cardinal principles in combination. Only time will tell whether or not it pointed to a new path of political-economic-social development.

Hu Jintao in Charge, 2003–2012

According to the rules set by Deng Xiaoping, Jiang Zemin retired from the offices of the general secretary of the CCP in 2003, the president of the PRC in 2004, and the chairman of the CMC in 2005. Hu Jintao succeeded him and largely followed the policies set by Deng and Jiang, focusing on economic growth measured by the GDP. China's economy grew steadily by exporting manufactured goods and importing oil and raw materials, encouraging foreign investment, and increasing Chinese investment in developing and developed countries. During Hu's ten-year tenure China maintained an annual growth rate of GDP at 9 to 10 percent and weathered the 2008 global recession with a ¥4 trillion stimulus plan. One historically significant development, and a result of the post-Mao reforms and economic growth, was the abolition in 2006 of the state agricultural taxes on peasants, which had existed for at least two and a half millennia. Ideologically, Hu promoted a "scientific view of development," a "harmonious society," and a "peaceful rise" of China in the world. These formulations were responses to domestic and international situations, while the transformation of the CCP continued in the Hu decade.

On Hu's watch, several long-term social-economic problems worsened, along with economic growth and social transformation. First, corruption in the form of bribery, embezzlement, selling offices, trading power for sexual favors, and keeping de facto concubines became rather common among Party and state officials, despite the CCP's efforts to rein in wayward officials.

Second, the promotion of a "harmonious society" actually pointed to rising social tensions due to the misconduct of corrupt officials and a growing income and wealth gap, tensions that often set off localized riots and violent incidents, called "mass incidents" (*qunti shijian*) in official reports.

Third, these social tensions were compounded by a "floating population" of several hundred million migrant workers from rural areas working or looking for work in cities, which led to a lack of labor protection, left-behind children and elderly in the countryside, the need for education of children brought by migrant parents into cities, broken family life, and exploitation of migrant workers by unscrupulous employers.

Fourth, the pressure to meet the demand for employment (each year around 20 million people entered the labor market) forced Beijing to stimulate growth by pouring state investment into manufacturing and infrastructure-building as well as by increasing exports, leading to industrial overcapacity, unbalanced economic structure, and high debts owed by local governments and enterprises.

Fifth, decades of pursuing GDP-oriented economic growth seriously degraded China's environment, depleted its natural resources, and contributed to global climate change, which the "scientific view of development" tried to address. The state began to emphasize that environmental protection and sustainable development were vital to China's economic future, as well as to the global fight against climate change, but such efforts and their results remained inadequate. The immediate demand for jobs and growth tended to push aside plans for long-term benefits, and local officials and private businesses engaged in a short-term calculus to make immediate profits at the expense of the environment and sustainability, defying the existing environmental protection laws and regulations. All these problems had implications for criminal and civil justice.

Xi Jinping in Charge, 2013–

It was in the face of these complex problems that Xi Jinping replaced Hu Jintao in 2013 as the head of the CCP, the PRC, and the CMC. As of this writing, Xi's tenure has seen a vigorous campaign to prosecute corruption among Party and state officials at all levels (including ministerial and provincial-level officials and the CCP political bureau members) and a consolidation of power in his own hands, which culminated in the CCP Nineteenth National Congress in October 2017. In March 2018 the National People's Congress amended the PRC Constitution to lift presidential term limits. It is expected that Xi will stay in power as China's top leader for a much longer time than his two predecessors.

In terms of policies, Xi has expressed a commitment to continuing and deepening Deng's reform and opening policies in a "new era of Socialism with Chinese characteristics." He has advocated governing the country by comprehensively insisting on the rule of law and governing the Party by comprehensively applying strict rules and discipline; again, these have implications for criminal justice. He has pushed for a long overdue restructuring of the economy to turn the growth pattern away from foreign export-oriented to domestic consumer-oriented, from environment-degrading to environment-friendly and sustainable, and from lower-end labor-intensive manufacturing to high-end technology-intensive manufacturing. He has spoken of helping the people realize a "China dream" as his vision of China's development and building a "community of a shared future for humankind" as his vision of China's relationship with the world. He has proposed an ambitious agenda for international economic growth known as the "Silk Road economic belt" and the "maritime Silk Road" (or Belt-Road Initiative), which has been welcomed by many developing countries as economic opportunities and is viewed by the United States as a challenge to American dominance. As these policies and commitments are still works in progress, their long-term outcomes are not preordained but contingent upon any number of variables.

Laws and Institutions of Criminal Justice

The 1997 Criminal Code

Soon after the enactment of the 1979 Criminal Code, the law was found to be inadequate to the rapidly changing political, social, and economic conditions in the country. According to a report from the National People's Congress Standing Committee (NPCSC), as early as 1982 central government lawmakers decided to study the revision of the Criminal Code, and in 1988 they proposed some preliminary changes. Prior to 1997 the National People's Congress made twenty-two separate amendments to the 1979 Code; in addition, 130 laws on administrative, economic, and civil matters invoked analogies to offenses in the Criminal Code, indicating a need for revamping the Code.[2] In March 1997 the Eighth National People's Congress Fifth Plenum enacted the new Code.

The 1997 Code was revamped in three areas where problems had arisen. First, some criminal offenses in the 1979 Code were vaguely defined, so that either they were difficult to prosecute or convictions were arbitrary. Second, certain crimes had grown to such a serious extent that penalties needed to be made harsher to fit them. Third, new crimes had emerged due to the changes in society that had not been addressed in the earlier code.

Accordingly, in the 1997 Code articles on offenses increased to 345 (from 103 in the 1979 Code), and each offense was more specifically defined. More critically, conviction by analogy was abolished. Article 3 provided that "what is defined in plain language by the law as a criminal act is to be convicted and punished according to the law; what is not defined in plain language by the law as a criminal act is not to be convicted and punished." The principle of equality before the law was also enshrined: "The law is equally applied to anyone who commits a crime; no one has the privilege of being above the law" (Article 4); so was the principle that the punishment must fit the crime (Article 5).

Much of the political vocabulary in the 1979 Code reminiscent of the Mao era and the Cultural Revolution was absent from the new code. Critically, "counterrevolutionary" as a category of criminal offenses disappeared. In its place the offense of "harming national security" was introduced. Offenses under this category were more specific and more clearly defined. On the other hand, certain offenses in the "counterrevolutionary" category under the 1979 Code were actually common crimes, so they were incorporated into relevant parts of the new code.

Hooliganism was another ill-defined offense, causing arbitrary convictions. In the new code, it was deleted. Related and better-defined offenses were placed under the category "disrupting social order." These included acting lewdly toward and molesting women; gathering people to engage in sexual indulgence; gathering people to engage in brawling; and picking fights and disrupting social order. The second of these would become controversial in recent years, as we shall see.

Responding to the rise in corruption, the 1997 Code raised the threshold of punishment for ill-gotten money in corruption and bribery cases from ¥2,000 to ¥50,000 in the 1979 Code to ¥5,000 to ¥100,000. The low end would result in a minimum of five years in prison, and the high end, a minimum of life imprisonment, up to the death penalty. The change had first been made in a 1988 amendment to the 1979 Code and was now incorporated into the new code. Reflecting the growth of corruption on increasingly larger scales, the new threshold would soon be surpassed by huge amounts of money in corruption cases involving Party and state officials.

Yet another offense in the 1979 Code that was superseded by reality was "speculating and profiteering" (*touji daoba*). In the late 1970s the term referred to people profiting by buying commodities at a lower price in one locale and shipping them to another locale to sell at a higher price. In other words, the 1979 Code criminalized profit-making itself, a conceptual holdover from the Mao era. In the course of the reforms, making money or profit had been legitimized. After the launch of the stock markets in the 1980s, it became philosophically and legally anachronistic and practically difficult to define either speculation or profit-making as a crime. To address the problem, lawmakers deleted the offense from the 1997 Code, and instead provided more specific offenses under the category "disrupting Socialist economic order," such as producing and selling fake or adulterated products, counterfeiting, disrupting financial markets (such as insider trading), signing fraudulent contracts, and buying and selling import-export permits.

Responding to newly emerging crimes, the 1997 Code added participating in organized crime; organizing, leading, or actively participating in terrorist groups; inciting hatred and discrimination against any nationality; money laundering; drug trafficking; using digital technology to commit crimes; securities fraud and insider trading; violating land regulations and transferring land use rights illegally; stealing commercial secrets; violating state safety standards in construction; illegally detaining people for debt payment; forcing other people to work by depriving them of personal freedom; illegally collecting and supplying blood; retaliating against a witness; and so on. These reflected the growth in kind and scale of various criminal activities, as the reform and opening to the world brought forth rapid and profound political, social, economic, and technological changes in the country. Opportunities to make money either legally or illegally and novel ways in which crimes were committed proliferated far beyond what anyone could have imagined in the Mao era.

The 1996 Criminal Procedural Law

The new criminal code was preceded in March 1996 by a new Criminal Procedural Law (CPL), with 245 articles (compared to 164 articles in the 1979 CPL).[3] The overall thrust of the law was to provide more safeguards for procedural justice. Such language in the 1979 version as "under the guidance of Marxism-Leninism-Maoism," "exercise proletarian dictatorship," and "strike at enemy" were deleted. Now the purposes of criminal procedures were "to accurately and timely find out facts of crimes, correctly apply the law, punish criminals, safeguard the innocent from criminal prosecution, and educate citizens to willingly follow the law and actively fight against criminal acts, in order to maintain the Socialist legal system, protect citizens' personal rights, property rights, democratic rights and other rights, and safeguard the steady progress of the enterprise of socialist construction."[4] Thus, at least to lawmakers, punishing criminals and protecting the innocent and citizens' rights were equally important.

Some of the provisions regarding rights protection are worth noting. Under Article 5 the court exercises the power to adjudicate independently in accordance with the law, and the procuracy exercises the power to prosecute according to the law, not subject to interference from administrative organs, social organizations, and individuals. Under newly added Article 12, without being convicted by the court in accordance with the law, no one should be considered guilty. Article 34 provided that the court might appoint an attorney for a defendant who could not afford one; the court *ought to* appoint an attorney for a defendant who had impaired hearing, vision, or speaking, was a minor, or faced the death penalty and did not already have a lawyer. Article 36 provided for lawyers' access to their clients and to all case documents. Article 37 allowed lawyers to conduct their own investigations into cases when representing defendants. Article 49 obligated the courts, the procuracies, and the public security organs to protect witnesses and their close relatives; threats, insults, assaults, and retaliations against witnesses were crimes to be prosecuted.

The 2012 Criminal Procedural Law

Problems in delivering procedural justice were widely discussed in the media and in judicial publications in China. Responding to public reaction, in March 2012 the Eighth National People's Congress Fourth Plenum adopted an amended version of the CPL to further emphasize procedural justice.[5] Article 2 added "respect and safeguard human rights." Although the 1997 Criminal Code had already replaced "counterrevolutionary" with "harming national security" as a criminal category, the 1996 CPL that preceded it by sixteen months did not reflect that change. In the 2012 CPL the phrase "counterrevolutionary cases" was deleted, and Article 20 provided that the intermediate courts would try cases of harming national security and terrorism and cases entailing the death penalty and life imprisonment.

With regard to the rights of the accused, Article 33 in the 1996 CPL had provided that a suspect had the right to obtain a lawyer when being charged, and the procuracy was obliged to inform the suspect of that right. In the 2012 CPL a suspect had the right to obtain a lawyer when being questioned by an investigating agency for the first time, and the agency had to inform the suspect of that right when questioning him or her for the first time; this was a straightforward adoption of the U.S. *Miranda* right.

In the same vein, the new law substantially enlarged the lawyer's capacity to defend the accused. Under newly added Article 36, defense lawyers could provide assistance to the suspect during the investigation period (before being formally charged), submit a statement and rebuttal, request removal of the restriction of personal movement of the suspect, request the investigating organs to provide information on the charge, and submit opinions.

Article 36 in the 1997 CPL defined lawyers' access to the defendants and to case documents, and the 2012 CPL separated the article into Articles 37 and 38. Article 37 provided that defense lawyers could meet and communicate with their client, and the place of detention had to arrange such meetings within forty-eight hours. In cases involving harming national security, terrorist activities, and especially serious bribery, lawyers were to get permission from the investigating agencies to meet with the defendant. From the day a case moved to prosecution, the defense lawyer could verify evidence with the defendant, and meetings between the lawyer and the defendant were not to be monitored.

Article 43 in the 1996 CPL prohibited the police, the prosecutor, and the court from using torture and threats or deception or other illegal means to obtain a confession or evidence. (This provision is more beneficial to suspects than in the U.S. judicial practice of permitting police officers to use deception when questioning a suspect.) The 2012 CPL added that judicial officers "must not force anyone to self-incriminate."

The 1996 CPL prohibited obtaining evidence illegally, but the law did not indicate the legal consequences for the police or the procurator who violated the law, and the procurator could still use the evidence believed to be reliable, even if it was collected illegally.[6] Now Articles 53, 54, and 55 of the 2012 CPL made clear that illegally collected evidence and testimonies were to be excluded from trials; evidence reported to be collected illegally had to be verified; and judicial personnel who committed crimes in illegally collecting evidence would be prosecuted.

The 2012 CPL had a direct impact on some well-publicized criminal cases. In Le county, Jiangxi province, a gruesome murder case took place on the night of May 23, 2000. A man and a woman on a date were hacked to death after being robbed and the woman being raped. Two years later four men were arrested. Tried at the Jingdezhen Intermediate Court, the four defendants were convicted of murder, rape, and robbery, and sentenced to death in July 2003. Noting their alibis and the lack of evidence, the four men's families and lawyers appealed to the Jiangxi Superior Court, which ordered a retrial. But the retrial by the Jingdezhen Intermediate Court resulted in the same verdict and sentence in 2004. At appeal the Jiangxi Superior Court changed the sentences to death with execution suspended for two years. The four men were still appealing their case as wrongful, when a serial killer arrested in 2013 confessed to the crime. In July 2015 the Jiangxi Superior Court began to reexamine the case under the 2012 CPL, and in December 2016 the court set the four men free. It stated that the initial conviction was based mainly on the defendants' confessions, which were inconsistent with the newly found material and forensic evidence; the possibility of coerced confessions could not be ruled out; and there were no clear facts or sufficient evidence for conviction. In 2017 the four men sued for state compensation under the law, and the Jiangxi Superior Court ruled for them in the amount of more than ¥2.27 million each.[7]

All these legal changes, which were informed by Western judicial practices, point to an effort to address the problems that lawyers encountered in defending criminal defendants or suspects. What may be considered standard criminal procedures in Western countries were still being gradually established in China in the twenty-first century. There is always a gap between what is intended by the law and what actually happens. Nonetheless, as more specific safeguards for due process are prescribed in the law, they at least allow the public to measure what is or is not done according to the existing law and try to hold state agents accountable.

Abolishing Reeducation through Labor

Since its inception in the 1950s, the system of reform through labor (*laogai*) has been an integral part of convicts serving time in prisons, as the Criminal Code (Articles 41 and 43) and the Criminal Procedural Law (Article 156) of 1979 made clear. At the same time, the parallel system of reeducation through labor (*laojiao*), set up in the 1950s, was deemed an innovative way to reform bad characters into morally and socially better persons, but the practice was in effect an extrajudicial penalty for people who violated some norms or rules but were not convicted of criminal offenses by any court. After the enactment of the 1979 Criminal Code, the National People's Congress issued Additional Regulations on Reeducation through Labor in 1981 to legitimize the practice. To better implement the State Council's 1957 decision on the matter, the regulations stated, provincial and municipal governments should establish *laojiao* administrative committees, staffed by heads of departments of civil affairs, public security, and labor. The committees would review and approve all cases of reeducation. The reeducation period would be one to three years, and might be extended for another year. Former reeducation inmates and their family members were not to be subject to discrimination. The procuracies at the provincial and municipal levels would supervise reeducation facilities.[8] In short, in the early decades of the post-Mao era, lawmakers did not find anything wrong with the system.

After the turn of the twenty-first century, as China became further integrated into the world, Chinese law and judicial practices received more and more international scrutiny. The international criticism of the systems of *laogai* and *laojiao* caused domestic debates among activists in nongovernmental organizations, lawyers, judicial officers, and Party and government officials. While few questioned the premise of the *laogai* system—that convicts should work and reform instead of idling away time—there was a growing consensus that *laojiao* should be abolished. First, since the system deprived citizens' freedom without due process and a court decision, it contradicted the spirit of the International Convention on Human Rights, the PRC Constitution, and the Law on Legislation (enacted in 2000) and lacked the legal basis to be legitimate. Second, it gave the public security organs too much power unchecked by any other institutions, since the *laojiao* administrative committees would routinely approve public security organs' decisions to throw people into the system. Third, as an administrative penalty the system was actually harsher than punishments under the Criminal Code (holding an inmate up to four years, while the sentences in the Criminal Code were as light as six months of supervised residence or one to six months of detention).

As the opinions against *laojiao* gained acceptance among CCP leaders and judicial officials, in November 2013 the CCP Eighteenth Central Committee Third Plenum adopted a number of resolutions on improving the judicial system to safeguard human rights. Specific measures included regulating the judicial procedures for confiscating and freezing property, improving mechanisms to prevent wrongful cases, strictly prohibiting torture for confession, prohibiting physical mistreatment, excluding inadmissible evidence from trials, reducing the number of capital crimes, and abolishing *laojiao*. Pursuant to the last point, in December 2013 the NPCSC adopted a resolution to end the law and the practice of *laojiao*. The system came to an end after fifty-six years. The development was widely supported as progress toward better protection of human rights.[9]

The 2015 Amendments to the Criminal Code

Since the 1997 Criminal Code was enacted, amendments have been made at different points in response to the changing society spawning new kinds of crimes and to the changing understanding of how to punish crimes properly. Here the focus is on the most recent amendments to the code. In August 2015 the National People's Congress adopted the ninth batch of amendments (fifty-one items) to the 1997 Code. These amendments reduced the number of capital crimes from fifty-five to forty-six by removing the death penalty for nine offenses, which was partly in response to the ongoing debates over the death penalty.[10] Another major change in these amendments was to include fines as one of the penalties for most offenses that did not entail fines in the 1997 Criminal Code.[11] Some of the more important amendments are as follows.

Article 120 was about the crime of terrorism. The amendments added several acts as criminal offenses in this category and added fines as penalties for all terrorist offenses. These included financing terrorist training, recruiting or transporting persons for terrorist activities or training or organizations, and spreading books or media of terrorism and extremism or inciting terrorist activities. These offenses would incur a prison term of five years or less (or more than five years for serious cases) and fines. A prison term of three years and fines would be imposed for the offenses of using violence or coercion to force others to wear attire or signs propagating terrorism or extremism, and knowingly possessing books and media propagating terrorism and extremism. Three to seven years plus fines were the penalties for the offense of using extremism to incite or coerce others to undermine the implementation of marital, judicial, educational, or social administrative systems established by state law; especially serious cases would receive a prison term of more than seven years. The additions were in response to the waves of terrorist violence against innocent civilians that took place in Xinjiang and elsewhere.

Articles 285, 286, and 287 were about cyber crimes. Several new acts were included as offenses, and "work unit" was added as a possible offender. The offenses included a service provider's failure to offer security measures required by law, causing a loss of sensitive data or criminal case evidence or the spread of illegal information or other serious consequences.

Article 307 was about obstruction of justice, to which a new offense was added: fabricating facts to launch civil lawsuits, impeding judicial order, or seriously infringing on others' legitimate rights and interests. The penalty was a prison term of three years; serious cases could lead to three to seven years. This addition reflected the fact that many people would launch malicious lawsuits simply to hurt targeted people, a traditional means of personal vendetta.

Article 358 was about the offense of organizing or forcing others to engage in prostitution. The amendment removed the death penalty for serious offenders. "Underage person" replaced "girls under fourteen" (to include boys). Relevant to this change, the offense of "sleeping with underage prostitutes" was deleted from Article 360 on prostitution, so that Article 360 became consistent with Article 236: sleeping with girls under fourteen (whether prostitutes or not) was rape, to be punished severely (from a prison term of ten years up to the death penalty). It is worth recalling for comparison that under the Qing penal code, having sex with a girl of twelve or under was rape and the penalty was death; under the Republican criminal code, having sex with a girl under sixteen was rape and the penalty was a prison term of seven years or more.

The Death Penalty

Since the pre-imperial era, the death penalty has been one of the standard penalties in Chinese criminal justice, because a common notion of justice, shared by elites and nonelites and known as "Heavenly reason," required that perpetrators of the most heinous crimes must pay the ultimate price or justice would not be served, victims would not rest in peace, and society would not be cleansed of evil; that is, yin and yang would not be in balance. Failure to punish evildoers properly by the death penalty to manifest the alignment of Heavenly reason, state law, and human relations would weaken the state's legitimacy as well as diminish the deterrent and didactical functions of law and justice. That is why in the imperial era the execution of capital offenders was a public spectacle, similar to what transpired in criminal justice in European countries prior to the early twentieth century.[12] China's legal-judicial reforms in the early twentieth century ended public executions in law, but in reality public executions of political offenders and common criminals still took place under the National government and during the Mao era. In general, the death penalty as a fitting punishment of heinous crimes was never questioned until the late twentieth and early twenty-first century, when the death penalty was gradually abolished in most Western countries. China's reform and opening policies, including legal-judicial reforms, unfolded precisely during the time the movement to abolish the death penalty had been gaining success in Europe and elsewhere, but the movement did not have an immediate impact on Chinese law.

Under the 1979 Code, death sentences had to be reviewed and approved by the Supreme Court, but in June 1981 the NPCSC adopted a resolution stating that, except in cases of counterrevolutionary acts and bribery, death sentences for common crimes, such as murder, robbery, rape, arson, causing an explosion, poisoning, and sabotage of water works, transportation, and power plants, need not be reviewed by the Supreme Court. The superior courts' decisions would be final, unless the defendant appealed.[13]

One study published in 2007 found that the mean age of offenders in all capital cases in China was 32.4 years old; an overwhelming majority of capital offenders were men (92.5 percent); 62 percent of capital offenders were unemployed or rural residents, and of those employed, 70 percent held low-status jobs. Capital cases took less time than noncapital cases to close, as did the second trial or first review of capital cases. But the judicial process was far longer for capital cases reviewed by the Supreme Court than those without such reviews. Compared to Western practices, capital offenders in China waited much less time on death row before being executed. Moral education and psychological counseling would continue for death-row inmates, who were encouraged to write to their families and their victims' families to express regret and remorse, and humanitarian measures were taken to alleviate psychological stress for those awaiting execution. Until 1997 the method of execution was a single shot to the back of head; after that date lethal injection was used.[14]

International debates over the death penalty did compel Chinese legal reformers to discuss the issue. Here it is important to point out how the Chinese public view the death penalty. While systematic national surveys are lacking, some online surveys and college student surveys suggest that public support for the death penalty in China is comparable to that in the United States, the United Kingdom, France, and Germany. Similar to Western countries, the death penalty is justified on the grounds of deterrence, retribution, and incapacitation. Most Chinese legal scholars believe that it would be premature to abolish the death penalty, in view of the political structure, economic development, and social conditions in the country, but they all support further reforms to improve the judicial process to safeguard the rights of the accused and prevent or minimize wrongful convictions and executions in capital cases.[15]

There have been such efforts in that direction. In January 2007 the Supreme Court took back the sole authority to approve death sentences, a power that was delegated to the superior courts in 1981, and has since disapproved some death sentences decided by the lower courts. In January 2007, for instance, Mr. Xuan, a bureau chief in the Suixi county government, Guangdong province, after having heard rumors that Mr. Chen, his deputy chief, would soon replace him, went to Chen's office and beat him unconscious with a wrench and then cut Chen's wrists, causing his death. Accompanied by his family members, Xuan turned himself in to the police the next day. The Zhanjiang Intermediate Court convicted Xuan of intentional homicide and sentenced him to death with immediate execution in December 2007. At Xuan's appeal, the Guangdong Superior Court held a second trial in September 2009 and sustained the conviction and sentence of the first trial. But Xuan was spared death by the newly restored authority of the Supreme Court to approve death sentences. The Supreme Court examined the case and opined that Xuan turning himself in was a cause for reduced punishment and immediate execution was unnecessary. The case was sent back to the Guangdong Superior Court for retrial. In April 2011 that court retried the case and sentenced Xuan to death with suspended execution, normally to be commuted to life imprisonment after the two-year suspension period.[16]

To prevent the lower courts from sticking to their previous errors in capital cases, in June 2016 the Supreme Court stated in a legal interpretation that effective June 24 a case in which the death penalty was disapproved by the Supreme Court should not be sent back for retrial to the court of the first trial.[17] This rule is of vital importance to the outcomes in some wrongful cases.

Another development was the reduction of capital crimes in the 1997 Criminal Code through a series of amendments. The code contained sixty-eight capital crimes. In February 2011 the NPCSC adopted a set of amendments to abolish the death penalty for thirteen nonviolent economic crimes (including the offense of bribing, but not that of accepting bribery by officials). As noted earlier, another nine capital crimes were abolished by the 2015 amendments.

One important issue related to the death penalty was using the organs of executed capital offenders for organ transplantation. For a long time, both the government and medical practitioners regarded the practice as a public good, since it made use of organs that would have been wasted to save patients who needed the medical procedure. But then the practice came under international scrutiny as a human rights issue. In March 2007 the State Council issued the Regulations on Human Organ Transplants, whereby organ donation must be voluntary and without compensation; buying and selling organs and taking any organs from persons under eighteen were prohibited; and if a person died without indicating his or her wish to donate organs, his or her spouse, adult children, and parents could jointly approve the donation in writing. Violations of these rules would be criminally prosecuted.[18] In 2013 the Ministry of Health established a nationwide computer network to monitor the donation, distribution, and transplantation of organs to make sure lawfully donated organs were equitably used in all provinces and to forestall organ buying and selling. In January 2015 the government completely prohibited using any organs coming from the judicial system, which was part of the effort to fight the illegal trafficking of human organs involving unscrupulous judicial personnel and medical practitioners.[19]

Another sign of Western influence on China's legal-judicial reforms was that the official discourse came to focus on human rights protection as one of the functions of law and justice. In September 2016 the State Council issued a white paper titled "New Progresses in Human Rights Protection in the Judicial Field." It described four areas of progress and ongoing efforts: building better mechanisms for judicial protection of human rights, improving procedures of judicial protection of human rights, increasing the rigor of enforcement in judicial protection of human rights, and ensuring the legal rights of the detained. According to the white paper, in the year 2015 the Chinese judiciary at all levels decided not to arrest 131,675 persons and not to prosecute 25,778 suspects due to lack of evidence or legal basis (accused acts were not crimes in the Code); it also corrected 6,591 cases of wrongful conviction or sentencing.[20]

Crime and Punishment in a Changing Society

The continuing reform and opening policies remained the driving force that transformed China and complicated Chinese society, giving rise to newly emerging crimes and reemerging old crimes. Certain criminal cases sampled here will illustrate the changes and continuities in criminal justice and in Chinese economy, society, and culture, and the complex interactions between the state and society.

Economic Crimes

Lai Changxing was born in a peasant family in Jinjiang county, Fujian province. In the early 1980s he tried his hand at different businesses before moving to Hong Kong in 1991 and setting up a company there in 1993. He returned as a Hong Kong businessman to invest in the mainland and founded the Yuanhua Group in Xiamen, one of the four special economic zones. He then began to run large-scale smuggling operations, bringing into China foreign goods (mostly oil) worth ¥53 billion and evading taxes in the amount of ¥30 billion in five years. He built a protection network by bribing officials at all levels, from the local police, the Maritime Customs office in Xiamen, and the municipal and provincial governments all the way to a vice minister in the Ministry of Public Security in Beijing, lavishing them with cash, goods, houses, club memberships, and prostitutes. After an informant exposed the case to the central government in Beijing in 1999, more than 600 people were investigated and more than 300 were prosecuted (over 160 of them had worked in the Xiamen customs office); 14 offenders were sentenced to death.

Alerted by his protection network, Lai escaped to Vancouver, Canada. The Chinese government requested Lai's extradition, but the Canadian government refused to cooperate for over a decade, until the 2011 amendments to the 1997 Criminal Code abolished the death penalty for economic crimes. In July 2011 Lai was returned to China. Tried by the Xiamen Intermediate Court, he was convicted and sentenced to life imprisonment in May 2012.[21]

Zhuang Rushun, deputy director of the Fujian Provincial Department of Public Security, who had taken bribes from Lai and tipped him off to escape, was convicted of bribery and abuse of office and sentenced to death in October 2000. Through several appeals and retrials, his sentence was commuted to death with suspended execution in 2003; to life imprisonment in 2006; and to a prison term of eighteen years in 2009. In 2012, 2014, and 2017, his term was cut three times, by a total of three years and seven months, for good behavior and poor health.[22]

In contrast, an accidental thief, for his one-time greed, almost received the same penalty as Lai. On April 21, 2006, Mr. Xu was using an ATM of the Guangzhou Commercial Bank in the city of Guangzhou, Guangdong province. He was surprised to find that when he took out ¥1,000, the ATM recorded only ¥1. With over ¥170 left in his account, he made 171 withdrawals, taking away ¥175,000. After the bank discovered the loss, Xu became a fugitive until he was caught in Shaanxi province one year later. He was convicted by the Guangzhou Intermediate Court of stealing huge sums from a financial institution and sentenced to life imprisonment and confiscation of all personal property.

But the case was controversial. Some believed the bank was responsible for what happened, others debated what law should be invoked to prosecute the case, and still others questioned whether the penalty was too harsh compared to other cases of economic crimes, such as the Lai case. Xu appealed his case to the Guangdong Superior Court, and in January 2008 the case was sent back for retrial. The Intermediate Court changed Xu's penalty to a prison term of five years and a fine of ¥20,000.[23]

Intentional Homicide

Murder (called "intentional homicide" in Chinese law) or attempted murder was not a new crime, but new motivations or circumstances for murder increased sharply in the post-Mao era because of the changes in society and the economy. A running theme, which is also familiar, was that money, sex, and power, often in varied combinations, were the most common motivations for the crime.

In August 2007 Ms. Mo of Shaoguan city, Guangdong province, went to a club to look for a job and encountered Mr. Guo, fifty-four, general manager of a pharmaceutical firm. They went to a hotel and had sex, and Guo paid Mo ¥2,000 as "wages." Thereafter they would meet once or twice a week, and Guo would pay Mo each time. Gradually, however, the payment from Guo dropped from ¥2,000 to ¥1,000 to ¥300. Resenting her devaluation, Mo began to conspire with two men, her brother and a friend named Su, to kidnap Guo for ransom. One day in July 2008 their kidnap attempt went wrong, and Guo was stabbed to death. The gang took his cash (¥4,500), jewelry (a ring and a bracelet), and cell phone before fleeing to another city. The police broke the case, and the gang was captured. In February 2009 they were convicted of robbery resulting in homicide. Su was sentenced to death with immediate execution, Mo's brother, death with suspended execution, and Mo, life imprisonment, all with confiscation of personal property. One more man participated in the plot but not in its commission, and he received eighteen months in prison and a fine of ¥1,000. Su appealed his sentence to the Guangdong Superior Court and lost in May 2010, and the Supreme Court approved his sentence in December 2010.[24]

A more complicated murder conspiracy transpired in 2009–2010. Mr. Ma owned a real estate business in Shaoxing city, Zhejiang province. He married Ms. Mao in 2005, a second marriage for both. Ms. Chen, Mao's daughter from her first marriage, claimed that over the years Ma had had an interest in her and her friend Ms. Huang, but they both loathed him. Mr. Dai, Chen's husband, knew about this and began to think of killing Ma. Besides Ma's assets being a strong motive for his murder, what pushed the plot into action was that Ma spent over ¥4 million to buy a house and another ¥900,000 on an Audi Q5 as gifts for his son's wedding in 2010, while Chen had received only a Volvo (worth ¥300,000) from Ma as a gift for her wedding earlier. With these "grievances," Dai, Chen, Mao, Huang, and Mr. Jiang (a friend of Dai's and a lover of Dai's wife) got together to arrange Ma's death. They made a remotely controlled bomb that Dai placed in Ma's car. On April 14, 2010, the bomb was detonated, but Ma survived with serious injuries. Convicted of attempted homicide, Dai received twelve years, Chen seven years, Mao five years, Huang eighteen months, and Jiang one year, according to their role in committing the crime.[25]

A rather unusual and highly publicized murder case took place in 2010. Mr. Yao, twenty, was a student at the Xi'an Conservatory. On the night of October 20, driving a car, Yao hit Ms. Zhang, twenty-six, who was riding an electric bike. Getting out of his car and finding Zhang was injured but alive, instead of trying to save her, Yao used a knife to stab Zhang six times to her death, before fleeing the scene and hitting and lightly injuring two more people along the way. On October 22, when questioned by the police, Yao denied any knowledge of Zhang's death. Next day, accompanied by his parents, he turned himself in.

The crime shocked the public conscience. With great media attention, Yao's trial began at the Xi'an Intermediate Court on March 23, 2011. The prosecution and the defense debated for over three hours. Since the facts of the crime were indisputable, the defense lawyers tried to present mitigating factors, such as Yao being a good person before the incident, his turning himself in, and his remorse. The prosecution rejected the argument that he turned himself in, since he initially denied his crime when questioned by the police. Being a good person before the incident was irrelevant, and his remorse was insufficient to mitigate his crime. On April 22 Yao was found guilty of intentional homicide. The court accepted that he did turn himself in when he was not suspected by the police, but it could not mitigate his despicable motive—just to evade his responsibility for an auto accident—and his cruelty in stabbing the injured Zhang to death in cold blood. Yao was sentenced to death with immediate execution, and his family was to pay civil damages to Zhang's family in the amount of ¥45,498. Yao's appeal to the Shaanxi Superior Court was rejected in May 2011. The Supreme Court approved the sentence, and Yao was executed with lethal injection in June 2011.[26] Why Yao, a twenty-year-old, was capable of committing such a heinous crime is to be understood in the evolving dynamics between the social-economic changes and civil justice, and between law and morality, in the post-Mao era.

Shifting Law on Sex Crimes

As the first two cases show, money and sex sometimes drive people to commit homicide. This was part of a larger social transformation in post-Mao China: the changes in sexual mores, following the passing of the Mao era with its puritanical legal and moral pressure on sexual conduct and on personal life in general. Such changes were reflected in both criminal justice and popular attitudes and their interactions. Two issues are in focus here: homosexual acts and group sex.

It may be recalled that in the imperial era homosexuality was not an offense in its own name under the penal code, although sodomy committed by certain men under certain circumstances was an offense by analogy to "bare sticks." In the same vein, the Republican law ignored homosexuality, as did the law of the PRC. Yet in the Mao era and the first two decades of the post-Mao era (prior to 1997), male homosexual acts could be and were punished as an offense of "hooliganism," while the term "sodomy" did not even appear in either the 1979 or the 1997 Criminal Code. The legality or illegality of punishing homosexual acts was never fully debated and resolved by legal scholars and judicial officials or by the public, but in practice consensual homosexual acts among adults were quietly decriminalized in the twenty-first century, along with an increasingly tolerant attitude among the public toward homosexual and bisexual people. (Same-sex marriage has not yet been legally recognized, however.)

To a degree, tolerance toward homosexuality was part of a growing permissive attitude among average Chinese (and Party officials, despite the CCP's moral code) toward any and all sexual relations and conducts. Such social-cultural changes came into conflict with the Criminal Code at least in one area: consensual group sex. As noted earlier, "hooliganism" in the 1979 Code was replaced in the 1997 Code by more specific offenses, one of which was "gathering people to engage in sexual indulgence" (*juzhong yinluan*), that is, group sex, under the category of "disrupting social order." In the puritanical Mao era, no one would have questioned whether consensual group sex in private was "disrupting social order." With the changing sexual mores in post-Mao China, however, such a criminal offense became questionable.

A case in point occurred in 2010. The police in Nanjing, the provincial capital of Jiangsu, broke a ring of fourteen men and eight women who engaged in group-sex parties prearranged online. The ring leader was Mr. Ma, fifty-three, an associate professor at a college in Nanjing. Twice divorced and lonely, Ma started the loosely connected group through online chat rooms in 2007. His initial idea was to call for couples to take tourist trips together. When responses were sparse, he changed the gathering purpose to wife-swapping parties, even though he was divorced. The requirement of "couples only" was soon dropped, as more people wanted to join and vetting in advance became impractical. Ma himself engaged in group-sex parties at least eighteen times. In May 2010 the Qinhuai District Court convicted Ma and other defendants. Ma was sentenced to three and half years due to his unrepentant attitude, and the rest received from two years to six months (fourteen of them had their penalties suspended) or no penalty (three).[27]

The case touched off a public debate in the print and online media. Legal scholars and sexologists argued that the offense should be removed from the Criminal Code since consensual sex among adults in private could not possibly constitute "disrupting social order." Whether or not the law changes, such prosecutions as Ma's might become rare, since the police, the prosecutors, and the judges are all aware of the changed and changing sexual mores and public opinions.

Wrongful Cases

As is true in all countries, a law on the books is one thing, and how the law is implemented or enforced is quite another. The best law may not have the best effect under all circumstances, and will certainly fail its intent when it is not enforced as designed. A key variable is the conduct of the enforcers—the police, the procuracy, and the court. Three wrongful cases demonstrate how they transpired for reasons that are both common in all countries and particular to Chinese society. In short, incompetence, corruption, a lack of integrity to admit mistakes, or a combination of these on the part of the police, the prosecutor, and the courts, as well as pressure from the public to identify and punish culprits quickly, were the most common causes of wrongful cases.[28]

Case 1: On January 20, 1994, Ms. Zhang, the wife of Mr. She, of Jingshan county, Hubei province, went missing. Three months later a woman's decomposing body was found in a pond in another village. Zhang's kin identified the body as hers. Mr. She became the immediate and only suspect because he was having an affair with another woman, but there was no physical evidence nor witnesses of what had happened. Nevertheless in June 1995 the Jingshan District Court convicted She of intentional homicide and sentenced him to fifteen years. The sentence being light for a homicide offense suggests that the procurator and the court were not confident that She was guilty but wanted to close the case. Unexpectedly, eleven years later, on March 28, 2005, Zhang showed up in her home village—alive and well! Upset about her marriage and mentally unstable, she had left home for Shandong province. (Thus the dead body found in the pond became a cold case.) Realizing its mistake, the district court formally absolved She and released him from prison. He sued for state compensation for his wrongful conviction and imprisonment for eleven years, and in September 2005 the Jingmen Intermediate Court awarded him ¥256,900.[29]

Case 2: On July 27, 2006, two families were having supper together in Aoqian village, Pingtan county, Fujian province. Several people who had eaten the same dishes soon had symptoms of food poisoning. After emergency medical care, two children (one from each family) died. The initial investigation on the scene by the county police found rat poison, and the suspect was a neighbor who fainted when questioned by the police. Yet, for reasons unexplained (it was said that the suspect's cousin was a county official), the police quickly shifted their focus away from the suspect onto another neighbor, Mr. Nian, thirty, and changed their conclusion about the cause of death from rat poison to a pesticide. The police produced test results showing that the substance was found in the blood and stomachs of the victims and that a trace of it was found on the doorknob of Nian's bedroom. Nian was arrested and tortured to confess.

In March 2007 the Fuzhou Intermediate Court began to try Nian, who stated that he had been tortured by the police to make a false confession. Because the police submitted a videotape of Nian's interrogation, from which a torture session of two hours was edited out, the court did not accept Nian's statement. He was convicted and sentenced to death with immediate execution in February 2008. Nian appealed to the Fujian Superior Court, which in December 2008 returned the case for retrial because of "unclear facts and insufficient evidence." In June 2009 the Fuzhou Intermediate Court rendered the same conviction and sentence, and Nian appealed again. In April 2010 the Fujian Superior Court now upheld the conviction and sentence. In October 2010, upon reviewing the case, the Supreme Court found it wanting in facts and evidence, and threw it back.

In September 2011 the Fuzhou Intermediate Court rendered the same conviction and sentence a third time! (This is why in June 2016 the Supreme Court prohibited such cases from going back to the court that gave the death sentence.) By that time the case had become national news thanks to the internet. Ms. Zhang, a defense lawyer, believed Nian was innocent and waived her fee while continuing to represent him. Several well-known lawyers also joined the case, and it was even turned into the subject of a law symposium in 2012. A series of acts of misconduct by the county police—fabricating the test results, editing the interrogation videotape, and suppressing crime scene evidence that pointed to Nian's innocence—was exposed by Zhang and others. Upon Nian's further appeal, the Fujian Superior Court took up the case but postponed the trial several times, until July 2013. After four days of sharp debate between the prosecution and the defense, the court was adjourned without a ruling. The trial was not resumed until June 2014. Finally, in August 2014, the Fujian Superior Court ruled that the Fuzhou Intermediate Court's conviction and sentence were annulled; Nian was innocent and was not responsible for civil damages to the two victims' families. Nian was exonerated, but the victims' families did not get justice, since the true murderer was still at large.[30] This case shows the importance of the Supreme Court being the sole authority to approve the death penalty, since it would be difficult for corruption in local society to reach that Court in such cases as Nian's.

Case 3: In March 1995 Mr. Yang, thirty, in Tianzhu county, Guizhou province, was arrested as a suspect for murdering a young woman whose decomposed body was found in a pond one hundred yards from where he was staying. In December 1996 Yang was convicted on that circumstantial evidence and sentenced to death with execution suspended. His appeal to the Guizhou Superior Court was overruled in March 1998. Yang's mother kept appealing for his retrial for nearly twenty years. At last, in August 2015, the Guizhou Superior Court held a retrial and ruled for Yang's innocence. After his release, Yang sued for state compensation of ¥13 million. The court granted him ¥2.03 million.[31]

Fighting Corruption

Corruption at all levels of the government has been a growing problem in recent decades, and the principal-agent relationship reached a crisis point in the early 2010s. The Tiananmen Incident of 1989 was set off by public indignation over official corruption. Yet corruption was not reduced thereafter but has only gotten even more ubiquitous, despite the CCP disciplinary rules and the state statutes designed to fight it. After Xi Jinping became the top leader in 2013, a more vigorous anticorruption campaign was launched. According to the 2016 State Council white paper, in the year 2015 alone, as many as 54,249 persons were investigated for corruption, of which 4,490 cases involved more than ¥1 million each, and cases of such scale jumped 22.5 percent over the previous year. Several cases illustrate what the official saying "Striking at tigers and flies at the same time" refers to.

Mr. Wu, a highway-patrol officer in Foshan city, Guangdong province, was approached by three con men who intended to fake auto accidents to defraud insurance companies. Wu accepted their offer. Between late 2013 and early 2015 he wrote and signed false certificates of auto accidents thirty-eight times in exchange for a total of ¥40,000, while the gang cheated insurance companies of ¥760,000. In September 2015 Wu was convicted of taking bribes and abusing his office and sentenced to twenty-one months.[32] Wu was a "fly."

Zheng Xiaoyu, who had retired in 2006 from the position of director of the China Food and Drug Administration, was arrested in May 2007 for corruption. The indictment stated that during 1997–2006 Zheng had used his office to grant permits for drugs and medical devices in exchange for bribes totaling ¥6.49 million. Six of the drugs he approved were fakes harmful to human health. Zheng was tried by the Beijing First Intermediate Court and convicted of taking bribes and dereliction of duty. He was sentenced to death with immediate execution and confiscation of all personal property for taking bribes, and seven years for dereliction of duty. His appeal to the Beijing Superior Court was rejected in June. The Supreme Court approved his conviction and sentence, and Zheng was executed in July 2007.[33]

Zheng was certainly a "tiger," but his case was the tip of the iceberg. Illegal production of unsafe food and medicine continued to threaten public safety, and such illegal activities were facilitated by both the absence of strict quality control and inspection regimens and the presence of corruption in the face of increasingly ingenious and hard-to-detect criminal methods. In 2015 the nation's prosecutors processed 1,646 cases of unsafe food and medicine involving 13,240 offenders, and the public security organs investigated 877 cases.[34] This is one of the ongoing fights in criminal justice.

One of the biggest "tigers" prosecuted after Xi Jinping took the helm of the CCP was Ling Jihua. A career Party official, Ling was the CCP center chief of staff in 2007–2008 and then the director of the CCP United Front Department in 2008 until December 2014, when he was arrested for corruption, abuse of office, and theft of state secrets. His indictment revealed that he took ¥77,085,383 in bribes. Among the bribers, three were provincial- or ministerial-level officials who paid Ling ¥7,610,000, ¥600,000, and ¥890,000, respectively. Ling was expelled from the CCP in July 2015 and his case was passed to the judiciary. Tried at the Tianjin First Intermediate Court (away from Beijing), he was convicted and sentenced to a life term in July 2016.[35]

In the same month, Guo Boxiong, a three-star general, vice chairman of the CMC, and CCP Politburo member, was given a life term by the military court for abusing his office and taking huge sums in bribes. Other "tigers" who were busted for corruption and abuse of office include Bo Xilai, CCP Politburo member and the Party head of the Chongqing municipality, Sichuan province, and Zhou Yongkang, CCP Politburo Standing Committee member in charge of (ironically) state security and law enforcement. Both were sentenced to life terms in September 2013 and June 2015, respectively.[36]

To put these high-profile cases in a legal context, it should be noted that in January 2016 the Supreme Court issued an opinion on sentencing in corruption and bribery cases, stating that those convicted of serious corruption and bribery shall normally not be sentenced to death with immediate execution; if the amount of ill-gotten goods exceeds ¥100 million, the convicted may be sentenced to a life term; and if the crime is committed under aggravating circumstances, causing especially pernicious influence on society and especially serious damage to the interests of the state and the people, the convicted may be sentenced to death with immediate execution.[37] What would constitute "especially pernicious influence" and "especially serious damage," of course, is at the discretion of the courts or their adjudicating committees or, in those high-profile cases, of the CCP Politburo. Indeed the CCP leaders can do no better than Emperor Kangxi did: be selective and deliberate in punishing agents of the principal.

In this connection, there is a procedural issue to note. Party officials who commit corruption and other crimes, such as Ling, Guo, Bo, and Zhou, are investigated first by the CCP Disciplinary Commission before they are turned over to the judiciary for prosecution when the investigation discovers evidence of crimes committed. The investigation would begin with the targeted person being taken into custody without warning—what is called *shuanggui*, i.e., they are to answer corruption charges "in designated time and place." As warranted by evidence discovered, such corrupt officials are stripped of CCP membership and dismissed from public office (called *shuangkai*) before they are sent to the judiciary for prosecution. The rationale for the *shuanggui* is that the measure will prevent guilty officials from destroying evidence of crimes committed and communicating with co-conspirators.[38] These procedures are applied only to CCP members who voluntarily joined the Party to abide by its disciplinary rules, even if the rules are not part of criminal procedures.

For comparison, Hong Kong and Singapore also rely on anticorruption commissions with wide powers and insulation from judicial challenges. One study found that such institutions were increasing in number worldwide, but there was no strong evidence that they helped reduce corruption. "It is unlikely in an effectively single-party authoritarian state that courts could be able to independently handle cases against senior government officials who are ultimately appointed by and responsible to the ruling party."[39]

"Naked Officials" and "Heavenly Net"

The reform and opening policies created one situation that had not existed in the Mao era, that is, the relative ease with which criminals, including corrupt officials, could evade law and justice by fleeing to other countries. Because Chinese law and the judicial system were not the same as their foreign counterparts, and because most Western countries had abolished the death penalty, the PRC faced many obstacles in extraditing criminal fugitives from Western countries, as seen earlier in the Lai Changxing case.

Another dimension of the situation was a phenomenon of China's officialdom since the 1990s: many officials would send their family members and assets abroad while they stayed alone in the country committing corruption; that way they could transfer their ill-gotten fortunes overseas and easily escape justice when their crimes were exposed. The public called such people "naked officials" because they were shameless and did not have baggage to slow them down when they had to flee abroad. During 1995–2005 there were 1.18 million officials' spouses and children staying overseas, and in Guangdong province alone there were 2,190 naked officials as of 2014.[40] In December 2013 the CCP Department of Organization issued a document on the selection and promotion of officials. It provided that those officials whose spouse had immigrated overseas, or who had no spouse but whose children had immigrated overseas, would not be considered for promotion.[41] Corrupt officials would certainly try to game the system and find loopholes to beat it.

Despite the obstacles, Chinese authorities have tried to catch as many fugitives as possible. In April 2015 the Ministry of Public Security began a program called Heavenly Net, in collaboration with law enforcement agencies and judiciaries in other countries, to capture corrupt officials and white-collar criminals who fled overseas. The code name comes from a Chinese saying coined by Lao Zi (sixth century BCE), "Heavenly net [law] is infinitely vast—while lenient to minor offenses, none of the guilty may slip through" (*tianwang huihui, shu er bulou*). In launching the program, the Ministry issued a "red notice," a list of one hundred "most wanted" criminal fugitives, including former officials who had committed crimes such as fraud, bribery, and embezzlement in China and were hiding from justice in foreign countries.

Yang Xiuzhu, the first on the wanted list and a former deputy head of the Zhejiang Provincial Department of Construction, fled the country in 2003 and moved through seven foreign countries until she was persuaded to return to China to face justice in November 2016. (The abolition of the death penalty for economic crimes was a factor in persuading fugitives to give up.)[42] It was reported that by the end of 2018 fifty-six of the one hundred most wanted fugitives had been returned to China.[43]

The Courts at Work

To gain a general sense of how Chinese criminal justice was functioning in recent years, a report made by the Supreme Court to the First Plenum of the Thirteenth National People's Congress in March 2018 may be cited. In 2013–2017 the Supreme Court processed 82,383 cases and closed 79,692, an increase of 60.6 percent and 58.8 percent over 2008–2012. All lower courts nationwide processed nearly 8.9 million cases and disposed of 8.6 million, with civil remedies totaling ¥20.2 trillion, an increase of 8.6 percent, 55.6 percent, and 44.6 percent over the previous five years. Of the 8.9 million cases closed, nearly 5.5 million were criminal cases, with 6.07 million offenders convicted. Of these criminal cases, 195,000 were of corruption and bribery, with 263,000 persons convicted; 571,000 of narcotics offenses; 131,000 of harming women and children; 4,685 of abducting-selling women and children; 42,000 of food and drug safety violations; and 88,000 of environmental law violations. The courts corrected a total of 6,747 cases of wrongful conviction and/or sentence, acquitted 4,879 defendants, and pardoned 31,527 convicts according to the law.[44] The data showed the general contour and amount of work done and the types of cases handled by the Chinese judiciary, even if the data might not be as accurate a depiction of the reality as one would like.

After 1996 the Chinese state continued to push reforms in criminal justice, with the enactment of and amendments to the Criminal Code and the Criminal Procedural Law. More protection of human rights and the rights of the accused was made possible by the reduction of capital crimes, the return of the authority to the Supreme Court for approving the death penalty; by the expansion of safeguards for due process and the rights of criminal suspects and defendants, the state compensation for victims of wrongful cases; and by the abolition of reeducation through labor, among other developments. At the same time, newly emerging crimes invited legal responses to them—the addition of new crimes and their penalties to the criminal code. The rising crime rate reflected both desires and opportunities in a rapidly changing society to make money legally and illegally. The widening gap of inequality in income and wealth also enticed individuals to resort to crime as a way to gratify their desires. A prominent part of the increasing criminality was official corruption, including judicial corruption, to which the state responded with more prosecutions of corrupt officials at higher levels. Given human nature, corruption and misconduct by a certain percentage of state agents, including those in the law enforcement and the judiciary, were unavoidable, while corruption-fighting measures were successful only in relative terms.

Globalization facilitated all these developments, both positive and negative, and connected China with the world in a paradoxical way. For all these reasons, the performance of Chinese criminal justice is an ongoing story of both achievements and defects.

11

"Look toward Money"

Civil Justice in Post-Mao China, 1977–2018

In the Mao era the abolition of private businesses and private property of substance after 1956 preempted most civil disputes other than marriage and divorce. In contrast, in the post-Mao era the market economy and private enterprises became the norm, and private property and personal wealth came under the law's protection. This transformation led to a dramatic rise in civil disputes over all kinds of matter: land-use rights, property ownership, breach of contracts, violation of trademarks, debts, marriage and divorce, inheritance, and newly emerging matters such as torts and intellectual property rights. Some disputes fall under the category of administrative lawsuits, that is, citizens suing the local government for violation of their property rights or other interests.

The Civil Law Regime

After the 1979 Criminal Code and the Criminal Procedural Law were enacted, Chinese lawmakers began to work on a civil code. In April 1986 the National People's Congress adopted the Normal Principles of Civil Law (NPCL; minfa tongze), marking the first phase of writing a civil code. With 150 articles, the NPCL functioned as the primary civil statute and was regularly invoked in civil adjudications. Five years later, in April 1991, the Civil Procedural Law was enacted, with 290 articles.[1] Amended in 2007 and 2012, this law greatly facilitated civil justice. In 2004 the National People's Congress Legal System Work Committee floated a draft civil code for discussion. In June 2016 the draft of the first book (out of nine) of the civil code, *General Principles (minfa zongze)*, was made public by the National People's Congress. Continually under revision, the entire civil code has not been enacted as of this writing. Since a complete civil code was not available, many individual civil statutes were enacted to supplement the NPCL, such as the revised Marriage Law (1980, 2001), the Inheritance Law (1985), the Trademark Law (1983), the Land Management Law (1986), the Enterprise Bankruptcy Law (1986), the Copyright Law (1990), the Adoption Law (1991), the Urban Real Estate Management Law (1994), the Company Law (1994), the Arbitration Law (1994), the Contract Law (1999), and the Law on Rights in Rem (2007). These laws addressed civil disputes arising from the market economy and issues regarding marriage and family, as these kinds of disputes and issues became far more frequent and complicated than before due to the reforms.

The 1980 Marriage Law

In September 1980 the National People's Congress enacted the new Marriage Law, with thirty-seven articles, which superseded the 1950 version (with twenty-seven articles).[2] Chapter 1, "General Principles," listed practice of marriage freedom, monogamy, and *gender equality*; protection of legitimate rights of women, children, and the elderly, and *practice of family planning*; and prohibition of interference in marriage freedom, of bigamy, of quest for money and property in the name of marriage, and of abandonment and mistreatment of *family members*. Unlike the old marriage law, the new law explicitly named the goal of gender equality and protected family members, which made it in effect a marriage *and* family law. A related new agenda was to help family planning, or the population control policy.

Article 5 raised the age of marriage from twenty to twenty-two for men and from eighteen to twenty for women and stated that later marriage and later pregnancy should be encouraged. This was part of the recently launched state effort to curb the fast population growth that would soon be known as the "one-child policy."

Consistent with the 1950 Marriage Law and the pre-1949 marriage statutes, Article 7 required registration with the government office that issues marriage certificates for a marriage to be legally valid. In reality, many peasant families would skip marriage registration for a variety of reasons, including to escape the state restrictions on the number of births allowed a married couple. In 1980, and again in 1986, the Marriage Registration Regulations were issued to help enforce marriage registration, with little success in rural China. In 1989 the Supreme Court recognized unregistered marriage as "de facto marriage"(or "common law marriage," in Western terms), which had important implications when divorce and property division between a divorcing couple were adjudicated.[3]

Article 8 provided that after marriage the woman may become a member of the man's family, and vice versa. Husband and wife could also choose to use their own names. Article 16 allowed children to use either their father's or their mother's surname, and Article 21 supported the mutual rights and obligations of stepparents and stepchildren.

Article 31 provided for consensual divorce. Article 32 stated that either the wife or the husband could "mediate or directly launch a divorce lawsuit at court." The language in Article 32 made it possible for either party to file for divorce without first going through mediation by work unit leaders or village leaders, even though mediation by courts would still occur, especially when disputes were about the terms of the divorce.[4]

Under Article 34, those who violated the law would be subject to administrative penalty or legal penalty, depending on the circumstances. Article 35 authorized the courts to enforce their rulings on cases involving alimony, maintenance, support, property division, inheritance, and so on.

The 1980 Marriage Law emphasized the protection of the rights of women, children, and the elderly and the prohibition of abandonment and mistreatment of family members. This came about because in post-Mao China the traditional values of filial piety and the social custom of the younger generation supporting the old were breaking down. It pointed to the larger issue of social security for the elderly that spawned criminal and civil lawsuits.

The 2001 Amended Marriage Law

The NPCSC amended the 1980 Marriage Law in April 2001.[5] The new version grew to fifty-one articles. Added to the general principles were the prohibition of married persons cohabiting with someone other than their spouse and of domestic violence. Again, these two additions reflected changes in post-Mao society: a dramatic increase in extramarital affairs, to the point of married men having de facto concubines, and a rising public awareness and criticism of domestic violence. The concern about domestic violence would lead to the enactment by the National People's Congress of the Anti–Domestic Violence Law in December 2015.[6]

One major change in 2001 was to define property owned by husband and wife jointly and separately, a critical issue in divorce cases, which were fast increasing. Article 13 in the 1980 law had provided that husband and wife would jointly own property acquired during marriage and have equal rights to dispose of it. Article 17 in the 2001 version provided more specific definitions: now jointly owned property included wages or salaries and bonuses, income from the production and management of any business the couple owned, income from intellectual property, inherited or gifted property, and other property that should be jointly owned. Husband and wife have equal rights to dispose of this property. This article was directly relevant to one of the cases discussed in next section.

Article 18 lists property belonging to one party only: property owned before marriage, compensation for work injuries or disabilities, inherited or gifted property named to one party, exclusively personal items, and other property that should belong to one party.

Under Article 19, husband and wife may reach a written agreement on how to own and dispose jointly and separately owned property; if there is no such agreement or an agreement is unclear, Articles 17 and 18 apply; the agreement will be binding to both parties; and if either husband or wife owe debts, he or she should pay them with separately owned property. These amendments indicated a growing trend of disputes over property between husband and wife upon seeking a divorce because the reforms made it common for married couples to own property, whereas such issues had not existed in the Mao era.

Amendments were also needed to define the relationship between parents and children. Article 30 provides that children should respect parents' rights to marriage and not interfere with parents' remarriage and their life after remarriage; children's obligation to support their parents does not change because of changes in parents' marital relationship. This addressed another new social phenomenon: divorce and remarriage and children objecting to parents' remarriage out of concern for property inheritance became common.

Under Article 38, after divorce, the parent who does not directly raise the children has the right to visit the children, and the other party is obliged to assist in the matter. If the two parties cannot agree on the terms of such visits, the court will decide; and if such visits are not beneficial to the children's mental and physical health, it is up to the court to void the right to visit until causes to void the right cease. These additions indicated that such issues had also become common.

Corresponding to the prohibition of domestic violence and abandonment or mistreatment of family members, Article 43 provides that victims of such violations have the right to ask their work unit and residents committee or villager committee for intervention and mediation; committees should assist victims, and public security organs should stop domestic violence. At the request of victims of domestic violence, public security organs should impose administrative penalties on the perpetrator according to the Security Administrative Management Regulations.

Article 44 requires the courts to rule for victims of abandonment or mistreatment to get financial support from the perpetrator. Under Article 45, perpetrators of bigamy, domestic violence, abandonment, or mistreatment are subject to criminal prosecution. Article 46 allows the no-fault party of a divorce to request compensation if divorce results from bigamy, spouse cohabiting with another person, domestic violence, abandonment, or mistreatment.

Under Article 47, upon divorce, if one party hid, transferred, sold, or destroyed jointly owned property or faked debts to take property of the other party, the party shall receive less or no property. Article 48 authorizes the courts to enforce decisions in cases of alimony, maintenance, support, property division, inheritance, visitation rights, and so on; individuals and work units are obliged to assist the court in this.

Comparing the Marriage Laws of 1950, 1980, and 2001, it is clear that the law has become a marriage and family law. It offers more legal protection for the rights and interests of women, children, and the elderly and of women seeking divorce, and stipulates more legal sanctions against violations of such rights and interests. The development of the legal framework for protection of these rights is a positive outcome of the legal reform. Several cases regarding family support and divorce in the next section will show how Chinese courts enforced the new law.

Civil Disputes in a Changing Society and Economy

The absence of a full-fledged civil code was partially remedied by the NPCL, the Civil Procedural Law, and individual civil statutes. Together these laws have guided the civil litigations that have proliferated since the 1980s. In 2003, for example, 51 percent (2,266,476) of all civil cases (4,410,236) filed throughout the country were disputes over contractual obligations, while marital, familial, and inheritance disputes totaled 29 percent (1,264,037), and other civil disputes made up 19.9 percent (879,723).[7] The last category includes lawsuits over environmental damages and other rights-claiming (*weiquan*) issues.[8] This proliferation of civil lawsuits indicates the rapidly changing economic and social conditions in China as well as citizens' awareness of their rights and of the legal means available to redress infringements on such rights.

From another perspective, however, as Confucius would have said, the rise of civil lawsuits, especially those regarding marriage, family, property, and tort, is indicative of the declining morality of average citizens, especially with regard to malicious lawsuits. Indeed the pervasive mindset for pursuit of material and monetary gains (called "look toward money") and sexual gratification (called "sexual happiness") has trumped both Confucian and Socialist moral values, such as filial piety, compassion, righteousness, trustworthiness, frugality, and marital fidelity.[9] At the same time, in adjudicating or mediating civil disputes, an effort by the courts at aligning Heavenly reason, state law, and human relations is discernible, even if not articulated as such. The following civil cases focus on civil lawsuits for matters other than commercial and contractual disputes.

Divorce and Property

The divorce rate shot up in China beginning in the 1980s, in part because the notion that divorce means moral decay and social chaos was replaced by the view that personal freedom and pursuit of happiness are legitimate rights. The courts now take a different approach to divorce cases than in the Mao era. They no longer go to the communities where a spouse seeking divorce lives or to his or her work unit to investigate circumstances. Instead the courts ask the divorce-seeking spouse to produce evidence to support his or her claims. The courts continue to encourage reconciliation but will grant a divorce when it is determined that the emotional relationship between husband and wife is broken and reconciliation untenable. They then rule on issues of property division, alimony, and so on under the Marriage Law and the NPCL.[10]

Mr. Wang and Ms. Shen got married in May 1989, when Wang had a son from a previous marriage. In June 2009 Shen filed for divorce at the district court and Wang objected. The court ordered that they try to reconcile within a year. In March 2010 Shen sued again for divorce. While the divorce case was pending, Shen filed a lawsuit against Wang, accusing him of dispersing property jointly owned by the couple. Wang had started a company in 2000 and owned 63.24 percent of its stock in 2009. In August 2009, after Shen's first filing for divorce, Wang transferred his stock to his son, who in turn transferred the stocks (28.83 percent) to his investment partner, Mr. Cheng. As a result, Wang's son and Mr. Cheng became the majority stockholders of the company; they also changed the name of the company. Shen's lawsuit claimed that, anticipating a divorce, Wang was illegally disposing of the property jointly owned by the couple so that Shen would not get her share after the divorce. The three defendants—Wang, his son, and Cheng—argued that the stock transfers were completed in accordance with the Company Law and the Regulations on Company Registration and Management and therefore were entirely legal.

The court focused on three legal questions: whether the stocks owned by Wang constituted jointly owned property; the nature and effect of the stock transfer; and whether the stock transfer was acquisition in good faith on the part of Wang's son and Cheng. The court concluded, first, that because the company was created during the couple's marriage, the stock owned by Wang was jointly owned property. Second, since the Company Law did not cover the transfer of property jointly owned by married couples, the transfer had to be examined under the Marriage Law. The stock transfer made by Wang was not approved by his wife and therefore it was not legally valid. Third, Wang's son and Cheng received their stock at a price far below the company's market value, which did not constitute acquisition in good faith. Based on these findings, the court ruled for Shen and ordered the stock transfers be annulled.

The defendants appealed, on the ground that Shen did not have a legal standing to file a lawsuit against the stock transfers; the stock transfers were made with the approval of the company's board of stockholders; and the court wrongly applied the Marriage Law to decide the case, which should be judged under the Company Law. At the second trial, the intermediate court again ruled for Shen, reaffirming that the stocks in question were jointly owned property and therefore Shen had standing to sue for her property; that Wang's son and his close friend Cheng knew or should have known about the pending divorce of Wang and Shen; and that the stock price at transfer was far below the company's value, so that they did not receive the transfer in good faith under Article 106 of the Law on Rights in Rem.[11] This case shows that the 2001 amended Marriage Law helps women to defend their rights to jointly owned property in divorce cases. The court did enforce the law, despite the efforts by the husband to confuse the Marriage Law with the Company Law.

Another case was also decided under the Marriage Law. Mr. Xiong of Liangping county, Sichuan province, hit a Lotto jackpot worth ¥4.6 million in February 2015. He hid the winnings from his wife, Yuan, and asked for a divorce. To sweeten the deal, he would pay the mortgage on a jointly owned house that was to be divided between them and would also pay off ¥100,000 in debt that Yuan's family owed. The couple registered a consensual divorce at the district court within a week of Xiong's winning. Next day Xiong secretly claimed his winnings. When she heard what Xiong had done, Yuan filed a lawsuit at the district court, claiming that the Lotto winnings were jointly owned property prior to the divorce. Xiong's mother filed to join the lawsuit, claiming it was she who bought the Lotto tickets. The district court decided that since Yuan could not prove Xiong bought the tickets, the prize was not a property that the couple jointly owned; instead the couple and Xiong's parents jointly owned the money, so Yuan should get one-quarter of it. Yuan appealed to the intermediate court. By examining the time sequence of the tickets purchase and the divorce, and analyzing the divorce agreement, the intermediate court ruled that the tickets must have been bought by Xiong and therefore the winning was property Xiong and his wife jointly owned, in which case Yuan should get half of it.[12]

Family Support

As noted earlier, the revised marriage laws pointed to the fact that the Confucian values of filial piety and the traditional practice of family members supporting the young and the elderly waned, if not altogether disappeared, in post-Mao China.

In March 1991 Ms. Zhao and Mr. Yu, both of Shanghai, reached a divorce agreement by which their daughter, Wenshu, would live with Yu. Seven months later Yu married Ms. Song, and Wenshu went to live with Zhao's mother in another city. In 1995 Yu brought Wenshu back to Shanghai for a better education. In April 1998 Yu died. His second wife, Song, did not marry again and continued to live with Wenshu. In the meantime Zhao had remarried in 1992, and both she and her second husband were laid off a few years later. They lived with the husband's parents and two siblings in a small apartment (about three hundred square feet).

In 1999 Song filed a civil suit at the Nanshi District Court to force Wenshu to live with her birth mother. Zhao's lawyer argued in court that the marriage between Yu and Song had created a supportive relationship between them and Wenshu, which should survive Yu's death, and that because Zhao did not have stable income and lived in a worse housing condition, she should not be forced to take her daughter. The court ruled for Zhao, both on the legal point Zhao's lawyer made and on the ground that it was in the best interest of Wenshu, who wished to stay where she was. Song appealed and again lost her case.[13] The case file did not reveal the real motive for Song's lawsuit (that she and Wenshu might be unable to get along when the child became a teenager), but her argument did not stand up to legal scrutiny.

A more complicated scenario began in 1995, when an old couple, Mr. Zhang and Ms. Wan, bequeathed the second floor of a two-story house they owned to their granddaughter Qian. One year later the whole house was demolished for a development project, and they were paid ¥123,000 in compensation by the developer. They made an agreement with their three children: first son Yinglong received ¥56,000, daughter Jinfeng ¥56,000, and second son Jinhai ¥10,000 since his daughter Qian had gotten the second floor of the house, for which she was paid a sum in compensation by the developer. The old couple would live with their three children by turns, four months at a time. But Yinglong lived in Beijing, and traveling to Beijing to stay with him for four months every year became a burden for the old couple. Moreover in 1999, when they were staying in Jinhai's home, he went into prison on a criminal conviction. Feeling abandoned, the old couple filed a civil suit at the district court, requesting that their three children be ordered to arrange a permanent place for them to stay and provide monetary support.

Yinglong claimed that he did not fail to provide monetary support. Jinfeng also denied that her parents were unsupported. Qian, in court on behalf of her father, Jinhai, admitted that her grandparents were not properly supported. Instead of adjudicating, the court made efforts to mediate among the litigants, resulting in an agreement: the old couple would stay in a nursing home and their three children would pay monthly support of ¥500; ¥150 each from Yinglong and Jinfeng, and ¥200 from Qian on behalf of her father.[14] It appears that the old couple's favor to their granddaughter had caused unhappiness to their older son and their daughter, who were therefore unwilling to support their parents by equal shares. In the end, the court-mediated agreement respected the old couple's wish but also obligated Qian to pay a larger share in supporting her grandparents on behalf her father, which made the settlement acceptable to Yinglong and Jinfeng.

Tort

Tort—a wrongful act, other than a breach of contract, for which the damaged party may seek legal relief in the form of a financial remedy or an injunction—is a type of civil lawsuit that emerged in China only in the 1980s. In the Mao era no relevant law existed, nor would anyone think of launching such a suit. After the enactment of the NPCL in 1986, which covered tort, however, civil tort lawsuits proliferated.

According to Mr. Xu, on October 13, 1996, he was walking by Mr. Chen, who suddenly played a prank on Xu by lifting and swinging him so that Xu's feet knocked against a tree. A dog that belonged to Mr. Jiang and was lying under the tree jumped up and bit Xu's penis. After spending a lot of money on medical treatment, Xu was left with a narrowed urine track. Xu sued both Chen and Jiang at the district court, invoking Article 127 of the NPCL and asking for ¥18,494 in damages and future treatment costs. In court, Chen denied playing a prank on Xu, and because Xu was unable to substantiate his story, his claim against Chen was rejected. The court did rule that Jiang was negligent in leaving his dog unattended when his whole family was away from home; that the amount Xu asked for was inconsistent with his actual medical costs (he did not ask for other damages beyond medical costs); and that Jiang should pay Xu ¥16,010. Using Xu's accusation of Chen playing a prank, Jiang appealed to the intermediate court in order for Chen to share the payment to Xu, but lost his case.[15]

Another case arose from a rather ordinary accident. Two students, Gu and Yang, collided into each other when they were doing an exercise in a physical education class at a private school. While Yang was not injured, Gu suffered injuries to his left eye and left side of his face, and ended up with reduced eyesight after medical treatment. Gu sued the school and Yang at the district court, on the ground that the teacher did not conduct the class properly and that Yang did not act properly, holding both responsible for his injury. He wanted ¥46,006 in damages. The court ruled that the teacher had failed to foresee and prevent the accident and was partially responsible for Gu's injury, and that because Yang was under age and could not have foreseen the accident, he was not responsible. Citing several articles of the NPCL, the court ordered the private school to pay Gu ¥17,531. Yang was willing to pay Gu ¥2,000 and the court had no objection.

Both the school and Gu appealed to the intermediate court, which ruled that this was a no-fault case. The teacher followed the school curriculum in asking students to do the exercise and could not have foreseen and stopped an accident that happened in an instant. Both Gu and Yang were following the teacher's instructions and so were not at fault. According to the law, the court observed, in a no-fault case, parties involved in an accident should share civil liability based on the actual circumstances. It decided that the district court decision be annulled, the private school pay Gu ¥16,576, Yang pay Gu ¥5,712, and litigation costs be shared by the school (¥2,206), Yang (¥1,320), and Gu (¥880).[16]

A third case reflects a different aspect of the changing society. A new type of social entity that had not exist in the Mao era emerged, the real estate management committee (REMC), after the housing reform led to private homeownership. In large cities private residences were mostly apartments. In one apartment building in Shanghai, the REMC rented a basement space of 200 square meters to Mr. Han, an entrepreneur, for two years (May 2008 to April 2010). Han used the space to store bananas and enhance their ripeness with certain equipment. His operations in the space created moisture, a smell, and noise that lessened the quality of life and living conditions of Mr. Zhang, the owner of the unit directly above the basement space. In 2009 Zhang sued the REMC and Han, asking that Han vacate the basement and both defendants pay him damages in the amount of ¥10,000. Citing the regulations on the REMC and the Law on Rights in Rem, the court ruled that Han's operations did cause harm to Zhang's health and his property rights, so his operations should cease; the amount of ¥10,000 that Zhang asked for did not have a reasonable base, however, but Han should pay Zhang ¥500. The REMC was also at fault in renting the space to Han without considering the interests of the homeowners that it represented, but it did not directly cause harm to Zhang. The court in effect annulled the rental agreement between the REMC and Han. Both defendants appealed to the intermediate court and lost their cases.[17]

As these examples show, excluding the factor of corruption, the court rulings in tort cases (and some other civil cases) tend to strive for balanced decisions that will be fair and just and financially reasonable to all parties, and also for mediated compromises in no-fault cases. Of course, this is not always possible, especially when corruption is involved.

Pengci and Malicious Lawsuits

One type of malicious act and lawsuit known as *pengci* (breaking porcelain) emerged out of torts. It began with an influential case that transpired in Nanjing in 2006. On November 20 Mr. Peng, twenty-seven, was stepping off a bus when a woman named Xu, sixty-five, stumbled and fell to the ground. Peng helped Xu get to the sidewalk. Xu made a phone call to her son, who worked in the municipal public security bureau. Peng waited for Xu's son to arrive and then went with her and her son to a hospital. Peng paid ¥200 for Xu's treatment. While they were in the hospital, and after Xu and her son talked in private, Xu began to accuse Peng of bumping into her to cause her fall. Peng denied it. He and Xu's son went to the local police precinct to give their testimonies of the incident. In January 2007 Xu filed her tort case against Peng at the Gulou District Court. Since this was a she-said–he-said case, it was rather difficult to adjudicate. And the police lost the written notes of their testimonies in the precinct on the day of the incident. In September 2007, however, Judge Wang ruled for Xu and ordered Peng to pay ¥45,876 in damages. Peng appealed, but before the second trial, the two parties reached a settlement, with a clause that both parties not disclose the content of the settlement.

The damage to the public interest was done, however. Judge Wang's ruling in the first trial was based on one thing only: his reasoning that Peng helped Xu because he must have bumped her and thus felt responsible for her fall. As the case was widely publicized from the start, Wang's ruling was a bombshell. Worst of all, the ruling and its reasoning set a pernicious precedent for similar cases and rulings to come, so much so that few people in China would dare to be a Samaritan to help anyone who fell to the ground or otherwise got injured.[18]

In the meantime, a practice called *pengci* came into fashion: individuals would extort drivers for money by claiming they had been hit and injured and threatening to file a lawsuit; some drivers would just pay a sum of money in order to avoid further troubles.[19] This was the social-cultural context of the case discussed in an earlier chapter in which a young man stabbed to death a woman he actually did hit and injure.

Online Defamation

The internet age has begotten new types of crime and legal responses to them. A landmark case for adjudicating online defamation took place in Shanghai. In the early morning of October 18, 2008, Mr. Xie, a well-known movie director, died of a heart attack in a hotel. Next day a man named Song uploaded an article with a sensational title onto his blog on Sina.com, saying that Xie died when he was having sex with a prostitute. Four days later Song uploaded another sensational blog article saying that Xie had an illegitimate son with an actress, and the boy, who was brain-damaged, was living in the United States. On October 28 Song uploaded both articles onto his blogs on Sohu.com and QQ.com as well. On that day and after, Mr. Liu, whom Song cited as his source, also uploaded blog articles on Sohu.com, giving his "eyewitness" account of Xie's encounter with a prostitute in the hotel where he happened to be staying at the time and his personal sighting of Xie's brain-damaged child in the United States. Responding to these blog articles in October and November 2008, reporters from one TV station and five newspapers interviewed Song and Liu by telephone, and the duo confirmed their stories.

In February 2009 Ms. Xu, Xie's widow, sued Song and Liu for defamation at the Jin'an District Court. She demanded that the defendants publish statements of retraction and apology on all the media that carried or reported their defaming articles and pay her ¥100,000 for her financial loss (the cost of her collecting evidence) and ¥400,000 in damages for her psychological suffering. The defendants claimed that they had not uploaded the articles in question but that their blogs were hacked; in other words, they did not argue that the articles were truthful. The court found that the defendants failed to provide evidence that their blogs were hacked; furthermore they never offered any statement to contradict the articles' claims, and their interviews with reporters confirmed what the articles had said. Thus the fact of defamation was established. Significantly, the court took into account one piece of evidence from the plaintiff that the defendants caused serious damage to Xie's personal reputation: an online search of the names of Xie and Song *together* returned 300,000 pages on Google; 700,000 on Yahoo; 3.54 million on Baidu; and 7.38 million on Sohu. Citing relevant articles in the NPCL and the Supreme Court legal interpretations of defamation cases, the court ruled for Xu, but reduced the damages for financial loss to ¥89,951 (the actual cost of her collecting evidence) and for psychological sufferings to ¥200,000 (based on the average living standards in Shanghai). The defendants appealed and lost their case.[20]

Real Property

One condition in defining rights to real property is unique to China. In the Mao era a peasant who was a member of a people's commune could build a house on a piece of land, known as "house foundation land" (HFL), that was legally owned by the commune. After the family responsibility system replaced the commune system in the early 1980s, the land rights regime did not change. A household head continued to hold user rights to HFL while receiving farmland allocated according to the number of household members.[21] The dual and separable rights to the house as the owner and to the HFL as the user would explain a civil decision at the Fengxian District Court in Shanghai.

The Pans were a married couple with a daughter born in 1986. In 1993 Mr. Pan had an extramarital affair that resulted in an illegitimate child. In 2002 the couple agreed to a divorce; their daughter would live with Ms. Pan, and Mr. Pan would provide ¥10,000 a year as alimony. But he never paid it. In 2007 Mr. Pan signed an agreement to bequeath the house that he and Ms. Pan jointly owned to their daughter. In 2011 the daughter, now twenty-five, filed a civil suit to establish her ownership of the house because her father was attempting to renounce the 2007 agreement. In court Mr. Pan said that the house had been built by his parents in 1984 and he did not want to give it away; in addition, he would not have a place to live if he couldn't live there. Ms. Pan testified to the 2007 agreement. The court ruled for the daughter on the basis of the 2007 agreement and the fact that the daughter allowed her father to stay in the house. At the same time, the court made it clear that because the three family members equally shared the user rights to the HFL, which was separate from house ownership, Mr. Pan's share would remain his. The court noted that in case the house was demolished for a development project, Mr. Pan would have his equal share of the compensation paid by a developer for the HFL. Mr. Pan appealed to keep his ownership of the house but lost his case in the second trial.[22]

"Nail Household"

The growth of the economy in general, and the growth of private homeownership and real estate development in particular, spawned many civil disputes over land and house between owners and developers (who were often backed by the local government). In 2001 the State Council issued the Regulations on Management of Urban Housing Demolition and Relocation.[23] These allowed local governments, for the purpose of urban development, to relocate owners of houses to be demolished. The owners could sue at the local court against such plans, but as long as they were offered compensation and replacement houses, demolition would continue during the litigation. But after the Law on Rights in Rem was enacted in March 2007, the Regulations contradicted the Law. So in August 2007 the NPCSC amended another statute, the Urban Real Estate Management Law, with a provision stating that, for the sake of public interest, the state may acquire houses on state-owned land that belong to individuals or work units and provide compensation for the acquisition according to law to safeguard the owners' lawful rights and interests; to acquire houses owned by individuals, the owners' living conditions should be protected.[24] In January 2011 the State Council replaced the 2001 Regulations with the Regulations on Acquiring and Compensating for Houses on State-Owned Land.[25] Critically, under the Land Management Law, urban land was state-owned land, as was land taken by the state from rural communities. In other words, urbanization was going to turn most land in the country into state-owned land, and all land transactions were essentially about user rights, not ownership rights.

Local governments had incentives to issue permits to developers for projects, since they would collect state-required fees from developers and expect tax revenues down the road. Even discounting corruption (bribes and kickbacks) that was common in such schemes, conflicts arose between developers armed with government permits to demolish houses for new projects and owners of those houses who were unwilling to accept the offer from developers for compensation. Two opposing scenarios existed: On the one hand, some owners would make unreasonable and unrealistic demands for compensation or simply did not want to leave their home for sentimental reasons; hence the phenomenon known as "nail household." On the other hand, some developers would offer subvalue compensation and forcibly remove owners and demolish their houses by any means, to the point of hiring thugs to brutalize resisting owners. Both scenarios led to civil (and criminal) lawsuits.

Many cases of this nature arrived in courts. In one case, Mr. Wu, owner of a house in the Jiulongpo district of the Chongqing municipality, Sichuan province, refused several offers from a developer to make room for a project. After dozens of attempts at a deal failed, his house stood alone in the middle of the project site, with the ground all around it dug 10 meters deep, as required by the project. The District Housing Management Bureau tried and failed several times to persuade Wu to move. In January 2007 the Bureau issued an administrative order for Wu to vacate in fifteen days. Wu did not act. The Bureau filed at the district court for an injunction. Supporting the Bureau, the court notified Wu that the date for demolishing his house was March 22. Climbing onto the roof of his house on March 21, Wu told onlookers that he would never leave his house. But nothing happened on March 22. Then, on March 24, Wu appealed against the district court injunction to the Chongqing Superior Court. The superior court sustained the district court injunction, however, and ordered Wu to vacate by April 10. Finally, on April 2, Wu signed an agreement to vacate. Apparently all the stunts Wu had performed was for the purpose of maximizing his compensation.[26] This local drama was but one example of how such disputes would occur, how litigants (both homeowners and developers) would fight, and how the courts handled them, but variations of the scenario were endless.[27]

The Problem of Civil Enforcement

In the Wu case just described, it appears that the district court took no action to enforce the injunction on March 22 in order to avoid a physical confrontation, and then another possible confrontation was avoided when Wu signed the agreement. In many civil cases, however, court rulings fail to be enforced, typically regarding payments of money or transfer of property. As Peerenboom points out, "In contrast to other countries that assign the task of enforcing court judgments and orders to a marshal or the police, PRC courts are responsible for enforcing their own judgments. Enforcement of civil judgments and arbitral awards is notoriously difficult in China, with as many as 50 percent of judgments and awards going unenforced."[28] Civil enforcement was as "notoriously difficult" in post-Mao China as it had been in the imperial and Republican eras, for the same reason: some litigants who lost cases did not respect court judgments, and there was little that could be done about it.

To help address the problem, the Supreme People's Court issued in 2013 (and amended in 2017) the regulations on publicizing in print media and online social media the identities of those who defy civil judgments without legitimate reasons; those who are identified could face damage to their credit in business or personal transactions.[29] Starting in 2014, for instance, the Sichuan Superior Court would periodically publish lists of defaulting litigants who lost their cases. Those on these blacklists faced restrictions on high-price consumption (e.g., purchasing luxury cars or flying first class). Between May and August 2017 the court published three lists of 11,359 enterprises and individuals. The third list, published in August, named 458 enterprises and 3,044 individuals; the largest amount owed by a single entity was ¥93.6 million and the smallest was ¥400. In response to the bad publicity, seventy-five enterprises paid their creditors ¥34.417 million in total, and 509 individuals paid their creditors ¥74.578 million (as of August 2017).[30] Obviously those who paid to honor civil judgments were still a minority of those blacklisted.

Finally, since the founding of the PRC there has been an official mechanism for citizens to bring their grievances, legal or otherwise, to the authorities by writing to or visiting the "offices of letters and visits" at all levels of the government above the county. Victims of wrongful suits or their families would try to right their wrongs through that mechanism and seek redress of their grievances that occurred at the local level. In recent decades, some local officials have tried to stop people visiting higher-level governments, including the central government in Beijing, by illegally abducting such visitors on their way to Beijing or provincial capitals. There have also been cases where no wrongs were committed but the losing parties in lawsuits simply refused to accept the court's decision and attempted to find ways outside the judicial process to overthrow such decisions.

Civil disputes tend to capture different facets and fabrics of the lived experiences of average citizens in a given society at a given time, and civil rulings in courts reflect the way the civil law and the judiciary deal with various social-economic issues in that society. This brief survey of civil justice in post-Mao China has attempted to convey the drastic and lasting changes engendered by the reform and opening policies since the early 1980s. Through the lens of civil disputes and rulings one may glimpse how

Chinese citizens lived, quarreled, and compromised in their changing social-economic environment, using the judicial process to achieve their objectives. From the Chinese state's perspective, resolving the mounting civil disputes in a fair and equitable way, through court mediation and adjudication, would go a long way toward maintaining social stability, considered essential for economic growth, and preventing civil disputes from escalating into violent conflicts that have to be dealt with by criminal justice. For all these reasons, the court's tradition of utilizing both mediation and adjudication has continued to find relevance in the twenty-first century. In a sense, court actions in civil cases often point to an interaction between laws on books and laws in action, reflecting an enduring effort to achieve justice as an alignment of Heavenly reason, state law, and human relations and feelings, even though the notion was rarely articulated in such language.

Conclusion

Heaven Has Eyes

The history of law and justice in China from ancient times to the twenty-first century has been a long play of change and continuity in a crucial dimension of state governance. Lawmaking and law-enforcing has taken place in multidimensional interactions among philosophical-moral, political, economic, social, and cultural factors and between rulers and officials, lawmakers and law-enforcers, state agents and social actors, and, in the past 150 years or so, between indigenous traditions and Western influences. It is these interactions that underlie the centuries-old accumulations and more recent transformations of philosophical-moral ideas, legal principles, state laws, juridical institutions, and judicial practices. These accumulations and transformations have largely informed laws and judicial practices in China today. The latter continue to evolve, amid similar interactions and with similarly intended and unintended consequences. Thus an interactive-contextual understanding of Chinese law and justice past and present is called for, and it may encourage a cautious belief in their continuous movement toward justice for all and human rights protection.

Context 1: Law and justice are imbedded in the country's dominant ideology, political system, economic patterns, social structures, and cultural practices. Interactions among all these factors resulted in the kind of law and justice that have been adopted and practiced in China. The Confucian ideology and the imperial system that came into being more than two millennia ago were the key determinants for the design of law and justice needed for governing society, while the patriarchal family and the agrarian society also informed the features of law and justice in the imperial era. In consequence, the imperial state's judicial functions and legal practices constituted part of the political-social-moral order. Ideally, justice was to be achieved by state law in an alignment with Heavenly reason (or ultimate morality) and with human relations (and/or feelings) found in Chinese society. The perceived alignment made the law and justice in the imperial era functional in maintaining peace and order, albeit with flaws that were either particular to Chinese conditions or common to all premodern societies. Importantly, imperial Chinese law and justice were not stagnant and unchanging, but dynamic and flexible, allowing spatial and temporal variations to a degree from the penal code and responding to the changes in the state, society, economy, demography, and culture during more than two millennia. It is a critical fact, however, that the most radical changes in Chinese law and justice came about in the twentieth century, hence the next context.

Context 2: Chinese law and justice may be roughly divided into two periods: prior to the arrival of Westerners in the sixteenth century and especially prior to the Opium War of 1840–1842, when the Chinese legal system and judicial practices developed independently of Western influences; and after 1842, when interactions between the Chinese state and Western nations and China's repeated defeats by the West eventually led to the reforms in Chinese law and justice in the twentieth century, starting in the final decade of the Qing dynasty and continuing to this day. Law and justice in Western nations also went through changes and reforms, evolving from Roman law and through the Middle Ages, when divine ordeals, the Inquisition, judicial tortures, and various cruel and unusual punishments were practiced, to modern laws and judicial practices based on natural rights, legal equality, the rule of law, judicial independence, and due process.

It was a decisive factor in the unfolding of modern world history that much of the legal-judicial reforms in Western nations had already begun when the encounters between China and the West first occurred, and had been largely completed when the Opium Wars transpired. For that reason, it is Chinese law and justice that have been moving much closer to their Western counterparts, and it is the Western-originated ideas and principles—the rule of law, judicial independence, and due process—that have guided the Chinese legal-judicial reform. Thus underpinning the reform was a key moral and philosophical shift, as Confucian familial, social, and political hierarchies were replaced by natural rights, legal equality, and the human dignity of all persons. These notions informed the reform goals, but living up to the goals in actual practice at all levels of the judiciary and the state system as a whole was and remains a challenge. The late Qing (1901–1911), the Republican (1912–1949), and the post-Mao (1977–) legal-judicial reforms, which were interrupted by the Mao era (1949–1976), were part of China's transformation into modernity in economic, social, political, legal, and cultural realms in the larger process of globalization.

The legal-judicial reforms were not an inexorable march toward the Western model, however. One might view the spread of Western theories and practices of law and justice throughout the non-Western world as an exercise of "legal Orientalism," an epistemology and a strategy of imperialism and colonialism; in parallel, Chinese efforts at reforming law and justice to approximate the Western model can be seen as the manifestation and result of "self-Orientalization."[1] In this light, Mao's endeavors to create a New China by breaking away from both Chinese tradition and the Western model, in the legal realm as well as others, may be seen as an imaginative but failed attempt to resist self-Orientalization. The reluctance among Nationalist officials to fully embrace the Western model may also be understood in the same vein.

Besides subjective inclinations of historical actors such as Nationalist and Communist officials, objective economic-social conditions in twentieth-century China did not offer enough necessary resources for the materialization of a Western-style judicial system, including modern prisons. Moreover Chinese law and judicial practices reformed in Western fashion would still uphold the prevailing political, social, and economic order in China of the twentieth and twenty-first century, which differed from those in the imperial era and in Western nations. Last, while Chinese legal principles and terminologies evolved in the twentieth century and beyond, the age-old notion of justice as an alignment of Heavenly reason, state law, and human relations or feelings was never far from the Chinese legal mind, with "Heavenly reason" or ultimate morality constantly redefined at various times.[2]

Context 3: Despite the international context, the everyday practices of Chinese law have involved constant interactions between state actions and societal responses rooted in the Chinese social and cultural soil. Three categories of players have figured in political-social-legal games. To begin with, the "state" is not an abstraction but material institutions and human beings who staff them. Two categories of players exist in the state system: policymakers and lawmakers (principals) and officials and functionaries who operate the system, including the judiciary (agents). The central government officials (principals) are instrumental in pushing reform agendas, making laws, and building judicial institutions, but equally essential are the ways in which state agents implement or enforce laws and operate the judiciary, or fail to do so. Besides the issue of professional competence, the dynamics of the principal-agent relationship—a certain percentage of agents break laws, rules, regulations, or professional ethics in performing their jobs for principal (so that mechanisms to monitor agents must be part of the system)—is a challenge to principals in implementing and enforcing policies and laws, a challenge that is universal and ubiquitous in all forms of state systems and large organizations.[3] The Chinese judiciary is no exception.

A third category of players—ordinary people governed by the legal-judicial system—is also crucial in shaping how law and justice work or fail to work as designed. Many variables in the convergence of interactions between principal and agents within the state system, and between the state system and society at large, make significant differences in legal outcomes and their social-political ramifications. Social actors and citizens—who are not monolithic but differentiated in social status, education, wealth or income, and access to power and resources—are not passive recipients of whatever laws the state enacts and actions the state takes. People engaging in criminality may be considered one type of societal response to the state. State-building, which involves an expansion of state power, entails more and more state laws and regulations. Resistance to the expansion of state power includes people breaking laws and violating rules and regulations, such as corruption committed by state agents and crimes by social actors. Such resistances lead to the cycles of lawmaking, lawbreaking, and law-enforcing (in criminal justice in particular) and actualize state power and its limits in a critical dimension. State power is daily contested and continually delineated by the practical boundary of societal compliance and state enforcement, within which the power is upheld and beyond which resistance to the power escapes penalty.[4]

Moreover, ordinary citizens adapt to the changing legal-judicial framework and its impact on their lives and use the law and court system to advance or protect their own interests to the fullest possible extent. Especially in the early twentieth century, when legal-judicial reforms began to unfold, citizens (and their lawyers) learned to use and manipulate laws and judicial procedures as additional tools in their cultural repertoire of daily struggle for a better life, along with informal, customary, and extralegal mechanisms embedded in the power structures of local society. It is natural and unavoidable that citizens will use and manipulate the law and court system for their own interests. Such use of state resources increases the cost of governing, of maintaining and operating the judicial system and the state system as a whole, which in turn affects the outcomes of state functions and of the legal-judicial reform.

This nexus of everyday interactions of lawmakers and state agents, and of law and state agents and social actors (both elite and nonelite), is at the heart of what transpires as law, legal culture, and judicial practices. It is as ancient as Chinese history, and has remained alive and active in the twenty-first century. The Confucian notion of "cultivated self, regulated family, well-governed state, and peace all under Heaven" is an ideal world to strive for. History tells us that in reality there is a constant tug of war between the state and society, between elites and nonelites, and among various interest groups of all social strata; consequently the normal state of affairs in the legal-judicial realm, as well as in others, is always a negotiated and managed balance between societal resistance to and societal compliance with state power, between state sanction and state suasion, and between yin and yang, as it were, to varying degrees in different times.

Context 4: The achievements and defects of Chinese law and justice in the past and in the present may be better understood from a comparative perspective, considering law and justice in other countries, both the developing and the developed nations. The design of laws and judicial institutions could have been worse or better under different historical conditions, thus making differences in legal and social outcomes. For this reason, legal-judicial reform in general was and is necessary and desirable in China (and elsewhere). Unfortunately, however, while judicial systems and practices are framed by laws, in practice they can deviate from laws for a variety of reasons. And whether or not they deviate, they may or may not fully achieve justice. Even with the best-designed laws and judicial systems, their legal and social outcomes in reality may not be as ideal or perfect as designed or desired, and substantive justice may not be fully achieved even when (or because) procedural justice is. Also, what constitutes substantive justice is not beyond debate; the controversy over the death penalty in different countries is a good example.

Why is perfect justice hard to come by, even with the best-designed law and judicial system? To answer the question, we quote from the dust jacket of a recent book on criminal justice in the United States:

> A child is gunned down by a police officer; an investigator ignores critical clues in a case; an innocent man confesses to a crime he did not commit; [and] a jury acquits a killer. The evidence is all around us: our system of justice is fundamentally broken.... Even if the system operated exactly as it was designed to, we would still end up with wrongful convictions, trampled rights, and unequal treatment. This is because the roots of injustice lie not in the dark hearts of racist police officers or dishonest prosecutors but within each and every one of us.[5]

That is, achieving perfect justice—both substantive and procedural justice—is a challenge for humankind, not for one country or one culture. Due to human fallibility, justice can be rendered only in relative, not absolute, terms, in China and elsewhere.[6] Yet striving for justice for all as an absolute goal is a necessary condition, if not a sufficient one, for justice to be done as much as humanly possible. Without such a goal or commitment, justice would not be done even in relative terms. In the end, it might be fitting to invoke the popular Chinese expression "Heaven has eyes" to convey the point: the legal-judicial reform in China should and will continue, and more justice and more human rights protections are to be achieved, in an ongoing and never-ending endeavor.

Notes

Introduction

1. The word "justice" as used in this book in two meanings: first, what is just, and second, judicial systems and practices. The proper meaning should be clear in context.
2. One scholar translated *tianli* as "natural reason" in this formulation. See Wejen Chang, *In Search of the Way: Legal Philosophy of the Classic Chinese Thinkers* (Edinburgh: Edinburgh University Press, 2016), 493.

Chapter 1

1. "Daxue Zhangju" (Passages and sentences in Great Learning), in *Sishu Wujing* (Beijing: Beijing guji chubanshe, 1994), 1:5.
2. Benjamin I. Schwartz, *The World of Thought in Ancient China* (Cambridge, MA: Harvard University Press, 1985), 350–356.
3. "Intellectual" source of law and justice in traditional China may also be called "spiritual" or "religious" source. For related discussion, see Yonglin Jiang, *The Mandate of Heaven and the Great Ming Code* (Seattle: Washington University Press, 2011).
4. "Tang Shi" (Oath by Shang Tang) and "Tai Shi" (Oath by King Wu), in *Sishu Wujing*, 1:383, 407–408.
5. *Sishu Wujing*, 1:417.
6. *Xun Zi* (Hangzhou: Zhejiang guji chubanshe, 1999), 276.
7. *Quan Tang Wen*, e-book, http://www.txshuku.net/book/0/562/index.html, accessed December 11, 2017, juan 6–9; Shen Jiaben, *Lidai Xingfa Kao* (Beijing: Zhonghua shuju, 1985), 616–617.
8. "Xingfazhi," in *Xin Tang Shu* (Shamghai: Kaiming shudian, 1934); *Zizhi Tongjian* (Beijing: Zhonghua shuju, 1956), 15:6830.
9. For a solid and insightful study of stories about Bao and common people's understanding of crimes, punishments, and legal practices reflected in such stories, see Xu Zhongming, *Baogong Gushi: Yige Kaocha Zhongguo Falü Wenhua De Shijiao* (Beijing: Zhongguo zhengfa daxue chubanshe, 2002).
10. Zhang Tian, *Bao Zheng Ji* (Beijing: Zhonghua shuju, 1962), 12–13, 16–19.
11. Jiang Liangqi, *Donghua Lu* (Beijing: Zhonghua shuju, 1980), 280–281.
12. Ibid., 173.
13. Ibid., 276.
14. Chen Tao, *Tongzhi Zhongxing Jingwai Zouyi Yuebian* (Shanghai: Shanghai shudian, 1985), 8:1–3. The memorials in the collection are undated. Page numbers cited here

are in the original edition in traditional binding where a page number sits at the fold of two pages, since no new page numbers are in the reprint edition.
15. Ibid., 6:32–33.
16. *Tangyin bishi* literally means "parallel cases in the shade of the pear tree," but would be better translated as "parallel cases solved by eminent judges" because "the pear tree" was a literary allusion referring to a wise and benevolent official. See Robert H. van Gulik, trans., *Crime and Punishment in Ancient China: Tang Yin Pi Shih* (Hong Kong: Orchid Press, 2007), 6.
17. Gui Wanrong and Wu Na, *Tangyin Bishi*, in *Siku Quanshu* (1779), Zi section.
18. For an easily accessible example, see Jonathan Spence, *The Death of Woman Wang* (New York: Penguin, 1979), 99–139.
19. For a longer discussion of the issue, see Brian E. McKnight, *Law and Order in Sung China* (New York: Cambridge University Press, 1992), 1–33.
20. *Sishu Wujing*, 1:42–43.
21. *Han Fei Zi* (Beijing: Zhonghua shuju, 2007), 285.
22. "Xingfazhi 1," in *Yuan Shi* (Shanghai: Kaiming Shudian, 1934).
23. On Confucianism and Legalism, also see Derk Bodde and Clarence Morris, *Law in Imperial China* (Philadelphia: University of Pennsylvania Press, 1973), 17–29; Geoffrey MacCormack, *The Spirit of Traditional Chinese Law* (Athens, GA: University of Georgia Press, 1996); Wejen Chang, *In Search of the Way: Legal Philosophy of the Classic Chinese Thinkers* (Edinburgh: Edinburgh University Press, 2016).
24. Meng refused to kill himself and was imprisoned. Later he was again ordered to kill himself or be killed. He took poison. See *Shi Ji* (Beijing: Zhonghua shuju, 1959), 8:2551, 2567–2570.
25. Mark E. Lewis, *The Flood Myths of Early China* (Albany: State University of New York Press, 2006), 132.
26. One Chinese scholar argues that some pieces of archaeological evidence of the Xia may have been found but have previously not been identified as such. See Sun Qingwei, *Dingzai Yuji* (Beijing: Sanlian shudian, 2018).
27. "Outburst Flood at 1920 BCE Supports Historicity of China's Great Flood and the Xia Dynasty," *Science* 353, no. 6299 (August 5, 2016): 579–582. For more on the myth about Yu and the flood, see Lewis, *The Food Myths of Early China*.
28. *Sishu Wujing*, 1:347.
29. Pu Jian, *Zhongguo Gudai Fazhi Congchao* (Beijing: Guangming ribao chubanshe, 2001), 1:12–14; Shen, *Lidai Xingfa Kao*, 9–13; Wu Shuchen et al., *Zhongguo Chuantong Falü Wenhua* (Beijing: Beijing daxue chubanshe, 1994), ch. 3.
30. "Xingfazhi," in *Han Shu* (Shanghai: Kaiming Shudian, 1934).
31. *Shi Ji*, 7:2231, 2236–2237.
32. Pu, *Zhongguo Gudai*, 1:195–241, 487–516. Prior to their conquest by the Qin, the Chu and other states also saw developments of law, legal philosophy, and judicial procedures, even though their influence on the imperial era is unclear. See Susan Roosevelt Weld, "Grave Matters: Warring States Law and Philosophy," in C. Stephen Hsu, ed., *Understanding China's Legal System: Essays in Honor of Jerome A. Cohen* (New York: New York University Press, 2003), 122–179.

33. Anthony J. Barbieri-Low and Robin D. S. Yates, *Law, State, and Society in Early Imperial China: A Study with Critical Edition and Translation of the Legal Texts from Zhangjiashan Tomb No. 247* (Leiden: Brill, 2015), 62–64.
34. "Xingfazhi," in *Han Shu*.
35. Up to the reign of Emperor He (89–105 CE), an imperial amnesty would allow convicts sentenced to death to be punished by castration, one grade reduction of punishment. After Emperor He abolished castration as a penalty sometime after 97, those who were spared death under an imperial amnesty would be punished by servitude in frontiers. See Xu Tianlin, *Donghan Huiyao* (Shanghai: Guji chubanshe, 1978), 508, 513–519; Shen, *Lidai Xingfa Kao*, 187–190.
36. *Han Fei Zi*, 53.
37. Pu, *Zhongguo Gudai*, 1:405–414.
38. Ibid., 1:524–525.
39. Ibid. 1:526–527.
40. Shen, *Lidai Xingfa Kao*, 892–895; Pu, *Zhongguo Gudai*, 1:587–589.
41. Pu, *Zhongguo Gudai*, 1:579–585; Xu, *Donghan Huiyao*, 506–507, 511; Yang Chen, *Sanguo Huiyao* (Beijing: Zhonghua shuju, 1956), 327–328.
42. Pu, *Zhongguo Gudai*, 1:578.
43. "Xingfazhi," in *Weishu* (Shanghai: Kaiming shudian, 1934); *Zizhi Tongjian*, 9:4279.
44. Shen, *Lidai Xingfa Kao*, 1800–1802.
45. Emperor Cheng (r. 32–6 BCE) of the Han dynasty said that judicial practices in the Zhou era (1045–221 BCE) already included five observations, eight deliberations, three interrogations, three nonliabilities, and three amnesties. The eight deliberations were the same eight categories discussed here. See "Xingfazhi," in *Han Shu*.
46. See Valerie Hansen, *The Open Empire: A History of China to 1800* (New Haven, CT: Yale University Press, 2015), 175, 178.
47. See Diana Lary, *Chinese Migrations: The Movement of People, Goods, and Ideas over Four Millennia* (Lanham, MD: Rowman and Littlefield, 2012), 39–40.
48. Starting in 1929, one *li* equals half a kilometer, or 500 meters, but in the imperial era, the distance of one *li* varied over many centuries, being more or less than 500 meters.
49. "Xingfazhi," in *Xin Tang Shu* (Shanghai: Kaiming shudian, 1934). The material and size of the flogging instruments varied in subsequent dynasties; inheriting the Ming practice, the Qing penal code of 1715 provided that heavy and light flogging instruments were canes and both were about 1.22 meter long, tapering from 11.2 cm (one end) to 7.7 cm (the other end) in diameter for heavy flogging and 9.45 cm to 5.95 cm for light flogging. They were to be applied on the buttocks only. Flogging as judicial torture was to use cane of the same length but thicker in diameter, and it was applied on the buttocks and thighs. See Shen, *Lidai Xingfa Kao*, 1214–1218; Shen Zhiqi, *Daq ing Lü Jizhu* (1715; reprint, Beijing: Falü chubanshe, 2000), 14.
50. Du Jiwen, *Fojiao Shi* (Beijing: Zhongguo shehui kexue chubanshe, 1991), 277–290; Qing Xitai and Tang Dachao, *Daojiao Shi* (Beijing: Zhongguo shehui kexue chubanshe, 1994), 92–109.
51. The English translation of these categories follows Wallace Johnson, trans., *The T'ang Code: Volume 2: Specific Articles* (Princeton, NJ: Princeton University Press, 1997).

52. "Xingfazhi," in *Xin Tang Shu*.
53. *Tanglü Shuyi* (Beijing: Zhonghua shuju, 1983), Article 48.
54. Hansen, *The Open Empire*, 239.
55. Ibid., 237, 246–248.
56. "Xingfazhi, 1," in *Song Shi* (Shanghai: Kaiming shudian, 1934).
57. Ibid.
58. Pu, *Zhongguo Gudai*, 3:488–490.
59. Hansen, *The Open Empire*, 331–332.
60. For a study of the 1291 code and an English translation of its reconstruction (the complete code was lost), see Paul Heng-chao Ch'en, *Chinese Legal Tradition under the Mongols: The Code of 1291 as Reconstructed* (Princeton, NJ: Princeton University Press, 1979).
61. "Xingfazhi, 1," in *Yuan Shi* (Shanghai: Kaiming shudian, 1934); *Dayuan Tongzhi Tiaoge* (Beijing: Falü chubanshe, 2000).
62. "Xingfazhi, 2," in *Xing Yuan Shi* (Shanghai: Kaiming shudian, 1934).
63. Ibid.
64. Hansen, *The Open Empire*, 349–350, 378–379.
65. "Xingfazhi, 1," in *Ming Shi* (Shanghai: Kaiming shudian, 1934).
66. *Da Ming Lü* (Beijing: Falü chubanshe, 1999), 20.
67. Shen, *Lidai Xingfa Kao*, 1136.
68. *Da Qing Lüli* (Beijing: Falü chubanshe, 1999), 4.
69. *Bo'an Huibian* (Beijing: Falü chubanshe, 2009), 26–28.
70. For a view that the case collections did not rise to the status of case law, see Wang Zhiqiang, *Qingdai Guojiafa Duoyuan Chayi Yu Jiquan Tongyi* (Beijing: Shehui kexue wenxian chubanshe, 2017), 137–172; for a view that the case collections and their use by officials in adjudications constituted "an indigenous case precedent system," see R. Randle Edwards, "The Role of Case Precedent in the Qing Judicial Process as Reflected in Appellate Rulings," in C. Stephen Hsu, ed. *Understanding China's Legal System* (New York: New York University Press, 2003), 180–209.
71. Wang, *Qingdai Guojiafa*, 27–65.
72. *Da Qing Lüli*, 122.
73. Yang Qiang, *Qingdai Menggu Fazhi Bianqian Yanjiu* (Beijing: Zhongguo Zhengfa daxue chubanshe, 2010), 39–56; Bai Jinglan, *Yiti Yu Duoyuan: Qingdai Xinjiang Falü Yanjiu, 1759--1911* (Beijing: Zhongguo zhengfa daxue chubanshe, 2013).
74. Wang, *Qingdai Guojiafa*, 2–26. Wang emphasized the interactions and power balances between the central government and provincial-local officials, which is a point well taken, but the perspective of the Qing as a multiethnic empire is to be noted as well.
75. For Qing officials' approaches to handling Miao people who were involved in violent conflicts with Han settlers, which included applying local customs instead of statutes, see Donald S. Sutton, "Violence and Ethnicity on a Qing Colonial Frontier: Customary and Statutory Law in the Eighteenth-Century Miao Pale," *Modern Asian Studies* 37, no. 1 (2003): 41–60; for more on the Qing legal pluralism and its modern ramifications, see Pär Cassel, *Grounds of Judgment: Extraterritoriality*

and Imperial Power in Nineteenth-Century China and Japan (New York: Oxford University Press, 2012).

76. Timothy Brook, Jérôme Bourgon, and Gregory Blue, *Death by a Thousand Cuts* (Cambridge, MA: Harvard University Press, 2008), 13–15.
77. For more on gruesome ways to execute offenders in imperial China, see Itaru Tomiya, ed., *Capital Punishment in East Asia* (Kyoto: Kyoto University Press, 2012), 1–127.
78. Brook, Bourgon, and Blue, *Death by a Thousand Cuts*, 90; also see Bodde and Morris, *Law in Imperial China*, 93–94.
79. Brook, Bourgon, and Blue, *Death by a Thousand Cuts*, 68–96.
80. One study finds that on average there were around five instances of dismemberment per year during the Qing dynasty; one-third of the condemned were punished for rebellions, and over half for killing an entire family or killing a parent or a senior member in the family, including a wife killing her husband or a servant killing a master. See Jérôme Bourgon and Julie Erismann, "Figures of Deterrence in Late Imperial China: Frequency, Spatial Repartition, and Types of Crimes Targeted by Dismemberment under the Qing Dynasty," *Crime, History & Societies* 18, no. 2 (2014): 49–84.
81. *Bo'an Huibian*, 295–297.
82. Brook, Bourgon, and Blue, *Death by a Thousand Cuts*, 89–94.
83. "Xingfazhi, 2," in *Xing Yuan Shi*.
84. Shen, *Lidai Xingfa Kao*, 71–81.
85. Joanna Waley-Cohen, "Collective Responsibility in Qing Law," in Karen G. Turner, James V. Feinerman, and R. Kent Guy, eds., *The Limits of the Rule of Law in China* (Stanford, CA: Stanford University Press, 2000), 112–131.
86. *Da Qing Lüli*, 668.

Chapter 2

1. For English translations of officials' titles in imperial China, this book follows Charles O. Hucker, *A Dictionary of Official Titles in Imperial China* (Stanford, CA: Stanford University Press, 1985).
2. "Xingfazhi, 1," in *Song Shi* (Shanghai: Kaiming shudian, 1934).
3. Zhang Jinfan, *Zhongguo Sifa Zhidu Shi* (Beijing: Renmin fayuan chubanshe, 2004), 270–272.
4. "Xingfa Zhi," in *Ming Shi* (Shanghai: Kaiming shudian, 1934); Zhang, *Zhongguo Sifa*, 311–315.
5. "Shizu benji er," in *Qingshi Gao* (Shanghai: Lianhe shudian, 1943).
6. Zhang, *Zhongguo Sifa*, 375.
7. On circuit judicial commissioners in the Song, see McKnight, *Law and Order in Sung China*, 230–250.
8. "Xingfazhi, 1," in *Song Shi*.
9. William Rowe, *China's Last Empire: The Great Qing* (Cambridge, MA: Belknap Press, 2009), 31–62.

10. "Shangshu-Lüxing," in *Sishu Wujing*, 1:475.
11. *Shi Ji*, 1:253; *Zizhi Tongjian*, 1:243.
12. Pu, *Zhongguo Gudai*, 1:472.
13. *Tanglü Shuyi* (Beijing: Zhonghua shuju, 1983), Article 487.
14. *Da Qing Lüli*, 206–207, 209–210, 214; Shen, *Daqing Lü Jizhu*, 260–265, 269–271, 290–293.
15. Wang, *Qingdai Guojiafa*, 66–89.
16. "Xingfazhi," in *Han Shu*.
17. "Xingfazhi," in *Tang Shu*.
18. "Xingfazhi," in *Song Shi*.
19. *Da Ming Lü* (Beijing: Falü chubanshe, 1999), 212.
20. "Xingfazhi, 3," in *Song Shi*.
21. Jiang, *Donghua Lu*, 294.
22. Ibid., 469–470.
23. R. Kent Guy, "Rule of Man and the Rule of Law in China: Punishing Provincial Governors during the Qing," in Karen G. Turner, James V. Feinerman, and R. Kent Guy, eds., *The Limits of the Rule of Law in China* (Stanford, CA: Stanford University Press, 2000), 88–111.
24. *Tanglü Shuyi*, Article 359.
25. *Da Ming Lü*, 174; *Da Qing Lüli*, 473.
26. For a survey of the practice evolving over time, see Qiang Fang, "Hot Potatoes: The Chinese Complaint Systems from the Early Times to the Late Qing (1898)," *Journal of Asian Studies* 68, no. 4 (2009): 1105–1135.
27. "Xingfazhi," in *Han Shu*.
28. *Da Qing Lüli*, 473–476.
29. "Xingfazhi, 2," in *Song Shi*. For the procedure of appealing to the emperor in the Qing dynasty, see Jonathan K. Ocko, "I'll Take It All the Way to Beijing: Capital Appeals in the Qing," *Journal of Asian Studies* 47, no. 2 (May 1988): 291–315.
30. Diyi Lishi Dang'an Guan, *Qingdai Tudi Zhanyou Guanxi Yu Diannong Kangzu Douzheng*, 2 vols. (Beijing: Zhonghua shuju, 1988), 1:17–20 (hereafter DLDG).
31. *Tanglü Shuyi*, Article 46.
32. *Sishu Wujing*, 1:94.
33. Pu, *Zhongguo Gudai*, 1:397.
34. *Tanglü Shuyi*, Article 352.
35. *Song Xingtong* (Beijing: Falü chubanshe, 1999), 423–424; *Da Ming Lü*, 179–180; *Da Qing Lüli*, 489. For the rationale offered, see Shen, *Daqing Lü Jizhu*, 839–840; Xue Yunsheng, *Duli Cunyi*, e-book, http://www.terada.law.kyoto-u.ac.jp/dlcy/index.htm, accessed January 10, 2018, juan 40, xinglü 16, susong 2, number 3.
36. "Xingfazhi 3," in *Song Shi*.
37. *Bo'an Huibian*, 522–524.
38. *Tanglü Shuyi*, Article 360.
39. Ibid., Article 480.
40. Ibid., Article 481.

41. For a photographed example, see *Longquan Sifa Dang'an Xuanbian*, in *Diyiji: Wanqing shiqi*, 2 vols. (Beijing: Zhonghua shuju, 2012), 2:694–702 (hereafter LSDX).
42. *Tanglü Shuyi*, Article 484.
43. Ibid., Article 450; *Da Ming Lü*, 205; *Da Qing Lüli*, 540.
44. *Xingbu Bizhao Jiajian Cheng'an* (Beijing: Falü chubanshe, 2009), 324 (hereafter XBJC).
45. *Tanglü Shuyi*, Article 490; *Song Xing Tong* (Beijing: Falü chubanshe, 1999), 556–557; *Da Ming Lü*, 221; *Da Qing Lüli*, 596–597. For more on criminal procedures in the Tang and subsequent dynasties, see Wallace Johnson and Denis Twitchett, "Criminal Procedure in T'ang China," *Asian Major* 6, no. 2 (1993): 116–117; Brian E. McKnight, "T'ang Law and Later Law: The Roots of Continuity," *Journal of the American Oriental Society* 115, no. 3 (1995): 410–420.
46. *Tanglü Shuyi*, Article 356.
47. See Melissa Macauley, *Social Power and Legal Culture: Litigation Masters in Late Imperial China* (Stanford, CA: Stanford University Press, 1998).
48. For English versions of these works, see van Gulik, *Crime and Punishment in Ancient China*, and Brian E. McKnight, trans., *The Washing Away of Wrongs: Forensic Medicine in Thirteenth-Century China* (Ann Arbor: University of Michigan Center for Chinese Studies, 1981).
49. See McKnight, introduction to *The Washing Away of Wrongs*, 5–18; *Da Qing Lüli*, 593.
50. *Da Ming Lü*, 441–442; *Da Qing Lüli*, 591–594.
51. He Ning, *Yi Yu Ji* (Shanghai: Fudan daxue chubanshe, 1988), 6.
52. For more on confession and judicial torture, see Judy Feldman Harrison, "Wrongful Treatment of Prisoners: A Case Study of Ch'ing Legal Practice," *Journal of Asian Studies* 23, no. 2 (February 1964): 227–244; Alison W. Conner, "True Confessions? Chinese Confessions Then and Now," in Karen G. Turner et al., eds., *The Limits of the Rule of Law in China* (Seattle: University of Washington Press, 2000), 132–162; Nancy Park, "Imperial Chinese Justice and Law of Torture," *Late Imperial China* 29, no. 2 (2008): 37–67.
53. Pu, *Zhongguo Gudai*, 1:320–331.
54. Zhou Ji'er, *Lichao Zheyu Zhuanyao* (Beijing: Quanguo tushuguan wenxian suowei fuzhi zhongxin, 1993), 31–33.
55. *Tanglü Shuyi*, Articles 476 and 477.
56. *Dayuan Shengzheng Guochao Dianzhang-Xingbu* (Taiyuan: Shanxi guji chubanshe, 2004), 16–22 (hereafter DSGDX).
57. *Da Qing Lüli*, 81.
58. *Tanglü Shuyi*, Article 485.
59. "Xingfazhi," in *Xin Tang Shu*; *Zizhi Tongjian*, 13:6087–6088, 6090.
60. *Tanglü Shuyi*, Article 497.
61. *Song Xingtong*, 561; "Xingfazhi," in *Song Shi*.
62. *Da Ming Lü*, 223; *Da Qing Lüli*, 600.
63. "Xingfa Zhi," in *Ming Shi*.
64. On the imperial court trials in the Ming and the Autumn Assizes in the Qing, see Bodde and Morris, *Law in Imperial China*, 135–143.

65. Bourgon and Erismann, "Figures of Deterrence in Late Imperial China."
66. Zhang Jinfan, *Qingchao Fazhi Shi* (Beijing: Falü chubanshe, 1994), 562–563.
67. Jiang, *Donghua Lu*, 423.
68. *Daqing Xinfaling* (Beijing: Shangwu yinshuguan, 2011), 9:127–128.
69. For the emphasis on mercy and compassion in the judicial process in imperial China and how county magistrates would write their capital case reports accordingly, see Thomas M. Buoye, "Bare Sticks and Naked Pity: Rhetoric and Representation in Qing Dynasty (1644–1911) Capital Case Reports," *Crime, History & Societies* 18, no. 2 (2014): 27–47.
70. Jiang, *Donghua Lu*, 503.
71. "Xingfazhi," in *Song Shi*; McKnight, *Law and Order in Sung China*, 455–460.
72. *Tanglü Shuyi*, Article 472.
73. DSGDX, 24–29.
74. *Xing'an Huilan*, 4 vols. (Beijing: guji chubanshe, 2004), 3:2227–2248.
75. "Xingfazhi, 2," in *Song Shi*. For similar behavior of county yamen runners in the Qing dynasty, see Bradly W. Reed, *Talons and Teeth: County Clerks and Runners in the Qing Dynasty* (Stanford, CA: Stanford University Press, 2000).
76. Sun Chengze, *Tianfu Guangji* (Beijing: Beijing chubanshe, 1962), 242–243; Gao Chao and Ma Jianshi, eds., *Zhongguo Gudai Faxue Cidian* (Tianjin: Nankai daxue chubanshe, 1989), 261–262.
77. Johnson and Twitchett, "Criminal Procedure in T'ang China," 135.

Chapter 3

1. *Zizhi Tongjian*, 15:6857. For articles in the Tang code regarding punishment of wayward officials, see Geoffrey MacCormack, "Liability of Officials under the Tang Code," *Hong Kong Law Journal* 17, no. 2 (1987): 142–162.
2. *Da Qing Lüli*, 89, 91.
3. *Xing'an Huilan*, 1:2211–2215.
4. Jiang, *Donghua Lu*, 360; *Li Xu Zouzhe* (Beijing: Zhonghua shuju, 1976), 97, 102–113, 126–128.
5. Not until 1910, as part of the legal reform at the time (see chapter 4), was the article in question changed to allow officials who committed offenses other than corruption, loss of cities, and dereliction of military or financial duties to be considered for being stayed (*huanjue*), pitied (*kejin*), or spared (*liuyang*). See *Daqing Xinfaling*, 9:129–130.
6. *Xing'an Huilan*, 3:1848–1849.
7. Ibid., 3:2206.
8. *Da Ming Lü*, 111; *Da Qing Lüli*, 317–318.
9. *Da Qing Lüli*, 181–183.
10. *Li Xu Zouzhe*, 194, 196, 202.
11. Ibid., 263, 282–283.
12. Jiang, *Donghua Lu*, 342, 365.
13. Guy, "Rule of Man and the Rule of Law in China," 106.
14. *Xing'an Huilan*, 1:439–440.

15. For a summary of how such crimes as robbery, extortion, and kidnapping were prosecuted and punished under the Qing law, see Robert J. Antony, *Unruly People: Crime, Community and State in Late Southern China* (Hong Kong: Hong Kong University Press, 2016), 239–256.
16. *Xing'an Huilan*, 3:1600–1601.
17. Ibid., 3:1599.
18. For an in-depth study of the imperial Chinese law on children's obligations to parents and grandparents, see Sun Jiahong, *Guanyu Zisun Weifan Jiaolin De Lishi Kaocha—Yige Weiguan Shixue De Changshi* (Beijing: Shehui kexue wenxian chubanshe, 2013).
19. Chang Jianhua, *Song Yihou Zongzu De Xingcheng Ji Diyu Bijiao* (Beijing: Renmin chubanshe, 2013), 264–300; William Rowe, *Saving the World: Chen Hongmou and Elite Consciousness in Eighteenth-Century China* (Stanford, CA: Stanford University Press, 2001), 393–404. For the durability of kinship networks and hierarchies from the Song to the Republic due to "bottom-up" demand, state promotion, and moral internalization, see Taisu Zhang, *The Laws and Economics of Confucianism: Kinship and Property in Preindustrial China and England* (New York: Cambridge University Press, 2017), 184–219.
20. *Qing Jiaqingchao Xingke Tiben Shehui Shiliao Jikan*, 3 vols. (Tianjin: Tianjin guji chubanshe, 2008), 1:7–8, 165–166, 190–191, 360–361 (hereafter QJXTSSJ).
21. For more on the issue, see Michael Dalby, "Revenge and the Law in Traditional China," *American Journal of Legal History* 25, no. 4 (1981): 267–307.
22. For more on the point, see Qu Tongzu, *Zhongguo Falü Yu Zhongguo Shehui* (Beijing: Zhonghua shuju, 1981), 72–93; also see Chang, *In Search of the Way*, 494.
23. *Da Qing Lüli*, 468.
24. Qu, *Zhongguo Falü*, 86–88.
25. *Xing'an Huilan*, 3:1650–1651.
26. Ibid.
27. Ibid., 3:1651–1652.
28. *Daqing Xinfaling*, 9:149.
29. *Da Ming Lü*, 202; Shen, *Lidai Xingfa Kao*, 1888; Xue, *Duli Cunyi*, juan 44, "Zafan" (various offenses).
30. *Da Ming Lü*, 434–435; *Da Qing Lüli*, 534–535.
31. In his annotations to the Qing code, Shen Zhiqi noted that the usurpation was a serious offense, so it was punished as severely as a parent deliberately killing an adopted child. See Shen, *Daqing Lü Jizhu*, 937–938.
32. Xue, *Duli Cunyi*, juan 44, "Zafan" (various offenses). Shen Zhiqi, in his annotations of the Qing code, did not find it necessary to make the point.
33. *Tanglü Shuyi*, Article 195; *Song Xingtong*, 257; *Da Ming Lü*, 66.
34. *Da Qing Lüli*, 203–204.
35. For the origin of the seven causes in the Han dynasty, see Pu, *Zhongguo Gudai*, 1:463–464.
36. *Tanglü Shuyi*, Article 189; *Song Xingtong*, 252; *Da Ming Lü*, 65; *Da Qing Lüli*, 212.
37. Yang Honglie, *Zhongguo Falü Fadashi* (1930; reprint, Shanghai: Shanghai shudian, 1990), 860–861. Yang mistook Liu Ji's comments for those of Song Lian, another

contemporary scholar. See Han Tao, "Yang Honglie's Zhongguo Falü Sixiangshi Zhongde Yili Cuowu Jiqi Liuchuan," in *Falüshi pinglun* (Beijing: Shehui kexue wenxian chubanshe, 2018), 11:123–130.
38. Pu, *Zhongguo Gudai*, 1:463–464; *Tanglü Shuyi*, Articles 189–190; *Song Xingtong*, 252; *Da Ming Lü*, 65; *Da Qing Lüli*, 212–213.
39. "Xingfazhi 3," in *Yuan Shi* (Shanghai: Kaiming shudian, 1934); DSGDX, 104.
40. *Da Ming Lü*, 151–152; *Da Qing Lüli*, 423–426.
41. *Da Qing Lüli*, 209–210.
42. Wang, *Qingdai Guojiafa*, 66–101.
43. Xue, *Duli Cunyi*, juan 11, "Hulü 3," "Hunyin 1," "Qu Qinshu Qiqie." Xue noted that death by strangulation delayed was lenient compared to the previous penalty of death by strangulation without delay.
44. *Xing'an Huilan*, 2:1202.
45. Ibid., 2:1200–1201.
46. QJXTSSJ, 1:33; for the substatute in question, see *Da Qing Lüli*, 468.
47. *Da Qing Lüli*, 521–523.
48. Vivien W. Ng, "Ideology and Sexuality: Rape Laws in Qing China," *Journal of Asian Studies* 46, no. 1 (February 1987): 57–70.
49. *Da Qing Lüli*, 521–523.
50. For more on this point, see Philip C. C. Huang, "Women's Choices under the Law: Marriage, Divorce, and Illicit Sex in the Qing and the Republic," *Modern China* 27, no. 1 (2001): 3–58.
51. Matthew H. Sommer, *Polyandry and Wife-Selling in Qing Dynasty China: Survival Strategies and Judicial Interventions* (Berkeley: University of California Press, 2015).
52. Matthew H. Sommer, *Sex, Law, and Society in Late Imperial China* (Stanford, CA: Stanford University Press, 2000). For favorable representations of male homosexual relationship in imperial China, see Bret Hinsch, *Passions of Cut Sleeve: Male Homosexual Tradition in China* (Berkeley: University of California Press, 1990); Mark Stevenson and Wu Cuncun, eds., *Homoeroticism in Imperial China: A Sourcebook* (London: Routledge, 2013); for a more nuanced reading of writings on male love in the Ming-Qing era, see Sophie Volpp, "Classifying Lust: The Seventeenth-Century Vogue for Male Love," *Harvard Journal of Asiatic Studies* 61, no. 1 (2001): 77–117.
53. Buoye, "Bare Sticks and Naked Pity: Rhetoric and Representation in Qing Dyansty (1644–1911) Capital Case Records," *Crime, History & Society* 18, no. 2 (2014): 27–47.
54. *Da Qing Lüli*, 401–403, 522–523.
55. These cases reached the Board of Punishment and ended up in the archives because they involved penalties of exile and death, while normal penalties for consensual sodomy (one hundred blows and wearing a *cangue*) would not be reviewed by the central government. In other words, it is not known how the county magistrate would typically handle cases of consensual sodomy or whether such cases would be reported to him at all when no other offenses were committed in connection to homosexual acts per se.
56. XBJC, 46.
57. *Da Qing Lüli*, 115–116.
58. XBJC, 307.

59. *Xing'an Huilan*, 3:1956–1957; XBJC, 303.
60. XBJC, 303–304.
61. For more on perceptions of the penetrated, see Sommer, *Sex, Law, and Society in Late Imperial China*.
62. See, e.g., Kathryn Bernhardt and Philip C. C. Huang, eds., *Civil Law in Qing and Republican China* (Stanford, CA: Stanford University Press, 1994); Philip C. C. Huang, *Civil Justice in China: Representation and Practice in the Qing* (Stanford, CA: Stanford University Press, 1996); Philip C. C. Huang, *Code, Custom, and Legal Practice: The Qing and the Republic Compared* (Stanford, CA: Stanford University Press, 2001); David Wakefield, *Fenjia: Household Division and Inheritance in Qing and Republican China* (Honolulu: University of Hawaii Press, 1998), 113–127; Linxia Liang, *Delivering Justice in Qing China: Civil Trials in the Magistrate's Court* (New York: Oxford University Press, 2008); Xiaoqun Xu, "Law, Custom, and Social Norms: Civil Adjudications in Qing and Republican China," *Law and History Review* 36, no. 1 (February 2018): 77–104.
63. Huang, *Civil Justice in China*, 140–141, 146–151; Thomas Buoye, *Manslaughter, Markets, and Moral Economy: Violent Disputes over Property Rights in Eighteen-Century China* (Cambridge, UK: Cambridge University Press, 2000), 197–218.
64. Pu, *Zhongguo Gudai*, 1:453–459; Valerie Hansen, *Negotiating Daily Life in Traditional China: How Ordinary People Used Contracts, 600–1400* (New Haven, CT: Yale University Press, 1995); Madeleine Zelin, Jonathan Ocko, and Robert Gardella, eds., *Contract and Property in Early Modern China* (Stanford, CA: Stanford University Press, 2004).
65. Zu Wei, *Zhongguo Gudai Zhengju Zhidu Jiqi Liju Yanjiu* (Beijing: Falü chubanshe, 2013), 123–149; Hansen, *Negotiating Daily Life in Traditional China*.
66. Xu, "Law, Custom, and Social Norms."
67. See Reed, *Talons and Teeth*.
68. Li Qian, *Mingguo Shiqi Qiyue Zhidu Yanjiu* (Beijing daxue chubanshe, 2005), 159.
69. Pu, *Zhongguo Gudai*, 2:498–500; Kathryn Bernhardt, *Women and Property in China, 960–1949* (Stanford, CA: Stanford University Press, 1999).
70. Kang Chao, *Man and Land in Chinese History: An Economic Analysis* (Stanford, CA: Stanford University Press, 1986); Zelin, "The Rights of Tenants."
71. In legal disputes and litigations over conditional sales of land, a party who was poorer but of higher social status in terms of advanced age and generational seniority would have an advantage against his richer opponent, which is found to be a significant factor in explaining why the kind of land concentration seen in early modern England did not happen in late imperial China. See Zhang, *The Laws and Economics of Confucianism*.
72. *Minggong Shupan Qingming Ji* (Beijing: Zhonghua shuju, 1987), 136–137 (hereafter MSQJ). This case is not in the English version translated by Brian E. McKnight and James C. T. Liu that is based on a different Chinese edition.
73. MSQJ, 131–132; Brian E. McKnight and James T. C. Liu, trans., *The Enlightened Judgments: Ch'ing-ming Chi: The Sun Dynasty Collection* (Albany: State University of New York Press,1999),159–161.

74. *Bo'an Huibian*, 600–602. For similar cases where disputes over property and rights led to violence in the Qing era, see Robert E. Hegel, *True Crimes in Eighteenth Century China: Twenty Case Histories* (Seattle: University of Washington Press, 2009), 30–36, 90–96, 123–133.
75. Wakefield, *Fenjia*, 200.
76. MSQJ, 126–127; McKnight and Liu, *The Enlightened Judgments*, 156–157.
77. MSQJ, 124–126. This case is not in the English version translated by McKnight and Liu that is based on a different Chinese edition.
78. *Bo'an Huibian*, 69–70.
79. Bernhardt, *Women and Property in China*, 47–72.

Chapter 4

1. Jonathan Spence, *The Chan's Great Continent: China in Western Minds* (New York: Norton, 1998), 87.
2. Ibid., 20–23.
3. See, e.g., Norbert Finzsch and Robert Jotte, *Institutions of Confinement: Hospitals, Asylums, and Prisons in Western Europe and North America, 1500-1950* (New York: Cambridge University Press, 1996); Norval Morris and David J. Rothman, eds., *The Oxford History of the Prison* (Oxford: Oxford University Press, 1995).
4. In mid-eighteenth-century France, on average 140 criminals per year were executed; 35 to 45 of them were killed by "breaking on the wheel." Compare these numbers to a few hundred executions per year in the Qing dynasty, of which 5 were by dismemberment. See Bourgon and Erismann, "Figures of Deterrence in Late Imperial China."
5. Brook, Bourgon, and Blue, *Death by a Thousand Cuts*, 200. Also see Li Chen, *Chinese Law in Imperial Eyes: Sovereignty, Justice, and Transcultural Politics* (New York: Columbia University Press, 2016), 156–200.
6. Shiming Zhang, "Painting and Photography in Foreigners' Construction of an Image of Qing Dynasty Law," *Frontier of History in China* 12, no. 1 (2017): 71.
7. Wang Jian, *Goutong Liangge Shijie De Falü Yiyi* (Beijing: Zhongguo fazheng daxue chubanshe, 2001), 39–41.
8. Ibid., 81–82.
9. Brook, Bourgon, and Blue, *Death by a Thousand Cuts*, 180.
10. Turan Kayaoğlu, *Legal Imperialism: Sovereignty and Extraterritoriality in Japan, the Ottoman Empire, and China* (Cambridge, UK: Cambridge University Press, 2010), 33.
11. R. Randle Edwards, "Ch'ing Legal Jurisdiction over Foreigners," in Jerome A. Cohen, R. Randle Edwards, and Fu-mei Chang Chen, eds., *Essays on China's Legal Tradition* (Princeton, NJ: Princeton University Press, 1980), 223–261; Chen, *Chinese Law in Imperial Eyes*. The analysis of the incident is based on Chen's book.
12. For the evolution of the institutions for practicing extraterritoriality, see Wesley R. Fishel, *The End of Extraterritoriality in China* (Berkeley: University of California Press, 1952), 11–18; Teemu Ruskola, *Legal Orientalism: China, the United States, and*

Modern Law (Cambridge, MA: Harvard University Press, 2013), 152–197; Jedidiah J. Kroncke, *The Futility of Law and Development: China and the Dangers of Exporting American Law* (New York: Oxford University Press, 2016), 63–66.

13. George W. Keeton, *The Development of Extraterritoriality in China* (Shanghai: Kelly and Walsh, 1928).
14. Ruskola, *Legal Orientalism*, 186–195. For more on the Mixed Court, see Fishel, *End of Extraterritoriality in China*, 18–25; A. M. Kotenev, *Shanghai: Its Municipality and the Chinese* (Shanghai: North China Daily News and North China Herald, 1927); Fei Chengkang, *Zhongguo Zujie Shi* (Shanghai: Shanghai shehui kexue chubanshe, 1991), 125–150; Thomas B. Stephens, *Order and Discipline in China: The Shanghai Mixed Court, 1911-1927* (Seattle: University of Washington Press, 1992).
15. Cassel, *Grounds of Judgment*, 39–62.
16. Douglas R. Reynolds, *China, 1898-1912: The Xinzheng Revolution and Japan* (Cambridge, MA: Harvard University Press, 1993), 202–203.
17. Wang, *Goutong Liangge Shijie*, 193–197.
18. Ibid., 236–239.
19. Li Guilian, *Ershi Shiji De Zhongguo Faxue* (Beijing: Beijing daxue chubanshe, 1998), 12–23.
20. HuangZunxian, *Riben Guozhi*, ebook, https://wenku.baidu.com/view/836b074c168884868762d6ad.html, accessed October 2, 2018, juan 27–31.
21. Xiaoqun Xu, *Trial of Modernity: Judicial Reform in Early Twentieth-Century China, 1901-1937* (Stanford, CA: Stanford University Press, 2008), 28.
22. Zheng Guanying, *Shengshi Weiyan* (1894; reprint, Changchun: Beifang funü ertong chubanshe, 2001), 122–149. For the connection between the New Policy reform and the intellectual trend on reforming cruel punishments going back to the earlier dynasties, see Jérôme Bourgon, "Abolishing 'Cruel Punishments': A Reappraisal of the Chinese Roots and Long-Term Efficiency of the Xinzheng Legal Reform," *Modern Asian Studies* 37, no. 3 (2003): 851–862.
23. John V. A. MacMurray, ed., *Treaties and Agreements with and concerning China, 1894-1919* (New York: Howard Fertig, 1973), 351, 414, 431; *Daqing Xinfaling*, 2:490, 515, 519.
24. *Daqing Xinfaling*, 1:457–458.
25. Ibid., 1:117, 120.
26. Xu, *Trial of Modernity*, 28–29.
27. For the text of the draft code and Shen Jiaben's explanations, see *Daqing Xinfaling*, 1:457–672.
28. For the texts of the revisions, see *Daqing Xinfaling*, 8:302–339.
29. Huang, *Code, Custom, and Legal Practice*, 58; also see Jérôme Bourgon, "Rights, Freedoms, and Customs in the Making of Chinese Civil Law, 1900–1936," in William C. Kirby, ed., *Realms of Freedom in Modern China* (Stanford, CA: Stanford University Press, 2003), 110.
30. For the text of the draft civil code, see *Daqing Minlü Cao'an-Minguo Minlü Cao'an* (Changchun: Jilin renmin chubanshe, 2005), 1–204 (hereafter DMC-MMC).
31. *Daqing Xinfaling*, 9:380–381.
32. Wang Qingqi, ed., *Gesheng Shenpanting Pandu* (Beijing: Beijing daxue chubanshe, 2007).

33. For the text of the law and Shen Jiaben's annotations, see *Daqing Xinfaling*, 1:418–456.
34. Bourgon, "Abolishing 'Cruel Punishments' "; Brook, Bourgon, and Blue, *Death by a Thousand Cuts*, 77–96.
35. Xu, *Trial of Modernity*, 46–47.
36. *Daqing Xinfaling*, 10:164–166, 11:42–44.
37. Xu, *Trial of Modernity*, 75–76, 144–145, 216–218.
38. Ibid., 49–50.
39. Ibid., 51.
40. See Jan Kiely, *The Compelling Ideal: Thought Reform and the Prison in China, 1901–1956* (New Haven, CT: Yale University Press, 2014).

Chapter 5

1. Xu, *Trial of Modernity*, 6–8, 149–183.
2. For the text of the PNCC with deletions from the 1907 version, see Yang, *Zhongguo Falü Fadashi*, 1101–1167.
3. Ibid., 1104.
4. Guo Wei, *Minguo Daliyuan Jieshili Quanwen* (Beijing: Zhongguo zhengfa daxue chubanshe, 2014), 546–547. A was not prosecuted for his false accusation because under Article 182 of the PNCC, he would get no penalty if his false accusation did not lead to the accused being punished.
5. *Da Qing Lüli*, 441–442, 481–486.
6. Guo, *Minguo Daliyuan*, 709.
7. *Daqing Xinfaling*, 1:607–611.
8. For more on the issue, see Jennifer M. Neighbors, *A Question of Intent: Homicide Law and Criminal Justice in Qing and Republican China* (Leiden: Brill, 2018), 172–180.
9. Xu, "Law, Custom, and Social Norms," 3.
10. Ibid.
11. See Shen Erqiao, ed., *Xianxing Lü Minshi Youxiao Bufen, Fu Hubu Zeli* (Hangzhou: Wulin yinshuguan, 1918).
12. Guo, *Minguo Daliyuan*, 345–346.
13. For the text of the 1925 draft civil code, see DMC-MMC, 205–417.
14. Xu, *Trial of Modernity*, 59–60.
15. Ibid., 247–274; Frank Dikötter, *Crime, Punishment and the Prison in Modern China* (New York: Columbia University Press, 2002).
16. Xu, *Trial of Modernity*, 61.
17. Ibid.
18. Guo, *Minguo Daliyuan*, 404–405, 1126–1127, 1166–1167.
19. Xu, *Trial of Modernity*, 62.
20. See *Daqing Xinfaling*, 1:418–420, 448–450.
21. Alison W. Conner, "Lawyers and the Legal Profession during the Republican Period," in Kathryn Bernhardt and Philip Huang, eds., *Civil Law in Qing and Republican China* (Stanford, CA: Stanford University Press, 1994), 215–248.

22. Xu, *Trial of Modernity*, 66–67. For more on the lawyer system in the Republican era as it operated in Shanghai, see Sun Huei-min, *Zhidu Yizhi: Minchu Shanghai De Zhongguo Lüshi (1912–1937)* (Taibei: Zhognyang yanjiuyuan jindaishi yanjiusuo, 2012).
23. Xu, *Trial of Modernity*, 75.
24. Guo, *Minguo Daliyuan*, 535.
25. Ibid., 79.
26. Ibid., 140–141.
27. U.S. Department of State, *Report of the Commission on Extraterritoriality in China, Peking, September 16, 1926*. Washington, DC: Government Printing Office, 1926, https://babel.hathitrust.org/cgi/pt?id=uc1.$b47432;view=1up;seq=6, 116–140; *Diaocha Faquan Weiyuanhui Baogaoshu*, Falü Pinglun Zengkan (1926), 36–70; Kayaoğlu, *Legal Imperialism*, 151. The report counted seventeen American consular courts, plus the U.S. Commissioner's Court and the U.S. Court in China. The last two courts were both in Shanghai, but the former was equivalent to consular courts in other treaty ports, and the latter was the appellate court above eighteen consular courts. Kayaoğlu's number of American courts does not include the U.S. Court in China. For more on that court, see Ruskola, *Legal Orientalism*.
28. U.S. Department of State, *Report of the Commission on Extraterritoriality in China*; also *Diaocha Faquan Weiyuanhui Baogaoshu*. For more on the negotiations in the 1920s and 1930s on ending extraterritoriality, see Kayaoğlu, *Legal Imperialism*, 171–181.
29. Xu, *Trial of Modernity*, 12.
30. Ibid., 91–92.
31. Ibid., 89.
32. Ibid.
33. Ibid., 90.
34. Ibid., 93.
35. Xie Shen, Chen Shijie, and Ying Jixi, eds., *Minxingshi Caipan Daquan* (Beijing: Beijing daxue chubanshe, 2007), 389–396.
36. Xu, *Trial of Modernity*, 95–96.
37. Ibid.
38. For the extrajudicial operations of the GMD special services, see Frederic E. Wakeman Jr., *Spymaster: Dai Li and the Chinese Secret Service* (Berkeley, CA: University of California Press, 2003); for assassinations carried out by the services, see 175–177, 344–346.
39. For the texts of both the criminal code and the criminal procedural law, see *Zhonghua Minguo Xianxing Fagui Daquan* (Shanghai: Shangwu yinshuguan, 1934), 123–141. 171–193 (hereafter ZMXFD).
40. Neighbors, *A Question of Intent*, 159–161.
41. *Beiping Difang Fayuan Xingshi Pandue Anjuan* (Beijing: Quanguo tushuguan wenxian suowei fuzhi zhongxin, 2005).
42. For the texts of the civil code and the civil procedural law, see ZMXFD, 15–69, 143–170. For the impact of the Civil Code on cases of marriage, property, succession, land rights, debt, and so on, see Bernhardt, *Women and Property in China*; Huang, *Code, Custom, and Legal Practice in China*; Margaret Kuo, *Intolerable Cruelty: Marriage, Law, and Society in Early Twentieth-Century China* (Lanham, MD: Rowman and

Littlefield, 2012); Lisa Tran, *Concubines in Court: Marriage and Monogamy in Twentieth-Century China* (Lanham, MD: Rowman and Littlefield, 2015).
43. Xu, "Law, Custom, and Social Norms."
44. Xu Wenxun, *Tajingting Andu* (Beijing: Beijing daxue chubanshe, 2007), 23, 36, 60.
45. Guo, *Minguo Daliyuan*, 279, 495, 768, 829–830.
46. Xu, "Law, Custom, and Social Norms"; Lu Jingyi, *Minchu Lisi Wenti De Falü Yu Caipan: Yi Daliyuan Minshi Panjue Wei Zhongxin* (Beijing: Beijing daxue chubanshe, 2004), 137–138, 156–169.
47. Xu, *Trial of Modernity*, 100.
48. Ibid., 102–103.
49. Ibid., 106–107.
50. Ibid., 109–110; also see Kiely, *The Compelling Ideal*, 176–186.
51. Kiely, *The Compelling Ideal*, 257.
52. Xiaoqun Xu, "The Chinese Judiciary under the Japanese Occupation: Criminal and Civil Justice in Jiangsu, 1938-1945," *Chinese Historical Review* 22, no. 2 (2015): 120–140.
53. Fishel, *The End of Extraterritoriality in China*, 207–215, 233–240; also see Kayaoğlu, *Legal Imperialism*, 182–190.
54. Xu, "The Chinese Judiciary under the Japanese Occupation."
55. For the phenomenon of making false accusations in the prewar period, see Xu, *Trial of Modernity*, 302–328.

Chapter 6

1. This section is largely based on Xu, *Trial of Modernity*, ch. 9.
2. Phil Billingsley, *Bandits in Republican China* (Stanford, CA: Stanford: Stanford University Press, 1988); Patrick Fuliang Shan, "Insecurity, Outlawry and Social Order: Banditry in China's Heilongjiang Frontier Region, 1900-1931," *Journal of Social History* 40, no. 1 (2006): 25–54. For a study of banditry as a survival strategy for the poor and the marginalized in Guangdong province in 1760–1845, see Antony, *Unruly People*.
3. Cases in this section are from Xu, *Trial of Modernity*, ch. 9.
4. For the criticisms of the banditry law, see Xu, *Trial of Modernity*, 280, 282–283, 287.
5. There is a large body of scholarship on how post–World War II European states dealt with collaborators. For example, see Istvan Deák, Jan T. Cross, and Tony Judt, *The Politics of Retribution in Europe: World War II and Its Aftermath* (Princeton, NJ: Princeton University Press, 2000). For the Chinese discourse on punishing collaborators, see Margherita Zanasi, "Globalizing *Hanjian*: The Suzhou Trials and Post–World War II Discourse on Collaboration," *American Historical Review* 113, no. 3 (2008): 731–751.
6. Judicial Archives, Baoshan County Archives, file number 43-1-017. Shanghai, China.
7. Frederic E. Wakeman Jr., "*Hanjian* (Traitors)! Collaboration and Retribution in Wartime Shanghai," in Wen-shin Yeh, ed., *Becoming Chinese: Passages to Modernity and Beyond* (Berkeley: University of California Press, 2000), 298–341; Frederic E.

Wakeman Jr., *The Shanghai Badlands: Wartime Terrorism and Urban Crime, 1937–1941* (New York: Cambridge University Press, 1996), 59–64, 69–74; Pan Min, *Jiangsu Riwei Jiceng Zhengquan Yanjiu, 1937–1945* (Shanghai: Shanghai renmin chubanshe, 2006), 230–231.

8. For the texts of these statutes, see *Zuixin Liufa Quanshu* (Shanghai: Chunming shudian, 1948), 235–237 (hereafter ZLQ).
9. *Shenxun Wangwei Hanjian Bilu* (Nanjing: Fenghuang chubanshe, 2004), 1441–1442 (hereafter SWHB).
10. ZLQ, 236; SWHB, 1442–1444.
11. SWHB, 61–90.
12. SWHB, 302–308, 1125.
13. "Legal Interpretations," *Sifa Jikan* (司法季刊, Justice Quarterly) no. 2 (April, 1947): 46.
14. "Wuhan Diqing Wenxian" (Historical data on Wuhan local society), "Chengzhi Hanjing" (Punishing Chinese traitors), and "Wenjian" (Documents), in *Wuhanshi Difang Zhi* (Wuhan municipal gazetteer), http://www.whfz.gov.cn:8080/pub/dqwx/dfwx/jfsl/ml/zz/201001/t20100117_13699.shtml, accessed January 11, 2014.
15. "Legal Interpretations," 45.
16. Pan, *Jiangsu Riwei Jiceng Zhengquan Yanjiu*, 233.
17. Ibid.
18. Judicial Archives, Baoshan County Archives, Shanghai, file number 43-1-265.
19. Ibid., file number 43-1-426.
20. Guo, *Minguo Daliyuan*, 585, 837–838, 932.
21. DMC-MMC, 174, 358.
22. Guo, *Minguo Daliyuan*, 262–263, 1033–1034; DMC-MMC, 174, 358.
23. Guo, *Minguo Daliyuan*, 515, 565.
24. Ibid., 536.
25. DMC-MMC, 176–177.
26. Guo, *Minguo Daliyuan*, 568–570, 577.
27. Ibid., 704–705.
28. Ibid., 993–994.
29. Ibid., 388–389, 709.
30. Jiangsu High Court Archives, Jiangsu Provincial Archives, Nanjing, file number 1047-41 (Statistics), 547.
31. DMC-MMC, 177.
32. ZMXFD, Chou: 60–61 (Articles 1049–1054).
33. DMC-MMC, 177, 364; Guo, *Minguo Daliyuan*, 1073.
34. Huang, "Women's Choice under the Law."
35. Cheng Yu, "Minguo Shiqi Qie De Falü Diwei Jiqi Bianqian," *Shi Lin*, no. 2 (2002): 74–83.
36. ZLQ, 222; Tran, *Concubines in Court*, 38–43.
37. Zhao Fengjie, *Zhongguo Funü Zai Falü Shangzhi Diwei*, revised edition (Shanghai: Shangwu yinshuguan, 1936), 126–127; Cheng, "Minguo Shiqi Qie De Falü Diwei Jiqi Bianqian," 80; Tran, *Concubines in Court*, 43.

38. Werner Levi, "The Family in Modern Chinese Law," The Far Eastern Quarterly, 4, 3 (1945): 272.
39. Zhao, *Zhongguo Funü Zai Falü Shangzhi Diwei*, 127–128.
40. Tran, *Concubines in Court*, 43–68.
41. For the development and the role of forensic science in China's judicial practices in the Republican era, see Daniel Asen, *Death in Beijing: Murder and Forensic Science in Republican China* (New York: Cambridge University Press, 2016).
42. Judicial Archives, Songjiang County Archives, Shanghai, file number 4-2-231.
43. Ibid.
44. Ibid., file number 4-2-236.
45. Ibid.
46. Baoshan County Archives, file number 43-1-410.
47. "Guizhou Sheng Zhi Renshi Xiguan (Social customs in Guizhou province)," *Falü Pinglun*, no. 116 (September 20, 1925): 19.
48. For more on the last point, see Kuo, *Intolerable Cruelty*.

Chapter 7

1. Zhang, *Zhongguo Sifa*, 564; Patricia E. Griffin, *The Chinese Communist Treatment of Counterrevolutionaries* (Princeton, NJ: Princeton University Press, 1976), 12–17.
2. Pan Junxiang and Shen Zuwei, *Jindai Zhongguo Guoqing Toushi* (Shanghai: Shanghai shehui kexueyuan chubanshe, 1992), 153, 158.
3. Zhang, *Zhongguo Sifa*, 566–570; Griffin, *The Chinese Communist*, 19–26; Hiroshi Oda, "Criminal Law and Procedure in the Chinese Soviet Republic," in W. E. Butler, ed., *The Legal System of The Chinese Soviet Republic, 1931-1934* (Dobbs Ferry, NY: Transnational Publishers, 1983), 53–59.
4. Zhang, *Zhongguo Sifa*, 578–583.
5. Griffin, *The Chinese Communist*, 36.
6. W. E. Butler, ed., *The Legal System of the Chinese Soviet Republic, 1931-1934* (Dobbs Ferry, NY: Transnational Publishers, 1983), 204–207.
7. Xiao Yongqing, *Zhongguo Fazhishi Jiaocheng* (Beijing: Falü chubanshe, 1987), 377–379.
8. Ibid., 379–381.
9. Zhang, *Zhongguo Sifa*, 583–587.
10. Griffin, *The Communist Treatment*, 32–36.
11. Oda, "Criminal Law and Procedure," 64–65; Griffin, *The Chinese Communist*, 60–62, 88–91.
12. Griffin, *The Chinese Communist*, 19–24, 39–40,
13. Ibid., 26–32, 83–88; Kiely, *The Compelling Ideal*, 242–246.
14. Based on the true story (the case files preserved in the Shannxi Provincial Archives), a feature movie about the Huang Kegong case was released in China in 2014.
15. Xiao, *Zhongguo Fazhishi*, 401–402.
16. For the CCP practices from the early 1940s onward, see Kiely, *The Compelling Ideal*, 242–396.

17. Griffin, *The Chinese Communist*, 109, 114.
18. Zhang, *Zhongguo Sifa*, 574–578; also see Oda, "Criminal Law, and Procedure," 67.
19. Zhang, *Zhongguo Sifa*, 613–614.
20. Jerome A. Cohen, "The Chinese Communist Party and 'Judicial Independence,' 1949–1050," *Harvard Law Review* 82, no. 5 (1969): 967.
21. *Dangdai Zhongguode Sifa Xingzheng Gongzuo* (Beijing: Dangdai zhongguo chubanshe, 1995), 22–30, 50–53 (hereafter DZSXG).
22. Ibid., 299; Zhang, *Zhongguo Sifa*, 619.
23. DZSXG, 304.
24. Ibid., 305–306.
25. Zhao Wenlong, *Jiancha Guande Shengya* (Zhengzhou: Haiyan chubanshe, 1997), 125–129.
26. Ibid., 129–133.
27. Bo Yibo, *Ruogan Zhongda Juece Yu Shijian De Huigu* (Beijing: Zhonggong zhongyang dangxiao chubanshe, 1993), 148–153.
28. Ibid. 144–145.
29. Maurice Meisner, *Mao's China and After: A History the People's Republic* (New York: Free Press, 1999), 123–124.
30. Li Hui, *Hu Feng Jituan Yuan'an Shimo* (Beijing: Renmin ribao chubanshe, 1989).
31. Jia Zhifang, *Yuli Yuwai* (Shanghai: Yuandong chubanshe, 1995).
32. Meisner, *Mao's China and After*, 155–188; Andrew G. Walder, *China under Mao: A Revolution Derailed* (Cambridge, MA: Harvard University Press, 2015), 135–151.
33. Bo, *Ruogan Zhongda Juece*, 618–619.
34. Wang, *Jianyu Suoji*, 152–159.
35. Meisner, *Mao's China and After*, 80–81.
36. On the persistent importance of natural villages to peasant life, see Yi Wu, *Negotiating Rural Landownership in Southwest China: State, Village, and Family* (Honolulu: University of Hawaii Press, 2016).
37. On residents committees and work units in the PRC's political structure, see Stanley B. Lubman, *Bird in a Cage: Legal Reform in China after Mao* (Stanford, CA: Stanford University Press, 1999), 44–47, 54–57; Kenneth Lieberthal, *Governing China: From Revolution through Reform* (New York: Norton, 1995), 167–168.
38. Kiely, *The Compelling Ideal*.
39. DZSXG, 155–158.
40. Ibid., 170–173.
41. James D. Seymour and Richard Anderson, *New Ghosts Old Ghosts: Prisons and Labor Reform Camps in China* (Armonk, NY: M. E. Sharpe, 1999), 25–26.
42. See ibid., chs. 2, 3, and 4; Klaus Muhlhahn, *Criminal Justice in China: A History* (Cambridge, MA: Harvard University Press, 2009), 230–232, 270–279.
43. Li Baiying, *Huiyi Wo De Gaizhao Shenghuo* (Beijing: Qunzhong chubanshe, 1984). For reformation as expected of prisoners, see Kiely, *The Compelling Ideal*, 287–288, 304–306.
44. DZSXG, 208–239.

45. Stuart Schram, ed., *Chairman Mao Talks to the People: Talks and Letters: 1956-1971* (New York: Pantheon Books, 1974), 179-180.
46. Meisner, *Mao's China and After*, 452.
47. For more on the Cultural Revolution, see Walder, *China under Mao*, 200-314.
48. Zhang, *Zhongguo Sifa*, 627-628.
49. Memoirs about tremendous human sufferings in the Cultural Revolution are numerous. One of the classics in English is Nien Cheng, *Life and Death in Shanghai* (New York: Grove Press, 1987).
50. Due to this scenario, at least one ministerial-level official and one factory worker were still serving time in the Beijing First Prison in the mid-1970s. See Wang, *Jianyu Suoji*, 120-121, 146.
51. In one case, a young man of eighteen was arrested early in the Cultural Revolution for killing a person in a fight between rebels. He was imprisoned without trial until late 1976, after Mao's death and the arrest of the Gang of Four, when he was sentenced to death and executed because Wu De, the mayor of Beijing at the time, tried to distance himself from the Gang of Four by showing his toughness toward "revolutionary rebels." See Wang, *Jianyu Suoji*, 164-165.
52. Zhang, *Zhongguo Sifa*, 263.
53. For more on the fall of Lin Biao and its aftermath, see Meisner, *Mao's China and After*, 376-385; Walder, *China under Mao*, 286-293.
54. Wang, *Jianyu Suoji*.
55. Ibid., 168-173, 177-178.
56. Lubman, *Bird in a Cage*, 71-72.

Chapter 8

1. Butler, *The Legal System*, 161-168.
2. Ibid., 177-182; Xiao, *Zhongguo Fazhishi*, 360-371.
3. Lubman, *Bird in a Cage*, 47.
4. Butler, *The Legal System*, 177-182.
5. Bai Chao, *Xiangchun Fa'an: 1940 Niandai Taihang Diqu Zhengfu Duan'an 63 Li* (Zhengzhou: Daxiang chubanshe, 2011). The editor of the source stated that the sixty-three case files were selected from over two thousand. Besides marriage and divorce, three other categories of cases were land dispute (twenty cases), debts and property (thirteen cases), and child support (five cases). For an in-depth study on the issue of marriage and divorce in another Communist base area, see Xiaoping Cong, *Marriage, Law and Gender in Revolutionary China, 1940-1960* (Cambridge, UK: Cambridge University Press, 2016).
6. Bai, *Xiangchun Fa'an*, 108-111.
7. Ibid., 123-132.
8. Cong, *Marriage, Law and Gender*, 33-51.
9. Ibid., 140-171.
10. Huang, *Chinese Civil Justice*, 74-82.

11. Zhang, *Zhongguo Sifa*, 593–594.
12. For the text of the 1950 Marriage Law in English translation, see Neil J. Diamant, *Revolutionizing the Family: Politics, Love, and Divorce in Urban and Rural China, 1949-1968* (Berkeley: University of California Press, 2000), 342–346.
13. Jennifer Altehenger, *Legal Lessons: Popularizing Laws in the People's Republic of China, 1949-1989* (Cambridge, MA: Harvard University Press, 2018).
14. See Huang, *Chinese Civil Justice*; Diamant, *Revolutionizing the Family*.
15. Zhang, *Zhongguo Sifa*, 593–594.
16. Diamant, *Revolutionizing the Family*, 58.
17. Ibid., 58–59.
18. Ibid., 71–72.
19. Ibid., 72–73.
20. Huang, *Chinese Civil Justice*, 37–38.
21. Huang, *Chinese Civil Justice*, 100–101.

Chapter 9

1. See, e.g., Sarah Biddulph, *The Stability Imperative: Human Rights and Law in China* (Vancouver: University of British Columbia Press, 2015), 22–27.
2. Randall Peerenboom, *China's Long March toward Rule of Law* (New York: Cambridge University Press, 2002), 3. Also see Randall Peerenboom, ed., *Judicial Independence in China: Lessons for Global Rule of Law Promotion* (New York: Cambridge University Press, 2010).
3. Tom Ginsburg and Tamir Moustafa, eds., *Rule by Law: The Politics of Courts in Authoritarian Regimes* (Cambridge, UK: Cambridge University Press, 2008), 4–11.
4. Meisner, *Mao's China and After*, 427–428.
5. Deng gave a long speech to elaborate the rationale for the four principles. See Deng Xiaoping, *Deng Xiaoping Wenxuan* (Hong Kong: Sanlian shudian, 1983), 144–170.
6. For more on the 1989 Tiananmen movement and its crackdown, see, e.g., Meisner, *Mao's China and After*, 499–511; Richard Baum, "The Road to Tiananmen: Chinese Politics in the 1980s," in Roderick MacFarquhar, ed., *The Politics of China: The Eras of Mao and Deng* (New York: Cambridge University Press, 1997), 441–463; Craig Calhoun, *Neither Gods nor Emperors: Students and the Struggle for Democracy in China* (New York: Cambridge University Press, 1994), 289–300.
7. "Deng Xiaoping Nanxun Jianghua," https://baike.baidu.com, accessed November 12, 2017. Also see Richard Evans, *Deng Xiaoping and the Making of Modern China* (New York: Penguin, 1997), 306–309.
8. See Wu, *Negotiating Rural Land Ownership*.
9. "Sanquan Fenzhi," https://baike.baidu.com, accessed January 29, 2018.
10. Meisner, *Mao's China and After*, 455.
11. For a study of the issue with a theory of authoritarian legality, see Mary E. Gallagher, *Authoritarian Legality in China: Law, Workers, and the State* (New York: Cambridge University Press, 2017).

12. For an in-depth analysis of the issue, see Shitong Qiao, *Chinese Small Property: The Co-Evolution of Law and Social Norms* (New York: Cambridge University Press, 2018).
13. See Benjamin van Rooij, *Regulating Land and Pollution in China, Lawmaking, Compliance and Enforcement: Theory and Cases* (Leiden: Leiden University Press, 2006); Benjamin van Rooij, Li Na, and Wang Qiliang, "Punishing Polluters: Trends, Local Practice, and Influences, and Their Implications for Administrative Law Enforcement in China," *China Law and Society Review* 3, no. 2 (2018): 118–176.
14. Deng, *Deng Xiaoping Wenxuan*, 136.
15. For more on the trial, see Alexander Cook, *The Cultural Revolution on Trial: Mao and the Gang of Four* (New York: Cambridge University Press, 2016).
16. This point was tellingly illustrated by Wu De, the mayor of Beijing in the late 1970s, who said that people who had opposed the Gang of Four before their arrest on October 6, 1976, were counterrevolutionaries nonetheless. See Wang Xuetai, *Jianyu Suoji* (Beijing: Sanlian shudian, 2013), 164.
17. For the text of the code, see *Zhonghua Renmin Gongheguo Falü Huibian, 1979–1984; 1985–1989*. 2 vols. (Beijing: Renmin chubanshe, 1991), Vol. 1:98–132 (hereafter ZRGFH).
18. Ibid., 1:114.
19. Ibid., 1:52–55.
20. Ibid., 1:133–167.
21. On torture used in the anticrime campaigns in the 1980s, see Harold M. Tanner, *Strike Hard! Anti-Crime Campaigns and Chinese Criminal Justice, 1979–1985* (Ithaca, NY: Cornell University Press, 1999), 121–122.
22. ZRGFH, 2:153–166.
23. Donald C. Clarke and James V. Feinerman, "Antagonistic Contradiction: Criminal Law and Human Rights in China," in Stanley B. Lubman, ed., *China's Legal Reforms* (Oxford University Press, 1996), 141.
24. See ZLQ, 434–443.
25. ZRGFH, 1:81–90.
26. Ibid., 1:98–132.
27. DZSXG, 173–174.
28. Peerenboom, *China's Long March*, 290.
29. Ibid., 290–294.
30. Tanner, *Strike Hard!*, 51–52; Peerenboom, *China's Long March*, 283–287.
31. Qianfan Zhang, "The People's Court in Transition: The Prospects of the Chinese Judicial Reform," *Journal of Contemporary China* 12, nos. 3–4 (2003): 83; Xin He, "Black Hole of Responsibility: The Adjudication Committee's Role in a Chinese Court," *Law and Society Review* 46, no. 4 (2012): 681–712.
32. Peerenboom, introduction to *Judicial Independence in China*, 17.
33. Kwai Hang Ng and Xin He, *Embedded Courts: Judicial Decision-Making in China* (New York: Cambridge University Press, 2017).
34. Ibid., 9–10.
35. ZRGFH, 1:195–199.
36. Zhang, *Zhongguo Sifa*, 649–659.

37. Peerenboom, *China's Long March*, 353.
38. William Alford, "Tasseled Loafers for Barefoot Lawyers: Transformation and Tension in the World of Chinese Legal Workers," in Stanley B. Lubman, ed., *China's Legal Reforms* (Oxford University Press, 1996), 22–38.
39. One understudied aspect of Chinese lawyers' role has been in the state-promoted legal-aid programs, providing reduced-fee or free legal services to the poor. See Benjamin L. Liebman, "Lawyers, Legal Aid, and Legitimacy in China," in William P. Alford, ed., *Raising the Bar: The Emerging Legal Profession in East Asia* (Cambridge, MA: Harvard University Press, 2007), 311–356.
40. Ping Yu, "Glittery Promise vs. Dismal Reality: The Role of a Criminal Lawyer in the People's Republic of China after the 1996 Revision of the Criminal Procedural Law," *Vanderbilt Journal of Transnational Law* 35, no. 3 (2002): 827–865. For more on Chinese lawyers' working environment, see Sida Liu and Terence C. Halliday, *Criminal Defense in China: The Politics of Lawyers at Work* (New York: Cambridge University Press, 2016).
41. William P. Alford, "Of Lawyers Lost and Found: Searching for Legal Professionalism in the People's Republic of China," in William P. Alford, ed., *Raising the Bar: The Emerging Legal Profession in East Asia* (Cambridge, MA: Harvard University Press, 2007), 295.
42. Liu and Halliday, *Criminal Defense in China*, 144–170; Scott Wilson, *Tigers without Teeth: The Pursuit of Justice in Contemporary China* (Lanham, MD: Rowman and Littlefield, 2015).
43. "Zhonghua Renmin Gongheguo Guojia Peichang Fa," http://www.baike.baidu.com, accessed October 23, 2016.
44. *Zhongguo Falü Nianjian, 2004* (Beijing: Falü nianjian she, 2004), 1055.
45. Clarke and Feinerman, "Antagonistic Contradictions," 138.
46. Tanner, *Strike Hard!*, 62.
47. ZRGFH, 1:382–386.
48. Ibid., 1:472–474.
49. Ibid., 1:475–476.
50. http://www.xinhuanet.org. March 4, 2007.
51. *Fazhi Wanbao* (Legal System Evening News), December 2, 2010.
52. *Yangcheng Wanbao* (Guangzhou Evening News), July 31, 2010.
53. Susan Trevaskes, *Courts and Criminal Justice in Contemporary China* (Lanham, MD: Lexington Books, 2007).
54. Tanner, *Strike Hard!*, 166.
55. Zhang Sihan et al., *Liuhai Anjian Falü Shiwu* (Beijing: Zhongguo zhengfa daxue chubanshe, 1993), 11–15.
56. *Zhonghua Renmin Gongheguo Falü Huibian, 1990* (Beijing: Renmin chubanshe, 1991), 145–149.
57. Zhang et al., *Liuhai Anjian*, 102–103.
58. Ibid., 109. One factory worker who recopied a hand-copied novel, *The Second Handshake*, which was not pornography but was about Chinese scientists and love, received a death sentence with suspended execution for that. See Wang, *Jianyu Suoji*, 116.

59. Zhang et al., *Liuhai Anjian*, 110–113.
60. Ibid., 115.
61. *Zhonghua Renmin Gongheguo Falü Huibian, 1990*, 151–155.
62. Zhang et al., *Liuhai Anjian*, 125.
63. Ibid., 145–146.
64. *Saohuang Dafei Anli Xuan* (Beijing: Renmin fayuan chubanshe, 2004), 177–179 (hereafter SDAX).
65. "Nuzi Xie Yinhui Xiaoshuo Maiqian Beipan Ruyu 10 Nian, Dui Haishi Cuo?," http://society.huanqiu.com/article/2018-11/13585880.html, accessed November 19, 2018. Online sources on criminal and civil cases cited in this book are not listed in the Selected Bibliography.
66. "Kaifa Shehuang Zhibo app IT Tiancai Mocai Bucheng Fan Ruyu," http://news.jstv.com/a/20180622/5b2c83c5b8318923afd38b9d.shtml, accessed December 30, 2018.
67. Zhang et al., *Liuhai Anjian*, 164.
68. Ibid., 164–167.
69. ZRGFH, 2:153–168.
70. Zhang et al., *Liuhai Anjian*, 170–171.
71. Tanner, *Strike Hard!*, 126–127.
72. Zhang et al., *Liuhai Anjian*, 210.
73. Ibid., 438–444.
74. Ibid., 213.
75. Ibid., 426–430.

Chapter 10

1. Hong Kong includes three pieces of land: the island of Hong Kong that was obtained by the British under the Treaty of Nanjing (1842), Kowloon Peninsula that was obtained under the Beijing Convention (1860), and New Territories that was leased in 1898 for ninety-nine years. New Territories is larger than the island and Kowloon put together, and with its lease expired in 1997, the island and Kowloon on their own are not viable economically. For one thing, they do not have power and water supplies to sustain residents' daily life. That is why all three pieces were returned to China in 1997.
2. *Zhonghua Renmin Gongheguo Xingfa—Zhonghua Renmin Gongheguo Xingshi Susongfa* (Beijing: Falü chubanshe, 1997), 130–131 (hereafter ZRGX-ZRGXS).
3. Ibid., 35–70.
4. Ibid., 189.
5. "Zhonghua Renmin Gongheguo Xingshi Susongfa, 2012 Nian Xiuzheng," http://www.gov.cn/flfg/2012-03/17/content_2094354.htm, accessed November 2, 2016.
6. Yuanyuan Shen, "Conceptions and Receptions of Legality: Understanding the Complexity of Law Reform in Modern China," in Karen G. Turner, James V. Feinerman, and R. Kent Guy, eds., *The Limits of the Rule of Law in China* (Stanford, CA: Stanford University Press, 2000), 33.

7. "Jiangxi Leping Yuan'an 4 Beigaoren Jiang Gehuo 227 Wan Guojia Peichang," https://news.china.com/news100/11038989/20170806/31043027.html, accessed December 21, 2017.
8. DZSXG, 211.
9. For more on this issue, see Biddulph, *The Stability Imperative*, 206–236.
10. The nine offenses were smuggling weapons and ammunition, smuggling nuclear materials, smuggling counterfeit currencies, making counterfeit currencies, large-scale financial fraud, organizing or forcing others to engage in prostitution, impeding execution of military duties, and spreading rumors to undermine military morale during wartime.
11. "Zhonghua Renmin Gongheguo Xingfa Xiuzheng An (9)," http://www.npc.gov.cn/zgrdw/npc/xinwen/2015-08/31/content_1945587.htm, accessed November 20, 2017.
12. See, e.g., Paul Freidland, *Seeing Justice Done: The Age of Spectacular Capital Punishment in France* (New York: Oxford University Press, 2012).
13. ZRGFH, 1:273.
14. Hong Lu and Terance D. Miethe, *China's Death Penalty: History, Law, and Contemporary Practices* (London: Routledge, 2007).
15. Ibid., 123.
16. *Guangzhou Ribao* (Guangzhou Daily), April 27, 2011.
17. "Zuigao Fayuan Guanyu Sixing Fuhe Sifa Jieshi," http://www.xinhua.org, accessed June 23, 2016.
18. "Renti Qiguan Yizhi Tiaoli," https://baike.baidu.com/item/%E4%BA%BA%E4%BD%93%E5%99%A8%E5%AE%98%E7%A7%BB%E6%A4%8D%E6%9D%A1%E4%BE%8B/3947933?fr=aladdin, accessed November 20, 2017.
19. "Zhongguo Quanmian Tingzhi Shiyong Siqiu Qiguan," https://www.chinacourt.org/article/detail/2015/02/id/1552799.shtml, accessed November 20, 2017.
20. "Zhongguo Sifa Lingyu Renquan Baozhang De Xin Jinzhan," http://www.cssn.cn/fx/fx_fxxf/201609/t20160913_3200586.shtml, accessed November 20, 2017.
21. "Lai Changxing Anjing," http://legal.people.com.cn/GB/17928008.html, accessed November 27, 2017.
22. "Zhuang Rushun Zaihuo Jianxing," http://news.sina.com.cn/c/nd/2017-07-11/doc-ifyhweua4808651.shtml.
23. http://www.news.qq.com, accessed November 28, 2017.
24. http://www.news.soho.com, accessed November 28, 2017.
25. http://chinanews.com, accessed November 28, 2017.
26. "Yao Jiaxin," http://www.baike.baidu.com, accessed November 28, 2017.
27. "Juzhong Yinluan An," https://baike.baidu.com/item/%E8%81%9A%E4%BC%97%E6%B7%AB%E4%B9%B1%E6%A1%88/2263361?fr=aladdin, accessed November 28, 2017.
28. For a study of how and why wrongful cases occurred in post-Mao China, see Jiahong He, *Back from the Dead: Wrongful Convictions and Criminal Justice in China* (Honolulu: University of Hawaii Press, 2016).
29. For a detailed analysis of the case, see ibid., 81–146.

30. "Nian Bin Toudu An," https://baike.baidu.com/item/%E5%BF%B5%E6%96%8C%E6%8A%95%E6%AF%92%E6%A1%88/1488296?fr=aladdin, accessed December 1, 2017.
31. "Yang Ming," http://www.baike.baidu.com. For the text of the Guizhou Provincial Superior Court Judgment on State Compensation for Yang Ming, see http://openlaw.cn/judgement/0aba597b3fd444c29e59ffda3af91de9, accessed December 1, 2017.
32. http://www.gd.qq.com. June 22, 2016.
33. "Zheng Xiaoyu," http://www.baike.sogou.com, accessed March 21, 2018.
34. http://www.spp.gov.cn, accessed March 13, 2016.
35. "Ling Jihua," http://www.baike.baidu.com, accessed March 21, 2018.
36. "Bo Xilai," "Zhou Yongkang," http://www.baike.baidu.com, accessed March 21, 2018.
37. "Zuigao Renmin Fayuan Guanyu Zhongda Tanwu Shouhui Fanzui Anjian Liangxing Yijian," http://www.baike.baidu.com, accessed March 21 2018.
38. "Shuang Gui," http://www.baike.baidu.com, accessed March 21, 2018.
39. Peerenboom, introduction to *JudicialIndependence in China*, 18.
40. "Luoguan," https://baike.baidu.com, accessed March 21, 2018.
41. "Dangzheng Lingdao Ganbu Xuanba Renyong Gongzuo Tiaoli," https://www.guancha.cn/FaZhi/2014_01_16_200015.shtml, accessed March 21, 2018.
42. *Zhejiang Xinwen* (Zhejiang News), May 25, 2017.
43. https://www.guancha.cn/politics/2018_12_29_485109.shtml, accessed September 10, 2018.
44. http://www.court.gov.cn/zixun-xiangqing-87832.html, accessed September 10, 2018.

Chapter 11

1. *Zhonghua Renmin Gongheguo Minshi Susongfa* (Beijing: Falü chubanshe, 1991).
2. http://www.law-lib.com.
3. Michael Palmer, "The Re-emergence of Family Law in Post-Mao China: Marriage, Divorce and Reproduction," in Stanley Lubman, ed., *China's Legal Reform* (New York: Oxford University Press, 1996), 118–122.
4. Huang, *Chinese Civil Justice*, 138–139, 204–208.
5. http://www.law-lib.com
6. http://www.npc.gov.cn. December 27, 2015.
7. *Zhongguo Falü Nianjian, 2004*, 1055.
8. For recent studies on the *weiquan* movement and related lawsuits, see Wilson, *Tigers without Teeth*; Biddulph, *The Stability Imperative*.
9. Both Chinese terms in this sentence are plays on puns that initially appeared as satirical usage but have become common usage. *Xiang qian kan* can mean "look to the future" or "look toward money," depending on which character is used for *qian* (the same pronunciation). Similarly, *xingfu* can mean "happiness" or "sexual happiness," depending on the character used for *xing*.
10. For more on divorce proceedings, and the legal thinking behind them, in post-Mao China, see Huang, *Chinese Civil Justice*, 125–144.

11. *2011 Shanghai Fayuan Anli Jingxuan* (Shanghai: Shanghai renmin chubanshe, 2012), 129–139 (hereafter SFAJ 2011).
12. *Chongqing Wanbao* (Chongqing Evening News), July 27, 2016, http://www.news.qq.com.
13. *1999 Shanghai Fayuan Anli Jingxuan* (Shanghai: Shanghai renmin chubanshe, 2000), 68–71).
14. Ibid., 72–75.
15. Ibid., 1–5.
16. Ibid., 6–11. For more on Chinese courts dealing with no-fault cases, see Huang, *Chinese Civil Justice*, 204–209.
17. SFAJ 2011, 78–81.
18. http://www.baike.baidu.com. "Peng Yu An."
19. https://baike.baidu.com. "pengci."
20. SFAJ 2011, 20–28.
21. Wu, *Negotiating Rural Land Ownership*, 98–99.
22. SFAJ 2011, 101–104.
23. http://www.law-lib.com.
24. http://www.china.com.cn. August 31, 2007.
25. http://www.law-lib.com.
26. Wang Maochang and Chen Shenggui, *Bubu Weiying: Da Fangwu Chaiqian Guansi* (Beijing: Zhongguo fazhi chubanshe, 2011), 21–22.
27. For more on this issue, see Biddulph, *The Stability Imperative*, 82–125.
28. Peerenboom, *China's Long March*, 287.
29. http://www.court.gov.cn/zixun-xiangqing-37172.html, March 2, 2017.
30. http://www.news.youth.cn. August 6, 2017.

Conclusion

1. Ruskola, *Legal Orientalism*, 51–52, 198–199.
2. In recent years, the alignment of Heavenly reason-state law-human relations has been increasingly discussed by legal scholars as a fine element of Chinese tradition. In an article published on the People's Supreme Court website on May 28, 2019, for example, the author argued that the highest achievement in legal adjudication was the convergence of (human) feelings, (Heavenly) reason, and (state) law; and that courts should respect the public's common values, respond to their concerns and desires, and draw from the fine experiences from the traditional Chinese justice. On the last point, the author cited Han Feizi's (3rd century BCE) saying that to bring chaos into order, law should be in alignment with Heavenly reason and human relations-feelings. See "Hao Panjue Yao Jiangjiu Qinglifa De Ronghe [好判决要讲究情理法的融合, Good adjusications should pursue the convergence of feeling, reason, and law]." https://baijiahao.baidu.com/s?id=1634749153319537088&wfr=spider&for=pc.
3. Francis Fukyuama, *Political Order and Political Decay: From the Industrial Revolution to the Globalization of Democracy* (New York: Farrar, Straus and Giroux, 2014), 507–508.

4. For a good example analyzing the issue through the phenomenon of smuggling, see Philip Thai, *China's War on Smuggling: Law, Economic Life, and the Making of the Modern State, 1842–1965* (New York: Columbia University Press, 2018).
5. Adam Benforado, *Unfair: The New Sciences of Criminal Injustice* (New York: Crown, 2015).
6. Among scholars who are critical of criminal justice systems in liberal democracies, Geoffroy de Lagasnerie characterizes the French version as that of the penal state: the state punishes a crime because the crime is a challenge to the state as a sovereign power. But he offers no solution as to how to change that. If the issue is not solvable, then it boils down to human fallibility. See Geoffrey de Lagasnerie, *Judge and Punish: The Penal State on Trial*, trans. Lara Vergnaud (Stanford, CA: Stanford University Press, 2018).

Selected Bibliography

Archival Sources

Judicial Archives. Baoshan County Archives, Shanghai, China.
Judicial Archives. Chuansha County Archives, Shanghai, China.
Judicial Archives. Songjiang County Archives, Shanghai, China.
Jiangsu High Court Archives. Jiangsu Provincial Archives, Nanjing, China.
Ministry of Justice Archives. Second Historical Archives, Nanjing, China.

Chinese Primary Sources

Bai Chao. *Xiangcun Fa'an: 1940 Niandai Taihang Diqu Zhengfu Duan'an 63 Li* [乡村法案: 1940 年代太行地区政府断案63例, Rural village legal files: 63 cases adjudicated by the (Communist) Taihang regional government in the 1940s]. Zhengzhou: Daxiang chubanshe, 2011.
Bao Weimin, ed. *Longquan Sifa Dang'an Xuanbian: Diyiji: Wanqing shiqi* [龙泉司法档案选编: 第一辑: 晚清时期, Selected compilations of judicial archives from Longquan county (Zhejiang province): Collection 1: The late Qing period]. 2 vols. Beijing: Zhonghua shuju, 2012.
Beiping Difang Fayuan Xingshi Panjue Anjuan [北平地方法院刑事判决案卷, Adjudication case files from the Beiping district court]. Beijing: Quanguo tushuguan wenxian suowei fuzhi zhongxin, 2005.
Bo'an Huibian [驳案汇编, A compilation of corrected cases]. Beijing: Falü chubanshe, 2009.
Bo Yibo. *Ruogan Zhongda Juece Yu Shijian De Huigu* [若干重大决策与事件的回顾, Looking back at certain significant policy decisions and events]. Beijing: Zhonggong zhongyang dangxiao chubanshe, 1993.
Chen Tao. *Tongzhi Zhongxing Jingwai Zouyi Yuebian* [同治中兴京外奏议约编, A collection of memorials from outside the capital during the Tongzhi restoration]. Shanghai: Shanghai shudian, 1985.
Da Ming Lü [大明律, Great Ming Code]. Beijing: Falü chubanshe, 1999.
Dangdai Zhongguo De Sifa Xingzheng Gongzuo [当代中国的司法行政工作, Judicial administrative work in contemporary China]. Beijing: Dangdai zhongguo chubanshe, 1995.
"Dangzheng Lingdao Ganbu Xuanba Renyong Gongzuo Tiaoli [党政领导干部选拔任用工作条例,Regulations on the work of selecting and promoting leading cadres]." https://www.guancha.cn/FaZhi/2014_01_16_200015.shtml. Accessed March 21, 2018.
Da Qing Fagui Daquan [大清法规大全, A complete collection of laws of the Great Qing]. Beijing: Zhengxueshe, 1909.

Da Qing Lüli [大清律例, Great Qing Code and substatutes]. Beijing: Falü chubanshe, 1999.

Daqing Minlü Cao'an—Minguo Minlü Cao'an [大清民律草案—民国民律草案, The Great Qing draft civil code—The Republic of China draft civil code]. Changchun: Jilin renmin chubanshe, 2005.

Daqing Xinfaling [大清新法令, New laws and ordinances of the Great Qing]. Beijing: Shangwu yinshuguan, 2011.

Dayuan Shengzheng Guochao Dianzhang—Xingbu [大元圣政国朝典章—刑部, Great Yuan Majestic Government present dynasty systems and rules: On punishment]. Taiyuan: Shanxi guji chubanshe, 2004.

Dayuan Tongzhi Tiaoge [大元通制条格, Great Yuan general edicts and substatutes]. Beijing: Falü chubanshe, 2000.

"Deng Xiaoping Nanxun Jianghua [邓小平南巡讲话 Deng Xiaoping's speeches during the tour of southern China]." Accessed November 12, 2017. https://baike.baidu.com.

Deng Xiaoping. *Deng Xiaoping Wenxuan* [鄧小平文選, Selected works of Deng Xiaoping]. Hong Kong: Sanlian shudian, 1983.

Diaocha Faquan Weiyuanhui Baogaoshu [调查法权委员会报告书, Report of the Commission on Extraterritoriality in China]. Falü Pinglun Zengkan [法律评论增刊, Special issue of the *Law Review*]. Beijing, 1926.

Diyi Lishi Dang'an Guan [Number one historical archives]. *Qingdai Tudi Zhanyou Guanxi Yu Diannong Kangzu Douzheng* [清代土地占有关系与佃农抗租斗争 Landownership relations and tenants' rent resistance in the Qing era]. 2 vols. Beijing: Zhonghua shuju, 1988.

Gui Wanrong and Wu Na. *Tangyin Bishi* [棠阴比事, Parallel cases ruled in the shade of a pear tree]. In *Siku Quanshu* [Complete repository of four treasures]. 1779.

Guo Wei. *Minguo Daliyuan Jieshili Quanwen* [民国大理院解释例全文, Complete texts of interpretations by the Supreme Court of the Republic]. Beijing: Zhongguo zhengfa daxue chubanshe, 2014.

Han Fei Zi [韩非子, Writings by Han Fei Zi]. Beijing: Zhonghua shuju, 2007.

"Hao Panjue Yao Jiangjiu Qinglifa De Ronghe [好判决要讲究情理法的融合, Good adjusications should pursue the convergence of feeling, reason, and law]." Accessed March 26, 2020. https://baijiahao.baidu.com/s?id=1634749153319537088&wfr=spider&for=pc.

He Ning. *Yi Yu Ji* [疑狱集, A collection of doubtful cases]. Shanghai: Fudan daxue chubanshe, 1988.

Huang Zunxian. *Riben Guozhi* [日本国志, A history of Japan]. ebook. Accessed October 2, 2018. https://wenku.baidu.com/view/836b074c168884868762d6ad.html.

Jia Zhifang. *Yuli Yuwai* [狱里狱外, Inside and outside prisons]. Shanghai: Yuandong chubanshe, 1995.

Jiang Liangqi. *Donghua Lu* [东华录, Emperor's words and deeds]. Beijing: Zhonghua shuju, 1980.

Li Baiying. *Huiyi Wo De Gaizao Shenghuo* [回忆我的改造生活, Reminiscence of my life of reformation]. Beijing: Qunzhong chubanshe, 1984.

Li Xu Zouzhe [李煦奏折, Memorials from Li Xu]. Beijing: Zhonghua shuju, 1976.

Minggong Shupan Qingming Ji [名公书判清明集, A collection of wise and clear legal judgments by well-known officials]. Beijing: Zhonghua shuju, 1987.

Minshi Xiguan Diaocha Baogaolu [民事习惯调查报告录, Reports on investigations into civil customs]. Beijing: Zhongguo zhengfa daxue chubanshe, 2000.

Minxingshi Caipan Daquan [民刑事裁判大全, A complete collection of rulings in criminal and civil cases]. Beijing: Beijing daxue chubanshe, 2007.

Pu Jian. *Zhongguo Gudai Fazhi Congchao* [中国古代法制丛钞, Compilation of sources on legal systems in ancient China]. 4 vols. Beijing: Guangming ribao chubanshe, 2001.

Qing Jiaqingchao Xingke Tiben Shehui Shiliao Jikan [清嘉庆朝刑科题本社会史料辑刊, Collection of social history sources in the cases reviewed by the criminal section of the Grand Secretariat during the Qing Jiaqing reign]. 3 vols. Tianjin: Tianjin guji chubanshe, 2008.

Quan Tang Wen [全唐文, Articles from the Tang dynasty]. e-book. Accessed December 11, 2017. https://www.txshuku.com/mulu/562.html.

"Renti Qiguan Yizhi Tiaoli [人体器官移植条例, Regulations on Human Organs Transplants]." Accessed November 20, 2017. https://baike.baidu.com/item/%E4%BA%BA%E4%BD%93%E5%99%A8%E5%AE%98%E7%A7%BB%E6%A4%8D%E6%9D%A1%E4%BE%8B/3947933?fr=aladdin.

"Sanquan Fenzhi [三权分置 system of separating three rights]." Accessed January 29, 2018. https://baike.baidu.com.

Saohuang Dafei Anli Xuan [扫黄打非案例选, Selected cases of sweeping the yellow (pornography) and striking illegal publications]. Beijing: Renmin fayuan chubanshe, 2004.

1999 Shanghai Fayuan Anli Jingxuan [1999 上海法院案例精选, The 1999 collection of cases tried by courts in Shanghai]. Shanghai: Shanghai renmin chubanshe, 2000.

2011 Shanghai Fayuan Anli Jingxuan [2011 上海法院案例精选, The 2011 collection of cases tried by courts in Shanghai]. Shanghai: Shanghai renmin chubanshe, 2012.

2014 Shanghai Fayuan Anli Jingxuan [2014上海法院案例精选, The 2014 collection of cases tried by courts in Shanghai]. Shanghai: Shanghai renmin chubanshe, 2014.

Shen Erqiao, ed. *Xianxing Lü Minshi Youxiao Bufen, Fu Hubu Zeli* [现行律民事有效部分,附户部则例, Effective parts of the current penal code on civil matters, with the Board of Revenue regulations attached]. Hangzhou: Wulin yinshuguan, 1918.

Shen Zhiqi. *Daqing Lü Jizhu* [大清律辑注, Collected annotations to the Great Qing Code]. 1715. Reprint, Beijing: Falü chubanshe, 2000.

Shenpan Wangwei Hanjian Bilu [审判汪伪汉奸笔录, A record of trials of the Chinese traitors of the Wang Jingwei puppet government]. Nanjing: Fenghuang chubanshe, 2004.

Shi Ji [史记, A record of the grand historian]. Beijing: Zhonghua shuju, 1959.

Sishu Wujing [四书五经, Four books and five classics]. 2 vols. Beijing: Beijing guji chubanshe, 1994.

"Shizu benji er" [世祖本记二, Biography of Emperor Shunzhi, part 2]. In *Qing Shi Gao* [清史稿, Draft History of Qing]. Shanghai: Lianhe shudian, 1942.

Song Ci. *Xiyuan Jilu* [洗冤集录, Washing away wrongs]. Fuzhou: Fujian kexue jishu chubanshe, 2005.

Song Xingtong [宋刑统, Song Penal Code]. Beijing: Falü chubanshe, 1999.

Sun Chengze. *Tianfu Guangji* [天府广记, Miscellaneous notes on Beijing]. Beijing: Beijing chubanshe, 1962.

Tanglü Shuyi [唐律疏义, Tang code and annotations]. Beijing: Zhonghua shuju, 1983.

Wang Maochang and Chen Shenggui. *Bubu Weiying: Da Fangwu Chaiqian Guansi* [步步为赢: 打房屋拆迁官司, Step by step to win: Launching lawsuits over housing demolition and relocation]. Beijing: Zhongguo fazhi chubanshe, 2011.

Wang Qingqi, ed. *Gesheng shenpanting pandu* [各省审判厅判牍, Trial documents from courts in various provinces]. Beijing: Beijing daxue chubanshe, 2007.

Wang Xuetai. *Jianyu Suoji* [监狱琐记, Random notes about prison]. Beijing: Sanlianshudian, 2013.

Xi Jinping. *Guanyu Dangfeng Lianzheng Jianshe He Fanfubai Douzheng Lunshu Zhaibian* [关于党风廉政建设和反腐败斗争论述摘编, Excerpts on Party discipline, incorruptible government, and struggle against corruption]. Beijing: Zhongyang wenxian chubanshe, 2015.

Xie Shen, Chen Shijie, and Ying Jixi, eds. *Minxingshi Caipan Daquan* [民刑事裁判大全, A complete compilation of civil and criminal verdicts]. Beijing: Beijing daxue chubanshe, 2007.

Xing'an Huilan [刑案汇览, Conspectus of penal cases]. 4 vols. Beijing: Guji chubanshe, 2004.

Xingbu Bizhao Jiajian Cheng'an [刑部比照加减成案, Board of Punishment cases of adding and reducing penalties by analogy]. Beijing: Falü chubanshe, 2009.

"Xingfazhi" [刑法志 Treatise on law and punishment]. In *Han Shu* [汉书 History of Han]. Shanghai: Kaiming shudian, 1934.

"Xingfazhi" [刑法志, Treatise on law and punishment]. In *Ming Shi* [明史, History of Ming]. Shanghai: Kaiming shudian, 1934.

"Xingfazhi" [刑法志, Treatise on law and punishment]. In *Qing Shi Gao* [清史稿, Draft History of Qing]. Shanghai: Lianhe shudian, 1942.

"Xingfazhi" [刑法志, Treatise on law and punishment]. In *Song Shi* [宋史, History of Song]. Shanghai: Kaiming shudian, 1934.

"Xingfazhi" [刑法志, Treatise on law and punishment]. In *Tang Shu* [唐书, History of Tang]. Shanghai: Kaiming shudian, 1934.

"Xingfazhi" [刑法志, Treatise on law and punishment]. In *Weishu* [魏书, History of Northern Wei]. Shanghai: Kaiming shudian, 1934.

"Xingfazhi" [刑法志, Treatise on law and punishment]. In *Xin Tang Shu* [新唐书, New history of Tang]. Shamghai: Kaiming shudian, 1934.

"Xingfazhi" [刑法志, Treatise on law and punishment]. In *Xin Yuan Shi* [新元史, New history of Yuan]. Shanghai: Kaiming shudian, 1934.

"Xingfazhi 1" [Treatise on law and punishment, 1]. In *Yuan Shi* [元史, History of Yuan]. Shanghai: Kaiming shudian, 1934.

Xu Wenxun. *Tajingting Andu* [塔景亭案牍, Case files from pagoda scenery pavilion]. Beijing: Beijing daxue chubanshe, 2007.

Xu Tianlin. *Donghan Huiyao* [东汉会要, Institutions and regulations of Later Han]. Shanghai: Guji chubanshe, 1978.

Xue Yunsheng. *Duli Cunyi* [读例存疑, Annotations on substatutes]. e-book. Accessed January 10, 2018. http://www.terada.law.kyoto-u.ac.jp/dlcy/index.htm.

Xun Zi [荀子, Xun Zi's writings]. Hangzhou: Zhejiang guji chubanshe, 1999.

Yang Chen. *Sanguo Huiyao* [三国会要, Institutions and regulations of Three Kingdoms]. Beijing: Zhonghua shuju, 1956.

Zhang Tian. *Bao Zheng Ji* [包拯集, A collection of Bao Zheng's writings]. Beijing: Zhonghua shuju, 1962.

Zhao Wenlong. *Jianchaguan De Shengya* [检察官的生涯, The life of a procurator]. Zhengzhou: Haiyan chubanshe, 1997.

Zheng Guanying. *Shengshi Weiyan* [盛世危言, Speaking danger in the prosperous era]. 1894. Reprint, Changchun: Beifang funü ertong chubanshe, 2001.

Zheng Ke. *Zheyu Guijian* [折狱龟鉴, Lessons for adjudications]. Shanghai: Fudan daxue chubanshe, 1988.

Zhongguo Falü Nianjian, 2004 [中国法律年鉴, Law yearbook of China, 2004]. Beijing: Falü nianjian she, 2004.

"Zhongguo Quanmian Tingzhi Shiyong Siqiu Qiguan [中国全面停止使用死囚器官, China completely stops the use of organs from executed capital offenders]." Accessed November 20, 2017. https://www.chinacourt.org/article/detail/ 2015/02/id/1552799.shtml.

"Zhongguo Sifa Lingyu Renquan Baozhang De Xin Jinzhan [中国司法领域人权保障的新进展, New Progresses in human rights protection in the judicial field]." Accessed November 20, 2017. http://www.cssn.cn/fx/fx_fxxf/201609/t20160913_3200586.shtml.

Zhonghua Minguo Xianxing Fagui Daquan [中华民国现行法规大全, A comprehensive collection of Chinese laws and regulations]. Shanghai: Shangwu yinshuguan, 1934.

Zhonghua Renmin Gongheguo Falü Huibian, 1979–1984; 1985–1989 [中华人民共和国法律汇编, A compilation of laws and regulations of the People's Republic of China, 1979–1985, 1985–1989]. 2 vols. Beijing: Renmin chubanshe, 1991.

Zhonghua Renmin Gongheguo Falü Huibian, 1990 [中华人民共和国法律汇编, A compilation of laws and regulations of the People's Republic of China, 1990]. Beijing: Renmin chubanshe, 1991.

Zhonghua Renmin Gongheguo Minshi Susongfa [中华人民共和国民事诉讼法, The People's Republic of China Civil Procedural Law]. Beijing: Falü chubanshe, 1991.

Zhonghua Renmin Gongheguo Xingfa—Zhonghua Renmin Gongheguo Xingshi Susongfa [中华人民共和国刑法-中华人民共和国刑事诉讼法, The Criminal Code of the People's Republic of China—The Criminal Procedural Law of the People's Republic of China]. Beijing: Falü chubanshe, 1997.

"Zhonghua Renmin Gongheguo Guojia Peichang Fa [中华人民共和国国家赔偿法]." Accessed October 23, 2016. http://www.baike.baidu.com.

"Zhonghua Renmin Gongheguo Xingfa Xiuzheng An (9) [中华人民共和国刑法修正案(九), The Amendments to the Criminal Code of the People's Republican of China (Ninth)]." Acceessed November 20, 2017. http://www.npc.gov.cn/zgrdw/npc/xinwen/2015-08/31/content_1945587.htm.

"Zhonghua Renmin Gongheguo Xingshi Susongfa, 2012 Nian Xiuzheng [中华人民共和国刑事诉讼法(2012年修正), The People's Republic of China Criminal Procedural Law (Amended 2012)]." Accessed November 2, 2016. http://www.gov.cn/flfg/2012-03/17/content_2094354.htm.

Zhou Ji'er. *Lichao Zheyu Zhuanyao* [历朝折狱篹要, Best selections of adjudications from all dynasties]. Beijing: Quanguo tushuguan wenxian suowei fuzhi zhongxin, 1993.

Zizhi Tongjian [资治通鉴, Eternal mirror in aid of governance]. Beijing: Zhonghua shuju, 1956.

"Zuigao Renmin Fayuan Guanyu Zhongda Tanwu Shouhui Fanzui Anjian Liangxing Yijian [最高人民法院关于重大贪污受贿犯罪案件量刑意见, The People's Supreme Court opinions on sentencing in severe criminal cases of corruption]." Accessed March 21 2018. http://www.baike.baidu.com.

Zuixin Liufa Quanshu [最新六法全书, The latest complete collection of the six laws]. Shanghai: Chunming shudian, 1948.

English Primary Sources

Commission on Extraterritoriality, Republic of China. *Laws, Ordinances, Regulations and Rules Relating to the Judicial Administration of the Republic of China*. Peking, 1923.

U.S. Department of State. *Report of the Commission on Extraterritoriality in China, Peking, September 16, 1926*. Washington, DC: Government Printing Office, 1926. Accessed October 28, 2018. https://babel.hathitrust.org/cgi/pt?id=uc1.$b47432;view=1up;seq=6.

Chinese Primary Sources in English Translation

Jiang, Yonglin, trans. *The Great Ming Code*. Seattle: University of Washington Press, 2014.
Johnson, Wallace, trans. *The Tang Code*. Vol. 2, *Specific Articles*. Princeton, NJ: Princeton University Press, 1997.
Jones, William C., and Tianhua Chen. *The Great Qing Code*. Oxford: Clarendon Press, 1994.
McKnight, Brian E., trans. *The Washing Away of Wrongs: Forensic Medicine in Thirteenth-Century China*. Ann Arbor: University of Michigan Center for Chinese Studies, 1981.
McKnight, Brian E., and James T. C. Liu, trans. *The Enlightened Judgments: Ch'ing-Ming Chi, the Sung Dynasty Collection*. Albany: State University of New York Press, 1999.
van Gulik, Robert H., trans. *Crime and Punishment in Ancient China: Tang Yin Pi Shih*. Hong Kong: Orchid Press, 2007.

Chinese Secondary Sources

Bai Jinglan. *Yiti Yu Duoyuan: Qingdai Xinjiang Falü Yanjiu, 1759–1911* [一体与多元: 清代新疆法律研究, One polity and pluralism: A study of laws in Xinjiang during the Qing, 1759–1911]. Beijing: Zhongguo zhengfa daxue chubanshe, 2013.
Chang Jianhua. *Song Yihou Zongzu De Xingcheng Ji Diyu Bijiao* [宋以后宗族的形成及地域比较, The formation of lineages and their regional comparison after the Song dynasty]. Beijing: Renmin chubanshe, 2013.
Cheng Yu. "Minguo Shiqi Qie De Falü Diwei Jiqi Bianqian [民国时期妾的法律地位及其变迁, The legal status of a concubine and its change in the Republican era]." *Shi Lin* [史林, Forest of history], no. 2 (2002): 74–83.
Du Jiwen. *Fojiao Shi* [佛教史, A history of Buddhism]. Beijing: Zhongguo shehui kexue chubanshe, 1991.
Fei Chengkang. *Zhongguo Zujie Shi* [中国租界史, A history of foreign concessions in China]. Shanghai: Shanghai shehui kexue chubanshe, 1991.
Gao Chao and Ma Jianshi, eds. *Zhongguo Gudai Faxue Cidian* [中国古代法学词典, A dictionary for ancient Chinese legal studies]. Tianjin: Nankai daxue chubanshe, 1989.
Han Tao. "Yang Honglie 'Zhongguo Falü Sixiangshi' Zhong De Yili Cuowu Jiqi Liuchuan" [杨鸿烈《中国法律思想史》中的一例错误及其流传, The spread of an error in A History of Chinese Legal Thought by Yang Honglie]. In Li Zan, ed. *Falüshi pinglun* [法律史评论]. Vol. 11, 123–130. Beijing: Shehui kexue wenxian chubanshe, 2018.
Li Guilian, *Ershi Shiji De Zhongguo Faxue* [二十世纪的中国法学]. Beijing: Beijing daxue chubanshe, 1998.
Li Hui. *Hu Feng Jituan Yuan'an Shimo* [胡风集团冤案始末, A complete story of the wrongful case of the Hu Feng clique]. Beijing: Renmin ribao chubanshe, 1989.
Li Qian. *Mingguo Shiqi Qiyue Zhidu Yanjiu* [民国时期契约制度研究, A study of contract system in the Republican era]. Beijing: Beijing daxue chubanshe, 2005.
Lu Jingyi. *Minchu Lisi Wenti De Falü Yu Caipan: Yi Daliyuan Minshi Panjue Wei Zhongxin, 1912-1927* [民初立嗣问题的法律与裁判: 以大理院民事判决为中心, Law and

adjudication on the issue of establishing an heir in the early Republic: Centering on the Supreme Court civil rulings, 1912–1927]. Beijing: Beijing daxue chubanshe, 2004.

Pan Junxiang and Shen Zuwei. *Jindai Zhongguo Guoqing Toushi* [近代中国国情透视, A transparent perspective on the national conditions of modern China]. Shanghai: Shanghai shehui kexueyuan chubanshe, 1992.

Pan Min. *Jiangsu Riwei Jiceng Zhengquan Yanjiu, 1937–1945* [江苏日伪基层政权研究, A study of local governments under the Japanese and puppet regimes in Jiangsu, 1937–1945]. Shanghai: Shanghai renmin chubanshe, 2006.

Pan Nianzhi et al. *Zhongguo Jindai Falü Sixiang Shi* [中国近代法律思想史, A history of legal theories in modern China]. Shanghai: Shehui kexue chubanshe, 1992.

Qing Xitai and Tang Dachao. *Daojiao Shi* [道教史, A history of religious Daoism]. Beijing: Zhongguo shehui kexue chubanshe, 1994.

Qu Tongzu. *Zhongguo Falü Yu Zhongguo Shehui* [中国法律与中国社会, Chinese law and Chinese society]. Beijing: Zhonghua shuju, 1981.

Shen Jiaben. *Lidai Xingfa Kao* [历代刑法考, A study of law and punishment in all dynasties]. Beijing: Zhonghua shuju, 1985.

Sun Huei-min. *Zhidu Yizhi: Minchu Shanghai De Zhongguo Lüshi (1912–1937)* [制度移植: 民初上海的中国律师, Institutional transplantation: The Chinese lawyers in Republican Shanghai, 1912–1937]. Taibei: Zhongyang yanjiuyuan jindaishi yanjiusuo, 2012.

Sun Jiahong. *Guanyu "Zisun Weifan Jiaoling" De Lish Kaocha—Yige Weiguan Shixue De Changshi* [关于"子孙违反教令"的历史考察——一个微观史学的尝试, The historical development of the law on "disobedient descendents" in traditional China from a perspective of microlegal history]. Beijing: Shehui kexue wenxian chubanshe, 2013.

Sun Qingwei. *Dingzai Yuji* [鼎载禹迹, Traces of Yu carried by ritual bronzes]. Beijing: Sanlian shudian, 2018.

Wang Jian. *Goutong Liangge Shijie De Falü Yiyi: Wanqing Xifangfa De Shuru Yu Falü Xinci Chutan* [沟通两个世界的法律意义：晚清西方法的输入与法律新词初探, Communicating between the legal meanings of the two worlds: A preliminary study of the importation of Western laws and new legal terms in late Qing]. Beijing: Zhongguo zhengfa daxue chubanshe, 2001.

Wang Zhiqiang. *Qingdai Guojiafa: Duoyuan Chayi Yu Jiquan Tongyi* [清代国家法: 多元差异与集权统一, State law in the Qing dynasty: Heterogeneous plurality and power centralization]. Beijing: Shehui kexue wenxian chubanshe, 2017.

Wu Shuchen et al. *Zhongguo Chuantong Falü Wenhua* [中国传统法律文化, Traditional Chinese legal culture]. Beijing: Beijing daxue chubanshe, 1994.

Xiao Yongqing. *Zhongguo Fazhishi Jiaocheng* [中国法制史教程, A historical outline of Chinese legal system]. Beijing: Falü chubanshe, 1987.

Xu Zhongming. *Baogong Gushi: Yige Kaocha Zhongguo Falü Wenhua De Shijiao* [包公故事: 一个考察中国法律文化的视角, Stories about Master Bao: A perspective from which to examine Chinese legal culture]. Beijing: Zhongguo zhengfa daxue chubanshe, 2002.

Yang Honglie. *Zhongguo Falü Fada Shi* [中国法律发达史, A history of the development of Chinese law]. 1930. Reprint, Shanghai: Shanghai shudian, 1990.

Yang Qiang. *Qingdai Menggu Fazhi Bianqian Yanjiu* [清代蒙古法制变迁研究, A study of changes in Mongol legal system during the Qing]. Beijing: Zhongguo Zhengfa daxue chubanshe, 2010.

Zhang Jinfan. *Qingchao Fazhi Shi* [清朝法治史, A history of the legal system in the Qing dynasty]. Beijing: Falü chubanshe, 1994.

Zhang Jinfan. *Zhongguo Sifa Zhidu Shi* [中国司法制度史, A history of the Chinese judicial system]. Beijing: Renmin fayuan chubanshe, 2004.

Zhang Sihan et al. *Liuhai Anjian Falü Shiwu* [六害案件法律实务, Practical legal issues in six-vices cases]. Beijing: Zhongguo zhengfa daxue chubanshe, 1993.

Zhao Fengjie. *Zhongguo Funü Zai Falü Shang Zhi Diwei* [中国妇女在法律上之地位, Chinese women's legal status]. Rev. ed. Shanghai: Shangwu yinshuguan, 1937.

Zu Wei. *Zhongguo Gudai Zhengju Zhidu Jiqi Liju Yanjiu* [中国古代证据制度及其理据研究, A study of evidence and reasoning system in ancient China]. Beijing: Falü chubanshe, 2013.

English Secondary Sources

Alford, William P. "Double-Edged Swords Cut Both Ways: Law and Legitimacy in the People's Republic of China." *Daedalus* 122, no. 2 (1993): 45–60.

Alford, William P. "Of Lawyers Lost and Found: Searching for Legal Professionalism in the People's Republic of China." In *Raising the Bar: The Emerging Legal Profession in East Asia*, edited by William P. Alford, 287–310. Cambridge, MA: Harvard University Press, 2007.

Alford, William P. "Tasseled Loafers for Barefoot Lawyers: Transformation and Tension in the World of Chinese Legal Workers." In *China's Legal Reforms*, edited by Stanley B. Lubman, 22–38. New York: Oxford University Press, 1996.

Altehenger, Jennifer. *Legal Lessons: Popularizing Laws in the People's Republic of China, 1949–1989*. Cambridge, MA: Harvard University Press, 2018.

Antony, Robert J. *Unruly People: Crime, Community, and the State in Late Imperial South China*. Hong Kong: Hong Kong University Press, 2016.

Asen, Daniel. *Death in Beijing: Murder and Forensic Science in Republican China*. New York: Cambridge University Press, 2016.

Barbieri-Low, Anthony J., and Robin D. S. Yates. *Law, State, and Society in Early Imperial China: A Study with Critical Edition and Translation of the Legal Texts from Zhangjiashan Tomb No. 247*. Leiden: Brill, 2015.

Baum, Richard. "The Road to Tiananmen: Chinese Politics in the 1980s." In Roderick MacFarquhar, ed., *The Politics of China: The Eras of Mao and Deng*, 441–463. New York: Cambridge University Press, 1997.

Benforado, Adam. *Unfair: The New Sciences of Criminal Injustice*. New York: Crown, 2015.

Bernhardt, Kathryn. *Women and Property in China, 960–1949*. Stanford, CA: Stanford University Press, 1999.

Bernhardt, Kathryn and Philip C. C. Huang. eds. *Civil Law in Qing and Republican China*. Stanford, CA: Stanford University Press, 1994.

Biddulph, Sarah. *The Stability Imperative: Human Rights and Law in China*. Vancouver: University of British Columbia Press, 2015.

Billingsley, Phil. *Bandits in Republican China*. Stanford, CA: Stanford University Press, 1988.

Bodde, Derk, and Clarence Morris. *Law in Imperial China*. Philadelphia: University of Pennsylvania Press, 1973.

Bourgon, Jérôme. "Abolishing 'Cruel Punishments': A Reappraisal of the Chinese Roots and Long-Term Efficiency of the Xinzheng Legal Reform." *Modern Asian Studies* 37, no. 3 (2003): 851–862.

Bourgon, Jérôme. "Rights, Freedoms, and Customs in the Making of Chinese Civil Law, 1900–1936." In *Realms of Freedom in Modern China*, edited by William C. Kirby, 84–112. Stanford, CA: Stanford University Press, 2003.

Bourgon, Jérôme, and Julie Erismann. "Figures of Deterrence in Late Imperial China: Frequency, Spatial Repartition, and Types of Crimes Targeted by Dismemberment under the Qing Dynasty." *Crime, History & Societies* 18, no. 2 (2014): 49–84.

Brook, Timothy, Jérôme Bourgon, and Gregory Blue. *Death by a Thousand Cuts*. Cambridge, MA: Harvard University Press, 2008.

Buoye, Thomas M. "Bare Sticks and Naked Pity: Rhetoric and Representation in Qing Dynasty (1644–1911) Capital Case Records." *Crime, History & Societies* 18, no. 2 (2014): 27–47.

Buoye, Thomas M. *Manslaughter, Markets, and Moral Economy: Violent Disputes over Property Rights in Eighteenth-Century China*. Cambridge: Cambridge University Press, 2000.

Butler, W. E., ed. *The Legal System of the Chinese Soviet Republic, 1931–1934*. Dobbs Ferry, NY: Transnational Publishers, 1983.

Calhoun, Craig. *Neither Gods nor Emperors: Students and the Struggle for Democracy in China*. Berkeley: University of California Press, 1994.

Cassel, Pär. "Excavating Extraterritoriality: The 'Judicial Sub-prefect' as a Prototype for the Mixed Court in Shanghai." *Late Imperial China* 24, no. 2 (December 2003): 156–182.

Cassel, Pär. *Grounds of Judgment: Extraterritoriality and Imperial Power in Nineteenth-Century China and Japan*. New York: Oxford University Press, 2012.

Chang, Wejen. *In Search of the Way: Legal Philosophy of the Classic Chinese Thinkers*. Edinburgh: Edinburgh University Press, 2016.

Chao, Kang. *Man and Land in Chinese History: An Economic Analysis*. Stanford, CA: Stanford University Press, 1986.

Chen, Li. *Chinese Law in Imperial Eyes: Sovereignty, Justice, and Transcultural Politics*. New York: Columbia University Press, 2016.

Ch'en, Paul Heng-chao. *Chinese Legal Tradition under the Mongols: The Code of 1291 as Reconstructed*. Princeton, NJ: Princeton University Press, 1979.

Cheng, Nien. *Life and Death in Shanghai*. New York: Grove Press, 1987.

Clarke, Donald C., and James V. Feinerman. "Antagonistic Contradictions: Criminal Law and Human Rights in China." In *China's Legal Reforms*, edited by Stanley B. Lubman, 135–154. New York: Oxford University Press, 1996.

Cohen, Jerome Alan. "The Chinese Communist Party and 'Judicial Independence': 1949–1959." *Harvard Law Review* 82, no. 5 (1969): 967–1006.

Cohen, Jerome Alan. *The Criminal Process in the People's Republic of China, 1949–1963*. Cambridge, MA: Harvard University Press, 1968.

Cong, Xiaoping. *Marriage, Law and Gender in Revolutionary China, 1940–1960*. Cambridge: Cambridge University Press, 2016.

Conner, Alison W. "Lawyers and the Legal Profession during the Republican Period." In *Civil Law in Qing and Republican China*, edited by Kathryn Bernhardt and Philip Huang, 215–248. Stanford, CA: Stanford University Press, 1994.

Conner, Alison W. "True Confession? Chinese Confessions Then and Now." In *The Limits of the Rule of Law in China*, edited by Karen G. Turner et al., 132–162. Seattle: University of Washington Press, 2000.

Cook, Alexander. *The Cultural Revolution on Trial: Mao and the Gang of Four*. New York: Cambridge University Press, 2016.

Dalby, Michael. "Revenge and the Law in Traditional China." *American Journal of Legal History* 25, no. 4 (1981): 267–307.

Deák, Istvan, Jan T. Cross, and Tony Judt. *The Politics of Retribution in Europe: World War II and Its Aftermath*. Princeton, NJ: Princeton University Press, 2000.

de Lagasnerie, Geoffroy. *Judge and Punish: The Penal State on Trial*. Translated by Lara Vergnaud. Stanford, CA: Stanford University Press, 2018.

Diamant, Neil J. *Revolutionizing the Family: Politics, Love, and Divorce in Urban and Rural China, 1949–1968*. Berkeley: University of California Press, 2000.

Dikötter, Frank. *Crime, Punishment and the Prison in Modern China*. New York: Columbia University Press, 2002.

Dikötter, Frank, et al. *Narcotic Culture: A History of Drugs in China*. Chicago: University of Chicago Press, 2004.

Edwards, R. Randle. "Ch'ing Legal Jurisdiction over Foreigners." In Jerome A. Cohen, R. Randle Edwards, and Fu-mei Chang Chen, eds., *Essays on China's Legal Tradition*. 223–269. Princeton, NJ: Princeton University Press, 1980.

Edwards, R. Randle. "The Role of Case Precedent in the Qing Judicial Process as Reflected in Appellate Rulings." In C. Stephen Hsu, ed., *Understanding China's Legal System*. 180–209. New York: New York University Press, 2003.

Escarra, Jean. *Chinese Law: Conception and Evolution, Legislative and Judicial Institutions, Science and Teaching*. 1936. Translated by Gertrude R. Brown. Seattle: University of Washington, 1961.

Evans, Richard. *Deng Xiaoping and the Making of Modern China*. New York: Penguin, 1997.

Fang, Qiang. "Hot Potatoes: Chinese Complaint Systems from the Early Times to the Late Qing (1898)." *Journal of Asian Studies* 68, no. 4 (2009): 1105–1135.

Finzsch, Norbert, and Robert Jotte. *Institutions of Confinement: Hospitals, Asylums, and Prisons in Western Europe and North America, 1500–1950*. New York: Cambridge University Press, 1996.

Fishel, Wesley R. *The End of Extraterritoriality in China*. Berkeley: University of California Press, 1952.

Freidland, Paul. *Seeing Justice Done: The Age of Spectacular Capital Punishment in France*. New York: Oxford University Press, 2012.

Fukuyama, Francis. *Political Order and Political Decay: From the Industrial Revolution to the Globalization of Democracy*. New York: Farrar, Straus and Giroux, 2014.

Gallagher, Mary. *Authoritarian Legality in China: Law, Workers, and the State*. New York: Cambridge University Press, 2017.

Ginsburg, Tom, and Tamir Moustafa, eds., *Rule by Law: The Politics of Courts in Authoritarian Regimes*. Cambridge, UK: Cambridge University Press, 2008.

Griffin, Patricia. *The Communist Treatment of Counterrevolutionaries, 1924–1949*. Princeton, NJ: Princeton University Press, 1976.

Guy, R. Kent. "Rule of Man and the Rule of Law in China: Punishing Provincial Governors during the Qing." In *The Limits of the Rule of Law in China*, edited by Karen G. Turner, James V. Feinerman, and R. Kent Guy, 88–111. Stanford, CA: Stanford University Press, 2000.

Hansen, Valerie. *Negotiating Daily Life in Traditional China: How Ordinary People Used Contracts, 600–1400*. New Haven, CT: Yale University Press, 1995.

Harrison, Judy Feldman. "Wrongful Treatment of Prisoners: A Case of Ch'ing Legal Practice." *Journal of Asian Studies* 23, no. 2 (February 1964): 227–244.

He, Jiahong. *Back from the Dead: Wrongful Convictions and Criminal Justice in China*. Honolulu: University of Hawaii Press, 2016.

He, Weifang. *In the Name of Justice: Striving for the Rule of Law in China*. Washington, DC: Brookings Institution Press, 2012.

He, Xin. "Black Hole of Responsibility: The Adjudication Committee's Role in a Chinese Court." *Law and Society Review* 46, no. 4 (2012): 681–712.

Hegel, Robert E. *True Crimes in Eighteenth Century China: Twenty Case Histories.* Seattle: University of Washington Press, 2009.

Hegel, Robert E., and Katherine Carlitz, eds. *Writing and Law in Late Imperial China: Crime, Conflict, and Judgment.* Seattle: University of Washington Press, 2007.

Hinsch, Bret. *Passions of Cut Sleeve: Male Homosexual Tradition in China.* Berkeley: University of California Press, 1990.

Huang, Philip C. C. *Chinese Civil Justice, Past and Present.* Lanham, MD: Rowman and Littlefield, 2010.

Huang, Philip C. C. *Civil Justice in China: Representation and Practice in the Qing.* Stanford, CA: Stanford University Press, 1996.

Huang, Philip C. C. *Code, Custom, and Legal Practice: The Qing and the Republic Compared.* Stanford, CA: Stanford University Press, 2001.

Huang, Philip C. C. "Women's Choices under the Law: Marriage, Divorce, and Illicit Sex in the Qing and the Republic." *Modern China* 27, no. 1 (2001): 3–58.

Hucker, Charles O. *A Dictionary of Official Titles in Imperial China.* Stanford, CA: Stanford University Press, 1985.

Jiang, Yonglin. *The Mandate of Heaven and the Great Ming Code.* Seattle: University of Washington Press, 2011.

Johnson, Wallace, and Denis Twitchett. "Criminal Procedure in T'ang China." *Asian Major* 6, no. 2 (1993): 113–146.

Kayaoğlu, Turan. *Legal Imperialism: Sovereignty and Extraterritoriality in Japan, the Ottoman Empire, and China.* Cambridge: Cambridge University Press, 2010.

Keeton, George W. *The Development of Extraterritoriality in China.* Shanghai: Kelly and Walsh, 1928.

Kiely, Jan. *The Compelling Ideal: Thought Reform and the Prison in China, 1901–1956.* New Haven, CT: Yale University Press, 2014.

Kotenev, A. M. *Shanghai: Its Municipality and the Chinese.* Shanghai: North China Daily News and North China Herald, 1927.

Kroncke, Jedidiah J. *The Futility of Law and Development: China and the Danger of Exporting American Law.* New York: Oxford University Press, 2016.

Kuo, Margaret. *Intolerable Cruelty: Marriage, Law, and Society in Early Twentieth-Century China.* Lanham, MD: Rowman and Littlefield, 2012.

Landry, Pierre. "The Institutional Diffusion of Courts in China: Evidence from Survey Data." In *Rule by Law: The Politics of Courts in Authoritarian Regimes*, edited by Tom Ginsburg and Tamir Moustafa, 207–234. Cambridge: Cambridge University Press, 2008.

Lary, Diana. *Chinese Migrations: The Movement of People, Goods, and Ideas over Four Millennia.* Lanham, MD: Rowman and Littlefield, 2012.

Lewis, Mark E. *The Flood Myths of Early China.* Albany: State University of New York Press, 2006.

Levi, Werner. "The Family in Modern Chinese Law," *The Far Eastern Quarterly*, Vol.4, No.3 (May 1945): 263–273.

Liang, Linxia. *Delivering Justice in Qing China: Civil Trials in the Magistrate's Court.* New York: Oxford University Press, 2008.

Liao Kuangsheng. "'Independent Administration of Justice' and the PRC Legal System." *Chinese Law and Government* 16, nos. 2–3 (1983): 123–152.

Lieberthal, Kenneth. *Governing China: From Revolution through Reform.* New York: W. W. Norton, 1995.

Liebman, Benjamin L. "Lawyers, Legal Aid, and Legitimacy in China." In *Raising the Bar: The Emerging Legal Profession in East Asia*, edited by William P. Alford, 311–356. Cambridge, MA: Harvard University Press, 2007.

Liu, Sida, and Terrence Halliday. *Criminal Defense in China: The Politics of Lawyers at Work*. New York: Cambridge University Press, 2016.

Lotverit, Trygve. *Chinese Communism 1931–1934: Experience in Civil Government*. Lund: Studentlitterature, 1973.

Lu, Hong, and Terance D. Miethe. *China's Death Penalty: History, Law, and Contemporary Practices*. London: Routledge, 2007.

Lubman, Stanley B. *Bird in a Cage: Legal Reform in China after Mao*. Stanford, CA: Stanford University Press, 1999.

Lubman, Stanley B., ed. *China's Legal Reforms*. New York: Oxford University Press, 1996.

Macauley, Melissa. *Social Power and Legal Culture: Litigation Masters in Late Imperial China*. Stanford, CA: Stanford University Press, 1998.

MacCormack, Geoffrey. "Liability of Officials under the Tang Code." *Hong Kong Law Journal* 17, no. 2 (1987): 142–162.

MacCormack, Geoffrey. *The Spirit of Traditional Chinese Law*. Athens: University of Georgia Press, 1996.

MacFarquhar, Roderick, ed. *The Politics of China: The Eras of Mao and Deng*. New York: Cambridge University Press, 1997.

MacMurray, John V. A., ed. *Treaties and Agreements with and concerning China, 1894–1919*. New York: Howard Fertig, 1973.

Matthews, Roger. *Doing Time: An Introduction to the Sociology of Imprisonment*. New York: St. Martin's Press, 1999.

McKnight, Brian E. *Law and Order in Sung China*. New York: Cambridge University Press, 1992.

McKnight, Brian E. "T'ang Law and Later Law: The Roots of Continuity." *Journal of the American Oriental Society* 115, no. 3 (1995): 410–420.

Meijer, Marinus J. *The Introduction of Modern Criminal Law in China*. Batavia: De Unie, 1950.

Meijer, Marinus J. *Murder and Adultery in Late Imperial China: A Study of Law and Morality*. Leiden: Brill, 1991.

Meisner, Maurice. *Mao's China and After: A History the People's Republic*. New York: Free Press, 1999.

Morris, Norval, and David J. Rothman. eds. *The Oxford History of the Prison*. Oxford: Oxford University Press, 1995.

Muhlhahn, Klaus. *Criminal Justice in China: A History*. Cambridge, MA: Harvard University Press, 2009.

Neighbors, Jennifer M. *A Question of Intent: Homicide Law and Criminal Justice in Qing and Republican China*. Leiden: Brill, 2018.

Ng, Kwai Hang, and Xin He. *Embedded Courts: Judicial Decision-Making in China*. New York: Cambridge University Press, 2017.

Ng, Vivien W. "Ideology and Sexuality: Rape Laws in Qing China." *Journal of Asian Studies* 46, no. 1 (February 1987): 57–70.

Ocko, Jonathan K. "I'll Take It All the Way to Beijing: Capital Appeals in the Qing." *Journal of Asian Studies* 47, no. 2 (May 1988): 291–315.

Oda, Hiroshi. "Criminal Law and Procedure in the Chinese Soviet Republic." In *The Legal System of the Chinese Soviet Republic, 1931–1934*, edited by W. E. Butler, 53–59. Dobbs Ferry, NY: Transnational Publishers, 1983.

"Outburst Flood at 1920 BCE Supports Historicity of China's Great Flood and the Xia Dynasty." *Science* 353, no. 6299 (August 5, 2016): 579–582.

Palmer, Michael. "The Re-emergence of Family Law in Post-Mao China: Marriage, Divorce and Reproduction." In *China's Legal Reform*, edited by Stanley Lubman, 110–134. New York: Oxford University Press, 1996.

Park, Nancy. "Imperial Chinese Justice and Law of Torture." *Late Imperial China* 29, no. 2 (2008): 37–67.

Peerenboom, Randall. *China's Long March toward Rule of Law*. New York: Cambridge University Press, 2002.

Peerenboom, Randall. ed. *Judicial Independence in China: Lessons for Global Rule of Law Promotion*. New York: Cambridge University Press, 2010.

Qiao, Shitong. *Chinese Small Property: The Co-Evolution of Law and Social Norms*. New York: Cambridge University Press, 2018.

Reed, Bradly W. *Talons and Teeth: County Clerks and Runners in the Qing Dynasty*. Stanford, CA: Stanford University Press, 2000.

Reynolds, Douglas R. *China, 1898–1912: The Xinzheng Revolution and Japan*. Cambridge, MA: Harvard University Press, 1993.

Rickett, W. Allyn. "Voluntary Surrender and Confession in Chinese Law: The Problem of Continuity." *Journal of Asian Studies* 30, no. 4 (1971): 797–814.

Rowe, William T. *China's Last Empire: The Great Qing*. Cambridge, MA: Belknap Press, 2009.

Rowe, William T. *Saving the World: Chen Hongmou and Elite Consciousness in Eighteenth-Century China*. Stanford, CA: Stanford University Press, 2001.

Ruskola, Teemu. "Law, Sexual Morality, and Gender Equality in Qing and Communist China." *Yale Law Journal* 103, no. 6 (1994): 2531–2565.

Ruskola, Teemu. *Legal Orientalism: China, the United States, and Modern Law*. Cambridge, MA: Harvard University Press, 2013.

Schram, Stuart, ed. *Chairman Mao Talks to the People: Talks and Letters: 1956–1971*. New York: Pantheon Books, 1974.

Schwartz, Benjamin I. *The World of Thought in Ancient China*. Cambridge, MA: Harvard University Press, 1985.

Seymour, James D., and Richard Anderson. *New Ghosts Old Ghosts: Prisons and Labor Reform Camps in China*. Armonk, NY: M. E. Sharpe, 1999.

Shan, Patrick Fuliang. "Insecurity, Outlawry and Social Order: Banditry in China's Heilongjiang Frontier Region, 1900–1931." *Journal of Social History* 40, no. 1 (2006): 25–54.

Shen, Yuanyuan. "Conceptions and Receptions of Legality: Understanding the Complexity of Law Reform in Modern China." In *The Limits of the Rule of Law in China*, edited by Karen G. Turner, James V. Feinerman, and R. Kent Guy, 20–44. Stanford, CA: Stanford University Press, 2000.

Spence, Jonathan. *The Chan's Great Continent: China in Western Minds*. New York: W. W. Norton, 1998.

Spence, Jonathan. *The Death of Woman Wang*. New York: Penguin, 1979.

Sommer, Matthew H. *Polyandry and Wife-Selling in Qing Dynasty China: Survival Strategies and Judicial Intervention*. Berkeley: University of California Press, 2015.

Sommer, Matthew H. *Sex, Law, and Society in Late Imperial China*. Stanford, CA: Stanford University Press, 2000.

Stephens, Thomas B. *Order and Discipline in China: The Shanghai Mixed Court, 1911–1927*. Seattle: University of Washington Press, 1992.

Stevenson, Mark, and Wu Cuncun, eds. *Homoeroticism in Imperial China: A Sourcebook.* London: Routledge, 2013.

Sutton, Donald S. "Violence and Ethnicity on a Qing Colonial Frontier: Customary and Statutory Law in the Eighteenth-Century Miao Pale." *Modern Asian Studies* 37, no. 1 (2003): 41–80.

Tanner, Harold M. *Strike Hard! Anti-Crime Campaigns and Chinese Criminal Justice, 1979–1985.* Ithaca, NY: Cornell University Press, 1999.

Thai, Philip. *China's War on Smuggling: Law, Economic Life, and the Making of the Modern State, 1842–1965.* New York: Columbia University Press, 2018.

Tomiya, Itaru, ed. *Capital Punishment in East Asia.* Kyoto: Kyoto University Press, 2012.

Tran, Lisa. *Concubines in Court: Marriage and Monogamy in Twentieth-Century China.* Lanham, MD: Rowman and Littlefield, 2015.

Trevaskes, Susan. *Courts and Criminal Justice in Contemporary China.* Lanham, MD: Lexington Books, 2007.

Trevaskes, Susan, Elisa Nesossi, Flora Sapio, and Sarah Biddulph, eds. *The Politics of Law and Stability in China.* Cheltenham, UK: Edward Elgar, 2014.

Turner, Karen G., James V. Feinerman, and R. Kent Guy, eds. *The Limits of the Rule of Law in China.* Seattle: University of Washington Press, 2000.

van Rooij, Benjamin. *Regulating Land and Pollution in China, Lawmaking, Compliance and Enforcement: Theory and Cases.* Leiden: Leiden University Press, 2006.

van Rooij, Benjamin, Li Na, and Wang Qiliang. "Punishing Polluters: Trends, Local Practice, and Influences, and Their Implications for Administrative Law Enforcement in China." *China Law and Society Review* 3, no. 2 (2018): 118–176.

Yu, Ping. "Glittery Promise vs. Dismal Reality: The Role of a Criminal Lawyer in the People's Republic of China after the 1996 Revision of the Criminal Procedural Law." *Vanderbilt Journal of Transnational Law* 35, no. 3 (2002): 827–865.

Volpp, Sophie. "Classifying Lust: The Seventeenth-Century Vogue for Male Love." *Harvard Journal of Asiatic Studies* 61, no. 1 (2001): 77–117.

Wakefield, David. *Fenjia: Household Division and Inheritance in Qing and Republican China.* Honolulu: University of Hawaii Press, 1998.

Wakeman, Frederic E., Jr. "*Hanjian* (Traitors)! Collaboration and Retribution in Wartime Shanghai." In *Becoming Chinese: Passages to Modernity and Beyond*, edited by Wen-shin Yeh, 298–341. Berkeley: University of California Press, 2000.

Wakeman, Frederic E., Jr. *The Shanghai Badlands: Wartime Terrorism and Urban Crime, 1937–1941.* New York: Cambridge University Press, 1996.

Wakeman, Frederic E., Jr. *Spymaster Dai Li and the Chinese Secret Service.* Berkeley: University of California Press, 2003.

Walder, Andrew G. *China under Mao: A Revolution Derailed.* Cambridge, MA: Harvard University Press, 2015.

Waley-Cohen, Joanna. "Collective Responsibility in Qing Law." In *The Limits of the Rule of Law in China*, edited by Karen G. Turner, James V. Feinerman, and R. Kent Guy, 112–131. Stanford, CA: Stanford University Press, 2000.

Weld, Susan Roosevelt. "Grave Matters: Warring States Law and Philosophy." In *Understanding China's Legal System: Essays in Honor of Jerome A. Cohen*, edited by C. Stephen Hsu, 122–179. New York: New York University Press, 2003.

Wilson, Scott. *Tigers without Teeth: The Pursuit of Justice in Contemporary China.* Lanham, MD: Rowman and Littlefield, 2015.

Wu, Yi. *Negotiating Rural Landownership in Southwest China: State, Village, and Family.* Honolulu: University of Hawaii Press, 2016.
Xu, Xiaoqun. "The Chinese Judiciary under the Japanese Occupation: Criminal and Civil Justice in Jiangsu, 1938–1945." *Chinese Historical Review* 22, no. 2 (2015): 120–140.
Xu, Xiaoqun. *Chinese Professionals and the Republican State: The Rise of Professional Associations in Shanghai, 1912–1937.* New York: Cambridge University Press, 2001.
Xu, Xiaoqun. "Law, Custom, and Social Norms: Civil Adjudications in Qing and Republican China." *Law and History Review* 36, no. 1 (February 2018): 77–104.
Xu, Xiaoqun. *Trial of Modernity: Judicial Reform in Early Twentieth-Century China, 1901–1937.* Stanford, CA: Stanford University Press, 2008.
Zanasi, Margherita. "Globalizing *Hanjian*: The Suzhou Trials and Post–World War II Discourse on Collaboration." *American Historical Review* 113, no. 3 (2008): 731–751.
Zelin, Madeleine. "The Rights of Tenants in Mid-Qing Sichuan: A Study of Land-Related Lawsuits in the Baxian Archives." *Journal of Asian Studies* 45, no. 3 (1986): 499–527.
Zelin, Madeleine, Jonathan Ocko, and Robert Gardella, eds. *Contract and Property in Early Modern China.* Stanford, CA: Stanford University Press, 2004.
Zhang, Qianfan. "The People's Court in Transition: The Prospects of the Chinese Judicial Reform." *Journal of Contemporary China* 12, nos. 3–4 (2003): 69–101.
Zhang, Shiming. "Painting and Photography in Foreigners' Construction of an Image of Qing Dynasty Law." *Frontier of History in China* 12, no. 1 (2017): 32–74.
Zhang, Taisu. *The Laws and Economics of Confucianism: Kinship and Property in Preindustrial China and England.* New York: Cambridge University Press, 2017.

List of Chinese Characters

bayi	八议
bi	比
bianxiu	编修
Bo'an huibian	驳案汇编
Caipanbu	裁判部
chengxu zhengyi	程序正义
chi	敕
chu	出
Dalisi	大理寺
Daqing xianxing xinglü	大清现行刑律
Dazongzhengfu	大宗正府
daishenshi	待审室
danghua sifa	党化司法
dao	道
dao	盗
daozei	盗贼
daozei zhongfa	盗贼重法
deli zongjian	得利纵奸
dianmai	典卖
dianquan	典权
dibao	地保
duanli	断例
Ducha yuan	督察院
Faguo lüli	法国律例
Fajing	法经
falü	法律
fanyi zhi guo	番夷之国
fei	匪
fengwen	风闻
ganhua zhuyi	感化主义
ge	格
gongjianfa	公检法

gongyi	公义
guaimai	拐卖
guandai guan	冠带官
Guizhou turen	贵州土人
guofa	国法
guojia falü	国家法律
Guojia zhengzhi baoweiju	国家政治保卫局
Hanjian	汉奸
hongfan	洪范
hongqi	红契
huanjue	缓决
huawai ren	化外人
Huijiang zeli	回疆则例
jianquan fazhi	健全法制
jiansheng	监生
jianshi juzhu	监视居住
jiantiao	兼祧
Jin-Ji-Lu-Yu	晋冀鲁豫
jinshi	进士
jinxing ri	禁刑日
jiudi zhengfa	就地正法
jiuqing	九卿
jiuqing huishen	九卿会审
junzi	君子
juren	举人
juzhong yinluan	聚众淫乱
ke	科
kejin	可矜
kugongdui	苦工队
laodong ganhuayuan	劳动感化院
laodong gaizhao	劳动改造
laodong jiaoyang	劳动教养
laogai	劳改
laojiao	劳教
laotian youyan	老天有眼
li	礼
li	里
li	例

liangren	良人
Lifan yuan	理藩院
Lifan yuan zeli	理藩院则例
ling	令
lingchi	凌迟
liqi	戾气
liucun yangqin	留存养亲
liuyang	留养
lu	路
lushi	戮尸
lü	律
Lüboshi	律博士
Menggu li	蒙古例
minben	民本
minfa tongze	民法通则
minfa zongze	民法总则
minquan	民权
mingxing bijiao	明刑弼教
mu	亩
Neiwufu	内务府
pingshi	平事
ping tianxia	平天下
pengci	碰瓷
qijia	齐家
qingguan	清官
qingli	情理
qingshi	情实
qiushen	秋审
qiushen tiaokuan	秋审条款
quanheng qingfa, yi ji qiping	权衡情法,以济其平
qunti shijian	群体事件
renmin	人民
renqing	人情
reshen	热审
Riben guozhi	日本国志
ru	入
sangqu	丧娶
sanquan fenzhi	三权分置

Shan-Gan-Ning	陕甘宁
shansha	擅杀
shaqi	杀气
Shengshi weiyan	盛世危言
shengyuan	生员
Shenxing yuan	审刑院
shi	式
shi'e	十恶
shixing fazhi	实行法治
shizu	氏族
shouji	收继
shourong	收容
shourong shencha	收容审查
shuize zaizhou, shuize fuzhou	水则载舟，水则覆舟
Shumi yuan	枢密院
shuanggui	双规
shuangkai	双开
sikepai lüshi	死磕派律师
sizhi	司直
sufa	俗法
sufan weiyuanhui	肃反委员会
Tanglü shuyi	唐律疏义
Tangyin bishi	棠阴比事
tian	天
tianli	天理
tianli ren liangxin	天理人良心
tianwei	天威
tianzi	天子
tiaoge	条格
Tingwei	廷尉
Tongwen guan	同文馆
touji daoba	投机倒把
tufei	土匪
Wanguo gongfa	万国公法
wanhun	完婚
weichi fenghua	维持风化
wei er bujian	伪而不奸
Weijing fafa	违警罚法

weiquan	维权
wenxing tiaoli	问刑条例
wufu	五服
wusha	误杀
xiang qian kan	向钱看
xiang qian kan	向前看
xiangyue	乡约
Xianxing lü	现行律
Xianxing lü minshi youxiao bufen	现行律民事有效部分
xianxing zeli	现刑则例
Xianzheng biancha guan	宪政编查馆
xiguan	习惯
Xing'an huilan	刑案汇览
Xingbu	刑部
Xingbu bizhao jiajian cheng'an	刑部比照加减成案
xingfa	刑法
xingfazhi	刑法志
xingfu	幸福
xingfu	性福
Xingke	刑科
Xingke tiben	刑科题本
xingzheng	刑政
xiushen	修身
Xiyuan luji	洗冤录集
Xuanzheng yuan	宣政院
yang	阳
yang	养
yida tianjie	以答天戒
yidang zhiguo	以党治国
yifa zhiguo	依法治国
yijue	义绝
yin	阴
yinhui wupin	淫秽物品
yin-yang	阴阳
yishi min wei bangben zhi yi	以示民为邦本之义
Yushitai	御史台
zei	贼

zhaozhi	诏制
zhengdang chengxu	正当程序
zhengxin	正心
Zhi'an guanli chufa tiaoli	治安管理处罚条例
zhiguo	治国
zhitian	职田
zhizuifa	治罪法
Zhouli sici	周礼-司刺
Zizheng yuan	资政院
Zongrenfu	宗人府
zongtiao jicheng	宗祧继承
zongzu	宗族
zu	族
zupu	族谱
zuzhang	族长
zuzheng	族正

Index

For the benefit of digital users, indexed terms that span two pages (e.g., 52–53) may, on occasion, appear on only one of those pages.

adjudicating committee, 240–41, 248
Anti-Rightist Movement, 186
appeals
   in Communist Base Areas, 179–80
   in imperial era, 50–52
   in People's Republic, 185, 246, 272–73
   in Republican era, 126, 148–49, 150, 154
Autumn Assizes, 61–63

Bandit Law, 148–51
bare sticks, 87–89, 205
Board of Punishment
   case review by, 68, 69–70, 73–74, 76–77, 81, 83–84, 88–90, 94–95, 97
   functions of, 41–43, 47, 48–49, 53–54, 61–63
   law making by, 34–35
   Ministry of Law, became, 113
Buddhism, 20, 26, 28–29

case backlogs, 47, 115, 126–27, 129, 137, 144, 151
Chiang Kai-shek, 118, 123–24, 132, 138–39, 147, 179
Chinese judiciary
   under Japanese occupation, 140–41
Chinese Traitors
   defining, 152–53
   punishing, 153–58, 178
Civil Code
   Civil Code of 1930, 135–36
   concubine, and, 163–65
   drafting, 111, 113, 121–22
   gender relations, and, 167–70
   marriage and divorce, and, 159–63
civil enforcement, 90, 127, 137, 143, 300–1

civil procedural law
   1909, 111–12, 114, 121–22, 128
   1930, 135
   1991, 285–86, 289–90
civil service examination, 25–26, 28–29, 30, 32, 45, 67
   punishing corruption in, 68–69
class struggle, 2, 176, 182–84, 190–91, 200
   shift away from, 223, 225–26, 245, 256
Communist quasi-state, 176–77, 178, 179, 180, 182–84, 207, 211
conditional sale, 92–93, 120–21, 122, 319n71
Confucianism, 7–8, 9, 12, 13, 15, 21–22, 26, 28–29, 31, 33–34
   neo-confucianism, 28–29
Confucius, 8–9, 12–13, 52, 290
contract, 90–91, 93–94, 96, 164, 207, 227–29, 230, 289–90, 294
   breach of, 285
   fraudulent, 90–91, 262
   Law (1999), 285–86
Counterrevolutionary Crimes
   abolishing, 256, 261, 263–64
   in Communist base areas, 180
   in Mao era, 191, 192, 193, 202, 203–5
   in National Government, 131–32
   in post-Mao era, 233, 234, 235–36, 245, 246, 269
Court of Judicial Review, 9–10, 41–43, 47, 51, 53, 60, 83–84
   Supreme Court, became, 113
court system
   in Late Qing and Early Republic, 111, 113–14
   in National Government, 137–38, 147
   in People's Republic, 186, 208–9

criminal code
    Criminal Code of 1928, 134–35, 163–64
    Criminal Code of 1935, 134, 164,
        165, 166–67
    Criminal Code of 1979, 234–36, 248–50,
        252, 253
    Criminal Code of 1997, 252, 254–55,
        256, 260–62
        2015 Amendments to Criminal
            Code, 267–68, 271
    Draft Criminal Code of 1907, 109–10,
        111, 112, 117
        Opposition to, 117
    Provisional New Criminal Code of
        1912, 120, 121, 148
Criminal Procedural Law
    Absent in Mao era, 182–83, 190–91, 205
    Criminal Procedural Law of 1909, 114
    Criminal Procedural Law of 1928,
        134, 158
    Criminal Procedural Law of 1979, 236,
        243, 246, 255, 265–66
    Criminal Procedural Law of 1996,
        256, 262–63
    Criminal Procedural Law of
        2012, 263–64
cruel and unusual punishments, 36–39
Cultural Revolution, 199–201
    lawlessness in, 201–5 (*see* Mao Zedong)

Daoism, religious, 20, 26, 28–29
death penalty, the, 36
    Bandit Law, under, 148–49
    Between Han and Sui Dynasties, 21
    Chinese Traitor, and, 152,
        153–54, 156–57
    Communist base areas, in, 178, 179, 180
    Criminal Code of 1997, under, 261
    Criminal Code of 1979, under, 234–35
    Criminal Code of 1928, under, 134
    Han Dynasty, in, 18
    Late Qing Reform, and, 111–12
    National government, and, 133
    Organ Transplant, and, 271–72
    People's Republic of China, in, 184,
        190, 204–5
    post-Mao era, in, 268–71
    pre-imperial era, in, 16

Provisional New Criminal Code of
    1912, under, 148
Review Procedures, in imperial era,
    49–50, 59, 61, 62
Song Dynasty, in, 29–30
Strike Hard Campaign, and, 246, 248–49,
    252, 253, 254–55
Tang Dynasty, in, 27
2015 Amendments, and, 267, 268
Yuan Dynasty, in, 30–31
Deng Xiaoping, 223, 225–28, 230, 232,
    233, 255, 256, 257–58, 260
Department of Censors, 41–43, 48–49, 54
divorce and property
    post-Mao era, in, 290–92
due process, 1–2, 304
    in late Qing, 101–2, 110–11, 114, 117
    in Mao era, 179, 181, 185, 206, 218–19
    in post-Mao era, 223, 224–25, 233, 256
    in Republican era, 118–19, 125, 126,
        144, 146, 152, 154, 159, 170–72

eight deliberations, 22
Empress Dowager, 107–8, 109–10
extraterritoriality, 106, 107
    efforts to end, 109–10, 120,
        128–29, 137–38
    end of, 140

false accusation, 52–53, 142–43, 157–58, 162
    penalty for, 53–54, 56, 58–59,
        88–90, 120–21
family support
    post-Mao era, in, 292–94
filial piety, 13, 14–15, 21–22, 52, 53, 75–76,
    80, 96–97
    waning of, 287, 290, 292
five punishments, 15, 18, 24, 27, 38–39,
    63, 77–78
Fu Su, 14–15, 36, 72–73

Gang of Four, 203
    arrest of, 225
    trial of, 233
gender inequality, 79–84, 112–13
generational inequality, 83–84. *See*
    filial piety
Ginsburg, Tom, 224

Han Fei, 12–13, 19
Heaven Has Eyes, 1–2, 233, 308
Heavenly Net, 282
Heavenly reason, 1–2, 11, 26, 39, 52, 80, 91, 92, 94, 97–98, 101–2, 111, 117, 122, 129, 134–35, 142, 144, 161, 166–67, 171–72, 175, 183, 206, 223, 268–69
homosexuality, tolerance of
   in imperial era, 86–90
   in Republican era and People's Republic, 275–76
hooliganism, 199, 205, 246–47
   abolished as crime, 261, 275–76
Hu Jingtao, 258–59
Huang, Philip, 211
Huang Zunxian, 109
human rights, 3–4, 110–11, 117, 179, 182–83, 190–91, 223, 263–64, 266–67, 271–72, 283–84, 303–4, 308

illicit sex, 16, 32, 68, 84–86. *See* homosexuality
imperial penal code
   in Han dynasty, 17–19
   in Ming dynasty, 32–33
   in Qin dynasty, 16–17
   in Qing dynasty, 34–36
   in Song dynasty, 29–30
   in Sui dynasty, 24–25
   in Tang dynasty, 26–28
   in Wei Kingdom, 20
   in Yuan dynasty, 30–31
imprisonment
   in imperial era, 39, 63, 77–78
     life, 61–62
   in People's Republic
     life, 190, 196, 205–6, 233, 234–35, 236, 245–47, 248–50, 261, 263–64, 270, 272–74
   in Republican era, 111–12, 115
     Communist base areas, 178
     life, 138–39, 152, 153–54, 156–57
inheritance
   in imperial era, 39, 92–93, 95–97
   in post-Mao era, 285, 287, 288, 289–90

Jiang Qing, 201, 203, 205, 225, 233. *See* Gang of Four
Jiang Zeming, 257–58
Judges Law, 239–40
judicial independence, 1–2, 304
   in late Qing, 101–2, 110–11, 117
   in Mao era, 175, 206, 218–19
   in post-Mao era, 223, 224–25, 233, 256
   in Republican era, 118–19, 144, 146, 170–72
   Nationalist Party, and, 120, 130–31
judicial torture
   banning
     in late Qing, 111, 114–15, 126
     in Communist base areas, 179, 182
     in People's Republic, 244–45, 246, 264, 266–67
   Beijing government, under, 105–6
   Europe, in, 101, 304
   imperial era, in, 11, 57–59, 109
   National Government, under, 133
   People's Republic, under, 237, 277–78
justice (what is just), 1–3, 101–2, 309n1

Kangxi, Qing Emperor, 10–11, 34, 48–49, 68–69, 70–71

land disputes
   in imperial era, 90–95
Lao Zi, 282
Lawyers Law, 241–43
Legal Imperialism, 104
Legal Orientalism, 305
legal pluralism, 27–28, 35–36, 43, 107
legal profession
   in People's Republic, 187–88, 241–44
   in Republican era, 125–26
legal scribes, 56, 125–26
legalism, 12–13
lineage, 44, 74–75, 90–91, 92–93, 96, 97
Liu Kunyi, 108, 114–15, 116
Liu Qingshan, 190
local bully and evil gentry, 131–33, 176, 178
local customs
   civil adjudication, and, 91, 114, 121–22, 136, 160, 171–72
   civil law, under, 111, 113
   ethnic minorities, of, 27–28, 35–36

Mandate of Heaven, 8–9, 10–11, 14–15, 17–18, 19, 20, 25, 26, 32, 33–34, 39, 47, 67, 133, 223–24
Mao Zedong, 118, 175–76, 180, 194, 196–97, 198, 203–4, 206
    Anti-Rightist Movement, and, 193
    Cultural Revolution, and, 199–203
    Hu Feng Affair, and, 191–92
marriage law
    in Communist base areas, 208
        impact of, 208–11
    Marriage Law of 1950, 208, 212–13
        impact of, 214–18
    Marriage Law of 1980, 286–87
    Marriage law of 2001, 287–89
        impact of, 290–92
mediation
    in Communist base areas, 208–9, 211
    in imperial era, 44, 47
    in Mao era, 212–15, 217–19
    in post-Mao era, 241, 287, 289, 301–2
    in Republican era, 136–37, 143–44
Mencius, 8–9
Ministry of Justice
    in People's Republic, 184, 186–88, 196–97, 239, 241–43, 253
    in Republican era, 10, 122, 123–26, 127, 130, 133, 137–39, 140, 141, 148–49, 156–57, 165
Mixed Courts, 106–7, 130–31, 140
Moustafa, Tamir, 224

nail household, 299–300

online defamation, 297–98
Opium War and aftermaths, 105–7

parent of the people
    emperor as, 8–9, 15, 20, 23, 52, 66, 75, 78
parental power
    in imperial era, 72–74 (*see* filial piety)
patrilineal succession, 122, 136
Peerenboom, Randall, 223–24, 300–1
pre-imperial law, 16
principal-agent relationship, 19, 48, 49, 190, 279, 305–6

prison condition
    in imperial era, 63–64
    in Republican era, 72, 138–39
prison reform, late Qing, 116–17
private castration
    prohibition of, 78–79
procedural justice, 2, 3–4, 57, 114, 151, 159, 171, 181, 183, 219, 236, 246, 256, 262–64, 307, 308
proletarian dictatorship, 175, 176, 205, 226, 234, 262–63
Provisional Regulations on Lawyers
    Provisional Regulations on Lawyers of 1912, 125
    Provisional Regulations on Lawyers of 1980, 241–42
    See also legal profession

Qianlong, Qing Emperor, 11, 33–34, 35, 37–38, 49, 51–52, 53–54, 76–78, 81, 94–95, 97

reeducation through labor, 198–99, 239
    abolishing, 265–67
reform through labor, 196–98, 203, 239, 265–66
residents committee, 194, 195, 213–14, 215–16, 289
revenge killing
    prohibition of, 75–78
rule of law, 1–2, 304
    late Qing, in, 101–2, 110–11, 112–13, 117
    Mao era, in, 218–19
    Nationalist Party, under, 120, 130–31, 175, 206
    post-Mao era, in, 223, 224–25, 232–33, 242–43, 256, 260
    Republican era, in, 118–19, 170–72

Shang Yang, 16–17, 25, 38
Shen Jiaben, 109–10, 112, 114–15, 116, 117, 120, 121, 125
Shen Junru, 184–85
Shi Liang, 184–85, 187–88
Sima Qing, 16–17
Song Ci, 56–57

substantive justice, 2–3, 57–58, 114, 171, 181, 183, 219, 307, 308
supreme court
  in People's Republic, 177, 184–86, 234, 236, 238, 239–40, 247, 249–50, 253, 269, 270–71, 273–74, 275, 278–79, 280, 281, 283–84, 286–87, 297–98
  in Republican era, 113–14, 123, 128, 134–35, 137, 154
    legal interpretations, 120–22, 124, 127, 136, 156, 160–61, 162–63

Taizong, Tang Emperor, 9–10, 26–27, 44, 47, 51, 53, 60
ten abominations, 22, 23, 27, 52, 61, 66, 72–73, 81
tort, 294–96
  malicious lawsuits, and, 296

urban residence registration, 194

Western Narrative of Chinese Law, 102–5
Wheaton, Henry, 107
work unit, 191, 192, 193, 195, 205, 213–14, 216, 218, 230–31, 290, 299

wrongful cases, 150–51, 171, 183, 193, 218–19, 246, 265, 277–79, 301, 307
  measures against
    in imperial era, 10–11, 41, 42, 48, 50, 51, 54, 57–58, 59
    in post-Mao era, 239, 244–45, 266–67, 270–72, 283–84
    in Republican era, 114–15, 128, 144, 149
Wu Tingfang, 112, 114–15, 116, 117

Xiaowen, Northern Wei Emperor, 21–22
Xi Jinping, 259–60
Xun Zi, 9

Yin-Yang balance, 7–8, 11, 14, 37–38, 39, 62, 63, 76–77, 268–69
Yongzheng, Qing Emperor, 34, 48–49, 62–63, 64–65

Zhang Fei, 21
Zhang Zhidong, 108, 109, 114–15, 116
Zhang Zishan, 190
Zheng Guanying, 109
Zhou Enlai, 189

www.ingramcontent.com/pod-product-compliance
Ingram Content Group UK Ltd.
Pitfield, Milton Keynes, MK11 3LW, UK
UKHW022152230426
12049UKWH00003BA/57